SOCIAL MEDIA IN TRAVEL, TOURISM AND HOSPITALITY

New Directions in Tourism Analysis

Series Editor: Dimitri Ioannides, E-TOUR, Mid Sweden University, Sweden

Although tourism is becoming increasingly popular as both a taught subject and an area for empirical investigation, the theoretical underpinnings of many approaches have tended to be eclectic and somewhat underdeveloped. However, recent developments indicate that the field of tourism studies is beginning to develop in a more theoretically informed manner, but this has not yet been matched by current publications.

The aim of this series is to fill this gap with high quality monographs or edited collections that seek to develop tourism analysis at both theoretical and substantive levels using approaches which are broadly derived from allied social science disciplines such as Sociology, Social Anthropology, Human and Social Geography, and Cultural Studies. As tourism studies covers a wide range of activities and sub fields, certain areas such as Hospitality Management and Business, which are already well provided for, would be excluded. The series will therefore fill a gap in the current overall pattern of publication.

Suggested themes to be covered by the series, either singly or in combination, include – consumption; cultural change; development; gender; globalisation; political economy; social theory; sustainability.

Also in the series

Tourists, Signs and the City
The Semiotics of Culture in an Urban Landscape
Michelle M. Metro-Roland
ISBN 978-0-7546-7809-0

Stories of Practice: Tourism Policy and Planning
Edited by Dianne Dredge and John Jenkins
ISBN 978-0-7546-7982-0

Sports Event Management
The Caribbean Experience
Edited by Leslie-Ann Jordan, Ben Tyson, Carolyn Hayle and David Truly
ISBN 978-1-4094-1855-9

Sex, Tourism and the Postcolonial Encounter
Landscapes of Longing in Egypt
Jessica Jacobs
ISBN 978-0-7546-4788-1

Social Media in Travel, Tourism and Hospitality

Theory, Practice and Cases

Edited by

MARIANNA SIGALA
University of the Aegean, Greece

EVANGELOS CHRISTOU
Alexander TEI of Thessaloniki, Greece

ULRIKE GRETZEL
University of Wollongong, Australia

LONDON AND NEW YORK

First published 2012 by Ashgate Publishing

2 Park Square, Milton Park, Abingdon, Oxon OX14 4RN
711 Third Avenue, New York, NY 10017, USA

Routledge is an imprint of the Taylor & Francis Group, an informa business

First issued in paperback 2016

British Library Cataloguing in Publication Data
Social media in travel, tourism and hospitality : theory,
practice and cases. -- (New directions in tourism analysis)
1. Tourism. 2. Hospitality industry. 3. Travel--Online
chat groups. 4. Tourism--Computer network resources.
5. Hospitality industry--Computer network resources.
6. Place marketing--Computer network resources. 7. Web
2.0--Economic aspects. 8. Web 2.0--Social aspects.
I. Series II. Sigala, Marianna. III. Christou, Evangelos.
IV. Gretzel, Ulrike.
338.4'791'02854693-dc23

Library of Congress Cataloging-in-Publication Data
Sigala, Marianna.
Social media in travel, tourism and hospitality : theory, practice and
cases / by Marianna Sigala, Evangelos Christou and Ulrike Gretzel.
p. cm. -- (New directions in tourism analysis)
Includes bibliographical references and index.
ISBN 978-1-4094-2091-0 (hbk)--ISBN 978-1-4094-2092-7 (ebk)
1. Tourism--Social aspects. 2. Hospitality industry--Social
aspects. 3. Social media. I. Christou, Evangelos. II. Gretzel, Ulrike. III. Title.

G155.A1S495 2011
910.68'8--dc23

2011030403

ISBN 978-1-4094-2091-0 (hbk)
ISBN 978-1-138-24759-8 (pbk)

Contents

List of Figures

List of Tables

List of Contributors

Daniela Attard specialises in online marketing, particularly in the implementation and use of Web 2.0 applications/technologies, social media strategies and affiliate marketing. She has a keen interest in tourism, especially in how Destination Marketing Organisations react to the global opportunities and threats presented by developments in Web 2.0 technologies. She is currently part of the Online Marketing team of one of the top online companies in the UK, where she manages the international affiliate marketing team for one of the company's main products. She has also been a guest speaker at conferences where she has presented her insight on developments in online marketing and has won awards for her contribution to the industry.

Anil Bilgihan is a PhD student in Rosen College of Hospitality Management. He earned his Master of Science degree from University of Delaware in Hospitality Information Management. His Bachelor of Science in Computer Technology and Information Systems is from Bilkent University. He became editorial assistant of the *International Journal of Contemporary Hospitality Management*. He has been working for numerous software companies and now he is teaching Hospitality Information Systems in Rosen College.

Jacques Bulchand-Gidumal has a major in Computer Sciences and a PhD in Business. He is Associate Professor at Las Palmas de Gran Canaria University, Spain, where he has been teaching since 1996. His research interests include IT, Social Media, Strategic Planning, Innovation and Entrepreneurship in the areas of tourism, public administrations and higher education. He has more than 15 years experience in both public and private companies, having been a CIO for 10 years in several organisations. His work has been published in journals such as *International Review of Administrative Sciences*, *Higher Education* and *Computers in Human Behavior*.

Kalotina Chalkiti is a Research Associate at the Northern Institute at Charles Darwin University, Australia. She holds a Master's degree in Business Administration from the University of Sunderland, United Kingdom. Her research explores knowledge management in environments of high labour turnover. Katolina's work has been published in international peer reviewed journals and edited book volumes. Her research interests focus on human resource management, organisational socialisation, new service development and knowledge management in dynamic labour environments.

Evangelos Christou is Professor of Tourism Marketing at the Department of Tourism Management of the Alexander Technological Institute of Thessaloniki, in Greece. He has long previous teaching and research experience at the University of the Aegean and the Hellenic Open University in Greece, and the University of Bolzano in Italy. He has a PhD in Tourism Marketing from the University of Wales in the UK, and he is a Chartered Marketer. His research interests include tourism and hospitality marketing, wine tourism and wine marketing, culture and heritage tourism, e-marketing, and tourism education. He has published extensively in refereed journals and conferences and has authored two books. He is editor of the refereed journal *Tourismos* and book reviews editor of the refereed journal *Managing Service Quality.*

John C. Crotts is Professor of Hospitality and Tourism Management in the School of Business at the College of Charleston, South Carolina, USA. Prior to this position, he lectured in the Advanced Business Programme on tourism subjects at Otago University, Dunedin, New Zealand and was Director of the Center for Tourism Research and Development at the University of Florida. His research encompasses the areas of economic psychology, tourism marketing and sales strategy, and management of cooperative alliances.

Boyd H. Davis is Bonnie E. Cone Professor of Teaching, Professor of Applied Linguistics/English at the University of North Carolina-Charlotte, USA. Her research currently focuses on how systems of appraisal, evaluation, agency and affect underlying question-answer dialogues and narrative in legal, medical and health situations, such as Alzheimer's. Her articles and books examine language use in a range of online and face-to-face environments, and she creates digital oral archives and related training materials.

Ricardo J. Díaz-Armas has a Bachelor's degree in Business Studies, a Degree in Economic Science and a PhD. He has developed his career at La Laguna University since 1996. He has participated in management consulting projects in different areas such as marketing research, technology, strategy and organisations. He is a full-time Professor of Marketing at the University of La Laguna, Spain, where he has taught Business Management, Marketing and Tourism Promotion. His research interests include the attitude of residents towards tourism and IT and Social Media in the area of tourism. He has published articles in several international journals and he has also published several book chapters.

Mehmet Erdem is Associate Professor in the Hotel College at UNLV. Prior to UNLV, he taught at University of New Orleans and at Purdue University. His area of research includes hospitality technology and human resource management. He regularly presents his work at research conferences and industry events. Dr. Erdem has over ten years of domestic and international hospitality operations experience. A technology operations and instructional design consultant, he serves as a corporate trainer for the International Gaming Institute (IGI) at UNLV. His professional affiliations include the International Hospitality Information Technology Association (iHITA), where he serves as the President.

Matthias Fuchs is full-professor in Tourism Management and Economics at European Tourism Research Institute, Mid Sweden University since 2008. Previously he directed the e-Tourism Competence Centre Austria where he also supervised four large-scale research projects in the area of mobile guides, online-auctions, technology impact and e-Learning. His research interest is focused on knowledge-retrieval and management, destination marketing, labour market, M-commerce, technology diffusion and impact. His articles appeared in tourism and management journals, respectively.

Ulrike Gretzel is Associate Professor of Marketing in the Institute for Innovation in Business and Social Research, University of Wollongong, and Director of the Laboratory for Intelligent Systems in Tourism. She received her PhD in Communications from the University of Illinois in Urbana-Champaign and holds a masters degree in International Business from the Vienna University of Economics and Business. Her research on social media deals with credibility judgements, motivations to create contents, privacy concerns, and influences on tourism experiences.

Desiderio Gutiérrez-Taño is Industrial Engineer and PhD. He has developed his career in EDEI Consultants since 1987 and he is currently a Managing Partner. He has participated in management consulting projects in different areas such as marketing research, technology, strategy and organisations. He is a part-time Professor of Marketing at the University of La Laguna, Spain, where he has taught Business Management, Marketing and Tourism Promotion. His research interests include the attitude of residents towards tourism and IT and Social Media in the area of tourism. He has published articles in several international journals and he has also published several book chapters.

Jim Hamill is a Web 2.0/Social Media evangelist, academic, author, consultant and executive educator. Jim is widely recognised as a leading international expert on social media strategy development for building sustained customer and competitive advantage. With over 25 years experience in international and e-business, Jim has successfully delivered on a broad range of consultancy assignments around the World. He has held Visiting Professorships or delivered Senior Executive Programmes in the US, Singapore, Hong-Kong, Malaysia, China, Norway, Italy, Lithuania, Latvia, France, Iceland, Malta, Russia and the UAE. Author of several books and numerous papers, he is a fully accredited EU ICT/e-Business Expert, Co-director and owner (with Alan Stevenson) of the social media strategy company Energise 2.0 (www.energise2-0.com) and the professional networking community for tourism industry professionals Tourism 2.0 (www.tourism2-0.co.uk).

Rob Law is Professor of Technology Management at School of Hotel and Tourism Management at the Hong Kong Polytechnic University. He has also worked at the Saskatchewan Institute of Applied Science and Technology, University of Regina, and Bell Northern Research/Northern Telecom in Canada. Dr. Law is an active researcher. He has received various research-related awards and honours, as well as external and internal research grants. He has authored/co-authored many research articles in first-tier academic journals, and has served different research journals and international conferences.

Hee Andy Lee is Assistant Professor at the School of Hotel and Tourism Management, the Hong Kong Polytechnic University. He earned his Masters degree from Michigan State University and his PhD from the Pennsylvania State University. Dr. Lee has industry experience at Seoul Hilton Hotel as a Food and Beverage Coordinator. His research interest is in information technology in restaurant and hotel industries and teaches hospitality technology classes at different universities.

Woojin Lee is Assistant Professor in the School of Community Resources and Development at Arizona State University. She earned her PhD from Texas A&M University and holds a masters degree in Hotel Administration from University of Nevada, Las Vegas. Her research focuses on the effects of mental imagery on attitudes and behavioural intentions toward visiting Websites of destination, and storytelling contained Consumer Generated Media. Additionally, she is currently involved in the research of the emotional marketing in tourism, the social media marketing in convention and meeting industry, the role of social networking sites for promoting local events and festivals and green initiative marketing in convention and hotel industry.

Daniel Hee Leung is a Research Student studying the Master of Philosophy in Hotel and Tourism Management at School of Hotel and Tourism Management at the Hong Kong Polytechnic University. Mr. Hee Leung earned his bachelors degree from SHTM, and he has industry experience at Marco Polo Hotels and other worldwide companies. Daniel's research interest is website evaluation and Web 2.0 or social media.

Peyton Mason takes a quantitative approach to market research and the analysis of consumers' language: see linguistic-insights.com. Prior to developing language analytic techniques, he had effectively provided over 20 years of research leadership to launch new products, turn around lagging sales and to move businesses forward; working for Unilever (Lipton), Anheuser-Busch, Kellogg's and Bank of America. He managed the market research for such established brands as: Pop Tarts, Lipton Pasta & Sauce, Lipton Rice & Sauce, Wyler's, Kellogg's children's cereals, Budweiser, and Busch Beer.

Athina Nella is a PhD candidate in the department of Business Administration, University of the Aegean (Greece) and a scholar of State Scholarships Foundation. Her PhD thesis focuses on the effects of consumer experience tourism on consumer behaviour. She holds a Bachelor's degree in Marketing and Communication and an MSc in Services Management, both from Athens University of Economics and Business, Greece. Among others, she has worked for Procter & Gamble as Consumer and Market Knowledge Associate Manager. Her research interests include services marketing, wine tourism and tourist behaviour.

Khaldoon "Khal" Nusair joined Rosen College of Hospitality Management team in 2007. He earned his PhD in Hospitality Management from The Ohio State University. He holds two Master of Science degrees both from The State University of New York at Stony Brook. Dr. Nusair's research interests include E-commerce and Information Systems. He is the author of one book and more than 20 refereed papers in leading academic journals and proceedings of international conferences. Dr. Nusair has received several awards for his research contributions. Dr. Nusair currently serves as the Vice President of International Hospitality Information Technology Association (iHITA).

Fevzi Okumus currently serves as the chair of the Hospitality Services Department at the Rosen College of Hospitality Management. He received his PhD in Strategic Hotel Management in 2000 from Oxford Brookes University, UK. His research areas include strategy implementation, change management, and competitive advantage. He has over 120 academic publications. His publications have been cited over 140 times by other academics and industry practitioners in numerous academic and industry publications. In 2007, he became editor of the *International Journal of Contemporary Hospitality Management*. He also serves on the editorial board of ten international journals including *Annals of Tourism Research.*

Bing Pan is Assistant Professor of Hospitality and Tourism Management and the Director of Office of Tourism Analysis in the School of Business at the College of Charleston located in Charleston, South Carolina, USA. Prior to this position, he obtained his PhD in Tourism Management from the University of Illinois at Urbana-Champaign before spending two years at Cornell University as a post-doctoral fellow. His research encompasses the areas of information technologies, search engine marketing, social media, research methodologies, and consumer behaviour research in tourism.

Eduardo Parra-López has a Bachelor in Business Studies and Degree in Economic Science and PhD. He has developed his career at La Laguna University since 1998 and he is currently a Reader in Strategic Management in Tourism in La Laguna University. He has participated in national projects (Spain) in different areas such as Supply Chain and technology and strategy. He is a full-time Professor of Strategic Tourism and e-Commerce at the University of La Laguna,

Spain. His research topics include: the supply chain management in tourism, Competitiveness in Small Island Destinations and IT and Social Media in the area of tourism, recently. He has published articles in several international journals and he has also published several book chapters.

Mary Ann Dávila Rodríguez is a Master's Student and member of the Laboratory for Intelligent Systems in Tourism (LIST) in the Department of Recreation, Park and Tourism Sciences at Texas A&M University. She holds a bachelor's degree in Touristic Culture from the University of Puerto Rico, Carolina. Her research focuses on the destination image, residents' perception of tourism visual representations, tourism experiences and travel photography.

Jun (Nina) Shao is Assistant Professor in the College of Landscape Architecture, Beijing Forestry University, China, and a researcher at Center for Recreation and Tourism Research, Peking University. She received her PhD in Human Geography from Peking University and was joint-educated by the Laboratory for Intelligent Systems in Tourism in the Department of Recreation, Parks and Tourism Sciences at Texas A&M University. She also holds a Master's degree in Computer Application Technologies from Beijing Institute of Technology. Her research focuses on online tourist behaviours, web-based destination marketing, as well as sense of place in the internet environment.

Katia L. Sidali is post-doctoral researcher at the University of Göttingen (Germany) since 2009. She took her PhD in a joint doctoral program between the University Alma Mater Studiorum of Bologna (Italy) and the University of Göttingen. Her research focuses on marketing of food and tourism, consumer behaviour and communication strategies in tourism. She has been awarded scholarships by the Italian Trade Commission (ICE) in 1993 and by the German Steinbeis Association in 2000. Her research appears in the following reviewed scientific journals: *Journal of Global Marketing Science*, *Journal of the Swiss Society of Agricultural Economics* and *Agricultural Sociology* and *Journal of the Canadian Association for Leisure Studies Leisure/Loisir*.

Marianna Sigala is Assistant Professor at the University of the Aegean, Greece. Before joining the University of the Aegean, she acquired extensive international teaching experience at the University of Strathclyde, Westminster University, Free University of Bolzano and Hellenic Open University. Her interests include service management, Information and Communication Technologies (ICT) in tourism and hospitality, and e-learning. She has professional experience from the Greek hospitality industry and contributed to several international research projects. She has published four books, and her work has been published in several refereed academic journals and international conferences. She is the co-editor of the journal *Managing Service Quality*. She is past President of EuroCHRIE and she has served at the Board of Directors of I-CHRIE, IFITT and HeAIS.

Achim Spiller is Professor and Chair of Marketing of Agricultural Products and Food, University of Göttingen, Germany, Department of Agricultural Economics and Rural Development since 2000. His research interests centre around quality management, consumer behaviour, branding and organic food marketing. He is a member of the Scientific Advisory Group of the Federal German Ministry of Agriculture and serves as Chair of the Stakeholder Board of the German Quality Certification System QS GmbH. His work has been published in both national and international journals (more details are available at: http://www.uni-goettingen.de/en/20076.html).

Alan Stevenson has over ten years experience working at the 'coalface' of e-business developments in the UK and internationally. He currently specialises in the development and successful implementation of Social-Media based marketing strategies for public and private sector organisations. Core competencies include 'Customer Led' Social Media Strategy Development, Implementation and Performance Measurement. He is internationally recognised as an expert in Social Media Monitoring and Analytics, Strategic Marketing, Market Research, Customer Relationship Management and the Balanced Scorecard. Co-director and owner (with Jim Hamill) of the social media strategy company Energise 2.0 (www.energise2-0.com) and the professional networking community for tourism industry professionals Tourism 2.0 (www.tourism2-0.co.uk), Alan is also a Visiting Lecturer at the University of Strathclyde and an EU approved management consultant.

Timothy J. Tyrrell is Director of the Center for Sustainable Tourism at Arizona State University. Dr. Tyrrell earned a PhD in Agricultural Economics from Cornell University, an MA in economics from the University of Tennessee and BA in Mathematics from the University of South Florida. He served as Professor of tourism economics at the University of Rhode Island until 2005, and as Professor of Tourism Development and Management at Arizona State University from 2005 until the present. He serves on the Leadership Council of International Association of Tourism Economists and is a member of the Travel and Tourism Research Association and the International Association of Scientific Experts in Tourism.

Dimitrios Vagianos is a PhD candidate at the Department of International and European Studies, University of Macedonia. His holds a BSc in Electrical Engineering and a MSc in Telecommunications. He is doing research in blog communication patterns.

Serena Volo is assistant professor and a member of the Competence Centre in Tourism Management and Tourism Economics at the School of Economics and Management of the Free University of Bozen-Bolzano. She holds a PhD in tourism marketing and has been a Fulbright Research Scholar at the Rosen School for Hospitality Management (University of Central Florida) and has conducted research on econometrics of tourism at the Faculty of Tourism and Food of the Dublin Institute of Technology. Her research interests include tourism marketing and communication, consumer behaviour in tourism, second-home tourism, tourism statistics and models for forecasting tourist demand.

Vasiliki Vrana is a mathematician and holds a PhD in Computer Sciences, Aristotle University of Thessaloniki, Greece. She is an Assistant Professor at the Department of Business Administration, Technological education Institute of Serres, Greece. Her research interests include the study of Web 2.0, of IT in tourism and hospitality industries and e-governance. She has published one book and many articles in international and Greek journals.

Kyung-Hyan Yoo is Assistant Professor in the Department of Communication at William Paterson University. She received her PhD in the Department of Recreation, Park and Tourism Sciences at Texas A&M University. She has published her research in the areas of travel recommender systems, online word-of-mouth, social media, online tourist information search and behaviour. Her current research focuses on online tourist behaviour, online trust, Web 2.0, and persuasion in human-technology interaction.

Kostas Zafiropoulos is an Assistant Professor at the Department of International and European Studies, University of Macedonia. He holds a PhD in applied statistics and has published articles in international and Greek journals. He is the author of three books about marketing research and research methodology (in Greek). His research interests include sampling and data analysis and research methods.

List of Abbreviations and Acronyms

AIDA	Attention, interest, desire and action
AVE	Average variance extracted
B2B	Business-to-business
B2C	Business-to-consumer
BIC	Schwarz's Bayesian Criterion
BSC	Balanced Scorecard
C2C	Consumer-to-consumer
CDT	Cognitive dissonance theory
CFA	Confirmatory factor analysis
CGM	Consumer generated media
CR	Composite reliability
CRM	Customer Relationship Marketing
DMO	Destination Marketing Organisation
DMS	Destination Management System
eCRM	electronic Customer relationship Marketing
eWom	electronic word-of-mouth/word-of-mouse
G2C	Government-to-consumer
GWCGN	Great Wine Capitals Global Network
HTB	Harbin Tourism Bureau
HRM	Human Resource Management
ICT	Information and Communication Technology
IS	Information systems
KM	Knowledge management
KPI	Key Performance Indicator
LIWC	Linguistic Inquiry and Word Count
MC	Merchant City (Glasgow)
MGC	Multi-group comparisons
MCTMC	Merchant City Tourism and Marketing Cooperative
MDS	Multidimensional Scaling
MICE industry	Meeting, Incentives, Conventions and Exhibitions industry
MMORPG	Massively multiplayer online role-playing game
MOA	motivation, opportunity and ability
MSN	Microsoft Social Network
NSD	New service development
OSN	Online social networking
PEST	Political Economical Social Technological
PLS	Partial Least Squares

RIA	Rich Internet Applications
ROI	Return On Investment
RSS	Really Simple Syndication
SEM	Search Engine Optimisation
SME	Small and medium-sized enterprises
SMM	Social Media Monitoring
TAM	Technology Acceptance Model
TBSP	Tourism Bureau of Sichuan Province
UGC	User-generated content
WHN	Wine and Hospitality Network
WOM	Word-of-mouth
WTO	World Trade Organization

Introduction

Social media, or Web 2.0 as it is usually called, are fundamentally changing the way travellers and tourists search, find, read and trust, as well as collaboratively produce information about tourism suppliers and tourism destinations. Moreover, applications of Web 2.0 such as, collaborative trip planning tools, social networks, and multi-player online social games, enable travellers to participate in all business operations and functions (e.g. marketing, new service development). Consequently, travellers become co-marketers, co-designers, co-producers and co-consumers of travel experiences. In using social media, the travellers co-produce and share a huge amount of information and knowledge namely user-generated content (UGC) and/or social intelligence. The latter is useful and it has a great impact not only on travellers' behaviour and decision-making processes, but it can also be exploited for informationalising and improving the effectiveness of business operations. For example, firms use UGC for enhancing their customer complaints management processes, improving their environmental scanning abilities and informationalising new service development. In this vein, travel, tourism and hospitality companies are currently changing and redefining their business models and operational practices in order to exploit the business opportunities offered by social media as well as to address the expectations and the behaviour of the new travellers' generation.

The wide application of social media by the travellers and the tourism industry alike has boomed research during the last decade. However, despite the increasing importance and impact of social media in the tourism industry, there is not any book yet addressing this topic from a holistic and overall perspective. To address this gap, this book consolidates under one cover leading-edge theory, research and case studies investigating the use and impacts of social media by both tourism demand and supply. The overall goal of this edited volume is to disseminate a coherent body of theory and practical based research that will provide insights for academics and professionals alike into the following issues: a) the profile, the behaviour and the changing roles of "travellers 2.0", and b) the ways in which travel, tourism and hospitality firms and destination organisations are transforming their business models and operations for accommodating and exploiting UGC and social network interactions.

The book chapters are contributed by an international group of leading experts. They also represent case studies and research findings from various countries, and different types of tourism, hospitality and leisure companies, which further enhance the contextualisation but also the generalisation of the book findings. The book chapters are organised into four parts, addressing the above-mentioned goals of the book.

Analytically the first part of the book aims to address the issue of the use and impact of social media in business operations and strategic models. To achieve that, the part includes four chapters providing practical examples and theoretical underpinnings on how firms can exploit social media for enhancing the following business operations and strategies: networking and collaboration; new service development; and travellers' engagement in destination marketing. The concluding chapter of this part also discusses the factors inhibiting and/or facilitating tourism firms to exploit social media.

Given the enormous impact of social media on the marketing function, the second part of the book focuses on the use and impact of Web 2.0 tools on tourism marketing. The part features six chapters analysing the use of social media for marketing tourism destinations and individual tourism firms. Practical evidence and findings are provided from Web 2.0 enabled marketing practices of international Destination Management Organisations, meeting planners and hotels.

The third part of the book addresses the book's aim to provide more insight into the impact of social media on travellers' behaviour. Unless firms know how social media affect tourism behaviour, it is impossible for them to address their new needs, expectations and ways of decision-making. To that end, five chapters provide findings about the antecedents of use, the types of use and impacts of use of social media on travellers' behaviour. In addition, book chapters address the question of whether all travellers are the same when it comes to social media perceptions and use. To that end, the book chapters provide findings regarding the impact and the use of social media for different personalities, age, gender and nationalities of travellers.

Information is currently one of the most important and competitive asset of the firms and the social media provide a valuable and important tool for identifying, sharing and creating competitive intelligence. In this vein, the last part of the book focuses on and analyses ways in which firms can exploit social media for enhancing their knowledge sharing and creation capabilities with external partners and firms, but also internally with their employees. To that end, three chapters provide theoretical underpinnings and findings on the following issues: the use of social media for knowledge management practices; content analysis of blogs' content; and the use of various tools for monitoring online reputation. The chapters demonstrate the use of various quantitative and qualitative methods that firms can use for exploiting UGC and informationalising their business operations.

Overall, the book provides a rich set of both theoretical background and industry evidence for exploiting and managing the impacts of social media both from a tourism demand and supply perspective. The book nicely integrates theoretical concepts with practical evidence gathered through a wide spectrum of international case studies and thorough literature reviews. The contributed book chapters also provide ideas for future research, which can hopefully further instill the readers to conduct more studies and further advance the knowledge in the field.

We hope you will enjoy reading this book.

Marianna Sigala,
Evangelos Christou,
Ulrike Gretzel,
2012

PART 1
Web 2.0: Strategic and Operational Business Models

Chapter 1
Introduction to Part 1

Marianna Sigala

1. The Integration and Impact of Web 2.0 on Business Operations and Strategies

During the last few years, we have experienced the mushrooming and increased use of web tools enabling Internet users to both create and distribute (multimedia) content. These tools referred to as Web 2.0 technologies can be considered as the *tools of mass collaboration*, since they empower Internet users to actively participate and simultaneously collaborate with other Internet users to produce, consume and diffuse the information and knowledge being distributed through the Internet. As information is the lifeblood of the tourism industry, Web 2.0 advances are having a tremendous impact on both tourism demand and tourism supply.

Web 2.0 is fundamentally changing the way travellers and tourists search, find, read, trust as well as (collaboratively) produce information about tourism suppliers and destinations (Cox et al., 2009). Moreover, Web 2.0 applications such as collaborative trip planning tools, social and content sharing networks as well as massive multi-player online social games such as Secondlife, empower travellers to get engaged with the operations of tourism firms (for example by designing and promoting a cultural trip/event). In fact, Web 2.0 affects all stages of the travellers' decision-making process (see Figure 1.1) in terms of the way travellers identify and realise that they have a need, for example user-generated content, UGC, is found to have an AIDA effect on travellers by creating attention, interest, desire and action (Pan et al., 2007); the sources that travellers use for searching and evaluating travel information (Kim et al., 2004); the channels that travellers use for booking and buying travel products, changing travel reservations and itineraries after purchase as well as for sharing and disseminating experiences and feedback after the trip (Yoo and Gretzel 2008). Overall, Web 2.0 transforms travellers from passive consumers to active prosumers (producers and consumers) of travel experiences, while changing the way in which travellers develop relations, their perceived image of and loyalty to, tourism firms (Christou 2003 and 2010).

In this vein, travel and tourism companies are currently changing and redefining their business models in order to address the needs and expectations of this new generation of travellers. Tourism firms are also trying to more actively involve travellers with their business operations in order to benefit from and exploit the intelligence and social influence of travellers' networks. In other

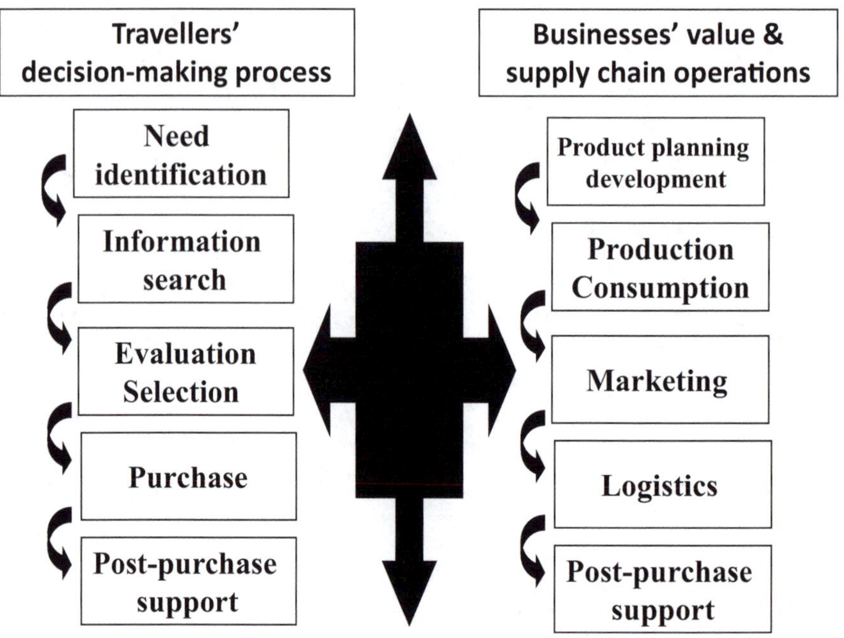

Figure 1.1 Web 2.0 Affects the Whole Process

words, Web 2.0 presses but also enables tourism firms to change the ways in which they traditionally conduct their internal and external business operations in order to integrate customers as a more active stakeholder of their business models. As a result, Web 2.0 has tremendous transformation power on the firms' value and supply chain operations (see Figure 1.1): more and more tourism firms exploit UGC and/or involve travellers' with their new Service Development (NSD) processes (i.e. travellers as co-designers) (Kohler et al., 2011); travellers' and their social networks play a more active role in the production and consumption of tourism experiences by influencing the way travellers design and perform their travel experiences (i.e. travellers as co-creators) (Sigala 2010); travellers and their social networks are being increasingly exploited for creating a positive image for a tourism firm, promoting and distributing its services (i.e. travellers as co-marketers and co-distributors) (Sigala 2011); and travellers' post-trip experiences and feedback are exploited for improving services as well as supporting other travellers to design their future trips.

Nevertheless, tourism firms differ in terms of the level and the degree to which they are integrating travellers into their operations. Similarly to the take-up of any technology, the adoption and exploitation levels of Web 2.0 by tourism firms are affected by numerous factors that are either internal to the firm (e.g. size of the firm and management commitment) and/or external to the firm (e.g. culture of travellers, see for example, Christou 2005). In this vein, it is not only interesting but also useful to study the diffusion level as well as the factors influencing the latter in order to better inform and support the tourism industry on how to fully and better exploit Web 2.0.

2. Overview of the First Part of the Book

The overall goal of the first part of this book is to provide practical examples and theoretical underpinnings on how tourism firms integrate and exploit Web 2.0 in their value and supply chain operations. The chapters in this part also aim to examine and give insight into the factors that can facilitate and/or inhibit the adoption of Web 2.0 technologies. Thus, the individual chapters offer useful practical implications to tourism professionals wishing to more effectively exploit Web 2.0.

Chapter 2 by Evangelos Christou and Athina Nella, analyses how Web 2.0 enables cooperation, networking and knowledge exchanges/dissemination amongst the various wine tourism stakeholders, such as wine tourists, wine clusters, wine tourism DMOs or tour operators, wine producers and distributors. To achieve that, the chapter analyses two Web 2.0 enabled wine networks, namely:

- the wineandhospitalitynetwork.com, a global network linking professionals of the wine and hospitality sectors, i.e. wineries, sommeliers, oenologists and other stakeholders of wine tourism destinations;
- the greatwinecapitals.com, a network of nine global wine tourism destinations that seek to create synergies, value and knowledge exchange for stakeholders of the member cities.

Chapter 3 is written by Marianna Sigala and investigates the ways, the benefits and the disadvantages of utilising Web 2.0 to involve customers with NSD processes. To achieve this, the chapter reviews and synthesises the related literature as well as analysing two case studies to show how two tourism firms are exploiting Web 2.0 for NSD practices: a) the social network of www.mystarbucksidea.com developed by Starbucks for engaging consumers with new service ideas generation and evaluation; and b) the exploitation of secondlife.com by Starwood to enable users to design, test and promote a new hotel concept namely, Aloft hotels. The chapter concludes by providing a holistic framework for studying customer involvement in NSD as well as practical implications and suggestions on how tourism firms can fully exploit the potential of Web 2.0 for NSD.

Chapter 4 is written by Jim Hamill and Alan Stevenson and presents a detailed case study of a local tourism industry collaborative effort aimed at building brand awareness and 'buzz' using the full potential of social media – the Merchant City (Glasgow) 'Creating the Buzz' Social Media Project. The case study shows that while a number of key project targets were met, organisational, people and internal political issues prevented the full realisation of expected project benefits. The chapter identifies and analyses the lessons that were learned from the case study and which are useful to other tourism networks embarking on similar collaborative social marketing efforts.

Chapter 5 is written by Daniel Hee Leung, Andy Lee, and Rob Law and examines how hotels can exploit Web 2.0 to enhance the design and functionality of the hotels' websites. Drawing on the findings from a content analysis of hotel websites and interviews with the hotel managers based in Hong Kong, the chapter also discusses the association between brand affiliation and the adoption of Web 2.0 technologies.

References

Christou, E. 2003. On-line buyers' trust in a brand and the relationship with brand loyalty: The case of virtual travel agents. *Tourism Today*, 3(1), 95-106.

Christou, E. 2005. Promotional pricing in the electronic commerce for holiday packages: A model of purchase behavior, in *Information and Communication Technologies in Tourism 2005*, edited by A.J Frew. Vienna: Springer Verlag.

Christou, E. 2010. Relationship marketing practices for retention of corporate customers in hospitality contract catering. *Tourism & Hospitality Management: An International Journal*, 16(1), 1-10.

Cox, C., Burgess, S., Sellitto, C. and Buultjens, J. 2009. The role of user-generated content in tourists' travel planning behavior. *Journal of Hospitality Marketing and Management*, 18, 743-764.

Kim, W.G., Lee, C. and Hiemstra, S.J. 2004. Effects of an online virtual community on customer loyalty and travel product purchases. *Tourism Management*, 25, 343-355.

Kohler, T., Fueller, J., Stieger, D. and Matzler, K. 2011. Avatar-based innovation: Consequences of the virtual co-creation experience. *Computers in Human Behaviour*, 27, 160-168.

Pan, B., MacLaurin, T. and Crotts, J.C. 2007. Travel Blogs and the Implications for Destination Marketing. *Journal of Travel Research*, 46, 35-45.

Sigala, M. 2010. Measuring customer value in online collaborative trip planning processes. *Marketing Intelligence and Planning*, 28, 418-443.

Sigala, M. 2011. eCRM 2.0 applications and trends: The use and perceptions of Greek tourism firms of social networks and intelligence. *Computers in Human Behavior*, 27, 655-661.

Yoo, K-H. and Gretzel, U. 2008. What motivates consumers to write online travel reviews? *Information Technology & Tourism*, 10, 283-295.

Chapter 2

Web 2.0 and Networks in Wine Tourism: The Case Studies of greatwinecapitals.com and wineandhospitalitynetwork.com

Evangelos Christou and Athina Nella

1. Introduction

Networks can act decisively for synergies and value creation in many sectors of the economy and wine tourism is not an exception. As Bras et al. (2010, p. 1639) state, "the fact that the tourism sector is composed of a diversity of services and resources, all of which contribute to the visitor's experience, enhances the need to have a destination management network that includes all regional stakeholders". Additionally, Buhalis and Kaldis (2008) and Sigala and Chalkiti (2007) emphasize the need for networks and clusters to define clear objectives enabling immediate access to various sources of information for all partners involved. The creation of wine tourism networks can lead to prompt and flexible reactions to market trends, increased efficiency and competitiveness while being a safe way to avoid all the drawbacks of centralized organizations (Dodd 2000; Sigala 2005). This can be achieved mainly through knowledge exchange and better coordination of activities among different wineries, wine tourism destinations and other key wine tourism stakeholders (Brown et al., 2007).

The value that wine tourism networks create significantly affects the supply side of wine tourism. Experience has shown that wine tourism stakeholders can share knowledge and experiences on best practices, work on solutions to similar problems they face and find partners with high expertise on wine, marketing and hospitality issues from all over the world (Alebaki and Iakovidou 2011). Moreover, they can collaborate in order to design better services and provide satisfactory tourism experiences or even establish common benchmarks for the improvement of their services (Roberts and Sparks 2006; Nella and Christou 2010; Sigala and Chalkiti 2008). The collaboration of wine tourism stakeholders into a regional or global network can create synergies not only for the improvement of their operations and services, but also for their communicational and promotional efforts.

Wine tourism networks may also benefit the demand side, i.e. the wine tourists or, more broadly, the wine-interested consumers. Wine consumers and tourists can be significantly assisted in evaluating information for particular wine varieties, wine brands and wine tourism destinations (Yuan et al., 2006; Kolyesnikova and Dodd 2008). Moreover, their interest in wine tourism could be further stimulated if well organized tourism experiences are offered to them on behalf of the members of the network.

Despite their importance and value, there is still great potential for network creation and expansion in the wine tourism sector, both locally and globally. Buhalis and Kaldis (2008) suggest that networks and clusters should exploit new technologies in order to increase interaction and collaboration. One area of improvement for wine tourism networks is to further exploit social media, since, "the wine industry is notoriously slow at embracing new technologies … although, especially in this industry, social media are predicted to evolve into social commerce".[1] Even today, there are many wine and wine tourism organizations that restrict their activities to the use of a sole website and the traditional one-way communication model (Christou et al., 2009).

Social media allow real time information sharing among network members, thus vastly facilitating communication, knowledge exchange, social interaction and collaboration not only at the regional and national level but globally as well (Rocha and Victor 2010; Sigala 2008). Moreover, Web 2.0 applications, due to the interactivity element that they offer can enhance the interest and engagement of current members. It is also easier for potential new members to be informed about the existence and the value of a network and evaluate whether to join it or not. Social media help to overcome the distance barriers and other communication obstacles.

Social media can also play a crucial role for consumer behavior towards wine. If we take for granted that community opinions can be more influential for intentions compared to advertising messages or professional reviews for wines, we realize the great impact that social media could have for brand awareness, brand acceptance, trial and other behavioural intentions. Quite apart from that, social media platforms and user generated content can contribute to creating or increasing the interest and engagement of wine consumers for a wine producing destination, a winery, a wine variety or a wine brand (Sigala 2006; Gill et al., 2007; Sigala 2010). If we accept that social media are playing an increasingly important role as information sources for travellers (Xiang and Gretzel 2010), we can realize the great potential that is untapped for wineries, wine festival organizers and wine tourism destinations (Christou and Nella 2010). Last but not least, social media can assist the members of wine tourism networks to gather valuable information on the profiles, motives, perceptions and attitudes of wine consumers and tourists.

Obviously, Web 2.0 enables every stakeholder to network (Sigala and Chalkiti 2011). There are different types of wine tourism stakeholders who may benefit from networks, e.g. wine tourists, DMO's, clusters of wine producers etc.

1 VinTank Report 2009. Available at: http://www.vintank.com/wp-content/uploads/2010/03/VinTank_SocialMediaReport.pdf [Accessed: 9 October 2010].

Various types of Web 2.0 social networks can be utilized according to the type of stakeholders. In this chapter, emphasis is put on business networks relating to wine tourism: two interesting cases of networks that, apart from creating significant value for their members, have eagerly utilized Web 2.0 tools (social media, blogs and online forums) in order to enhance their efforts are:

- wineandhospitalitynetwork.com: a global network linking professionals of the wine and hospitality sectors, i.e. wineries, sommeliers, oenologists and other stakeholders of wine tourism destinations.
- greatwinecapitals.com: a network of nine global wine tourism destinations that seek to create synergies, value and knowledge exchange for stakeholders of the member cities.

2. The Great Wine Capitals Global Network (GWCGN)

Collaboration practices are common in the business arena, partly due to the pressures of rapidly intense competition, changing technologies and market turbulence. Currently, the competitive advantages of an organization do not solely depend on its internal capabilities and resources but also on the strength of its network, such as the type and scope of its relationships with other organizations (Lee and Cavusgil 2006). The issues of organizational alliances, clusters and networks have been well documented in the management and strategy literature while the benefits and drawbacks of such strategies and structures have also been discussed extensively. As noted by Reuer et al. (2006), inter-organizational alliances do not only offer great benefits but pose challenges as well. Among the benefits of strategic alliances, Dacin et al. (1997) mention the abilities for sharing risks, exchanging resources, accessing new markets, achieving economies of scale, obtaining synergies and competitive advantages. Gomes-Casseres et al. (2006) argued that knowledge flows between alliance partners is greater than flows between pairs of non-allied firms.

In the tourism literature, co-ordination, defined by Schianetz et al. (2007) as formal inter-organizational relations (e.g. networks and partnerships) and its importance to maintain and increase the competitiveness and sustainability of tourism destinations have been discussed extensively (e.g. Bramwell and Lane 2000; Saxena 2005). Several attempts have been made using networking, clustering and agglomeration theories to explain the role of tourism in influencing local growth and stimulating regional development (Novelli et al., 2006).

When referring to tourism destination networks, it is most common that authors examine the relationship among tourism stakeholders within a specific destination. In the case study presented in this section the term network extends to link nine global wine tourism destinations and their main stakeholders.

The Great Wine Capitals Global Network (GWCGN) is a network owned by nine major global cities that share a key economic and cultural asset: their internationally renowned wine-producing regions. GWCGN constitutes a significant link for the destinations of Bilbao-Rioja in Spain, Bordeaux in France, Cape Town in South Africa, Christchurch-South Island in New Zealand, Firenze in Italy, Mainz-Rheinhessen in Germany, Mendoza in Argentina, Porto in Portugal and San Francisco-Napa Valley in the USA. Created in 1999, it is the only network that encompasses the so-called 'Old' and 'New' worlds of wine. It primarily aims at heightening the wine experience for visitors and helping the cities themselves to make the most of their culture, heritage and geographical locations.

The network strongly encourages travel, education and business exchanges among the destinations. The Permanent Secretary of GWCGN has the task of organizing and managing the Network and its member cities. The common budget of the network is financed by each member city on an equal basis and is managed by the Permanent Secretary, according to the different programs led by the four Thematic Committees (Tourism, Education & Research, Business & Investment and Marketing & Communication). The brand "Great Wine Capitals Global Network" and the logo are registered. Technical and/or commercial exploratory trips to the member wine regions are encouraged, since knowledge-sharing is a crucial and integrative part of the network. The network also exploits Web 2.0 in order to create a point of interactive contact between interested stakeholders.

The benefits of being a member of the GWC global network are commonly recognized by key-stakeholders of the nine regions. As mentioned by representatives of the member capitals (source: GWCGN website) these benefits "assist to strengthen economic and institutional bonds among some of the most famous wine regions in the world, create potential for joint partnerships among private and public organizations, successfully project the cities' image, remain up to date with international developments, share knowledge and ideas, create benchmarks and adopt best practices, enhance the country's reputation in the industry, facilitate international wine tourism, create economic and academic links, keep lines of communication opening, leverage positions in the world of wine, maintain status and provide opportunities to meet with business, government and industry people from the global wine and tourism business".

Some of the main activities of the network include the following:

- Symposiums of experts on investments in the wine sector and education initiatives in wine and conferences held to debate and illuminate crucial issues that affect the wider world of wine.
- A business network with extensive training and information seminars, forums and tastings. Business facilities are also provided for visits between member cities.
- An international annual competition; the 'Best of Wine Tourism' awards, designed to recognize excellence and encourage wider participation in wine tourism initiatives in the member cities. The categories of the awards include Accommodation, Architecture, Parks and Gardens, Art and Culture,

Innovative Wine Tourism Experiences, Sustainable Wine Tourism Practices, Restaurants and Wine Tourism Services. Wineries, hotels, restaurants, museums, and other wine tourism-related businesses can be nominated for these awards.

- An annual International Student Grant that aims at promoting excellence and innovativeness in wine research and encourages research in topics interesting the Network (wine tourism, wine marketing, sustainability).
- The Business Services Network. Within the GWCGN, commercial, industrial and services firms of the member cities can benefit from a range of services, thanks to existing partnerships. These services aim at facilitating the welcoming, business contacts and logistics for companies during their business trips abroad. Companies from the nine member cities can use the Business Services Network when they consider going through an activity of internationalization. The Network can provide businesses with partner research for production agreement, commercial agreements, license or representation agreement, financial agreement, joint ventures and subcontracts, franchising, technological and know-how transfer, consulting and marketing services etc.
- Technical and /or commercial exploratory trips to each of the nine member regions. Knowledge-sharing is a crucial part of the network, as is the idea behind this that each city can benefit from the strengths of their neighbours in the network.
- A Travel Network to facilitate travel between the regions, where travel agencies in each city develop custom-made food and wine itineraries and are able to handle all travel requirements to and between the GWC. The Travel Network is a global alliance of travel agencies (one per city) endorsed for their proven track record in developing custom-made wine and food itineraries for both individuals and groups. It aims to develop the offer of tourism services and market standards, co-operate to generate awareness of wine tourism for the nine regions of GWC, co-operate in the offer and sales of programs evolving more than one GWC region, improve expertise by sharing experiences for quality improvement and 'best practices' that should be implemented. The co-operation between the networks' travel agencies has enabled them to organize educational trips to the destinations of GWC for travel agents and promote the regions and travel services in major events.

After this extensive description of the network and its activities, the Web 2.0 tools it uses are presented in the following section.

Web 2.0 Tools Used by GWCGN

The wide activities of the network are facilitated through their website and the Web 2.0 tools that the network uses, which provide:

- Alternative options for various wine tourism stakeholders of the nine regions to connect and stay in touch with the network (Facebook, Twitter, LinkedIn, GWC blog); wine tourists and wine interested consumers may also join the social media that the network uses and keep up with latest events and news.
- Extensive tourism information on the nine wine producing regions (e.g. travel and accommodation options), newsletters and press releases.
- A file management platform specially intended for partners/capitals of GWC; this tool serves as a knowledge sharing platform for the members of the network.
- Recommended links to related content (e.g. wine blogs, wine tourism destinations, resorts and attractions, wine producers and retailers, wine education, communication and marketing services etc.); website visitors may also suggest links to related content.

GWCGN seems to acknowledge the importance of social networks, such as Facebook, Twitter and LinkedIn for information exchange, social interaction, targeting, market penetration and brand acceptance. As stated in one of their newsletters (February 2010), "these three networks provide a good variety of connections to people and companies that share our interests … they also help promote both our brand as a Global Network and our individual wine Capitals. It also gives us an opportunity to build relationships that develop our international wine tourism community".

Facebook (http://www.Facebook.com/GreatWineCapitals)

More than 1,000 Facebook users "like" GWCGN while there are many comments, news and information on the relevant Facebook page regarding upcoming wine tasting and winery events, publications concerning wine, awards nominees and winners, innovations taking place in the industry, new wine labels, business and scientific seminars, symposia and conferences, wine tourism experiences, wine festivals, meetings and public relations activities of the wine industry etc. Wine related photo albums and videos are also shared through Facebook. Moreover, there are more than 500 links with wine blogs and wine-related websites.

Twitter (http://twitter.com/GWCGN)

There are more than 600 followers of GWC, 300 friends and 1,200 tweets. There are also approximately 60 lists following GWCGN, including lists of wine blogs, professional chambers, tourism and travel organizations, gastronomic and wine industry organizations. The RSS feed of GWCGN's tweets is available while updates can be sent via sms.

LinkedIn (http://www.linkedin.com/groups?gid=1931378&trk=hb_side_g)

While LinkedIn is used purely for professionals, it is probably one of the most overlooked networks for professionals of the wine industry, according to the VinTank Social Media report (Bromley and Wark 2009). Though, LinkedIn provides an excellent tool for interaction between professionals of the same business fields, such as sommeliers, oenologists, tasting room managers etc. GWCGN utilizes this important tool to encourage and facilitate interaction among its members.

The GWC blog (http://www.greatwinecapitals.com/?1&it=blog&LG=1)

The blog is an addition to the wealth of information already available on the network's website. Its posts mainly concern issues such as wine trails, wine tourism events, wine festivals, wine tourism destinations, awards, winery architecture, wine exhibitions, wine markets and other issues that attract the interest of wine interested publics. For wine tourists, organizing a trip to a wine region can be a major challenge. Unlike the majority of ordinary travel guides, there are few guides to specifically orient the wine tourist through the maze of wineries and events taking place in wine producing countries around the world.

The wine travel blog created by the GWCWN can give answers to questions such as when is the best time to visit a wine region, which are the best places to visit, where visitors can get a good meal etc. Written collectively by experts from the Network, the blog leads readers to the "hottest" places to go and things to do in these vibrant cities and their nearby wine regions. For example, where to sample Grand Cru Bordeaux by the glass, which are the dates of the most popular wine festivals in southern New Zealand, the Western Cape in South Africa and Mendoza, where are the best tapas bars in Rioja and the most distinctive restaurant in the Napa Valley etc. In addition, guest posts are contributed by wine, food and tourism experts from around the world. A link to the blog is at the home page of the GWC website while in the blog there are links to Facebook, LinkedIn and Twitter groups.

The GWCGN website (http://www.greatwinecapitals.com)

Quite apart from the social media tools, a content-rich website is available. Website visitors have the opportunity to be informed on events organized in the capitals through a calendar tool while they can also subscribe to newsletters and complete information request forms. The website also hosts a guests' book where visitors can express their opinion and comments. Many testimonials and recommended links to other websites and blogs of relative interest are also available (e.g. http://newbordeaux.blogspot.co.uk, http://legendarynapavalley.org, http://vinography.com, www.openwineconsortium.org, www.wine.co.za). Finally, website visitors may subscribe to the newsletter in order to be informed on recent news or access photos and videos from a multimedia gallery. RSS technology is used in order to connect and get the latest updates for GWC news, events and blog.

Challenges and Suggestions

GWCGN is a network making continuous efforts to enrich its activities and promote them for the common benefit of its member cities. Perhaps its impact could be further strengthened if more wine producing regions join it in the near future. Although this could cause issues of increased complexity and would demand increased co-ordination efforts it could definitely create greater synergies and enhance its image as a global and leading network for wine tourism destinations.

3. The Wine and Hospitality Network (WHN)

In today's world, online collaboration constitutes a major resource for professionals. The World Wide Web opened up new possibilities for people to collaborate and to form networks of business interest. Online communities can be an excellent means for professionals to maintain currency of knowledge, access the expertise of peers and share resources (Bowes 2002). Professional networks, like LinkedIn and Plaxo, have attracted millions of dedicated global users and provided powerful tools to enable them to digitally recreate professional needs, such as sharing professional details and linking with colleagues (Ianella 2009). Moreover, social sources of opportunity-related information, such as informal industry networks and participation in professional forums proved to have direct, positive effects on opportunity recognition by entrepreneurs (Shane 2003; Ozgen and Baron 2007). In this section, an exemplary network for professionals is presented.

The Wine and Hospitality Network (wineandhospitalitynetwork.com) is a world-wide community for professionals in the beverage, hospitality, hotel, restaurant, wine and related industries. It serves as a social network that addresses mainly professional groups that are involve with wine and hospitality, such as bartenders, independent hoteliers, consultants, retailers, importers and distributors, sommeliers, tasting room managers, wine makers, wine bloggers and other related professional groups. It is a valuable industry resource containing relative blogs, forums, events calendar, news, magazines, videos, jobs, surveys and other sources of information that can help a professional build their career. Serving as a communication network, it allows professionals to search for partners, exchange views, pose questions or share best practices.

The network is owned and operated by "Outside the Lines, Inc", a consulting company that offers business solutions for the wine and hospitality industries. The company also owns and operates WineAndHospitalityJobs.com – a job site for the wine and hospitality industry, with over 110.000 registered users, and Wine &

Hospitality Ezine – an ezine for wine and hospitality professionals, emailed out in HTML weekly to over 85,000 industry professionals.

The WHN has approximately 2,800 active members, more than 400 blog posts and 300 discussions around wine and tourism, thousands of photos and videos and provides information for hundreds of wine related events. As these numbers imply, the network is very active in terms of Web 2.0 exploitation; it uses blogs, Facebook, Twitter and discussion forums in order to connect these industry professionals. The network is a point of direct and synchronous contact of highly skilled and interested professionals from all over the world. A description of the Web 2.0 activities of the network follows.

Web 2.0 Tools used by the Wine and Hospitality Network

Facebook (http://www.Facebook.com/whnetwork)

On the Facebook page WHN is described as "Social networking for professionals in the beverage, hospitality, hotel, restaurant, wine and related industries". There are approximately 4,500 Facebook users who "like" it and more than 1,100 links to wine producing regions and wine varieties, wine awards and publications, wine festivals and tastings, wine and food pairings and many other wine related issues. Facebook users can easily subscribe to the newsletter or become members of WHN, while interesting wine events are communicated in a special section.

Blog (http://blogs.wineandhospitalitynetwork.com/index.php/whnblog/)

Not surprisingly, the majority of blog topics refer to wines while others refer to business, winery, marketing and sales issues. Some of the most popular blog posts concern news that relates to wine production or specific wine regions, hospitality issues, current trends or proposed business solutions for wineries, restaurants and other professional groups. In order to add comments, one has to be a member of the Wine and Hospitality Network.

Twitter (twitter.com/winehospitality) and forums (wineandhospitalitynetwork.com/forum)

There are approximately 800 followers of WHN, 65 lists following WHN and approximately 1,000 tweets. Updates can be sent via sms. Online discussion forums are divided into four broad content categories: a) winery/ wine industry (where users discuss about wine suggestions, tasting rooms, wine clubs, issues of wine storage etc.), b) culinary, restaurant, food and beverage (e.g. dining service techniques, cost control tips, help on management and chef decisions), c) hotel, hospitality and lodging (e.g. hotel management, quality issues) and d) general topics that cannot be included in the other listing categories (e.g. best practices, use of social media etc.). Users may ask for or provide suggestions and pieces of advice on wine varieties and brands. They can also discuss business issues (e.g. software appropriateness and alternative techniques concerning wine production) or even search for partners, such as sales representatives to promote a wine abroad.

Website content (http://wineandhospitalitynetwork.com)

Rich website content is available at the site, which is structured in the following main sections:

1. "Invite": this section gives members the opportunity to invite friends and colleagues to join the network.
2. "My page": where members can manage their profile page in the network.
3. "Members": which contains details and information for all of the members of the network.
4. "Media", with the following sub-sections: "Our bloggers", "Member blogs", "Press releases & submissions", "Photos", "Videos", "Free industry magazine subscriptions" and "Articles" (articles can be submitted via e-mail).
5. "Education": "E-learning" (Online classes, certifications, etc.) and "Groups", such as geographic and professional groups (e.g. bartenders, beverage sales, catering, independent hoteliers, consultants, customer service, retailers, importers and distributors, sommeliers, tasting room managers, wine makers, wine bloggers, wine club management etc.).
6. "Social": events calendar and submission of recipes.
7. "Jobs": which serves as a link to wineandhospitalityjobs.com, a job site for the wine and hospitality industry, with over 110,000 registered users.
8. "Advertising" (advertising opportunities for companies, products, events, trade shows or conferences, offers).
9. "Wine and Hospitality Ezine" (an ezine for wine & hospitality professionals, emailed out in HTML weekly to over 85,000 industry professionals).

4. Conclusions and Practical Recommendations

Despite the continuously increasing adoption and usage rates of social media and user generated content, there are not many wine tourism networks that fully exploit them. It may be argued that the two cases that are described here are not particularly innovative or pioneering in the use of Web 2.0 tools, at least not if compared to companies and organizations from other sectors of tourism; However, GWC and WHN are among the first networks in the field of wine tourism to have realized the contribution of Web 2.0 tools in achieving their objectives and their importance, predicted to grow even more. In particular, it may be concluded that GWC exploits Web 2.0 tools in order to build and strengthen relationships among various stakeholders in the wine and tourism sectors, both private and public, that develop their international wine tourism community. WHN's objectives seem rather different, as it appears to invest in social media in order to connect different wine tourism professionals and help them to expand their activities, exchange information, knowledge and experiences. Perhaps, these two cases could provide paradigms for other wine and tourism networks in order to further expand the use of social media in wine tourism.

Online social networks and user generated content concerning wine in general are numerous, more active than those concerning wine tourism and highly popular. In this vein, it may be safely assumed that there is a significant opportunity for wine tourism stakeholders to take advantage of the existing pool of the "wine interested" market segment and further stimulate this segment's interest so as to include wine tourism activities. Networks can act decisively in this direction, as they can create direct and indirect benefits for their members and additional value for wine tourists. Web 2.0 tools can certainly facilitate this attempt and as their use is constantly becoming more popular, it becomes evident that the wine tourism sector should not let itself get left behind.

The use of Web 2.0 tools is expected to become mandatory for all social and business networks in the future. Given the vast opportunities that remain untapped for creating global networks in wine tourism, there is still a long way to go. The necessity for wine tourism organizations to create synergies and business alliances becomes even more imperative in a highly turbulent market environment and an era of intense and constantly growing global competition.

References

Alebaki, M. and Iakovidou, O. 2011. Market segmentation in wine tourism: A comparison of approaches. *Tourismos*, 6(1), 123-140.

Bowes, J. 2002. *Building Online Communities for Professional Networks: Proceedings of the Global Summit of Online Knowledge Networks* (Adelaide, Australia, March). Available at: http://www.educationau.edu.au/ globalsummit/papers/jbowes.htm [accessed: 23 December 2010].

Bramwell, B. and Sharman, A. 1999. Collaboration in local tourism policy making. *Annals of Tourism Research*, 26(2), 392-415.

Brás, J.M., Costa, C. and Buhalis, D. 2010. Network analysis and wine routes: The case of the Bairrada Wine Route. *The Service Industries Journal*, 30(10), 1621-1641.

Bromley, D. and Wark, T. 2009. *The State of Wine Industry Social Media*. VinTank 2009 Report. Available at: http://www.vintank.com/wp-content/uploads/2010/03/VinTank_SocialMediaReport.pdf [accessed: 23 December 2010].

Brown, G.P., Havitz, M.E. and Getz, D. 2007. Relationship between wine involvement and wine-related travel. *Journal of Travel & Tourism Marketing*, 21(1), 31-46.

Buhalis, D. and Kaldis, K. 2008. Enabled internet distribution for small and medium sized hotels: The case of Athens. *Tourism Recreation Research*, 33(1), 67-81.

Chalkiti, K. and Sigala, M. 2008. Information Sharing and Knowledge Creation in online forums: The case of the Greek online forum "DIALOGOI". *Current Issues in Tourism*, 11, 381-406.

Christou, E., Kassianidis, P., Sigala, M. and Tsiakali, K. 2009. Electronic marketing systems of wine and wine tourism: Best practices and growth prospects. E-business Forum Report. Available at: http://www.ebusinessforum.gr/teams/teamsall/view/index.php?ctn=119&language=el [accessed: 19 December 2010].

Christou, E. and Nella, A. 2010. A review of wine-tourism research from 1995-2010: Analysis of 111 contributions. *Journal of Hospitality & Tourism*, 8(1), 112-123.

Dacin, M.T., Hitt, M.A. and Levitas, E. 1997. Selecting partners for successful international alliances: Examination of US and Korean firms. *Journal of World Business*, 32(1), 3-16.

Dodd, T. 2000. Influences on cellar door sales and determinants of wine tourism success: Results from Texas wineries, in *Wine Tourism Around the World: Development, Management and Markets*, edited by C.M. Hall, L. Sharples, B. Cambourne and N. Macionis. Oxford: Elsevier Science, 136-149.

Gill D., Byslma B. and Ouschan R. 2007. Customer perceived value in a cellar door visit: The impact on behavioural intentions. *International Journal of Wine Business Research*, 19(4), 257-275.

Gomes-Casseres, B., Hagedoorn, J. and Jaffe, A. 2006. Do alliances promote knowledge flows? *Journal of Financial Economics*, 80(1), 5-33.

Iannella, R. 2009. *Industry Challenges for Social and Professional Networks*. W3C Workshop on the Future of Social Networking, Spain.

Kolyesnikova, N. and Dodd, T. 2008. Effects of winery visitor group size on gratitude and obligation. *Journal of Travel Research*, 47(1), 104-112.

Lee, Y. and Cavusgil, T. 2006. Enhancing alliance performance: The effects of contractual-based versus relational-based governance. *Journal of Business Research*, 59, 896-905.

Nella, A. and Christou, E. 2010. Investigating the effects of consumer experience tourism on brand equity and market outcomes: An application in the wine industry. 63rd Annual I-CHRIE Convention. Available at: http://scholarworks.umass.edu/refereed/CHRIE_2010/Friday/14 [accessed: 23 December 2010].

Novelli, M., Schmitz, B. and Spencer, T. 2006. Networks, clusters and innovation in tourism: A UK experience. *Tourism Management*, 27(5), 1141-1152.

Ozgen, E. and Baron, R.A. 2007. Social sources of information in opportunity recognition: Effects of mentors, industry networks, and professional forums. *Journal of Business Venturing*, 22(2), 174-192.

Reuer, J., Arino, A. and Mellewigt, T. 2006. Entrepreneurial alliances as contractual forms. *Journal of Business Venturing*, 21(2), 306-325.

Roberts, L. and Sparks, B. 2006. Enhancing the wine tourism experience: The customers' viewpoint, in *Global Wine Tourism: Research Management and Marketing*, edited by J. Carlsen and S. Charters. Wallingford: CAB International, 47-66.

Rocha, Á. and Victor, J.A. 2010. Quality of hotels websites: Proposal for the development of an assessment methodology. *Tourismos*, 5(1), 173-178.

Saxena, G. 2005. Relationships, networks and the learning regions: Case evidence from the Peak District National Park. *Tourism Management*, 26(2), 277-289.

Schianetz, K., Kavanagh, L. and Lockington, D. 2007. The learning tourism destination: The potential of a learning organisation approach for improving the sustainability of tourism destinations. *Tourism Management*, 28(6), 1485-1496.

Shane, S. 2003. *A General Theory of Entrepreneurship: The Individual-Opportunity Nexus*. Cheltenham, UK: Edward Elgar.

Sigala, M. 2005. Networking in the tourism supply chain: Evaluating the readiness of small and medium tourism enterprises of an island economy, in *Situación actual, implicaciones y perspectivas futuras del turismo en Canarias. Vol.2*, edited by Garcia Francisco Calero and Eduardo Parra-López. Escuela Universitaria de Ciencias Empresariales (EUCE) University de la Laguna: Tenerife, Spain, 27-39.

Sigala, M. 2006. e-Customer relationship management in the hotel sector: Guests' perceptions of perceived e-service quality levels. *Tourism*, 54(4), 334-344.

Sigala, M. 2008. WEB 2.0, social marketing strategies and distribution channels for city destinations: Enhancing the participatory role of travellers and exploiting their collective intelligence, in *Information Communication Technologies and City Marketing: Digital Opportunities for Cities around the World*, edited by Mila Gascó-Hernández and Teresa Torres-Coronas. Hershey, PA: IDEA Publishing, 220-244.

Sigala, M. 2010. Measuring customer value in online collaborative trip planning processes. *Marketing Intelligence and Planning*, 28(4), 418-443.

Sigala, M. and Chalkiti, K. 2007. Improving performance through tacit knowledge externalization and utilization: preliminary findings from Greek hotels. *International Journal of Productivity & Performance Management*, 56, 456-483.

Sigala, M. and Chalkiti, K. 2011. Knowledge Management and Web 2.0: Preliminary findings from the Greek tourism industry, in *Social Media in Travel, Tourism and Hospitality: Theory, Practice and Cases*, edited by M. Sigala, E. Christou and U. Gretzel. Farnham: Ashgate.

Xiang, Z. and Gretzel, U. 2010. Role of social media in online travel information search. *Tourism Management*, 31(1), 179-188.

Yuan J., Morrison, A., Cai, L. and Linton, S. 2008. A model of wine tourist behaviour: A festival approach. *International Journal of Tourism Research*, 10(2), 207-219.

Chapter 3

Web 2.0 and Customer Involvement in New Service Development: A Framework, Cases and Implications in Tourism

Marianna Sigala

1. Introduction

As global competition intensifies and tourism demand becomes more sophisticated, new service development (NSD) is not only a competitive but a survival necessity in the tourism industry (Sigala and Chalkiti 2007). Nowadays, Web 2.0 advances offer new and numerous opportunities to tourism firms to actively engage their customers with NSD processes. In reviewing the literature on customer engagement and NSD, Sigala (2008) identified four streams of current research advocating the business benefits for involving and exploiting customers' intelligence into NSD: customer partnerships (e.g. Gruner and Homberg 2000; von Hippel 2001; Magnusson et al., 2003); open innovation (e.g. Chesbrough 2003); customer co-creation and service-dominant logic (e.g. Vargo and Lusch 2004); and customer empowerment and innovation through Web 2.0 tools (e.g. Dahan and Hauser 2002; Pitta and Fowler 2005; Sigala 2008; Kohler et al., 2009). By exploiting the customer intelligence of Web 2.0, firms can better understand and address customer needs and market trends and so reduce innovation failure rates, as the latter have been traditionally attributed to a lack of a market understanding and orientation (Menor et al., 2002; Martin and Horne 1995). However, despite these theoretical arguments, empirical studies provide divergent results regarding the benefits, risks and problems created when involving customers into NPD processes (Enkel et al., 2005; Leonard and Rayport 1997). Moreover, there has been limited research on the role and the impact of customer involvement on the effectiveness of NPD processes, not only in general (Akamavi 2005), but also in the Web 2.0 literature (Kohler et al., 2009; Sigala 2008). Thus, research investigating how to effectively exploit Web 2.0 for successfully integrating customers into NSD is guaranteed that is important and needed to be conducted.

This chapter aims to address this gap by reviewing the existing literature on customer involvement and Web 2.0 as well as by analysing two related case studies from the tourism industry. The practical implications of these case studies are identified and discussed in order to provide tourism firms with more suggestions on how to fully exploit the innovation potential of Web 2.0. Overall, the chapter provides a holistic framework based on which tourism firms can identify the ways in which they can exploit the two features of Web 2.0 (namely customer intelligence and social networks) for actively engaging customers into NSD processes.

2. Customer Involvement in NSD: Benefits and Disadvantages

Information about customer and market trends is a necessary resource in all stages of NPD to reduce uncertainty and risk regarding the market conditions, including customer expectations and needs, and other competitive issues (Zahay et al., 2004; Carlile 2001; Christou and Kassianidis 2002; Christou 2006). There are many sources of such information, but customers are recognized as the most valuable source for gaining direct and reliable market intelligence (Sigala and Chalkiti 2007; Christou and Kassianidis 2010). However, although, understanding customers is very important, mere understanding and knowledge of customer needs are often not sufficient for successful NPD. In addition, the customer has to be active participating and providing valuable feedback in as many NPD stages as possible. As a result, several studies and streams of research currently advocate the need to actively involve customers with NSD (e.g. Franke and Piller 2004; Chesbrough 2003). This notion was initially argued by Von Hippel (1976) who introduced the customer active paradigm (CAP) whereby the customer is active in NPD, as opposed to the manufacturing active paradigm (MAP) in which the manufacturer generates the new product ideas and conducts all problem solving. The key difference lies in the role that the customer plays during the NPD process. The CAP was later extended to an interaction perspective, called the lead user concept (von Hippel 1988), which suggests that interaction with certain customers (i.e. the lead users who face needs that will be general in a marketplace) can result in new product success. Currently, there is a plethora of definitions of customer involvement in NSD (e.g. Matthing et al., 2004; Kristensson et al., 2008), but all of them conceptualize it as interactions and partnerships between current (or potential) customers and firms with the goal to produce superior mutual benefits to both parties. In sum, customer involvement reflects a shift of NSD from *'designing for customers'* to *'designing with'* and *'design by'* customers that transforms customers from a passive audience to active players of the NSD processes (Sigala 2012).

Numerous studies report the benefits of customer involvement in NSD. For example, Magnusson et al. (2003) demonstrates that user involvement makes ideas for new products more original and it enhances new products' perceived value by users, while, it can also makes users' ideas less producible. Other studies (e.g. von Hippel 2001; Lagrossen 2005; Sanberg 2007; Alam 2002; Matthing et al., 2004; Enkel et al., 2005) have demonstrated that by integrating consumers in NPD processes, firms can achieve a wide range of benefits related to NPD success, such as: the development of products that match and satisfy customers' needs; public relations and development/improvement of relationships with customers; better understanding of market needs; reduction of market failure and errors in the early NPD stages; reduction in time to market; speed up the NPD process; high new product acceptance rates; superior quality and a differentiated service; user education; and rapid diffusion of innovation.

On the other hand, the literature also provides opposing views regarding user involvement in NPD. These views mainly refer to the limitations of the information that the firm can gain from customers either indirectly (e.g. by conducting market research) or directly (e.g. by involving customers in NPD processes). Analytically, Sigala (2008) summarized three reasons for which satisfying consumers' articulated needs will lead to product failures: a) consumers can only perceive what they currently relate to; b) consumers cannot express and verbalize their needs because they do not know what is technologically feasible; and c) expressed consumer needs may change until the new product is developed and launched in the market. Leonard and Rayport (1997) and Christensen (1997) agreed with this by advocating customers' insufficient technical knowledge and inability to express their perceived or latent needs in order to produce breakthrough and disrupting innovations. von Hippel (1986) defined the human tendency to fixate on the way products or services are normally used as functional fixedness and they also recognized that the latter can significantly hinder firms' ability to engage in radical innovations, because users have a tendency to focus solely on improving existing products rather than finding and suggesting a new one. Deszca et al. (1999) emphasized that gaining information about customers and their needs is more difficult in the case of radical innovations, whereby the firm may not even know who the future potential customers of the new product may be or even if the customers are identified they may not be able to articulate their needs for a new product. Enkel et al. (2005) summarize the risks of customer integration in NPD as follows: loss of know-how since information is shared; over-dependence on customer views, personality and demands and difficulties in selecting appropriate users; limitation to mere incremental innovation; serves a niche market only if the customers involved are not representative of the marketplace.

On the contrary, recent research (Sigala 2012; Hoyer et al., 2010; Alam 2006) attributes the limitation of customer involvement of addressing the real customer needs, not to the abilities and characteristics of the customers per se, but: a) to the inabilities of the classical methods of customer involvement in NPD (e.g. focus groups, market researches, direct interviews, surveys) to explore the deeper determinants of customer affection and real wants, as these methods solely focus on gathering the rational and conscious customer needs; and b) to the managers and researchers who do not know how to interact with customers, how to listen to and interpret their voice and obtain the correct and tacit input from them. To resolve the problem of the information quality gleaned from the customers, firms need to develop richer interactions and communication processes with their customers than simply information-processing approaches. Web 2.0 advances empower firms to enhance customer involvement in NSD by fostering highly interactive customer interactions and communications which in turn provide a greater depth and breath of market intelligence. The role of Web 2.0 in supporting and enhancing customer involvement is analysed below.

3. Web 2.0 and Customer Involvement in NSD

Traditional research about customer involvement in NSD (e.g. Alan 2002) has shown that it is possible and suggested to engage customers into all stages of NSD. Actually some researchers (e.g. Kujala 2003) recommend involving the user at early stages since the cost involved in making changes increases during the later stages of development. Currently, Web 2.0 has also accelerated and mushroomed the possibilities to engage customers into all stages of NSD. Indeed, research demonstrates how the two features of Web 2.0 (namely social intelligence and networking) can be exploited for supporting and enhancing customer involvement. For example, studies (Sigala 2011; Evans and Wolf 2005) have emphasized the need to identify and use user-generated content for: conducting quick and reliable market research; identifying customers' needs and suggestions for product and process improvements; and informating and reducing the risks of NSD processes. Erat et al. (2006) discussed how the different types of online communities of practice (e.g. B2C, C2C) can be used for acquiring and sharing customer knowledge in order to improve business processes and performance. Pitta and Fowler (2005) also examined the use and benefits of using communities of practice for identifying, accessing lead users and using them in NPD stages such as, idea generation and screening, product – service testing and piloting, product design, delivery preferences and price testing. They specifically argued that lead users participating in online communities not only receive great credibility by their peers, but they also have access to a large-scale distribution method of their opinions and so, they can have a significant potential influence over the buying habits of others.

Beyond simply collecting and analysing customer knowledge, firms can use online social communities for actively co-operating and interacting with individual customers or customer communities in order to: generate and evaluate new ideas, design and test new products (Rowley et al., 2007; Lagrosen 2005; Dahan and Hauser 2002; Fuller et al., 2009); and develop/support social innovation communities (e.g. Nambisan 2002; Dahan and Hauser 2002) aiming to create and maintain customer bonds with the firm, its services and processes. Meeuwesen and Berends (2007) provided evidence that communities of practice can have a significant impact on NPD team's performance, because they allow participants to: identify and communicate with appropriate individuals; remove organizational structure barrier and different time zones; use efficient communication channels; engage in effective knowledge creation and management practices (e.g. storage and easy retrieval of expertise, information etc.); enhance learning; and increase trust. Overall, online innovation communities can play a major role in creating, shaping and disseminating innovation activities.

Table 3.1 Exploiting Web 2.0 for Engaging Customer into all Stages of NSD

Stage of the NSD	Activities	Examples of Web 2.0 applications that can support the activities
Idea generation and screening	Identify, collect and analyse UGC for understanding customer needs, preferences and wants and for scanning the environment Collect and use customer feedback for service improvements and upgrades Analyse customer views about competitors' offerings Engage customers in online idea brainstorming and generating sessions Identify lead users and knowledgeable customers and VC that can help with idea generation Involve customers in idea evaluation and screening Analyse user-generated content for understanding customers' criteria and features for evaluating services	Online interviews Online focus groups Online suggestion box Online forums Online brainstorming communities Online creativity groups Applications for analysing user-generated content Online idea competitions Online brand communities Social networks Crowdsourcing applications RSS for collecting social intelligence Customer review websites Blogs Podcasting networks Tags and tag clouds for analysing UGC
Service concept development and design	Engage customers and VC in developing service blueprint, features and characteristics Engage customers and VC in service co-creation and co-production	User toolkits for enabling customers to design services Wikis 3D words for developing virtual services Crowd funding initiatives whereby customers can contribute financial resources for a new service development, e.g. www.sellaband.com/www.kickstarter.com/, ww.indiegogo.com/
Service concept testing	Engage customers and VC for: testing the service blueprint testing the marketing plan and mix identifying improvements and changes determine customer acceptance and intensions to adopt new services	online simulations of service experiences, e.g. 3D words virtual tests of the marketing mix (4Ps) of new services, e.g. initiate and test a campaign in secondlife
Launch and commercialization	Engage customers and VC in service marketing and promotion Identify customer networks and opinion leaders for promoting new services	e-word-of-mouth brand communities social networks blogs podcasting networks

Kim et al. (2008) identified three types of innovations that firms can develop by exploiting 3D words such as secondlife: a) immersive prototyping for evaluating the design of spaces, products or services and receiving feedback on how to improve implementation and delivery in the real environment; b) immersive event simulation to simulate real-world events to study people's reactions and behaviours (e.g. a disaster for emergency services, festivals, wedding services etc.); and c) immersive commerce which can be used for increasing commercial activity in the real world (e.g. launch and promotion of a new product, education of the new market of the use of the new product etc.). Kohler et al. (2009) have also analysed how 3D words can be used for engaging customers into the design and testing of services' prototypes.

In summary, by summarizing and synthesizing the previous literature, Table 3.1 provides a holistic framework on how Web 2.0 can be exploited for supporting and enhancing customer involvement in NSD. It should be noted that in all NSD activities supported by Web 2.0, firms can use three interaction modes for collecting social intelligence created and diffused through the Web 2.0: convert, overt and mixed modes. In a convert interaction an employee becomes a community member and without disclosing its identity, it asks questions to the virtual community (VC) for collecting information and feedback. A convert interaction also includes Web 2.0 applications that collect and analyse user-generated content (UGC) without the customer knowing it. In an overt interaction, the customer is aware of the firms' activities, as the firm identifies itself and the employee(s) interacts with the VC as an outsider. Of course, firms may also use and mix both modes for collecting UGC and interacting with their customers for NSD activities. For example, the firm's "community member" might uncover some valuable product information and in his interaction he/she might reveal his identity. Later, the firm may use this information to design a new product and then, use the VC to verify customers' interest on this.

Overall, it becomes evident that customers assume three major roles in Web 2.0 supported NSD processes: a resource for identifying and evaluating opportunities and new ideas; a co-creator for designing and improving new services; and a user for promoting/marketing the adoption and commercialization of new services. In addition, Web 2.0 tools and applications serve the following functions and roles in Web 2.0 supported NSD: a platform for collaborating, gathering, sharing and evaluating new ideas; a tool for motivating and instilling brainstorming sessions and idea generation; a tool for gathering, categorizing, visualizing and analysing social intelligence.

4. Case Studies and Implications of Web 2.0 Supported NSD in Tourism

www.mystarbucksidea.com

Starbucks developed an online social network (www.mystarbucksidea.com) for providing its current individual and corporate customers (e.g. store franchisors) a platform for contributing, evaluating, discussing and further improving ideas about new services for Starbucks. Analytically, the social network allows its users to post their ideas about new services, evaluate/vote and/or comment on the ideas contributed by others as well as develop and participate in online dialogues developed around the submitted services' ideas. Users can contribute and discuss service ideas by uploading them into specific idea categories. Three categories of new services have been defined by Starbucks in order to facilitate the online organization and search of submitted ideas and each category in sub-divided into other subgroups of ideas: product ideas (e.g. coffee, tea, food and merchandizing etc.); experience ideas (e.g. ordering, payment, atmosphere etc.) and involvement ideas (building community, social responsibility etc.).

To motivate customers to submit and comment on new service ideas, Starbucks is using normative and not functional mechanisms (Sigala 2010). In this vein, the homepage of the social network publishes on a weekly basis its top users in terms of the number of ideas and dialogue comments they have submitted, as well as the number of ideas for which they have voted. In other words, users are instilled to contribute to the online idea generation and evaluation community for obtaining social recognition and prestige from other members. So far, no financial rewards are provided to any community user.

Starbucks' staff also participates and contributes to the online social community in two ways: a) by contributing to the online dialogues/debates developed around the submitted new services ideas; and b) by maintaining a company blog which aims to inform customers about which new service ideas have been reviewed, positively evaluated and adopted by Starbucks, and the timeline for launching the new service ideas. By participating in the online dialogues, Starbuck's staff aims to inform users about the technical and business feasibility of their ideas, as well as to nurture and instil debates amongst users in order to obtain more in depth qualitative feedback and responses about customers' needs and purchase behaviour intentions. The role of the blog is twofold. First, it supports and motivates users to further contribute to the idea social networks, as it provides evidence that Starbucks does hear the voice of the customers and it takes action to address it. Consequently, customers believe that it is worth it proposing new ideas, as it is very likely that they can be implemented so that they can get services that match their needs and preferences). Secondly, the blog helps with the launch and e-marketing of the new services, as it creates buzz and awareness about the dates of the introduction of the new services. In addition, by keeping the customer informed about the progress stage of new ideas, it maintain customers' interest and anxiety to try and adopt the new services immediately after they are introduced in the market.

The use of social communities for generating and evaluating new service ideas and involving customers into the ideation stage of NSD is not new. However, in surveying tourism professionals, Sigala (2008) identified several implications and risks that firms have to address when using UGC for NSD. These are categorized and summarized below:

- The quality of UGC: is it authentic and real? Are views biased and/or manipulated by competitors and/or others?
- Appropriateness of customers involved: is the customer sample representative of the firms' current and potential customers? Are the customers involved capable to generate/evaluate new ideas (e.g. have technical and business abilities etc.)? What about unreliable customers?
- Effectiveness of the platform: is the website easy-to-use for submitting and evaluating ideas? Are customers motivated to submit ideas and comments? Has sufficient time be allowed to instill customer activity on the platform?
- Role of company staff: how does it support and instill customer activity in the short and long term? How does it moderate customers' interactions? How new service development teams are integrated with customers' participation/role in NSD? Train customers for getting involved in NSD?

In addition, firms should also address the following issues (Sigala 2012). Who owns the copyright of ideas submitted and/or discussed/improved on brainstorming platforms? Does the customer obtain any intellectual property rights and/or is the customer entitled to obtain some of the company's profits resulting from the new services? Such issues may become critically important in the future. In addition, making NSD and innovation public, the firm is also risking loosing competitive advantage and knowledge to other firms. Web 2.0 has also resulted in a huge mass of UGC, that firms have to become highly efficient to not only identify but also appropriately analyse it. Previous studies have showed the benefits of the following methodologies for analysing UGC: social network analysis, monte carlo techniques, content analysis, and linguistics approaches. Sigala (2012) used netnography for analysing customers' contributions in www.mystarbucksidea.com and concluded that in order to empower customers to propose successful new service ideas, the firms need to support and instill dialogues amongst customers, because the latter enable customers to reflect on their own and others' experiences, identify their problems, express their latent needs and, so propose new service solutions that effectively addressed the drivers of their real needs.

Aloft hotel in secondlife

Aloft hotel is a very representative case showing how Starwood Hotels have exploited an online 3D world (ww.secondlife.com) for involving customers into all stages of NSD. Before building a new hotel concept in the physical world, Starwood supported users of Secondlife to create a prototype of a new hotel concept, design and use the new hotel building and hotel rooms for testing the new product and suggesting improvements. Secondlife users also voted for the name of the new hotel concept which was titled the Aloft, and they also contributed to the launch and e-marketing of this new hotel by creating e-word-of-mouth (Schiller 2007). Currently, there are more than 15 Aloft hotels in the real word, which achieve high occupancy rates and performance, which provide evidence of the positive impact of customer involvement in the success of NSD.

In order to fully exploit the customer potential in 3D words supporting NSD, Kohler et al. (2011) highlighted the importance of several socio-technical factors of the platform that need to managed in order to provide a compelling experience to the customer and motivate/enable him to participate. These factors are the following:

- Offer customers information and guidance/training about the platform/ technologies used.
- Offer customers information about the product and the firm.
- Enable the customers to perceive themselves as members of the group community, e.g. organize events, discussion forums, welcome areas etc.
- Enhance the quality of human-computer interaction.
- Create a platform and a community environment that is mentally stimulating, enjoyable, entertaining and a source of pleasure and fun for the customers.

Unless, the customers' experience on the virtual word is gratifying, enjoyable and engaging, the customers will not get involved and contribute to their maximum potential.

5. Conclusions and Further Implications

Web 2.0 provides numerous opportunities for exploiting customer intelligence and involving customers more actively in NPD processes. The chapter has reviewed the ways in which Web 2.0 can enable customers to become more actively involved in NSD, as well as the roles and activities that customers and firms have to engage in order to exploit the innovation potential of customers. The benefits and disadvantages of Web 2.0 supported NSD have been discussed, while two case studies were also analysed for revealing and analysing in more depth the implications that firms have to manage for supporting, motivating and managing customer involvement in NSD practices. The chapter has shown that firms need to exploit Web 2.0 for being both reactive and proactive in NSD and innovation. For example, when a firm is examining blogs' content for identifying customer needs, it adopts a reactive approach to customer requests. On the contrary, when a firm creates and/or participates in a blog with the aim to influence the customer needs' and requirements by changing their cognitive processes and social values, it adopts a proactive approach to innovation for addressing customers' needs, since the firm influences the formation and shape of customers' perceptions and preferences in advance and before customers become aware of their articulated needs.

In summary, before engaging customers in NSD, firms have to address the following strategic questions:

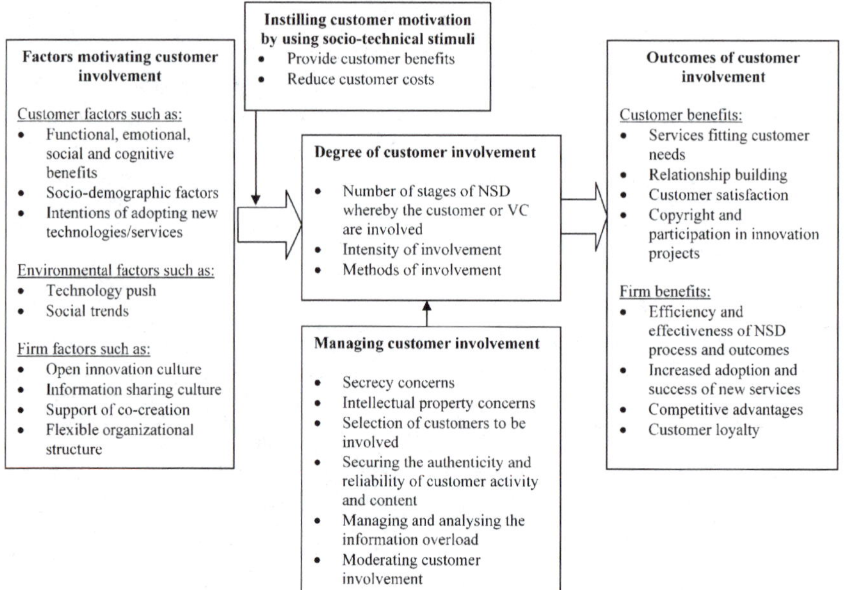

Figure 3.1 A Holistic Framework for Managing Customers Involved in Web 2.0 NSD Processes

- The objective/purpose of involvement: e.g. gaining ideas, reducing cycle time and/or improve customer relations.
- Stage(s) of NSD that customers get involved.
- Intensity of involvement: the degree of customer involvement which is described as a continuum from passive listening/observation to extremely intense whereby the customer is part of a development team.
- Methods of involvement: the ways in which input and information are obtained from the customer such as online interviews, brain storming communities, online focus groups etc.

Figure 3.1 also summarizes the chapter arguments by suggesting a holistic framework that includes all the issues that firms have to manage when exploiting Web 2.0 for engaging customers into NSD. The framework is also very useful because, it also provides directions and ideas for future research. For example, future studies may focus on: measuring the impacts of Web 2.0 customer involvement on the outcomes/success of NSD; the reasons and factors motivating customers to get involved in NSD; the types of customers and/or degrees of customer involvement that are most effective for Web 2.0 supported NSD.

References

Akamavi, R. 2005. A research agenda for investigation of product innovation in the financial services sector. *Journal of Services Marketing*, 19(6), 359-378.

Alam, I. 2002. An exploratory investigation of user involvement in new service development. *Journal of the Academy of Marketing Science*, 30(3), 250-261.

Alam, I. 2006. Removing the fuzziness from the fuzzy front-end of service innovations through customer interactions. *Industrial Marketing Management*, 35(4), 468-480.

Carlile, P. 2001. A pragmatic view of knowledge and boundaries: Boundary objects in NPD. *Organization Science* 13(4), 442-455.

Chesbrough, H.W. 2003. *Open Innovation: The New Imperative for Creating and Profiting from Technology*. Harvard: Harvard Business School Press Books.

Christensen, C. 1997. *The Innovator's Dilemma: When New Technologies Cause Great Firms to Fail*. Boston: Harvard Business School Press.

Christou, E. 2006. A qualitative analysis of consumer attitudes on adoption of online travel services. *Tourism: An International Interdisciplinary Journal*, 54(4), 323-331.

Christou, E. and Kassianidis, P. 2002. Consumers perception and adoption of online buying for travel products. *Journal of Travel & Tourism Marketing*, 12(4), 93-107.

Christou, E. and Kassianidis, P. 2010. Adoption of mobile commerce in the air travel sector: A qualitative survey of attitudes. *Turizam International Scientific Journal*, 14(1), 41-52.

Dahan, E. and Hauser, J.R. 2002. The virtual customer. *Journal of Product Innovation Management*, 19, 332-353.

Deszca, G., Munro, H. and Noori, H. 1999. Developing breakthrough products: Challenges and options for market assessment. *Journal of Operations Management*, 17(6), 613-630.

Enkel, E., Kausch, C. and Gassmann, O. 2005. Managing the risk of customer integration. *European Management Journal*, 23(2), 203-213.

Erat, P., Desouza, K., Schafer-Jugel and Kurzawa, M. 2006. Business customer communities and knowledge sharing: Studying the critical issues. *European Journal of IS*, 15, 511-524.

Evans, P. and Wolf, B. 2005. Collaboration Rules. *Harvard Business Review*, 83 (July-August), 96-104.

Franke, N. and Piller, F. 2004. Value creation by toolkits for user innovation and design: The case of the watch market. *Journal of Product Innovation Management*, 21(6), 401-415.

Fuller, J., Mätzler, K. and Hoppe, M. 2008. Brand Community Members as a Source of Innovation. *Journal of Product Innovation Management*, 25(6), 608-623.

Gruner, K.E. and Homburg, C. 2000. Does customer interaction enhance new product success? *Journal of Business Research*, 49(1), 1-14.

Hoyer, W.D., Chandy, R., Dorotic, M., Krafft, M. and Singh, A. 2010. Consumer Cocreation in New Product Development. *Journal of Service Research*, 13, 283-296.

Kim, H., Lyons, K. and Cunningham, M.A. 2008. Towards a framework for evaluating immersive business models: Evaluating service innovations in Second Life. Proceedings of the 41st Hawaii International Conference on System Sciences.

Kohler, T., Fueller, J., Stieger, D. and Matzler, K. 2011. Avatar-based innovation: Consequences of the virtual co-creation experience. *Computers in Human Behaviour*, 27, 160-168.

Kohler, T., Matzler, K. and Fuller, J. 2009. Avatar-based innovation: using virtual worlds for real-world innovation. *Technovation*, 29, 345-407.

Kristensson, P., Matthing, J. and Johansson, N. 2008. Key strategies for the successful involvement of customers in the co-creation of new technology-based services. *International Journal of Service Industry Management* 19(4), 474-491.

Kujala, S. 2003. User involvement: A review of the benefits and challenges. *Behaviour and Information Technology*, 22(1), 1-16.

Lagrosen, S. 2005. Customer involvement in new product development: A relationship marketing perspective. *European Journal of Innovation Management*, 8(4), 424-436.

Leonard, D. and Rayport, J.F. 1997. Spark Innovation through empathic design. *Harvard Business Review*, 75(6), 102-113.

Magnusson, P.R., Matthing, J. and Kristensson, P. 2003. Managing user involvement in service innovation: Experiments with innovating end users. *Journal of Service Research*, 6(2), 111-124.

Martin, C. and Horne, D. 1995. Level of success inputs for service innovations in the same firm. *International Journal of Service Industry Management*, 6(4), 4-56.

Matthing, J., Sanden, B. and Edvardsson, B. 2004. New service development: Learning from and with customers. *International Journal of Service Industry Management*, 15(5): 479-498.

Meeuwesen, B and Berends, H. 2007. Creating communities of practices to manage technological knowledge: An evaluation study at Rolls-Royce. *European Journal of Innovation Management*, 10(3), 333-347.

Menor, L., Tatikonda, M. and Sampson, S. 2002. New service development: Areas for exploitation and exploration. *Journal of Operations Management*, 20(2), 135-157.

Nambisan, S. 2002. Designing virtual customer environments for new product development: Towards a theory. *Academy of Management Review*, 27, 392-413

Pitta, D.A. and Fowler, D. 2005. Online consumer communities and their value to new product developers. *Journal of Product & Brand Management*, 14(5), 283-291.

Rowley, J., Teahan, B. and Leeming, E. 2007. Customer community and co-creation: A case study, *Marketing Intelligence & Planning*, 25(2), 136-146.

Sandberg, B. 2007. Customer-related proactiveness in the radical innovation development process. *European Journal of Innovation Management*, 10(2), 252-267.

Schiller, M. 2007. *Virtual aloft re-opening on Tuesday, 8 May. Aloft in Second Life: A Developers Report*. Available at http://www.virtualaloft.com [accessed: January 2008].

Sigala, M. 2008. WEB 2.0 tools empowering consumer participation in New Product Development: findings and implications in the tourism industry. Annual International Council for Hotel, Restaurant and Institutional Education, (I-CHRIE) Convention *Welcoming a New Era to Hospitality Education*. Atlanta, Georgia, USA: 30 July-2 August 2008.

Sigala, M. 2010. Measuring customer value in online collaborative trip planning processes. *Marketing Intelligence and Planning*, 28(4), 418-443.

Sigala, M. 2011. eCRM 2.0 applications and trends: The use and perceptions of Greek tourism firms of social networks and intelligence. *Computers in Human Behavior*, 27, 655-661.

Sigala, M. 2012, in press. Social networks and customer involvement in New Service Development (NSD): The case of www.mystarbucksidea.com. *International Journal of Contemporary Hospitality Management.*

Sigala, M. and Chalkiti, K. 2007. New Service Development: preliminary findings on process development and assessment from the Greek hotels. *Advances in Hospitality and Leisure*, 3, 131-153.

Vargo, S.L. and Lusch, R.F. 2004. Evolving to a new dominant logic for marketing. *Journal of Marketing*, 68, 1-17.

Von Hippel, E. 1976. The dominant role of users in the scientific instrument innovation process. *Research Policy*, 5 (December), 212-239.

Von Hippel, E. 1988. *The Sources of Innovation*. New York: Oxford University Press.

von Hippel, E. 2001. User toolkits for innovation. *Journal of Product Innovation Management*, 18(1), 247-257.

Zahay, D., Griffin, A. and Fredericks, E. 2004. Sources, uses, and forms of data in the new product development process. *Industrial Marketing Management*, 33, 657-666.

Chapter 4
'Creating the Buzz': Merchant City (Glasgow) Case Study

Jim Hamill and Alan Stevenson

1. Case Study Background and Context

About Merchant City Tourism and Marketing Cooperative (MCTMC)

Glasgow's Merchant City (MC) has all the elements in place to be a significant and successful tourist area. From being a run down part of the city, considerable infrastructure investment has taken place over the last three decades to develop the Merchant City as a 'must visit' area. In addition to its rich history and architecture, MC has a lively arts and culture scene, along with niche retail outlets and a very popular food, bar and nightlife area. MC also benefits from its very close proximity to Glasgow city centre, the main shopping areas and the new River Clyde Waterfront Development.

Merchant City has been identified as a key priority in the 'Glasgow Tourism Strategy, 2007 to 2016' which aims to deliver an additional 1 million visitors by 2016, with expected spending of over £1 billion per annum. The area is seen as a 'hidden gem' with the potential to deliver a vibrant cultural, retail and leisure experience with a 'sense of place' provided by the large number of niche, independent businesses and art distributors.

Established in 2007 by a group of local businesses, Merchant City Tourism and Marketing Cooperative (MCTMC) is a non-profit, grassroots organisation whose main objective is to raise awareness of, market and promote the Merchant City as a 'must visit' destination; to increase footfall (new and return) and visitor spend in the area. It is fully constituted and made up of representatives from local visitor attractions, the wider business community and partner organisations. MCTMC works very closely with other public sector agencies promoting tourism in Glasgow, (Visitscotland and Glasgow City Marketing Bureau); also with agencies delivering complementary services, Glasgow City Council, Scottish Enterprise and the Merchant City Initiative.

MCTMC has agreed key targets and performance measures for 2008 to 2013, together with an Action Plan for 'getting there':

- Increase visitors to the area from 1.1 million (2007) to 1.19 million (2011).
- Raise awareness of Merchant City among visitors to Glasgow from

26 per cent (2007) to 50 per cent (2011) (A visitor survey carried out in 2007 showed that only 26 per cent of visitors to Glasgow had heard of the MC and only 4 per cent were visiting the City specifically for the MC).

- Increase visitor spend in the Merchant City from £15 million (2007) to £18 million (2011).

A number of marketing initiatives have been launched to support these objectives and to raise brand awareness of the Merchant City as a 'must visit' destination including a 200,000 print run of a Merchant City Guide Map which has been widely distributed; the initial launch of the MC Website in May 2008 and relaunch in the Autumn of 2009 (www.merchantcityglasgow.com); a national advertising campaign (print, outdoor advertising and radio); development of a new brand identity and improved signage together with a planned programme to more fully leverage Merchant City Events – especially the annual MC Festival, Glasgay! and Radiance Festivals. A 'Web 2.0/Social Media Workshop' was delivered to local businesses in May 2009 to raise awareness and build enthusiasm for the use of new media. This generated a high level of enthusiasm for moving forward in this area.

The 'Creating the Buzz' Social Media Project represented a logical extension to and was intended to be fully integrated with these other marketing initiatives. The overall objective of the project was to develop and implement a proactive, integrated and coordinated online marketing strategy – one that fully leveraged emerging social media opportunities for 'creating a buzz' about the Merchant City, building a strong online network of MC 'advocates'. The social media strategy was fully aligned with and supportive of agreed business goals relating to visitor numbers and spending. With the planned relaunch of the MC website in the Autumn of 2009, the time was right to support this with a proactive online marketing strategy leveraging the full potential of new media for engaging with and energising the MC 'groundswell' – in other words, building a strong online community of MC advocates, maximising e-word-of-mouth effects to create a 'buzz' about the area.

There was a clear 'strategic fit' between the project and the 'Scottish Executive's Tourism Framework for Change 2005-2015'. This set out five key product segments to meet visitor demand and build on Scotland's core strengths. MC fits within 'City Breaks' with particular strengths in food tourism, shopping and nightlife and with strong links to the business tourism, culture and heritage segments. VisitScotland's brand plan for developing Scotland's cities had already acknowledged the Merchant City as a very important key differentiator for Glasgow.

Case study context

The context of the case study is the growing importance of social media in tourism and hospitality, the opportunities and threats presented to local tourism/hospitality associations but also the dearth of good case study material on local tourism industry collaboration in this area.

There is a growing volume of literature relevant to this chapter including the general literature on destination marketing and destination branding – Aaker (1991), Blain et al. (2005), Kotler and Gertner (2002), Morgan et al. (2002), Morgan et al. (2003), Pike (2004); online destination marketing – Douglas and Mills (2004), Gertner et al. (2006), Park and Gretzel (2007), So and Morrison (2003), Wang and Fesenmaier (2006); customer empowerment and the customer experience – Buhalis et al. (2007), Hamill and Stevenson (2006), Nykamp (2001), Thompson (2006); the emerging literature on Web 2.0 – Eikelmann et al. (2007), O'Reilly (2006), Tapscott and Williams (2006), Li and Bernoff (2008); and specifically, Web 2.0 in the travel and tourism industry – Ellion (2007), O'Connor (2008), Reactive (2007), Schegg et al. (2008), Sigala (2007). More recent publications relevant to the topic include Baker and Cameron (2008), Schmallegger and Carson (2008), Tapscott (2008), Elowitz and Li (2009), Inversini, Cantoni and Buhalis (2009), Weber, L. (2009), Hofbauer, Stangl and Teichmann (2010), Sigala (2008), Tapscott and Williams (2010) and Xiang and Gretzel (2010). Sigala's (2009) study of the internal political and management issues that arose in the implementation of Destination Management Systems (DMS) in Greece is also highly relevant to this case study (see final section).

These studies have examined a wide range of strategic and operational marketing issues relating to tourism 2.0, including the use of social media for brand awareness, reputation management, e-CRM, e-marketing, word-of-mouth effects and so on. By comparison, very little has been written on social media project management, organisation and people issues or the key success factors in successful social media implementation – the main focus of this chapter. While there is a growing literature on tourism and social media, there is an almost complete dearth of good case study material relating to local tourism/hospitality industry collaboration for social media leverage; what works and doesn't work; the "do's and don't's" of social media cooperation; and lessons learned.

2. Project Vision and Objectives

The overall vision of 'Creating the Buzz' was to establish a solid foundation for achieving sustained growth in visitor numbers and spending through leveraging the full potential of social media for building a quality customer base, engaging with and energising a strong online community of Merchant City 'advocates' thereby maximising e-word-of-mouth effects.

Based on the above, the following key strategic objectives were agreed:

- Build brand awareness, loyalty and advocacy of the MC as a 'must visit' destination; the 'hidden gem' of Glasgow.
- Achieve sustained increase in visitor numbers and spending.

- Build a 'quality customer base' – a strong base of high value, high growth potential customers providing MC with sustained growth in visitor numbers and spend. A strong network of loyal customers who become advocates of the MC as a 'must visit' destination in various online communities.
- Ensure that the project makes a significant contribution to the medium-term strategic goals and objectives of the MCMTC, Visit Scotland Growth Fund, Glasgow City Tourism and the Scottish Executive's Tourism Framework.
- Maximise the net economic impact of Merchant City tourism on Glasgow and Scotland generally.
- Achieve Return on Investment from project investments.
- Maximise MCMTC marketing effectiveness and marketing efficiency.
- Build a strong network of local businesses, tourism partners and MC residents, working in collaboration to position MC as a 'must visit' destination and to achieve sustained growth in visitor numbers and spend.
- Achieve self-sustained growth and a self-financed MCMTC by 2012.

A key element of the initial proposal was the issue of 'sustainability' and the use of social media for building strong collaborative working relationships between MCTMC, local residents and businesses. Collaborative working was seen as being critical to achieving sustained growth in visitor numbers and spend and to the sustainability of social media initiatives on completion of the 12-month project.

The strategic objectives listed above translated into a number of key targets and performance measures as follows:

- Increase the percentage of visitors to Glasgow with awareness of the Merchant City from 26 per cent (2007) to 50 per cent (2011).
- Increase visitor numbers to the MC from 1.1 million (2007) to 1.19 million (2011).
- Increase visitor spending in the MC from £15 million (2007) to £18 million (2011).
- Targets were agreed for the '4Is' of online community – Involvement, Interaction, Intimacy and Influence. These are the main 'lead drivers' contributing to a sustained increase in visitor numbers and spend (see below).
- To make a significant contribution to achieving the challenging growth targets of the 'Glasgow Tourism Strategy' – a minimum 60 per cent increase in Glasgow tourism revenues by 2016 and to the Scottish Executive's goal of a 50 per cent increase in tourism value.
- To achieve a marketing ROI from the project in excess of £11 per pound of Growth Fund spend.
- 150 local businesses and partners to be actively involved in the MCMTC Online Business Network by year end 2010.
- 150 local residents to be actively involved in the MCMTC Online Residents Community by year end 2010. The active participation and involvement

of local residents and businesses is critical to achieving sustained growth in visitor numbers and spend.
- MCMTC to become self-financing by 2012.

3. Key Actions and Initiatives

Implementation of 'Creating the Buzz' involved key actions and initiatives in nine main areas:

Action 1: Channel development

A major project objective was to significantly enhance the online customer experience and raise brand awareness of the MC as a 'must visit' destination. This was to be achieved in two main ways:

- By delivering 'Rich Internet Applications' on the new Merchant City website, enhancing site interactivity, functionality and the user experience including downloadable guide books, trails and interactive maps (mobile ready); videos and podcasts; online media pack; image library; foreign language versions of the site; interactive educational pack for schools/young people; MC blog; user generated content and feedback.
- Full development of a number of interactive Web 2.0/Social Media Channels aimed at building a robust online community of MC 'advocates' and maximising eword-of-mouth effects including, an MC Facebook community, Flickr, YouTube and Twitter channels and a MC wiki.

Action 2: Website marketing strategy (1.0)

Use of 'traditional' Web 1.0 tactics to develop and implement a proactive e-marketing strategy to support the new website including search engine positioning strategy, proactive links strategy and the implementation of an e-communications strategy using advanced e-mail newsletter software supported by a robust, but low cost hosted CRM system. A target of 25,000 unique site visits per month was agreed representing a significant increase from the pre-project average of just less than 5,000.

Action 3: 'Creating the buzz'/Social media engagement strategy

Development, implementation and ongoing management of an integrated and coordinated Web 2.0/Social Media Engagement Strategy building on the 2.0 channels established in Action 1. The overall aim was to build a solid foundation for achieving sustained growth in visitor numbers and spending through energising online communities of MC 'advocates'. Success in this area would be measured using the '4Is' of social media engagement discussed above.

Action 4: Building customer insight, knowledge and understanding

Develop actionable customer insights from offline visitor research, web analytics, social media monitoring tools, customer/business feedback through the new website and MC online communities.

Action 5: Offline media advertising

While the core focus of 'Creating the Buzz' was online marketing and social media, this would be supported by a limited amount of offline media advertising closely linked to an online 'call-to-action' e.g. sign up for the e-newsletter, join the MC Twitter and Facebook communities etc.

Action 6: Partnership working and collaboration

Development, implementation and on-going management of a professional networking site for local businesses and partners. This was seen as being critical to achieving sustained growth in tourism numbers and spending through on-going industry collaboration. A target of 150 local businesses actively involved in the online business community was agreed.

Action 7: Residents

Development, implementation and ongoing management of an online community site for local residents. As above, the active involvement of local residents was seen as being critical to achieving sustained growth in tourism numbers and spending. A target of 150 local residents actively involved in the online residents' community was agreed.

Action 8: Project monitoring and evaluation

To ensure that online marketing and social media efforts were fully aligned behind and supportive of agreed business objectives, and to deliver high ROI on project spend, it was strongly recommended that a simplified Balanced Scorecard (BSC) approach should be used for project management. This would establish a clear 'cause and effect' relationship between key project objectives and targets to be achieved; how these will be measured (Key Performance Indicators); and the core online marketing and social media initiatives and actions required for 'getting there'. The proposal recommended that all activity should be geared towards encouraging a 'call to action' by the customer e.g. visit the new website, register for the e-mail newsletter, view/comment on MC YouTube videos, register to receive Twitter updates, respond to Twitter promotions, join and participate in the MC online community etc.

The proposal recommended agreed procedures for monitoring project progress on a regular basis with a strong emphasis on performance measurement, project effectiveness, efficiency and ROI. MCTMC was already a performance driven organisation. Progress in achieving the main goals and objectives of the 'Action Plan, 2008 to 2013' is closely monitored on an ongoing basis using a range of mechanisms including, Economic Impact Studies conducted by Scottish Enterprise (SE)(2007 and 2012), annual targeted visitor surveys, regular monitoring of footfall, business feedback etc. MCTMC submits monthly budget reports to SE together with quarterly reports on key marketing initiatives measured against agreed milestones.

'Creating the Buzz' added a number of other important performance measures relating to the key online actions and initiatives to be taken. Detailed web analytics, e-mail campaign monitoring software and advanced social media monitoring tools were to be used for measuring the overall 'buzz' being created about the MC. Particular attention was paid to measuring the '4Is' of social media performance – Involvement, Interaction, Intimacy and Influence (see below); both for individual social media channels and across all social media generally. These are not abstract, difficult to measure criteria; in fact, almost the complete opposite. The '4Is' and their impact on visitor numbers and spending can be measured with a very high degree of accuracy. In a Web 2.0 era, Involvement, Interaction, Intimacy and Influence become the main drivers of future competitiveness and growth.

- Involvement – the level of customer involvement in various social media channels e.g. YouTube and Flickr views, numbers participating in MC online communities, time spent, frequency, geography etc.
- Interaction – actions taken by online community members e.g. read, post, comment, review, recommend.
- Intimacy – the level of affection or aversion shown to the brand; community sentiments, opinions expressed etc.
- Influence – advocacy, viral forwards, referrals and recommendations, social bookmarking, retweets etc.

Summarising the above, a hybrid approach was to be used in evaluating project performance and impact including: Economic Impact Studies (with Scottish Enterprise), visitor surveys, regular monitoring of footfall, customer, business and resident feedback in online communities, user generated content through the new website, detailed web analytics, e-mail campaign software and the use of advanced social media monitoring tools, Facebook insights, Twitter analytics etc.

Action 9: Project management and organisation

It was strongly recommended that professional project management procedures should be followed at all stages to ensure that the project was delivered 'on time, within budget' and that agreed business objectives were achieved. Successful implementation would also depend on having an appropriate organisational structure in place, with clear agreement on roles, responsibilities and reporting relationships. A key element of the proposal was the appointment (for one year) of a full-time online marketing/social media officer to develop, implement and manage MCTMC's e-marketing and social media strategy, working under the supervision of the project advisers. It was recommended that a small Steering Group be set up to manage the project and to ensure that key deliverables were being achieved. This was to comprise the two members of MCTMC most closely involved in the preparation of the initial proposal, the external project adviser, together with representatives from Scottish Enterprise, Visit Scotland and the local business community.

4. Progress and Performance

Following Visit Scotland approval of the project proposal in September 2009, a project start date of 1 December was agreed. At the time of writing this chapter (January 2011), it is too early to evaluate the net economic impact of the project in terms of increased visitor numbers, visitor spend and return on project costs. However, given that 13 months have passed since project inception, an initial assessment can be made of project progress and performance benchmarked against a number of the key goals, objectives and performance indicators.

Four main comments are worth making in this respect:

- The project successfully achieved some of its key goals and objectives, especially in relation to certain aspects of the social media component of the project. Successful Facebook and Twitter groups were established providing MCTMC with low cost channels for on-going communications and customer engagement. The MC Facebook group at www.facebook.com/merchantcityglasgow currently has over 4,700 'likers' (January 2011). It has grown to become the main customer communications channel for MCTMC. With 2,867 followers on the MC Twitter page (www.twitter.com/merchantcity) a strong foundation has been established for further development of this channel. However, with an overall Klout Score of just 40, considerable scope for improvement exists (this is more fully explained by going to www.klout.com; use 'merchantcity' as the Twitter username).
- While the project successfully delivered in terms of Facebook and Twitter, it failed to achieve agreed goals and objectives in most other areas. Benchmarked against the previous discussion of project goals, objectives, key actions and initiatives (Sections 3 and 4 above), the project failed to deliver in the following areas:
  - Recommended improvements to the MC website were not implemented (Action 1 above – Rich Internet Applications)
  - A coordinated, integrated and proactive e-marketing strategy to

support the new MC website was not implemented (Action 2 – Search engine positioning, links strategy, e-communications, CRM etc.). As a consequence, the project failed to achieve one of its key targets – 25,000 unique site visits per month. Due to the failure to support the site with a proactive e-marketing strategy, the average number of site visits stagnated at its pre-project level of approximately 5,000 per month

– No attempt was made to develop actionable customer insight and understanding from the two-way dialogue being encouraged on social media (Action 4).
– The most serious weakness of the project was its failure to actively involve local businesses and residents in 'Creating the Buzz'. Building a strong network of local businesses, tourism partners and MC residents, working in collaboration to position MC as a 'must visit' destination, was seen as being critical to achieving sustained growth in visitor numbers and spend; also to the sustainability of the project after the initial twelve months. As stated previously, specific targets and KPIs were agreed in these two areas – 150 local businesses and partners to be actively involved in the MCMTC Online Business Network by year end 2010; 150 local residents to be actively involved in the MCMTC Online Residents Community by year end 2010. Almost no action was taken to achieve these objectives. The online business and resident networks have not been established.

- It is a condition of Visit Scotland Growth Fund support that all projects have clearly agreed goals and objectives and that professional project management and performance measurement procedures are put in place to ensure successful project delivery 'on time, within budget' and that agreed business objectives are achieved. A considerable amount of time and effort was invested at the project proposal stage to ensure that 'Creating the Buzz' was a professionally developed and implemented project. It was strongly recommended that a simplified Balanced Scorecard approach should be used for project management and performance measurement ensuring that the key actions and initiatives taken were fully aligned behind and supportive of agreed business objectives, targets and KPIs. The failure to achieve key project objectives was entirely due to poor project execution and implementation rather than strategy. In particular, the project experienced major organisational, people and internal political problems which prevented the full achievement of expected project benefits. This started with a nine-week delay in project inception due to internal disputes over project management and control leading to the resignation of the two main MCTMC board members most closely involved in preparing the initial project proposal. In addition to causing a major delay in project start date, internal control of the project was now the responsibility of someone who had no involvement at all in drawing up the initial project specification; someone who also had their own internal political agenda. The decision to appoint a part-time rather than full-time e-marketing/social media officer (as

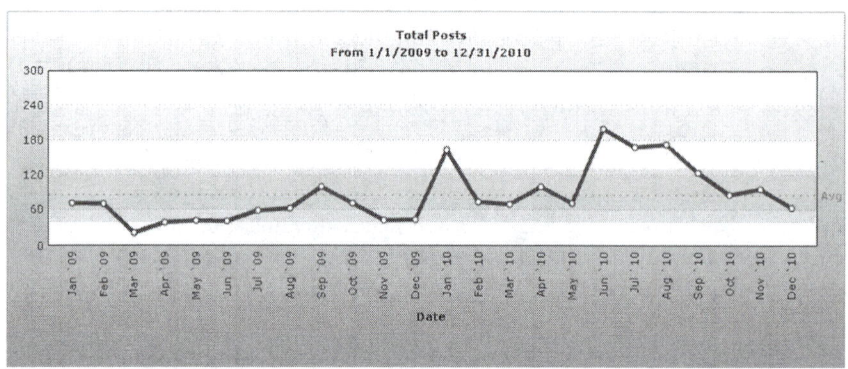

Figure 4.1 Number of Online Marketing Mentions about the 'Merchant City Glasgow'

Source: The authors.

stated clearly in the project proposal) was a major error. A list of key tasks and responsibilities of the e-marketing/social media officer had been listed in detail in the project proposal. The failure to create a full-time position resulted in many key tasks remaining undone due to time constraints. Other project management problems included the failure to follow agreed project management and performance measurement procedures and the single minded focus on Facebook and Twitter to the exclusion of other important aspects of the project. The failure to engage with and actively involve local businesses and residents was a major failing.

- As a consequence of the above, the project failed to deliver on the key objective of creating a sustained increase in online 'buzz' about the Merchant City. This can be shown using advanced social media monitoring tools such as Social Radar. As shown in Figure 4.1 above, the total number of social media mentions about the Merchant City increased significantly after the (delayed) project start date of February 2010, reaching a peak in June, coinciding with the annual Merchant City Festival. However, the project management problems listed above resulted in a significant decline in online mentions about the MC over the last six months of the project. The current level of online buzz about the MC has fallen to pre-project levels.

5. Discussion and Implications

Used properly, social media provides local tourism and hospitality groups with a low cost but very effective global marketing, communications and customer engagement platform. With growing recognition of the potential of social media, it can be expected that more and more local tourism and hospitality groups will embark on collaborative efforts in this area. From the detailed case study presented in this chapter, the following advice can be offered:

- Ensure that the project is business led – that clear business goals and objectives are agreed covering visitor numbers, spend and ROI.
- Agree specific targets for each project objective and the Key Performance Indicators to be used in monitoring on-going progress.
- Ensure that the key social media actions and initiatives taken are fully aligned behind and supportive of agreed business goals and objectives
- Follow professional project management procedures at all stages and ensure ongoing performance measurement benchmarked against agreed objectives.
- Support project delivery with an agreed organisational structure, decision-making and reporting procedures. Ensure that the right people are in place to ensure 'on time, within budget' delivery and that key business goals and objectives are met.
- Ensure strong project management, leadership and on-going commitment
- Be prepared for 'internal politics'.

6. Further Research

There is now wide recognition and acceptance within global tourism and hospitality of the critical importance of social media for building sustained customer and competitive advantage. However, as the case study presented in this chapter has shown, implementing a successful social media strategy is no easy task. Successful implementation requires the integration of strategy, people, processes, systems, technology, organisation, culture and people to achieve agreed business goals and objectives. Especially in projects requiring local industry collaboration, a great deal of attention needs to be paid to nurturing and encouraging a culture of cooperation for mutual benefit.

The internal political and management issues involved in the successful implementation of e-tourism projects were also identified by Sigala (2009) in her study of Destination Management Systems (DMS) in Greek DMOs. The paper concluded that most DMS in Greece failed due to poor project management and implementation with beauracracy andinternal politics being the main barriers to successful DMS implementation and performance.

Given the time, effort and resources required to develop and implement a successsful social media strategy, the next few years will witness a significant increase in collaborative efforts in this area. Additional case study material is needed in terms of what works and doesn't work, and the key management issues that arise in local industry collaboration to leverage the full potential of social media.

References

Aaker, D.A. 1991. *Managing Brand Equity*. New York: Free Press.

Baker, M.J. and Cameron, E. 2008. Critical success factors in destination marketing. *Tourism and Hospitality Research*, 8(2), 17, April, (19), 79-97.

Blain, C., Levy, S.E. and Brent Ritchie, J.R. 2005. Destination branding: Insights and practices from destination management organizations. *Journal of Travel Research*, 43(May), 328-338.

Buhalis, D., Niininen, O. and March, R. 2007. Customer empowerment in tourism through consumer centric marketing (CCM). *Qualitative Market Research: An International Journal*, 10(3), 265-281.

Douglas, A. and Mills, J.E. 2004. Staying afloat in the tropics: Applying a structural equation model approach to evaluating national tourism organization websites in the Caribbean. *Journal of Travel & Tourism Marketing*, 17(2/3), 269-293.

Eikelmann, S., Hajj, J. and Peterson, M. 2007. *Web 2.0 Profiting from the Threat*. Available at: http://www.strategybusiness.com/li/leadingideas/li00037 [accessed: 12 February 2011].

Ellion, R. 2007. *Web 2.0 and the Travel Industry: Practical Strategies for Exploiting the Social Media Revolution*. White Paper. Available at: http://www.ellion.co.uk/sectors/travel/index.php [accessed: 12 February 2011].

Elowitz, B. and Li, C. 2009. The World's Most Valuable Brands. Who's Most Engaged? Available at: www.engagementdb.com [accessed: 12 February 2011].

Gertner, R., Berger, K. and Gertner, D. 2006. Country-dot-com: Marketing and branding destinations online. *Journal of Travel & Tourism Marketing*, 21(2/3), 105-116.

Hamill, J. and Stevenson, A. 2006. *Manage the Customer Experience and the Relationship will Follow*. University of Strathclyde, Glasgow. Available at: http://msc.market.strath.ac.uk/BB/index.php?showtopic=1865 [accessed: 12 February 2011].

Hofbauer, J., Stangl, B. and Teichmann, K. 2010. Online destination marketing: Do local DMOs consider international guidelines for their website design?, in *Information and Communication Technologies in Tourism*, edited by U. Gretzel, R. Law and M. Fuchs, ENTER 2010, Proceedings of the International Conference in Lugano, Switzerland. Vienna: Springer Verlag.

Inversini, A., Cantoni, L. and Buhalis, D. 2009. Destinations' information competition and web reputation, *Information Technology & Tourism*, 11(3), 221-234.

Kotler, P. and Gertner, D. 2002. Country as brand, product, and beyond: A place marketing and brand management perspective. *Journal of Brand Management*, 9(4/5), 249-261.

Li, C. and Bernoff, J. 2008. *Groundswell: Winning in a World Transformed by Social Technologies*. 1st ed. Boston, MA: Harvard Business School Press.

Morgan, N., Pritchard, A. and Pride, R. 2002. *Destination Branding*. 1st ed. Oxford: Butterworth-Heinemann.

Morgan, N., Pritchard, A. and Piggott, R. 2003. Destination branding and the role of the stakeholders: The case of New Zealand. *Journal of Vacation Marketing*, 9(3), 285.

Nykamp, M. 2001. *The Customer Differential: Complete Guide to Implementing Customer Relationship Management CRM*. 1st ed. AMACOM.

O'Connor, P. 2008. User generated content and travel: A case study on TripAdvisor.com, in *Information and Communication Technologies in Tourism 2008*, edited by P. O'Connor, W. Höpfen and U. Gretzel. Proceedings of the International Conference in Innsbruck, Austria, 2008. Vienna: Springer Verlag.

O'Reilly, T. 2006. *Web 2.0 Principles and Best Practices*. O'Reilly Radar [Internet]. Available at: www.oreilly.com/catalog/web2report/chapter/web20_report_excerpt.pdf [accessed: 12 February 2011].

Park, Y.A. and Gretzel, U. 2007. Success Factors for Destination Marketing Websites: A Qualitative Meta-Analysis. *Journal of Travel Research*, 46, 46-63.

Pike, S. 2004. *Destination Marketing Organisations*. 1st ed. Oxford: Elsevier.

Reactive 2007. *Web 2.0 for the Tourism and Travel industry*. Reactive Media Pty Ltd. – White Paper. Available at: http://blogs.reactive.com/RequestWhitepaper.aspx [accessed: 12 February 2011].

Schegg, R., Liebrich, A., Scaglione, M. and Syed Ahmad, S.F. 2008. An Exploratory Field Study of Web 2.0 in Tourism, in *Information and Communication Technologies in Tourism 2008*, P. O'Connor, W. Höpfen and U. Gretzel. Vienna: Springer Verlag, 152-163.

Schmallegger, D. and Carson, D. 2008. Blogs in tourism: Changing approaches to information exchange. *Journal of Vacation Marketing* April, 14(2), 99-110.

Sigala, M. 2007. *Web 2.0 in the Tourism Industry: A New Tourism Generation and New E-business Models*. Travel Daily News. Available at: http://www.traveldailynews.com/pages/show_page/20554 [accessed: 12 February 2011].

Sigala, M. 2008. WEB 2.0, social marketing strategies and distribution channels for city destinations: Enhancing the participatory role of travellers and exploiting their collective intelligence, in *Information Communication Technologies and City Marketing: Digital Opportunities for Cities around the World*, edited by M. Gascó-Hernández and T. Torres-Coronas. Hershey, PA: IDEA Publishing, 220-244.

Sigala, M. 2009. Destination Management Systems: A reality check in the Greek tourism industry, in *Information and Communication Technologies in Tourism 2009*, edited by R. Law, W. Höpfen and U. Gretzel. Vienna: Springer Verlag.

So, A. and Morrison, M. 2003. Destination marketing organisations' website users and nonusers: A comparison of actual visits and revisit intentions. *Information Technology and Tourism*, 6, 129-139.

Tapscott, D. and Williams, A.D. 2006. *Wikinomics: How Mass Collaboration Changes Everything*. London: Atlantic Books.

Tapscott, D. 2008. *Grown Up Digital: How the Net Generation is Changing Your World.* New York: McGraw-Hill.

Tapscott, D. and Williams, A.D. 2010. *Macrowikinomics: Rebooting Business and the World.* New York: Blackwell.

Xiang Z. and Gretzel, U. 2010. Role of social media in online travel information search. *Tourism Management*, 31(2), 179-188.

Wang, Y. and Fesenmaier, D.R. 2006. Identifying the success factors of web-based marketing strategy: An investigation of convention and visitors bureaus in the United States. *Journal of Travel Research*, 44, 239-249.

Weber, L. 2009. *Marketing to the Social Web: How Digital Customer Communities Build Your Business.* New York: John Wiley & Sons.

Chapter 5

Examining Hotel Managers' Acceptance of Web 2.0 in Website Development: A Case Study of Hotels in Hong Kong

Daniel Hee Leung, Andy Lee and Rob Law

1. Introduction

Over the past 30 years, information technology has been an essential source of, and for, sustainable competitive advantages (Lam, Cho and Qu 2007) and a key factor for effective lodging industry operations (Winston 1997). In particular, the emergence and prevalence of the Internet in the late 1990s has transformed industry practices and structure dramatically (Buhalis 2003). With various benefits from the Internet (Lee and Morrison 2010; O'Connor 2003; Chung and Law 2003), the majority of hotel companies have exploited the potential of the Internet by utilizing their own websites.

Though hoteliers develop and expect their websites to be an effective marketing tool for disseminating product information, promoting sales and attracting customers (Buhalis 2003), findings from recent studies have indicated that Internet users tend to trust what other users create, or user-generated content (UGC) more than what marketing departments or advertising agencies create (Kardon 2007). Park, Lee and Han (2007) stated that UGC is often considered more trustworthy and credible than marketer-generated information since the contents generated by the marketer tend to conceal negative aspects. Consequently, Internet technologies known collectively as Web 2.0 or social media have become an influential form of travel information dissemination and consumption over the last five years (Pan, MacLaurin and Crotts 2007) as travellers now prefer informal and personal communication to formal and organizational information sources (Bansal and Voyer 2000). In response to the popularity of Web 2.0 among travellers, many travel-related companies started to integrate these functions into their websites to enhance customers' travel information searching experiences. Fuchs, Scholochov and Höpken (2009) also asserted that the use and diffusion of Web 2.0 in the tourism and hotel industry has been proliferating rapidly.

While information technology undoubtedly projects opportunities and benefits for hotel companies, its success largely depends on how hotels adopt and implement new technology (Nyheim, McFadden and Connolly 2004). Technology adoption and implementation are sophisticated tasks for hospitality organizations as there are many internal and external variables affecting their technology adoption decisions (Wang and Qualls 2007). Of all the influential factors, hotel brand affiliation (i.e. chain or independent) plays a tremendous role in a hotel's inclination towards IT adoption (Siguaw, Enz and Namasivayam 2000). Au Yeung and Law (2004) found that discrepancies in website usability and performance are attributable to the difference in financial and technical support between chain and independent hotels. Hence, this chapter will examine the adoption of Web 2.0 technologies on chain and independent hotel websites in Hong Kong, a leading tourist destination in Asia with many international hotels. A previous study (Leung, Lee and Law 2011) examined the adoption of Web 2.0 among all hotel websites in Hong Kong, but did not come to a consensus on factors influencing IT adoption. This study further examines the issue by investigating the interviews with hotel managers (Lefebvre, Mason and Lefebvre 1997). To achieve these objectives, this study conducts a case study that integrates observations of hotel websites and interviews with key persons in the adoption of information technology by hotels in Hong Kong.

2. Web 2.0 in Tourism and Hospitality

Web 2.0 refers to the second generation of web-based services that have gained massive popularity by allowing people to collaborate and share information in previously unavailable ways (Reactive 2007). Web 2.0 in tourism, also referred to as Travel 2.0, describes a new generation of travel websites encouraging and facilitating a higher level of social interaction among travellers. By providing a medium in which to share travel information and experiences, Web 2.0 allows travellers to share their first-hand experiences with fellow consumers who consider this information credible and useful when planning possible future journeys (Casaló, Flavián and Guinalíu 2010). At the same time, Web 2.0 provides tourism companies with unprecedented opportunities for understanding a market's reaction to their offering and subsequently feeding this information into their product development and quality control processes (Dellarocas 2003). For instance, hotel managers can analyse comments on TripAdvisor.com (Zehrer, Crotts and Magnini 2011) to better understand what their guests like and dislike about them and even their competitors. Hotel and tourism companies can also feed the information gathered from Web 2.0 to their product development and quality control processes to reflect customer and business value (Sigala 2008).

In view of the rapidly growing trend towards and potential benefits of Web 2.0, more hotels are embracing and benefiting from Web 2.0 applications (Fuchs et al., 2009). The increasing trend towards integrating Web 2.0 has also drawn tourism researchers' attention in recent years (Schegg et al., 2008; Sigala 2007; Sigala 2008; Yoo and Gretzel 2011). Table 5.1 summarizes the types of Web 2.0 applications reported and discussed in some prior tourism studies. Among all types of Web 2.0 applications, blogs in particular have proliferated rapidly within travel-

Table 5.1 Summary of Web 2.0 Applications Discussed in Prior Tourism Studies

Author	Blogging	Wiki	Podcast /Vodcast	Social networking	Really Simple Syndication	Tagging /Folksonomy	Bookmark	Mashup	Virtual community /Virtual world	Forums/Online discussion	Review Sites and Ratings	Online photo sharing	Social Search engines/Metasearch	Instant messaging/Email	Travel themed sites
Bray and Schetzina 2006					•	•	•				•		•		
Carroll 2006											•				
Conrady 2007				•		•		•					•		
Dippelreiter et al., 2008	•	•	•		•	•						•			
Ettestad 2008				•							•				
Lo et al., 2011	•			•						•		•		•	•
Sigala 2007	•	•	•	•	•	•		•	•						
Sigala 2008	•	•	•	•	•	•	•		•	•	•		•		
Xiang and Gretzel 2010	•		•	•					•		•				

related businesses as a medium to promote their products and to build customer relationships. Blogging thus helps define the image of a company and keeps the company in touch with its consumers. Schmallegger and Carson (2008) as well as Schmollgruber (2007) claimed that blogs can help increase incoming traffic and improve search engine ranking. Social networking sites are another application offering dynamic ways to inform and entertain consumers (*TIME* 2007). Nowadays many hotels have an account on social networking sites such as Facebook.com and Myspace.com to promote their products through increased web presence and high value links back to their homepages (Ettestad 2008). In addition, hotels leverage these sites to communicate to their customers directly and increase understanding of their actual needs (Sigala 2007). Establishing virtual communities is another strategy used by tourism companies to attract potential, and connect existing, customers online. By engaging customers through social interactions, companies can manage customer relations effectively in virtual tourist communities (Wang and Fesenmaier 2004).

In addition to the above three applications, Sigala (2007) analysed six other major applications of Web 2.0 technologies commonly used in the tourism and hospitality industries; Really Simple Syndication (RSS), podcasting, massively multiplayer online role playing game (MMORPG), tagging, mashups, and wikis. As information is the lifeblood of the tourism industry, it is believed that the diffusion of Web 2.0 will have a substantial impact on tourism demand and supply (Sigala 2007; Sigala 2011). In this vein, Sigala (2007) analysed the major Web 2.0 applications in the tourism and hospitality industry by presenting their impacts on both demand and supply.

3. Information Technology Adoption in the Hospitality Industry

In a highly competitive hospitality business environment, information technology (IT) has become essential and ubiquitous. Its adoption in the hospitality industry is attributed to the rapid development in information technology, fear of lagging behind competitors as well as the increasing demands of customers, who look forward to flexible, specialized, accessible, and interactive products and communication with principals (Buhalis 1998; Sigala 2003; Srinivasan, Lilien and Rangaswamy 2002). Prior studies have acknowledged that the hotel industry implements information technologies to improve operational efficiencies (Bacheldor 1999), refine customer service (Sweat and Hibbard 1999), increase revenue, and minimize costs (Huo 1998). In view of the benefits that IT provides to the hospitality industry, the active adoption of technology appears to be inevitable (Ham, Kim and Jeong 2005; Siguaw et al., 2000).

Given the growing appreciation of the role of IT in enhancing a company's competitive advantages and contributing to business success, hospitality academic researchers and industry practitioners have conducted numerous studies on technology adoption. Davis (1989) postulated the Technology Acceptance Model (TAM), which suggests that an individual's intention to adopt technology is dependent on its perceived usefulness and ease of use. Subsequent researchers modified and extended TAM with different antecedents, moderating and mediating variables to increase its applicability (Shih 2004; Venkatesh and Davis 2000). Of various variables explaining users' IT adoption, brand affiliation has been suggested as one of the most significant factors dictating a hotel's technology adoption and diffusion (Wang and Qualls 2007). With their relatively greater financial and human resources from which they can draw, chain or affiliated hotels generally have a longer history of technology adoption than non-affiliated or independent hotels (Scaglione, Schegg, Steiner and Murphy 2005). By analysing almost 3,000 Swiss hotels, Scaglione et al. (2005) found that larger, affiliated and luxury hotels adopted a domain name earlier than their smaller, budget and non-affiliated competitors. Similar findings were also identified in Siguaw et al.'s (2000) study. Drawing on the findings from these studies, hotel brand affiliation is likely to affect directly a hotel's inclination towards IT adoption.

A plethora of empirical studies has already examined the association between brand affiliation and information technology adoption in hotels (Sigala 2011). As Web 2.0 technology is an innovative way for customers to get involved in direct communication with hotels and other customers online, its adoption and implementation by existing websites may or not require relatively fewer financial and human resources. Thus, an empirical study on the association of Web 2.0 technologies adoption with brand affiliation would present how chain and independent hotels are in making a decision on technology adoption.

4. Web 2.0 Adoption among Chain and Independent Hotels in Hong Kong

In order to examine the trend of adopting Web 2.0 technologies, content analysis was conducted. Manual observations were adopted and all Hong Kong hotel websites, including both homepage and all subpages, were reviewed. Every Web 2.0 application adopted by each hotel was coded based on written instructions. One point was given to a hotel if a link or access to Web 2.0 applications was detected on its website (1 = adopted; 0 = not adopted). All data were monitored and cross-verified by different researchers to ensure validity. Data were collected quarterly from February 2010 to August 2010, and a longitudinal approach was employed to verify the proliferation of hotels adopting Web 2.0 applications.

From the websites of all 109 members of the Hong Kong Hotels Association including 87 chain and 22 independent hotels, content analysis identified a trend of more hotels adopting Web 2.0 technologies. As shown in Table 5.2, the percentage of hotels adopting Web 2.0 applications has continuously increased over the last three quarters of 2010 (February 2010 to August 2010). By February 2010, only 27 per cent of all 22 independent hotels had integrated Web 2.0 applications. However, the corresponding number increased to 36 per cent and 41 per cent in the following two quarters, respectively. Similarly, of the 87 chain hotels, the adoption rate increased from 29 per cent in February 2010 to 32 per cent in May 2010. In August 2010, more than a half of them (51 per cent) integrated at least one Web 2.0 application into their websites. These figures clearly revealed the increasing trend towards adoption of Web 2.0 technology among Hong Kong's hotels. Though this trend was found among both chain and independent hotel websites in Hong Kong, the adoption rate varied between the groups. Specifically, the adoption rate of chain hotels was mostly higher than that of independent hotels in the study period (Please refer to the "Overall" column in Table 5.2). In a comparison of the average number of Web 2.0 applications used by the chain and independent hotels, chain hotels were found to adopt more Web 2.0 applications. In August 2010, chain hotels adopted an average of 2.1 Web 2.0 applications; whereas independent hotels adopted an average of 1.4 applications.

Table 5.2 Adoption of Web 2.0 Technologies by Chain and Independent Hotels

	Facebook	Twitter	RSS	TripAdvisor	Company Blog	Flickr	Guest Comment	Bookmark	Google Buzz	Google Maps	YouTube	Overall *	Mean #
Independent Hotels (N=22)													
February	23%	9%	0%	5%	0%	0%	5%	0%	0%	0%	0%	27%	1.5
May	23%	9%	0%	5%	0%	0%	14%	0%	0%	0%	0%	36%	1.4
August	27%	9%	0%	5%	0%	0%	14%	5%	0%	0%	0%	41%	1.4
Chain Hotels (N=87)													
February	17%	14%	7%	5%	5%	0%	0%	0%	0%	0%	1%	29%	1.6
May	22%	16%	8%	5%	5%	2%	0%	7%	3%	0%	2%	32%	2.2
August	25%	16%	6%	8%	8%	2%	0%	11%	3%	21%	6%	51%	2.1
All Hotels													
February	18%	13%	6%	5%	4%	0%	1%	0%	0%	0%	1%	28%	1.6
May	22%	15%	6%	5%	4%	2%	3%	6%	3%	0%	2%	33%	2.0
August	26%	15%	5%	7%	6%	2%	3%	10%	3%	17%	5%	49%	2.0

Note: The percentage refers the proportion of hotels adopting that particular Web 2.0 application to the total number of hotels in each category. * Overall refers to the percentage of hotels adopting at least one Web 2.0 application to the total number of hotels in the category. # Mean refers to the average number of Web 2.0 applications adopted by hotels in the category.

Source: Leung, Lee and Law (2011).

Of 11 Web 2.0 applications identified from all Hong Kong hotel websites, chain hotels implemented nearly all applications except "Guest Comment"; whereas independent hotels implemented five applications. Social networking sites, particularly Facebook, were the most-used Web 2.0 applications on both chain and independent hotel websites. More than a quarter of chain and independent businesses had a Facebook page for promoting their offerings and networking with their in-group members. Microblogging such as Twitter was the second most popular Web 2.0 application on the websites of both hotel groups. Hotels usually posted the latest promotional messages to their Twitter pages linked to company websites. These findings imply that brand affiliation is associated with their inclination to Web 2.0 technology adoption, and the adoption rate of chain hotels is relatively higher than independent hotels.

5. Factors Influencing Web 2.0 Adoption

For further investigation of factors influencing hotels' Web 2.0 technology adoption, four semi-structured interviews were conducted using a series of open-ended questions around a set of key themes. The sample consisted of managers from both chain and independent hotels because Mikkelsen (1995) claimed that interviewees who have special knowledge on a given topic are characterized as key informants providing insightful implications. In this study, all interviewees were recruited via convenience and snowball sampling. All respondents were identified as key persons in the adoption, design and implementation of information technology in their respective companies. An interview was conducted with a revenue manager of a chain property (*Manager A*) and an IT Manager of an independent hotel (*Manager B*), respectively, which had adopted Web 2.0 technologies on their websites. Another interview was with a public relations manager from a chain hotel (*Manager C*) and an IT Specialist from an independent hotel (*Manager D*), respectively, which had not adopted Web 2.0 technologies. Each interview lasted for 40 to 60 minutes and the discussion content of all interviews was recorded and transcribed for coding and analysis. Open coding was conducted and the result was cross verified by researchers in order to ensure validity and reliability.

Each interview started with the question "To your knowledge, what are Web 2.0 technologies?". As managers who have better knowledge in the subject field would have fewer cognitive barriers in adopting new technology (Wöber and Gretzel 2000), this question measuring the managers' knowledge of Web 2.0 technologies was included to examine the association between managers' knowledge and IT adoption. *Manager A* from a chain hotel adopting Web 2.0 replied that Web 2.0 is "a series of online platforms for all Internet users to group together and share anything about themselves". In another interview, *Manager C* from another chain hotel not adopting Web 2.0 answered, "Web 2.0 represents Facebook, YouTube, and other tools allowing Internet users to convey their thoughts and share comments on specific issues". Although the technology adoptions in these two chain hotels were different, the chain hotel managers had similar understanding about Web 2.0. *Manager B* from an independent hotel adopting Web 2.0 defined Web 2.0 as "a digital space for sharing personal thoughts and knowledge"; whereas *Manager D* from another independent hotel answered, "Web 2.0 is a place that can group people with similar interests together for sharing". Regardless of whether they work for chain or independent hotels and whether their hotels adopted Web 2.0, all of the managers had similar knowledge and understanding of Web 2.0 technologies.

The question "What factor(s) motivate your hotel to adopt and integrate Web 2.0 technologies on your website?" was asked to the managers whose affiliated hotels had adopted Web 2.0 applications. *Manager A* from a chain hotel replied that the factor would be the top management perception of the potential benefits of Web 2.0. The senior management at the headquarters with which *Manager A* is affiliated believes that Web 2.0 is "an effective channel to retain existing customers and approach new customers with insignificant cost". *Manager A* claimed that Web 2.0 provides "informal channels" to indicate customers' views on how well or badly his hotel does because the content and evaluation created by customers on Web 2.0 is honest, unfiltered and realistic. The analysis of the contents of these media allows hotels not only to realize their performance but also to "better understand the customers' needs and subsequently customize the offerings". In view of the positive belief the top management held, the corporate headquarters require all their affiliated properties to implement certain Web 2.0 applications and provide technical support. The viewpoint of *Manager B,* from the independent hotel, of the motivating factor was somewhat different from the chain hotel. *Manager B* replied that they had adopted Web 2.0 because "competitors are using social media". As its competitors had already adopted these media, the top management thought that they should follow this approach otherwise they would lag behind. Moreover, the top management of *Manager B*'s hotel acknowledged the potential of Web 2.0 as a promotion channel, rather than a communication channel for understanding customers.

Both managers (*C* and *D*) from the hotels that did not adopt Web 2.0 applications said that they acknowledge the importance of Web 2.0 in their business and plan to integrate these technologies into their websites. In order to understand the impediments affecting their original decision, the question "What factor(s) inhibit your hotel's original decision on adoption Web 2.0 technologies?" was asked. The managers thought that they had limited financial resources for IT development and that top management did not perceive Web 2.0 as a useful tool for revenue generation. *Manager C* stated that their top management originally "thought that the function of Web 2.0 applications was similar to their website as a medium to provide customers with information" and that top management "did not recognize what additional benefit Web 2.0 could bring to them". *Manager D* shared the similar view that their top management "disbelieved the ability of Web 2.0 in generating revenue or other benefits to the hotel". However, *Manager D* added that since the adoption of Web 2.0 was becoming common in the hotel industry, the top management had started to recognize its potential benefits and consider its implementation as an Internet marketing strategy. Similar to the managers from hotels adopting Web 2.0 applications, *Managers C* and *D* suggested that "top management's realization of the benefits of Web 2.0" and "their agreement to its adoption" were the crucial determinants of this new technology's adoption. The findings from the interviews imply that the perceived benefits of Web 2.0 from the perspective of top management directly affect a hotel's inclination towards adopting Web 2.0 technologies.

6. Conclusions and Implications

Content analysis of 109 hotel websites identified a trend of increasing adoption of Web 2.0 applications among the hotels in Hong Kong. The difference in adoption rate of Web 2.0 technologies was associated with brand affiliation – chain hotels in Hong Kong generally have a higher inclination towards the adoption of Web 2.0 applications than independent hotels. Managers, regardless of whether they work for chain or independent hotels or whether their hotels adopted Web 2.0, had similar understanding of Web 2.0 technologies. Hence the difference in their adoption decisions may not be associated with their knowledge of technology. Also, the managers did not identify resources available within their organizations as a constraint on technology adoption although technology projects are usually dependent on an IT budget (Au Yeung and Law 2004; Wang and Qualls 2007). In a study on the applicability of Web 2.0 in learning and research, Ullrich, Borau and Luo (2008) demonstrated that the costs associated with introducing and adding Web 2.0 applications into existing channels are insignificant to a company. In the hotel context, a hotel can open an account on Facebook.com at no extra cost. Therefore scarce financial resources were not identified as the critical inhibitor against Web 2.0 adoption.

On the other hand, Lefebvre, Mason and Lefebvre (1997) suggested that top management plays an important role in the decision-making process on technology adoption and resource allocation. Also, the findings of this study reconfirmed the theoretical meaningfulness of top management's attitude and perception in dictating a company's tendency towards technology adoption. In addition, the interviews with the hotel managers revealed that the top managements of chain hotels hold different views on the perceived benefits of Web 2.0 from those of independent hotels. As stated by *Managers B* and *D*, their top management perceived Web 2.0 adoption as a defense mechanism against the fear of lagging behind the competition. In contrast, the top management of chain hotels perceived Web 2.0 adoption as a strategic decision for marketing, and understanding and retention of customers. Phillips, Calantone and Lee (1994) suggested that the more benefits organizations can foresee from using the technology, the more likely they are to adopt it given sufficient support and facilitation. Hence, chain hotels are more likely to adopt this technology because they realize more benefits from it.

Lincoln (2009) concluded her book by stating that the sooner a business adopts Web 2.0, the better results it gets. From the practical perspective, this study discovered that there is still room for Hong Kong hotels to exploit the potential of Web 2.0 technology as only about half of them have adopted it. The interviews identified that top management's perception plays an important role in Web 2.0 technology adoption so hotel managers need to provide their top management with adequate information about how Web 2.0 can help improve their business and competitive advantage. The findings of this study cannot claim to be generalizable owing to the limited geographical region and the number of managers interviewed. Future research can be extended to hotels in other regions and more hotel managers should be interviewed in order to gain more insight along with quantitative research approaches. This would be of benefit to both researchers and practitioners.

References

Au Yeung, T. and Law, R. 2004. Extending the modified heuristic usability evaluation technique to chain and independent hotel websites. *International Journal of Hospitality Management*, 23(3), 307-313.

Bacheldor, B. 1999. Hospitality & Travel: A Trip to Grandma's Goes High Tech. *Information Week*, 27 September, 189.

Bansal, H.S. and Voyer, P.A. 2000. Word-of-mouth processes within a services purchase decision context. *Journal of Service Research*, 3(2), 166-177.

Bray, J. and Schetzina, C. 2006. Travel 2.0 Harnessing the Power of User-Generated Content and Tagging. *Hospitality Upgrade* (Fall 2006), 28-29.

Buhalis, D. 1998. Strategic use of information technologies in the tourism industry. *Tourism Management*, 19(5), 409-421.

Buhalis, D. 2003. *eTourism: Information Technology for Strategic Tourism Management*. New York: Financial Times Prentice Hall.

Carroll, D. 2006. Travel community present online players with opportunities. *Travel Weekly Australia*, 8 September, 6-7.

Casaló, L., Flavián, C. and Guinalíu, M. 2010. Understanding the intention to follow the advice obtained in an online travel community. *Computers in Human Behavior*, 27(2), 622-633.

Chung, T. and Law, R. 2003. Developing a performance indicator for hotel websites. *International Journal of Hospitality Management*, 22(1), 119-125.

Conrady, R. 2007. Travel technology in the era of Web 2.0, in *Trends and Issues in Global Tourism 2007*, edited by R. Conrady and M. Bucks. Heidelberg and Berlin: Springer Verlag, 165-184.

Davis, F.D. 1989. Perceived usefulness, perceived ease of use and user acceptance of information technology. *MIS Quarterly*, 13(3), 319-339.

Dellarocas, C. 2003. The digitization of word-of-mouth: Promise and challenges of online feedback mechanisms. *Management Science*, 49(10), 1407-1424.

Dippelreiter, B., Grun, C., Pottler, M., Berger, H. and Dittenbach, M. 2008. Online Tourism Communities on the Path to Web 2.0: An Evaluation. *Information Technology & Tourism*, 10(4), 329-353.

Ettestad, S. 2008. Easy Travel 2.0 Strategies Hotels Can Implement Today. *Hospitality Upgrade* (Summer 2008), 172.

Fuchs, M., Scholochov, C. and Höpken, W. 2009. E-Business adoption, use, and value creation: An Austrian Hotel Study. *Information Technology & Tourism*, 11(4), 267-284.

Ham, S., Kim, W.G. and Jeong, S. 2005. Effects of information technology on performance in upscale hotels. *International Journal of Hospitality Management*, 24(2), 281-294.

Huo, Y.H. 1998. Information technology and the performance of the restaurant firms. *Journal of Hospitality & Tourism Research*, 22(3), 239-251.

Kardon, B. 2007. They're saying nasty things. *Marketing News*, 41(20), 30.

Lam, T., Cho, V. and Qu, H. 2007. A study of hotel employee behavioral intentions towards adoption of information technology. *International Journal of Hospitality Management*, 26(1), 49-65.

Lee, J.K. and Morrison, A.M. 2010. A Comparative Study of Website Performance. *Journal of Hospitality and Tourism Technology*, 1(1), 50-67.

Lefebvre, L., Mason, R. and Lefebvre, E. 1997. The influence prism in SMEs: The power of CEOs' perceptions on technology policy and its organisational impacts. *Management Science*, 43(6), 856-878.

Leung, D., Lee, H.A. and Law, R. 2011. Adopting Web 2.0 technologies on chain and independent hotel websites: A case study of hotels in Hong Kong, in *Information and Communication Technologies in Tourism 2011*, edited by R. Law, M. Fuchs and F. Ricci. Vienna and New York: Springer Verlag, 229-240.

Lincoln, S.R. 2009. *Mastering Web 2.0: Transform your Business Using Key Website and Social Media Tools*. London: Kogan Page.

Lo, I.S., McKercher, B., Lo, A., Cheung, C. and Law, R. 2011. Tourism and online photography. *Tourism Management*, 32(4), 725-731.

Mikkelsen, B. 1995. *Methods for Development Work and Research: A Guide for Practitioners*. London: Sage Publications.

Nyheim, P., McFadden, F. and Connolly, D. 2004. *Technology Strategies for the Hospitality Industry*. Upper Saddle River, NJ: Pearson Prentice Hall.

O'Connor, P. 2003. Room rates on the Internet: Is the web really cheaper? *Journal of Services Research*, 1(1), 57-72.

Pan, B., MacLaurin, T. and Crotts, J.C. 2007. Travel Blogs and the Implications for Destination Marketing. *Journal of Travel Research*, 46(1), 35-45.

Park, D.H., Lee, J. and Han, I. 2007. The effect of online-consumers reviews on consumer purchasing intention: The moderating role of involvement. *International Journal of Electronic Commerce*, 11(4), 125-148.

Phillips, L., Calantone, R. and Lee, M. 1994. International technology adoption: Behavior structure, demand certainty and culture. *Journal of Business and Industrial Marketing*, 9(2), 16-28.

Reactive. 2007. *Web 2.0 for the Tourism and Travel Industry: A White Paper. Reactive Media Pty Ltd.* Available at: http://blogs.reactive.com [accessed: 2 September 2010].

Schegg, R., Liebrich, A., Scaglione, M. and Ahmad, S.F.S. 2008. An Exploratory Field Study of Web 2.0 in Tourism, in *Information and Communication Technologies in Tourism 2008*, edited by P. O'Connor, W. Höpken and U. Gretzel. Vienna and New York: Springer Verlag, 463-474.

Scaglione, M., Schegg, R., Steiner, T. and Murphy, J. 2005. Investigating Domain Name Diffusion across Swiss Accommodation Enterprises, in *Information and Communication Technologies in Tourism 2005*, edited by A.J. Frew. Vienna and New York: Springer Verlag, 360-370.

Schmallegger, D. and Carson, D. 2007. Blogs in tourism: Changing approaches to information exchange. *Journal of Vacation Marketing*, 14(2), 99-110.

Schmollgruber, K. 2007. *Hotel 2.0 – Interview with Opus Hotel CEO Blogger Daniel Craig*. Available at http://passionpr.typepad.com/tourism/2007/04/hotel_blog_opus.html [accessed: 30 August 2010].

Shih, H.P. 2004. Extended technology acceptance model of Internet utilization behavior. *Information & Management*, 41(6), 719-729.

Sigala, M. 2003. The Information & Communication Technologies productivity impact on the UK hotel sector. *International Journal of Operations and Production Management*, 23(10), 1224-1245.

Sigala, M. 2007. *Web 2.0 in the Tourism Industry: A New Tourism Generation and New E-business Models* [Online]. Available at http://195.130.87.21:8080/dspace/handle/123456789/386 [accessed: 7 September 2010].

Sigala, M. 2008. Developing and Implementing an eCRM 2.0 Strategy: Usage and Readiness of Greek Tourism, in *Information and Communication Technologies in Tourism 2008*, edited by P. O'Connor, W. Höpken and U. Gretzel. Vienna and New York: Springer Verlag, 463-474.

Sigala, M. 2011. eCRM 2.0 applications and trends: The use and perceptions of Greek tourism firms of social networks and intelligence. *Computers in Human Behavior*, 27, 655-661.

Siguaw, J., Enz, C. and Namasivayam, K. 2000. Adoption of Information Technology in U.S. Hotels: Strategically Driven Objective. *Journal of Travel Research*, 39(2), 192-201.

Srinivasan, R., Lilien, G.L. and Rangaswamy, A. 2002. Technological opportunism and radical technology adoption: An application to E-business. *Journal of Marketing*, 66(3), 47-60.

Sweat, J. and Hibbard, J. 1999. Customer disservice. *Information Week*, 21, 65-78.

TIME 2007. *50 Best Websites 2007*. Available at: http://www.time.com/time/specials/2007 [accessed: 24 August 2010].

Ullrich, C., Borau, K. and Luo, H. 2008. Why Web 2.0 is Good for Learning and for Research; Principles and Prototypes, in *Proceeding of the 17th International Conference on World Wide Web*, edited by J. Huai., R. Chen., H.W. Hon and Y. Liu. New York: Association for Computing Machinery, 705-714.

Venkatesh, V. and Davis, F.D. 2000. A theoretical extension of the technology acceptance model: Four longitudinal field studies. *Management Science*, 46(2), 186-204.

Wang, Y. and Qualls, W. 2007. Towards a theoretical model of technology adoption in hospitality organizations. *International Journal of Hospitality Management*, 26(3), 560-573.

Winston, M. 1997. Leadership of renewal: Leadership for the twenty-first century. *Global Management*, 31, 31-33.

Wang, Y. and Fesenmaier, D. 2004. Modelling participation in an online travel community. *Journal of Travel Research*, 42(3), 261-270.

Wöber, K. and Gretzel, U. 2000. Tourism Managers' Adoption of Marketing Decision Support Systems. *Journal of Travel Research*, 39(2), 172-181.

Xiang, Z. and Gretzel, U. 2010. Role of social media in online travel information search. *Tourism Management*, 31(2), 179-188.

Yoo, K-H. and Gretzel, U. 2011. Influence of personality on travel-related consumer-generated media creation. *Computers in Human Behavior*, 27(2), 609-621.

Zehrer, A., Crotts, J. and Magnini, V. 2011. The perceived usefulness of blog postings: An extension of the expectancy-disconfirmation paradigm. *Tourism Management*, 32(1), 106-113.

PART 2
Web 2.0: Applications for Marketing

Chapter 6
Introduction to Part 2

Evangelos Christou

1. Web 2.0 and Its Applications for Marketing

Traditional marketing approaches for the tourism, travel, hospitality and leisure industries focused on identifying the product features and benefits that would satisfy the needs, wants and demands of tourists and travellers, as well as the appropriate price, an integrated promotion and communication mix, and the management of distribution channels. Many marketing managers focus their efforts and activities on exploiting promotional tools including advertising, sales promotion, public relations, special events, publicity, and brand awareness. But in the current social, economic and business environment, marketing managers in tourism need to have Web 2.0 applications and techniques as part of their overall marketing plans.

Contemporary web technologies tend to provide more interactive and richer techniques for small and medium tourism firms and destination organizations to target new market segments and to effectively develop, promote and distribute a more competitive and personalized offering (Christou and Kassianidis 2002; Ellis-Green 2007). It may be argued that the growth of social media, of Web 2.0 applications, is a dramatic change for tourism, travel, hospitality and leisure marketing just as the printing press was for written communications. Previous research has established that Web 2.0 marketing offers a significant advantage: information technology today makes it possible, reliable and convenient to measure the results of marketing activities (Gretzel and Yoo 2008; Sigala 2010). For example, by using tools such as conversion-tracking services web traffic can be analysed to establish the exact number of website visitors who actually do what marketers desire (i.e., study information about products, order products or make bookings, etc.). With the right approach, a tourism firm can efficiently exploit Web 2.0's impressive reach and the opportunity it provides to connect with existing and potential tourists in a completely new manner (Kracht and Wang 2010).

Perhaps the most significant benefit of using Web 2.0 applications in marketing is that it offers an opportunity to actively engage consumers (Conrady 2007). An increasing number of tourism marketers are using social networking tools to work in partnership with customers on product development, service value enrichment, promotion and marketing communication (O'Connor 2008; Xiang and Gretzel 2010). Tourism firms and destination management organizations can utilize social media tools to enhance cooperation with both its industry associates and clients.

Small and medium-sized tourism firms have developed competitive advantages by using Web 2.0 marketing tools to effectively compete with larger firms. At the same time, social media are used to diminish the gap between tourism businesses and clients, by becoming more intuitive and user friendly by offering information that is accessed effortlessly by the final user.

2. Overview of the Part: Web 2.0 Applications for Marketing

This part of the book is particularly concerned with social media applications for marketing in tourism, travel, leisure and hospitality. It explores the use patterns as well as the types of use and impacts of use of contemporary Web 2.0 marketing tools. The cases presented are diverse in nature and geographical focus, drawing knowledge and best practices from various tourism, hospitality, travel and leisure sectors and regions.

Chapter 7 focuses on providing a review of contemporary theories of social media applications in tourism marketing, the construction of a relevant integrated meta-framework, and on examining implications for hospitality and tourism marketing research and the tools of promotion for hospitality and tourism businesses through social media.

Chapter 8 describes and presents a categorization of social media marketing opportunities for Destination Management Organizations (DMOs), and discusses in-depth case studies of DMOs who exploit social media marketing; these case studies are representative of DMOs in countries where use of social media is significant but under-researched.

Chapter 9 details updated findings concerning the Web 2.0 social media progress made by Europe's leading National DMOs; the methodology used includes measures of social media depth of engagement as well as channel presence.

Chapter 10 investigates meeting planners' use of social media and the perceived usefulness of the different types of Web 2.0 tools within the Meetings, Incentives, Conferences and Exhibitions (MICE) industry, and examines why meeting planners use social media by discussing the case of professional meeting planners in Arizona.

Chapter 11 explores the impact of Web 2.0 in creating transparency about hotel prices. The paper investigates and provides evidence on how consumers use UGC for understanding and comparing hotel prices in relation to the hotel offerings, quality of services and the additional "hidden" charges that an hotel price may involve.

Lastly, Chapter 12 explores the nature, use and role of blogs in online tourism information search and the potential of social media to supplant or to supplement the more traditional marketing communication functions; the case of Tourism British Columbia's use of social media is discussed to illustrate the changing facets of the current tourism market communication paradigm.

References

Christou, E. and Kassianidis, P. 2002. Consumers perception and adoption of online buying for travel products. *Journal of Travel & Tourism Marketing*, 12(4), 93-107.

Conrady, R. 2007. Travel technology in the era of Web 2.0, in *Trends and Issues in Global Tourism 2007*, edited by R. Conrady and N. Buck. Berlin and Heidelberg: Springer Verlag, 165-184.

Ellis-Green, C. 2007. *The Travel Marketer's Guide to Social Media and Social Networking*. McLean, VA: Hotel Sales and Marketing Association International.

Gretzel, U. and Yoo, K-H. 2008. Use and impact of online travel reviews, in *Information and Communication Technologies in Tourism 2008*, edited by P. O'Connor, W. Hopken and U. Gretzel. Vienna: Springer Verlag, 35-46.

Kracht, J. and Wang, Y. 2010. Examining the tourism distribution channel: Evolution and transformation. *International Journal of Contemporary Hospitality Management*, 22(5), 736-757.

O'Connor, P. 2008. *User-generated Content and Travel: A Case Study on TripAdvisor.com*. Vienna: Springer Verlag.

Sigala, M. 2010. Web 2.0, social marketing strategies and distribution channels for city destinations: Enhancing the participatory role of travelers and exploiting their collective intelligence, in *Web Technologies: Concepts, Methodologies, Tools, and Applications*, edited by A. Tatnall. New York: Information Science Reference.

Xiang, Z. and Gretzel, U. 2010. Role of social media in online travel information search. *Tourism Management*, 31(2), 179-188.

Chapter 7

Theoretical Models of Social Media, Marketing Implications, and Future Research Directions

Bing Pan and John C. Crotts

1. Introduction

Social media is becoming increasingly crucial to hospitality and tourism businesses as a result of the intangibility and the experiential nature of tourism products and the lowering of technological barriers for average travellers enabling them to contribute information online. Different from the one-way communication in most mass media channels, social media represents two-way communication between consumers. Social media has revived the older decision-making processes prevalent before the emergence of mass media, when the exchange of opinions between one's families, relatives, friends, and neighbours was the basis for purchasing decisions. As the digital version of word-of-mouth, social media represent the materialization, storage, and retrieval of word-of-mouth content online. However, the large-scale, anonymous, ephemeral nature of the Internet induces new ways of capturing, analysing, interpreting, and managing social media content. Some traditional theories, such as social exchange theory, social penetration theory, and social network theory, could be valid paradigms for studying and explaining how people form networks, express their opinions, and pass information to each other. For example, Buckner's (1965) theory on rumour transmission indicates that the accuracy and speed of rumour-passing were affected by the structure of the network and the mental sets of individual actors in the network. This chapter will focus on the review of relevant theories, the construction of an integrated meta-framework, and, more importantly, the implications for hospitality and tourism marketing research and the principles of marketing hospitality and tourism businesses, through social media.

2. Background

Social media is becoming increasingly crucial to hospitality and tourism enterprises. On one hand, hospitality and tourism industries offer intangible and experiential products and visitors must rely on the information delivered to them,

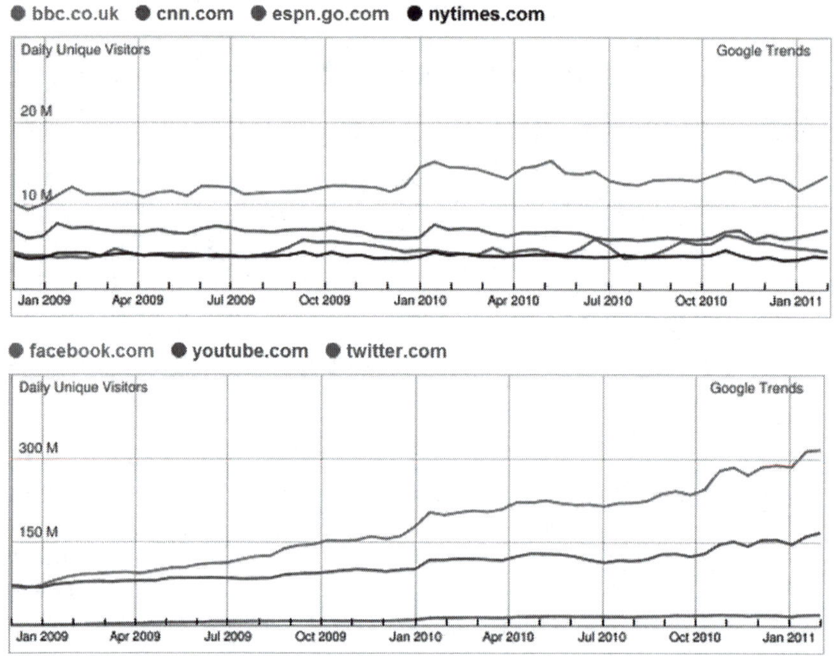

Figure 7.1 Traffic Volumes of Top Mass Media Sites versus Top Social Media Sites

Source: http://trends.google.com/websites/ as of 2 March 2011.

either online or offline, to identify and evaluate the product alternatives. On the other hand, the development of Internet technologies has lowered the barrier for contributing information online and user reviews and comments are experiential in nature and perceived as highly trustable. Almost anyone with Internet access can easily blog, tweet, review, comment, and update his or her Facebook status. These communication tools have led to an explosion of social media content. In September 2010, Facebook was ranked as the number one website online which can reach 39.2 per cent of the Internet population; YouTube was ranked number two with 31.8 per cent (Google 2010). More importantly, the traffic on these websites continues to increase, dwarfing the most popular mass media sites, while consistently increasing their number of daily, unique visitors (Figure 7.1).

Faced with the explosive volume of social media and its increasing influence, hospitality and tourism enterprises are searching for ways to make sense of this media and manage it to their advantage. Placing the phenomenon into an appropriate theoretical context that better describes the complex and dynamic relationships inherent in social media will help enhance our understanding of it.

Different from the one-way model of communication of most mass media, social media represent two-way communication between consumers and the materialization of the communication content. As the digital version of word-of-mouth, social media includes the solidification, storage, and retrieval of word-of-mouth content online. However, the large-scale, anonymous, ephemeral nature of the Internet induces new ways of capturing, analysing, interpreting, and managing social media content (Dellarocas 2003). In-depth theoretical and behavioural understanding of this content might be crucial for making sense of these media.

However, do theories *really* matter for our usage of social media? Facebook was created because a Harvard undergraduate student wanted to connect with his fellow students (Mezrich, Chamberlain and Publishing 2009); Twitter came from a brainstorming session by its founder Evan Williams (Johnson 2009); neither was created as a result of deep understanding of social network theories. More importantly, in today's online world, a huge amount of behavioural data can be captured and analysed instantaneously, and new ideas can be tested easily through various social media platforms. Some tools based on these ideas will fly and become popular; some others will just die off due to a lack of participation. Businesses can test new marketing methods and ideas easily online and get instant feedback from their customers. For example, Amazon has become the largest online social science 'laboratory' as a result of testing many models of consumer purchase behaviour (Contractor 2009). As Chris Anderson announced, online data deluge will make theories obsolete (Anderson 2008).

However, theories are still crucial to enable researchers and businesses to understand and take advantage of this media. First, relevant theories can help interpret and make sense of data. One can easily capture many types of behavioural data about customers, such as clicks, impressions, search volumes, comments, reviews, etc., but what do they represent? Appropriate theoretical models can help make sense of this data.

Secondly, theoretical frameworks can help the discovery of new opportunities in the field. After all, the core technology of Google was invented by adopting the aged theories of biliometrics in order to solve the problem of finding quality web pages online (Vise and Malseed 2006). Potential opportunities may exist when we survey relevant theories in communications, sociology, and computer and information sciences. For example, complex interactions exist between informational artifacts and actors in social networks; you can share and recommend a piece of text, picture, or video to friends, and other people may discover you through shared information artifacts and add you as a friend. Understanding this complex and dynamic relationship is important for harnessing the power of social networks for marketing purpose, for example, discovering opinion leaders.

Thirdly, theoretical frameworks could help avoid technological dominance over our lives and society. Fast development of technologies could easily overwhelm users, both as business managers and consumers. Understanding their implications through a global and abstract view could help them deal with the inundation of information technologies.

3. Theoretical Foundations

This section reviews major theoretical frameworks which may be applicable to the study and understanding of social media. One can separate these theories into three schools: micro-theories dealing with studying the dynamics of the contribution of information online and communication of individual social actors; macro-theories looking at the structure and dynamics of social actors and social media content through global or abstract views and pseudo-theories which include the recent conceptual frameworks in marketing and social media proposed mostly by non-academics. Pseudo-theories may make sense intuitively, but have yet to be tested empirically. All these schools of thought and frameworks might contribute to our understanding of the nature of social media, why people contribute, how they form relationships, and how one can find opinion leaders and valuable social media content.

Micro-theories

Word of mouth/psychological ownership theory and perceived control

Historically, tourism researchers have found that advice from friends and relatives is the most frequently obtained and influential source of information used by consumers in their travel decision-making (Crotts 1999; Perdue 1993). The information communicated by friends and relatives is construed as more credible, honest, and trustworthy than that generated by marketers, since the communicators are not compensated for the referral. Advances in the Internet and Web 2.0 technologies now allow consumers to access personally meaningful critiques not only from friends and relatives but also from strangers (e.g. travel blogs, which continue to grow in popularity). As an illustration, TripAdvisor currently purports to have over 40 million reviews attracting over 50 million unique users each month (Dépêches 2010).

Asatryan and Oh (2008) applied Psychological Ownership Theory to explain why former guests are motivated to offer Word-of-mouth feedback. On one level, some customers develop feelings of connections with firms they are loyal to that manifest into a sense of ownership, as evidenced by the 'mine', 'my', 'our' language they use in their reviews. In such circumstances, one would assume that a loyal guest would provide positive feedback to others, directing their negative feedback to management (Mattila 2001). However, where no such loyalty exists, the motive to write either a negative or positive review may be a desire to control or influence the business indirectly by communicating with its future potential customers. Loyal consumers' motives in posting positive reviews on travel blogs are attempts to reward firms; the motives of non-loyal customers are purportedly based on the satisfaction of being helpful to other consumers. According to Pierce, Kostova and Dirks (2003), the desire by the consumer to control through such communications may result in feelings of efficacy, intrinsic pleasure, and extrinsic satisfaction in providing such advice to others.

These propositions point to strategies in which a firm can leverage customer feedback and social media for its own strategic benefit. On one hand, firms should enhance the perception of psychological ownership and control among their customer base through loyalty and guest feedback and service recovery programs; they should keep more negative evaluations internal and positive feedback external. On the other hand, firms that do not emphasize customer loyalty or guest feedback should expect customers to both reward and punish their performance through social media.

Social exchange theory

Given that all social media are dependent on users providing content, an understanding of their motives appears to be fundamental. Social exchange theory originated from sociology studies exploring exchange between individuals or small groups (Emerson 1976). The theory mainly uses a cost-benefit framework and comparison of alternatives to explain how human beings communicate with each other, how they form relationships and bonds, and how communities are formed through communication exchanges (Homans 1958). The theory states that individuals engage in behaviours they find rewarding and avoid behaviours that have too high a cost. In other words, all social behaviour is based on each actor's subjective assessment of the cost-benefit of contributing to a social exchange. They communicate or exchange with each other contingent on reciprocal actions from the other communicating party (Emerson 1976). The mutual reinforcement could be analysed through a micro-economic framework, though the rewards are often not monetary but social, such as opportunity, prestige, conformity, or acceptance (Emerson 1976). The theory was arguably best summarized by Homans (1958, p. 606) when he wrote:

> Social behavior is an exchange of goods, material goods but also non-material ones, such as the symbols of approval or prestige. Persons that give much to others try to get much from them, and persons that get much from others are under pressure to give much to them. This process of influence tends to work out at equilibrium to a balance in the exchanges. For a person in an exchange, what he gives may be a cost to him, just as what he gets may be a reward, and his behavior changes less as the difference of the two, profit, tends to a maximum.

Hence, the reasons why people engage in a social exchange have been posited as a) an expected gain in reputation and influence on others; b) an anticipated reciprocity on the part of others; c) altruism; and d) direct reward. Given that participation in the social media is not compensated, the first three reasons appear to have particular relevance to why people participate in social media.

Travel blogs and social media sites have long recognized that there are far more people consuming information than generating it. On YouTube, for example, though subscribers have uploaded over 2 billion videos and audio tracks to the site since its founding in 2005, it is accessed by more than 10 million unique visitors daily, indicating that there are far more viewers than contributors. The Global Web Index (2009) (Li 2010; TrendsStream Limited 2010), which tracks this phenomenon, suggests that users of social media can be segmented into four main groups. These are: (1) watchers (79.8 per cent of US social media users), who consume content only to help with their decision-making; (2) sharers (61.2 per cent), who upload and forward information to others in order to help others and demonstrate knowledge; (3) commenters (36.2 per cent), who both review and rate products and comment on those who do in an effort to participate and contribute; and (4) producers (24.2 per cent), who create their own content in an effort to express their identity and garner recognition. Framed in social exchange theory, watchers take but do not reciprocate from the exchange suggesting that they consider the cost of posting or commenting too high, or fear offering their opinion or raising their profile.

Though far more research is needed to test the validity of such groupings, segmenting users as to their exchange behaviours has a certain level of face-value validity. Given such a hierarchy of users based on their active exchanges, firms attempting to leverage social media to their advantage should attempt to engage consumers of all four segments. For watchers, the task is to first identify the specific social media they use, what information they seek, and what makes it engaging, in an effort to develop and position content that is relevant. The same strategy and content should be useful for sharers as well. However, the tendencies of sharers should be facilitated by marketers by simplifying the process of forwarding content (e.g., Retweet and Facebook forward links) as well as recognizing and rewarding the desired behaviour. Facebook's OpenGraph has allowed a user to "like" or "comment" on any content on the web (Zuckerberg 2010). Firms may find advantages in getting ahead of this trend by proactively adding a commenting feature to each of their webpages. By doing so, they can directly manage the content of such comments which in effect will discourage spammers and trolls. Lastly, with regard to producers, attempts by firms to engage with their customers or to create unique platforms for their customers may produce dividends at the brand or chain level. Publicly recognizing sites that are helpful to the firm and increasing their visibility through search engine marketing are options.

Social penetration theory

Similar to social exchange theory, social penetration theory explains how human exchange forms relationships (Altman and Taylor 1973). However, social penetration theory focuses more on the individual and dyadic levels while social exchange theory could explain behaviour at aggregated and organizational levels.

Social exchange theory states that human beings form close relationships through self-disclosure. Using an analogy of peeling off the layers in an onion, one must disclose him or herself through the continuing process of exposing one's inner self and identity. It starts with public, visible, and superficial information, such as gender, clothing preferences, and ethnicity; slowly, as the relationship progresses, one starts to share feelings; at the deepest level, one will expose his or her goals, ambitions, and beliefs (Altman, Vinsel and Brown 1981).

In the online social world, we may be able to design social networks in a way which separates these different layers of information. By default, certain information will be disclosed to the public, while private and semi-private information could be confidential. There might be ways to determine the levels of relationships from the mode and frequency of communications, which could easily be tracked online through social media sites. A recent privacy lawsuit against Facebook highlighted the importance of following the layered intimacy levels of social penetration when disclosing one's information (Gaudin 2010).

Macro-theories

Social network analysis

Social network theory views the community of individuals as connected actors, and uses mathematical models to study its structure, development, and evolution (Wasserman and Faust 1994). Social network analysis treats individual actors in a community as nodes; the communications between those actors are deemed to be ties, edges, links, or connections. Social networks can form at many levels, from individual people, to families, communities, and nations. Those ties could be communication frequency, friendship, kinship, financial exchange, sexual relationships, or common interests or beliefs. Together they form a complex graph structure.

Mathematical calculation on many indices could be performed on this complex graph, including the following:

> Betweenness: the extent of a node lying between other nodes.
> Centrality: how connected is a node to the network.
> Closeness: how one node is near all other nodes in the network.
> Density: all the ties in a network in proportion to all the possible ties.
> Structural hole: the node which connects other nodes. Those nodes are disconnected without the first node.

These measurements determine the importance and structural positions of individual actors, and the characteristics of the partial or whole networks. The measurements could be used to study the social network, improve the network structure, and help increase the efficiency of information flows within the network. Network analysis software such as UCINET could be used to measure those indices (Borgatti, Everett and Freeman 1992).

Traditional social network analysis views individuals or organizations as nodes in the network, and the communication between them as edges. However, social media content is exactly the materialization and solidification of the chatter, comments, or reviews. The recent emergence of a multi-dimensional social network framework is crucial when studying the interaction between social actors and information artifacts (Contractor 2009). By treating social media content as nodes one can perform mathematical calculations on those information artifacts, such as what are the important pieces shared by many people, how one can connect users through artifacts, where are the structure holes of social media by connecting which the network could be more tightly integrated?

Buckner's (1965) theory on rumour transmission indicates that the accuracy and speed of rumour passing were affected by the structure of the network and the mental sets of individual actors in the network. Connecting this line of research with social network analysis of online social network sites could inform businesses of the best methods for promoting themselves through organic word-of-mouth. Recent applications of multidimensional social network analysis to Web 2.0 has generated some fruitful results (Kazienko, Musial and Kajdanowicz 2011).

McLuhan's media theory

McLuhan is a Canadian philosopher and educator, the author of the famous quote "the media is the message"(McLuhan 1995). He argued that the media itself, rather than its actual content, will transform people and society. The actual messages people are communicating won't be any different on the new media; the interactivity and frequency of new communication patterns will change our behaviour forever. Thus, the media's effects on society are much greater than their content. He separates media into "cool" and "hot" media. The former requires a viewer to exert effort and participation in understanding the content, e.g. television, seminars, or cartoons; the latter enhance one sense, so the viewers do not need to exert much effort, e.g. films, radio, and photography (McLuhan 1995).

If we use McLuhan's arguments, social media will transform the users not as a result of it content but because of the mode of communication it entails. For example, Twitter is just a microblogging service with a limit of 140 characters. Theoretically one can perform all the Twitter functions through a blog service. However, it is precisely this limiting factor that made Twitter more nimble and 'real-time'. Many breaking news stories have been spread via Twitter, such as China's Sichuan earthquake and the terrorist attack in Mumbai in 2008 (Parr 2009). As business managers and consumers, we need to realize the changes in behaviour caused by the usage of new social media services and adopt an attitude of acceptance toward those technologies and behaviour.

Pseudo-theories

The social media landscape is fast changing due to the low cost of innovation in an era of open-source movement. The long distance between academia and the industry and the slow process of the formal publishing cycle pose a challenge to researchers in academic institutions. Many social media and online marketing agencies are actually more innovative and ahead of the curve regarding social media for marketing purposes. This section views two frameworks trying to make sense of the social media landscape.

Carlene Li and Jeremiah Owyang from Altimeter Group are the major contributors to the socialgraphics framework (Jowyang 2010). They argued that instead of studying the demographic, geographic, or psychographic profiles of your customers, businesses also need to develop a social strategy termed socialgraphics. Marketers and managers need to ask the following questions: which websites are my customers on? What are my customers' social behaviours online? What social information or people do my customers rely on? What is my customers' social influence? The answers to these questions could separate your customers into layers of engagement: from curating, producing, commenting, sharing, to watching. Businesses need to separate their customers into these layers and provide tools and platforms to facilitate their particular social interactions.

Another line of framework, Social Feedback Loop, links consumer purchase funnel with social media. Dave Evans (2008) has argued that traditional purchase funnel has three stages (awareness, consideration, and purchases) during which a marketer could influence a consumer's decision-making. However, the purchase funnel concept treats customers as though they are living in a vacuum. A customer, after purchase, will use the product, form opinions, and talk about it at a later stage. Some of the experience after purchase will be materialized and posted online, this will loop back to other customers' purchase decision-making processes. This social feedback cycle is driven mostly by word-of-mouth which is further driven by actual use, trial, or sampling experience. Harnessing this feedback loop might be even more important than marketing on the mass media through the first three stages of consumer decision-making.

These two frameworks make intuitive sense: marketers should switch focus from effects of mass media on pre-purchase decision-making to post-purchase word-of-mouth; one needs to study the different levels of engagement by customers in order to adopt different strategies for encouraging the spread of social media and influence the direction of consumer conversation. However, the frameworks don't specify the exact methods for segmenting engagement groups and the behaviours to adopt in order to differentiate stages of pre-purchase decision-making and post-consumption and the ways to influence them.

4. An Integrated Meta-Framework

The aforementioned theories look at social media and social actors through individual, global, or marketing and business perspectives. An integrated framework needs to be reductionistic, quantifiable, and applicable to business and marketing settings. Social network analysis, especially multi-dimensional social network analysis, with rigorous methodology and measurements, seems to be an overall framework for studying the interaction between information artifacts, human actors, and the interaction and evolution of the two. Thus, multidimensional network is at the centre of the framework. On one hand, the macro- and micro-theories, such as McLuhan's media theory, social exchange and social penetration theory, could inform the analysis and modelling of social network analysis. On the other hand, social network analysis can actually quantify socialgraphics and link social media content with purchase funnels through quantitative analysis. Social network analysis could be adopted to explore various aspects of those behavioural theories online. For example, on one hand, one needs to look at social penetration theory and start linking different layers of private information with different levels of relationships; on the other hand, the frequency of posting and commenting and number of friends on social networks could be the basis for differentiating levels of participation in the socialgraphic profile of a business's customer base. Figure 7.2 displays a meta-framework which connects the theories and frameworks discussed in this chapter, with the questions they could address in the social media world.

5. Future Trends and Research

A few major theoretical and behavioural frameworks are reviewed in this chapter, including word-of-mouth research, social exchange theory, social network analysis, McLuhan's media theory, socialgraphics, and purchase funnel and social media. Social network analysis, especially multi-dimensional social network analysis, could be the general framework for investigating social networks, information artifact networks, and the dynamic evolution between the two. On one hand, the behavioural frameworks could inform the development and directions of multidimensional networks; on the other hand, the methodologies of multidimensional social network could be used to inform and validate other general theories and frameworks; more importantly, the quantifiable nature of the methodology and the ease of capturing behavioural data online could finally validate the socialgraphic framework and quantify different stages of the decision-making process and inform marketers of ways to influence their customers through social feedback loop.

For future research efforts, more specifically, we need more studies combining data mining and data modelling on the web with behavioural frameworks. For example, we need to capture the social generated media and metadata existing on current social media websites, such as Facebook, LinkedIn and Twitter. Adopting

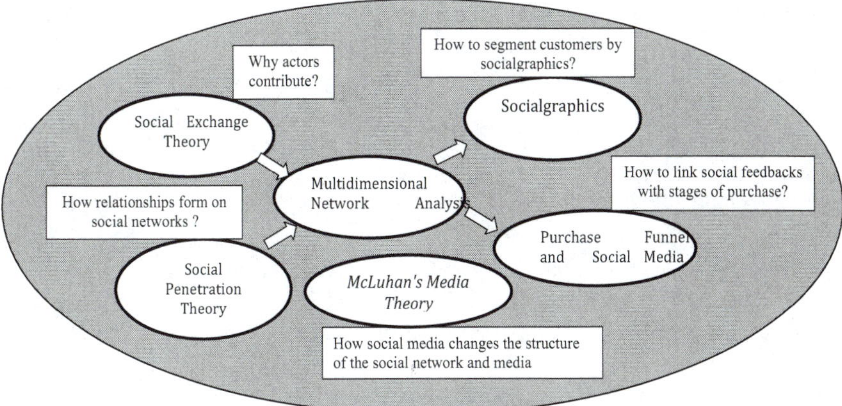

Figure 7.2 The Connections between Theoretical Models and Applicable Questions

multidimensional social network analysis in studying online social networks and knowledge networks could result in more in-depth understanding of the phenomenon and inform social media marketing practices for hospitality and tourism businesses (Contractor 2009).

Acknowledgements

The authors would like to thank Kevin Smith in the Office of Tourism Analysis in the College of Charleston for his meticulous copy-editing support.

References

Altman, I. and Taylor, D. 1973. *Social Penetration: The Development of Interpersonal Relationships.* New York: Holt, Rinehart and Winston.

Altman, I., Vinsel, A. and Brown, B. 1981. Dialectic conceptions in social psychology: An application to social penetration and privacy regulation. *Advances in Experimental Social Psychology*, 14(1), 107-160.

Anderson, C. 2008. The end of theory: The data deluge makes the scientific method obsolete. *Wired Magazine*, 16(7) (16 July).

Asatryan, V. and Oh, H. 2008. Psychological ownership theory: An exploratory application in the restaurant industry. *Journal of Hospitality and Tourism Research*, 32(3), 363.

Borgatti, S., Everett, M. and Freeman, L. 1992. *Ucinet X: Network Analysis Software.* Columbia, SC: Analytic Technologies.

Contractor, N. 2009. The emergence of multidimensional networks. *Journal of Computer Mediated Communication*, 14(3), 743-747.

Crotts, J.C. 1999. Consumer decision making and prepurchase information search, in *Consumer Behavior in Travel and Tourism*, edited by A. Pizam and Y. Masfeld. New York: The Haworth Hospitality Press, 149-168.

Dellarocas, C. 2003. The digitization of word of mouth: Promise and challenges of online feedback mechanisms. *Management Science*, 49(10), 1407-1424.

Dépêches 2010. *TripAdvisor Becomes the First Travel Brand to Break the 40 Million Unique Monthly Visitors Barrier* [online, 1 November]. Available at: http://www.aeroweb-fr.net/depeches/2010/09/tripadvisor-becomes-the-first-travel-brand-to-break-the-40-million-unique-monthly-visitors-barrier [accessed: 1 December 2010].

Emerson, R. 1976. Social exchange theory. *Annual Review of Sociology*, 335-362.

Evans, D. 2008. *Social Media Marketing: An Hour a Day*. Indianapolis, IN: Sybex.

Gaudin, S. 2010. *Facebook Slapped with Class-Action Privacy Lawsuit* [online 8 July]. Available at: http://www.computerworld.com/s/article/9178993/Facebook_slapped_with_class_action_privacy_lawsuit [accessed: 1 November 2010].

Google 2010. *The 1000 Most-Visited Sites on the Web* [online, 1 October]. Available at: http://www.google.com/adplanner/static/top1000/ [accessed: 5 November 2010].

Homans, G. 1958. Social behavior as exchange. *American Journal of Sociology*, 63(6), 597-606.

Johnson, S. 2009. How Twitter Will Change the Way We Live, *Time* [online, 5 June 2009]. Available at: http://www.time.com/time/printout/0,8816(1902604),00 [accessed: 5 November 2010].

Jowyang, J. 2010. *Socialgraphics Help You to Understand Your Customers: Slides and Webinar Recording* [online, 21 January 2010]. Available at: http://www.web-strategist.com/blog/category/socialgraphics/ [accessed: 1 November 2010].

Kazienko, P. and Musial, K. 2007. *Discovering Multidimensional Social Communities in Web 2.0: Proceedings of The 3rd European Symposium on Nature-inspired Smart Information Systems* (26-27 November 2007, St Julians, Malta).

Kazienko, P., Musial, K. and Kajdanowicz, T. 2011. Multidimensional Social Network and Its Application to the Social Recommender System. *IEEE Transactions on Systems, Man and Cybernetics-Part A: Systems and Humans*, 41(4), July, 746-759. doi: 10.1109/TSMCA.2011.2132707.

Li, C. 2010. *Open Leadership: How Social Technology Can Transform the Way You Lead.* San Francisco, CA: Jossey-Bass.

Mattila, A. 2001. Emotional bonding and restaurant loyalty. *The Cornell Hotel and Restaurant Administration Quarterly*, 42(6), 73-79.

McLuhan, M. 1995. *Understanding Media: The Extensions of Man.* Cambridge, MA: The MIT Press.

Mezrich, B. and Chamberlain, M. 2009. *The Accidental Billionaires.* Harpswell, ME: Anchor.

Parr, B. 2009. *10 Most Extraordinary Twitter Updates* [online, 12 March]. Available at: http://mashable.com/2009/04/10/extraordinary-twitter-updates/ [accessed: 1 November 2010].

Perdue, R.R. 1993. External information search in marine recreational fishing. *Leisure Sciences*, 15(3), 169-187.

Pierce, J., Kostova, T. and Dirks, K. 2003. The state of psychological ownership: Integrating and extending a century of research. *Review of General Psychology*, 7(1), 84-107.

TrendsStream Limited 2010. *Global Web Index* [online, 1 March]. Available at: http://globalwebindex.net/ [accessed: 1 November 2010].

Vise, D. and Malseed, M. 2006. *The Google Story: Inside the Hottest Business, Media, and Technology Success of Our Time*. Surrey, UK: Delta.

Wasserman, S. and Faust, K. 1994. *Social Network Analysis*. Cambridge: Cambridge University Press.

Zuckerberg, M. 2010. *Building the Social Web Together* [Online, 21 April]. Available at: http://blog.Facebook.com/blog.php?post=383404517130 [accessed: 1 October 2010].

Chapter 8
Riding the Social Media Wave: Strategies of DMOs Who Successfully Engage in Social Media Marketing

Jun (Nina) Shao, Mary Ann Dávila Rodríguez and Ulrike Gretzel

1. Introduction

The emergence of new technologies challenges existing marketing paradigms. It requires innovative approaches to take advantage of marketing opportunities provided through technological capabilities and to address changes in consumer behaviours and expectations due to the technological shift. It also requires holistic and strategic thinking rather than short-term fixes and piecemeal approaches (Li and Petrick 2007). For marketers invested in current activities, which are evaluated based on existing performance measurement schemes, such transitions are not easy. Problems with marketers adjusting to new realities were already very evident when Internet use increased and more and more organizations tried to establish a Web presence in the late 1990s. The need to strategically think about the implications of technological change in relation to marketing activities was not always recognized and led to an application of old ways of doing things in the new marketing environment (Gretzel, Yuan and Fesenmaier 2000, Hanson 1999). A technology-driven shift is again occurring now with the broad adoption of Web 2.0 technologies by both consumers and organizations.

Such changes in technologies and the resulting challenges for marketers have a great impact especially on destination marketing organizations (DMOs). Gretzel, Fesenmaier, Formica and O'Leary (2006) discuss the unique situation of DMOs and emphasize their need to critically reflect on their technology use in order to engage in effective marketing when technological parameters change. Existing literature on technology use in DMOs shows that innovation, especially continuous innovation, is not very common (Zach, Gretzel and Xiang 2010). It also shows that the capacity of DMOs to innovate and successfully adopt new information technologies differs greatly among organizations (Yuan, Gretzel and Fesenmaier 2003, Wang and Fesenmaier 2006). While some DMOs are still struggling with fully taking advantage of Web 1.0 applications, others have already embraced the new Web 2.0 paradigm and are active users of social media-based strategies in their marketing efforts, riding high on the social media wave.

Stankov, Lazić and Dragićević (2010) explored Facebook use among national DMOs in Europe and found that not only did many in their sample not have a Facebook presence; even more important, those who had a Facebook presence were not using it in ways that would allow them to really seize the advantages of this social medium. The chapter by Hamill, Stevenson and Attard (2011) included in this book also shows that few DMOs in Europe are really engaged in social media marketing and that the majority of organizations analysed have yet to develop sophisticated and comprehensive social media strategies.

One issue related to successfully shifting marketing strategies and developing innovative approaches is understanding what is important from a theoretical perspective but also learning about what is possible in practice. In accordance with this, this chapter will describe and categorize social media marketing opportunities for DMOs. It will then provide in-depth case studies of DMOs that are highly engaged in social media marketing. The case studies are selected to represent DMOs in countries where social media use is high but which are usually not researched. The social media efforts of these DMOs will be described in detail and compared to the framework of social media marketing opportunities established in the beginning of the chapter. The chapter concludes with a discussion of future opportunities and challenges with respect to marketing travel destinations using social media.

2. Social Media Marketing: Concepts and Approaches

Web 2.0 technologies have created a conversation space in which messages about brands are not only designed and promoted by marketers but increasingly also initiated and published by consumers. In such an environment, marketers are conversation managers in a bigger social network that communicates continuously through various media avenues as well as directly with one another. Social media marketing, then, involves developing methods for strategically shaping conversations (Mangold and Faulds 2009). These methods have to acknowledge the realities of the new conversation space while meeting marketer needs. They also require letting go of traditional beliefs of what marketing is. Kaplan and Haenlein (2010) stress the importance of acknowledging that social media marketing is essentially about participation, sharing, and collaboration rather than straightforward advertising and selling. Steenburgh, Avery and Dahod (2009) specifically address the notion of push versus pull marketing and propose that Web 2.0 marketing means pulling consumers to the brand through the use of Web 2.0 applications such as blogging and fan pages. Similarly, Vargo and Lusch (2004) emphasize that marketing in this new paradigm should consider consumers as partners who collaborate and co-create value together with marketers by exchanging resources and information.

Yoo and Gretzel (2010) identified several areas in which active participation in marketing conversations by consumers, and the resulting changes in expectations,

Table 8.1 Social Media Marketing Functions (Yoo and Gretzel 2010)

Marketing Functions	Traditional Marketing	Web 2.0 Marketing
Customer Relations	- One-way communication - Offline customer service center - Limited customer data - Limited C2C communication - Delayed response	- Feedback from customer - Online customer service - Customer identification with data mining - Virtual customer communities - Real-time communication
Product	- Limited product information - Mass products for mainstream markets - Company-created products	- Value added information on products: Pictures, video, catalogue, consumer reviews etc. - Product customization - Co-creation with consumers - Digital/virtual Product
Price	- One-price pricing - Limited payment options	- Flexible pricing (Price transparency) - Online payment
Promotion	- Offline promotions - One promotion message - Partnerships with traditional partners - Targeting customers - Mediated through mass media	- Online promotions - Customized promotion messages - Non-traditional partnerships - Customer participation - Facilitated by Web 2.0 tools
Place	- Intermediaries - Required time to process order/booking - Offline distribution of products	- Dis-/Re-intermediation - Real-time ordering and processing - Online distribution of products
Research	- Delayed results - Push - Encouraged through incentives - No follow-up - Mediated - Sporadic - Costly - Response limited to numbers and text	- Real-time info through RSS or email alerts - Pull - Based on altruistic motivations - Immediate reaction - Unmediated - Continuous - Free data - Multiple formats
Performance Measurement	- Leads - Discrete times - Hard sales/visitor numbers	- Conversations - Continuous - Consumer sentiment

require new approaches. These areas include customer relationship management, product development, promotion, pricing, distribution, market research as well as performance measurement (Table 8.1). The list of functional areas clearly shows that social media marketing requires a holistic approach that encompasses all

Table 8.2 Marketing Paradigm Shift (Birch 2011)

Classic Marketing	21st Century Marketing	Social Media Marketing
Product	Experience	Relevance
Price	Exchange	Revenue
Place	Everyplace	Reach
Promotion	Evangelism	Reputation

marketing functions, including research and performance evaluation. Customer participation is a central issue across all areas. Success in social media marketing is not about return on investment but rather return on engagement (Frick 2010).

Similarly, Brand Karma, a social media marketing agency, argues that social media marketing is all-encompassing and fundamentally different from the traditional marketing paradigm centered on the 4P's (Birch 2011). Table 8.2 identifies the specific differences and describes social media marketing as essentially focused on 1) Relevance; 2) Revenue; 3) Reach; and 4) Reputation. A marketing strategy based on this paradigm has to engage customers but also continuously track results to ensure relevance and monitor reputation.

Numerous books are proposing ways in which social media marketing should be tackled. There are essentially two big issues to be addressed: which social media among the plethora of different types to choose, and how to communicate within a specific medium? Kaplan and Haenlein (2010) emphasize the importance of choosing social media outlets carefully and taking advantage of already existing applications. They also strongly argue for ensuring activity alignment across social media, integration of social media efforts with other online and offline marketing strategies, as well as making certain that employees stand fully behind the company's social media engagement.

As discussed by Hamill et al. (2011), mere presence is not enough for achieving social media marketing success. Social media marketing is a conversation that needs to be held with the right audience, needs interesting input, and requires trust to be established (Brogan and Smith 2009). Gunelius (2011) identified "10 Laws of Social Media Marketing" based on the social media marketing paradigm (Table 8.3). These guidelines suggest as well that social media marketing requires well-planned, active, and continuous engagement with influential consumers. Riding the wave of social media marketing thus needs to be understood as a deliberate effort to navigate social media waters, focused on staying on top of developments in the conversation space.

3. Social Media Marketing Cases

The value of cases lies in presenting the specific to illustrate the general. The concepts and approaches presented above described general assumptions that

Table 8.3 Social Media Marketing Laws (Gunelius 2011)

Social Media Marketing Law	Implications
1. Law of Listening	Learning how consumers engage in a specific social media type and what is important to them
2. Law of Focus	Diversity of social media types makes it impossible to be present in all – most relevant have to be selected
3. Law of Quality	Connecting to a small group of active and influential consumers is more important than reaching all
4. Law of Patience	Long haul commitment
5. Law of Compounding	Consumers will share quality content with others
6. Law of Influence	Identifying consumers who have the greatest influence
7. Law of Value	Interesting content and trust adds value to a conversation
8. Law of Acknowledgment	Acknowledging everyone who reaches out to establish relationships
9. Law of Accessibility	Being available to the audience on a continuous basis.
10. Law of Reciprocity	Sharing content published by others

should guide social media marketing efforts. However, destination marketing organizations are faced with very specific challenges (Gretzel et al., 2006) and, thus, social media marketing for destinations needs to be discussed within this specific context. While most research on DMOs looks at organizations in North America and Europe, an effort was made to look at DMOs in Asia and Latin America as regions where social media penetration is high. A note of caution should be added here as previous research has found significant national differences in social media structures, which influence uses (Gretzel, Kang and Lee 2008). The social media marketing strategies presented have to be understood as embedded in this national social media use context. Consequently, the focus of the cases is on linking the specific innovative activities to overall concepts so that their relevance becomes clearer and they can be understood as examples rather than universal recipes for social media marketing success.

"The Year of Chengdu" Marketing Campaign

Chinese New Year, also called Spring Festival, is a very important traditional holiday in China. The national holiday connected to the Spring Festival lasts for seven days and usually takes place in late January or early February. Every year since 2008 the municipal government of Chengdu in the southeast region of China has run a marketing campaign coined "The Year of Chengdu" to promote Spring

Festival tourism to Chengdu city. In 2010, the Chengdu Municipal Tourism Administration together with other agencies interested in promoting tourism to Chengdu hosted the third winter marketing campaign for "The Year of Chengdu" with the specific theme of "Create and Share Together". The official website of DMOs in Chengdu, Pandahome.com, cooperated with ten other websites including Microsoft MSN in China in the effort to promote Chengdu through social networks. MSN China invited its users to insert the phrase "I am enjoying Chinese New Year in Chengdu" into their individual MSN titles (similar to status updates in Facebook) and to vote for the "Top Ten Favourites of Winter Tourism in Chengdu". The winners were rewarded with ski tickets to Xiling Snow Mountain in the suburbs of Chengdu. Further, a promotional video for "The Year of Chengdu" was broadcast to users via the platform of MSN instant messenger.

This online promoting program stirred up a wave of responses to the "The Year of Chengdu" campaign. According to the Chengdu Daily, during the first week alone (up to 1 February 2010), the special link entitled "The Year of Chengdu" posted in MSN China was clicked over 400,000 times (http://www.chengdu.gov.cn/news/detail.jsp?id=307490) and users happily followed the invitation to change their MSN titles. The most favourite titles among MSN users were "I am enjoying Chinese New Year in Chengdu – skiing at Xiling Snow Mountain", and "I am enjoying Chinese New Year in Chengdu – viewing pandas, enjoying Lantern Fair, wandering through old towns, eating hotpots". According to Chengdu Business Daily, during the Spring Festival Golden Week (from 14 February to 20 February), the number of visitors in Chengdu reached 5,167,800, which represents an increase of 10 per cent over the same period in 2009. Most tourist areas received the highest number of visitors in their history. The number of tourists visiting Xiling Snow Mountain was 78,000, which reflects a growth of 20 per cent over the same period in the previous year, marking an all-time record. Moreover, the stream of incoming tourists did not finish with the end of the Golden Week. Tourists continued to travel to Chengdu the week after the holiday and flocked to the specific attractions mentioned in the MSN titles, such as the Lantern Festival (http://news.xinmin.cn/rollnews/2010/02/21/3697766.html).

Finally, on 4 March 2010, nearly 500,000 users voted on the "Top Ten Favourites of Winter Tourism in Chengdu" on the MSN China website. The results were: 1) Favourite festival – Chengdu Lantern fair; 2) The most unique folklore festival – Chengdu Great Temple Fair; 3) Tourism Area with Best Quality Services – Dujiangyan Scenic Area; 4) The most popular winter tourist destination – Xiling Snow Mountain; 5) The most popular winter destination abroad – Australia; 6) Best eco-tourism destination – Mount Qingchengshan; 7) Favourite Tianfu town – Pingle ancient town; 8) The most special New Year's Eve dinner – Ginkgo South Pavilion; 9) Favourite hotels – Homeland Hotel; 10) The most popular tourist souvenir – Tianhe Gift. This contest allowed the tourism organizations in Chengdu to reinforce the campaign and extend engagement beyond the actual holiday period.

Case study insights

"The Year of Chengdu" social media campaign illustrates several important aspects of the social media marketing paradigm. First, consumers were invited to not only engage in a conversation about Chengdu but to actually determine the topic of the conversation. Second, the structure of the campaign allowed MSN users to easily share their opinions with others, increasing the reach of the campaign. Third, the campaign took advantage of tourists' desire to share their experiences while traveling. Further, the contest allowed the conversation to continue long after the holiday and encouraged those who had traveled to yet again think about their experience. Thus, the campaign successfully addressed both the participatory as well as continuous nature of social media marketing.

Destination Marketing through Sina Microblog

A microblog is a broadcast medium that differs from a traditional blog in that its content is much smaller, with a limit of 140 Chinese characters. A microblog can be published much more conveniently via both computers and cell phones, and can be shared more easily by clicking "forward it". A microblog entry can consist of a short sentence fragment within the 140 Chinese character limit and can be created with or without an image or embedded video.

In China, microblogs have become more and more popular as this instant representation style is in line with Chinese people's modern pace of life and habits. According to a forecast by the Data Center of the China Internet, by the end of 2010, the number of active registered accounts of Chinese microblogs will exceed 65 million, and the number will exceed 100 million in 2011. The four biggest web portals in China, including sina.com, sohu.com, tencent.com, and netease.com, have each launched their own microblog services. Following the traditional blog and the online forum, the microblog has become a standard product of Chinese web portals. Sina Microblog (t.sina.com.cn) was launched in August 2009 and became the first microblog service in China.

Recognizing the potential opportunity for marketing via microblogs, several DMOs in China have registered at Sina Microblog. Harbin Tourism Bureau (HTB) was the first Chinese destination marketing organization at the city level to register at Sina Microblog on 24 January 2010 to promote its attractions online. Up to 28 October 2010, HTB had attracted 4,475 fans and published 703 messages. The Tourism Bureau of Sichuan Province (TBSP), a DMO at the province level, registered at Sina Microblog on 26 July 2010. Although starting half a year later than HTB, TBSP has slightly more fans (4,908 fans) but has only published 604 messages.

Tags are important for blogs and microblogs to become searchable. Both tourism bureaus are aware of the need to create these tags. The HTB microblog has the following tags: backpacker, individual travel, prevent sunstroke, ice and snow, food, Harbin, ice city and summer resort, tourism and travel. TBSP's microblog site features the respective tags: Panda Home, travel strategy, travel notes, classic articles, promotions, activities, information, news, Sichuan, tourism.

In addition to publishing information on and photos of specific tourist sites in Sichuan, the Sichuan Tourism Bureau organizes reward activities to encourage participation in tourism policy making. For instance, in order to collect suggestions for the Twelfth Five-year Plan (from 2011 to 2015), which will guide tourism development in Sichuan for the next five years, TBSP published a short description with a web link on its microblog. Tourists and residents alike can access a web survey and then give their personal advice or voice expectations for the future development of Sichuan province. Ten respondents will be rewarded with the designation "Best Advice" and an admission ticket to Mount Emei or Chengdu Happy Valley. In general, online quizzes and competitions are very frequently-found features on Sina Microblog.

Case study insights

Co-creation and consumer feedback are essential components of a successful social media marketing strategy. The case study presented a concrete example of how such co-creation can be structured. It fits inherently with the notion of seeing consumers as true partners in social media marketing efforts instead of mere receivers of promotional messages. The engagement of Chinese DMOs on Sina Microblog also shows that marketing efforts have to take the specific affordances of the social media type into account. Marketing on a microblog site is fundamentally different from marketing in a social networking site or marketing through a company-sponsored traditional blog. Further, social media content benefits from increased searchability and both DMOs seem to be very aware of this fact.

Marketing Brazil on YouTube

The national DMO of Brazil (Embratur) has whole-heartedly adopted social media marketing. It is present on Twitter, Facebook, Flickr and YouTube. The DMO website not only includes links to these social media sites but actively encourages website visitors to engage with the social media through an ad-like section in the upper half of the website. Each of the social media sites not only includes a link to the website but also links to the other social media sites.

Embratur created its YouTube presence in June of 2009. Its YouTube channel now has close to 2000 subscribers and has been viewed over half a million times. The YouTube channel page (http://www.youtube.com/visitbrasil) links to Google Maps, making it easy to assign videos to geographic destinations. Further, videos are categorized by type of destination into five different themes (sun and beach, culture, ecotourism, sport, and business and events). A separate playlist features videos of testimonials and yet another playlist gives consumers access to Embratur's promotional videos. Users are invited to leave comments on the YouTube channel page. Most importantly, it is obvious from the postings that Embratur takes these consumer contributions seriously and regularly responds to comments posted in this section. The page has pictures of famous Brazilian attractions as its background and is prominently branded with the Visit Brazil logo and the "Brazil – Sensational!" slogan. Links to Embratur's Facebook, Twitter and FlickR pages are also included on the YouTube channel page.

Case study insights

The above case study stresses the importance of integrated marketing communication and the creation of a coherent brand image across channels. Not only are the various online activities linked, the offline logo and the promotional videos are also integrated. However, in accordance with the true spirit of honesty and pull marketing, these promotional videos are clearly identified as such and not disguised as user-generated content. Most importantly, the YouTube page is not used as just another broadcast medium but as a real platform for communication among consumers and between consumers and the DMO. Embratur acknowledges postings and through that encourages the conversation to continue. Further, Embratur has clearly focused on a few selected social media types and actively promotes these.

4. Future of Social Media Marketing

The popularity of existing social media types changes rapidly and new forms of social media are certainly going to appear in the near future. Geographic and cultural differences are also evident in the popularity of certain social media in specific regions or even countries. However, while the specifics of social media campaigns differ depending on the social media type selected, the overall assumptions of social media marketing are the same and will continue to be relevant. While there might be another marketing paradigm shift in the future, it will be based on the social media marketing paradigm, not on traditional marketing. Thus, it is important to understand the basic assumptions of social media marketing.

Conversations are fundamental elements of tourism information search processes and tourism content is often inherently engaging. Yet, DMOs have to learn how to be relevant in these conversations without falling back into the old sales and push mode. Managing but not over-managing these conversations to influence destination reputation and to increase reach is a critical strategy in the social media environment. This means that measures of success will have to be adjusted accordingly to reflect the new realities. Counting the number of fans as a performance indicator, for instance, clearly violates the laws of social media marketing. Continuous and active engagement in these conversations will also require investments beyond the creation of a Facebook page or YouTube channel and have personnel implications.

The social media wave is only gaining in momentum and drowning in it is a real danger for many DMOs. This chapter outlined and illustrated fundamental principles of social media marketing that should make it possible for DMOs to strategically engage in this new form of marketing and actually enjoy the ride.

References

Birch, D. 2011. *Travel & Tourism is A Mature Business – Nothing Much Changes or Does It? Proceedings of the ENTER 2011 18th International Conference on Information and Communication Technology in Travel and Tourism* (Innsbruck, Austria, 26 January).

Brogan, C. and Smith, J. 2009. *Trust Agents*. Hoboken, NJ: John Wiley & Sons.

Frick, T. 2010. *Return on Engagement: Content, Strategy, and Design Techniques for Digital Marketing*. Burlington, MA: Focal Press.

Gretzel, U., Fesenmaier, D.R., Formica, S. and O'Leary, J.T. 2006. Searching for the future: Challenges faced by destination marketing organizations. *Journal of Travel Research*, 45(2), 116-126.

Gretzel, U., Kang, M. and Lee, W. 2008. Differences in consumer-generated media adoption and use: A cross-national perspective. *Journal of Hospitality Marketing and Management*, 17(1/2), 99-120.

Gretzel, U., Yuan, Y. and Fesenmaier, D.R. 2000. Preparing for the new economy: Advertising strategies and change in destination marketing organizations. *Journal of Travel Research*, 39(2), 146-156.

Gunelius, S. 2011. 10 Laws of Social Media Marketing. Available at: http://www.entrepreneur.com/article/218160# [accessed: 16 February 2011]

Hamill, J., Stevenson, A. and Attard, D. 2011. National DMOs and Web 2.0, in *Social Media in Travel, Tourism and Hospitality: Theory, Practice and Cases*, edited by M. Sigala, E. Christou and U. Gretzel. Farnham: Ashgate.

Hanson, W. 1999. *Principles of Internet Marketing*. Cincinnati, OH: South-Western College Publishing Company.

Kaplan, A.M. and Haenlein, M. 2010. Users of the world, unite! The challenges and opportunities of Social Media. *Business Horizons*, 53(1), 59-68.

Li, X. and Petrick, J.F. 2008. Tourism marketing in an era of paradigm shift. *Journal of Travel Research*, 46(1), 235-244.

Mangold, W.G. and Faulds, D.J. 2009. Social media: The new hybrid element of the promotion mix. *Business Horizons*, 52(3), 357-365.

Stankov, U., Lazić, L. and Dragićević, V. 2010. The extent of use of basic Facebook user-generated content by the national tourism organizations in Europe. *European Journal of Tourism Research*, 3(2), 105-113.

Steenburgh, T.J., Avery, J.J. and Dahod, N. 2009. *Hubspot: Inbound Marketing and Web 2.0.* HBS Case No. 509-049; Harvard Business School Marketing Unit. Available at: SSRN: http://ssrn.com/abstract=1491111.

Vargo, S.L. and Lusch, R.F. 2004. Evolving to a new dominant logic for marketing. *Journal of Marketing*, 68, 1-17.

Wang, Y. and Fesenmaier, D.R. 2006. Identifying the success factors of web-based marketing strategy: An investigation of convention and visitors bureaus in the United States. *Journal of Travel Research*, 44(3), 239-249.

Yoo, K-H. and Gretzel, U. 2010. *Web 2.0: New Rules for Tourism Marketing: Proceedings of the 41st Travel and Tourism Research Association Conference* (San Antonio, TX, 20-22 June 2010. Lake Orion, MI: Travel and Tourism Research Association).

Yuan, Y., Gretzel, U. and Fesenmaier, D.R. 2003. Internet technology use by American convention and visitors bureaus. *Journal of Travel Research*, 41(3), 240-255.

Zach, F., Gretzel, U. and Xiang, Z. 2010. Innovation in the web marketing programs of American convention and visitor bureaus. *Journal of Information Technology & Tourism*, 12(1), 47-63.

Chapter 9
National DMOs and Web 2.0

Jim Hamill, Alan Stevenson and Daniela Attard

1. Introduction

A previous chapter by the authors, based on 2008 research, examined the strategic response of National Destination Marketing Organisations in Europe to the global marketing opportunities and threats presented by the Web 2.0/social media revolution (Hamill, Stevenson and Attard 2009). The chapter concluded that National DMOs, from the leading tourist destinations in Europe, had made only limited progress in this area. Of the 25 DMOs examined, only three could be described as 'progressive adopters' of Web 2.0 and social media. The National DMOs surveyed did exhibit a high level of awareness and understanding concerning the global marketing and customer engagement potential of new media and there was considerable enthusiasm for moving forward in this area. However, major barriers to Web 2.0 adoption were identified, especially in relation to internal resource constraints, organisational culture and mindset, the lack of a clear social media vision and strategy, concerns about the loss of control and potential negative brand impact of user generated content.

Given the rapid growth of social media over the last few years, what progress has been made since our 2008 research? Are National DMOs in Europe still 'laggards' in their use of social media for building sustained customer and competitive advantage?

Based on research undertaken in late November 2010 and using a similar but revised methodology, this chapter reports updated findings concerning the Web 2.0/social media progress made by Europe's leading National DMOs. The updated methodology includes measures of social media depth of engagement as well as channel presence. While some progress has been made since the previous study, the 2010 results show that few national DMOs in Europe are fully utilising the interactive power of Web 2.0 for building strong customer and network relationships; for engaging with and energising online communities. This is a worrying conclusion given the revolutionary impact of Web 2.0/social media on the global travel, tourism and hospitality industry.

2. Research Background and Approach

This section presents the background to and importance of the research undertaken. A detailed explanation of the research approach and benchmark criteria used is also presented.

Online social networks

In reviewing the existing state of knowledge in this area, the previous chapter drew on five key strands of the relevant literature including the general literature on destination marketing and destination branding – Aaker (1991), Blain et al. (2005), Kotler and Gertner (2002), Morgan et al. (2002), Morgan et al. (2003), Pike (2004); online destination marketing – Douglas and Mills (2004), Gertner et al. (2006), Park and Gretzel (2007), So and Morrison (2003), Wang and Fesenmaier (2006); customer empowerment and the customer experience – Buhalis et al. (2007), Hamill and Stevenson (2006), Nykamp (2001), Thompson (2006); the emerging literature on Web 2.0 – Eikelmann et al. (2007), O'Reilly (2006), Tapscott and Williams (2006), Li and Bernoff (2008); and specifically, Web 2.0 in the travel and tourism industry – Ellion (2007), O'Connor (2008), Reactive (2007), Schegg et al. (2008), Sigala (2007). More recent publications relevant to the topic include Baker and Cameron (2008), Schmallegger and Carson (2008), Tapscott (2008), Elowitz and Li (2009), Inversini, Cantoni and Buhalis (2009), Weber, L. (2009), Hofbauer, Stangl and Teichmann (2010), Sigala (2010), Tapscott and Williams (2010) and Xiang and Gretzel (2010).

The model shown in Figure 9.1 was used to summarise the impact of Web 2.0/ social media on the global travel, tourism and hospitality industry.

From the above, the background to and importance of the research reported in this chapter is the rapid growth of social media; the revolutionary impact it is having on consumer behaviour in the global travel, tourism and hospitality industry; the global marketing opportunities, but also threats, for National DMOs; and the lack of previous research in this area. To the best of our knowledge, our 2008 and 2010 studies have been the only comprehensive evaluations undertaken of National DMO social media progress.

The progress being made needs to be seen in the context of the potential business benefits to be derived by National DMOs from proactive social media engagement. These can be summarised under five main headings:

- Market/Customer Knowledge and Insight: the potential for the DMO to build more detailed market knowledge and customer insight through user generated feedback, comments, ratings and reviews; and the use of advanced Social Media Monitoring Tools to monitor who is saying what about the brand, where online and the positive/negative sentiments being expressed. One of the major trends in social media over the last few years has been the emergence of a very wide range of Social Media Monitoring

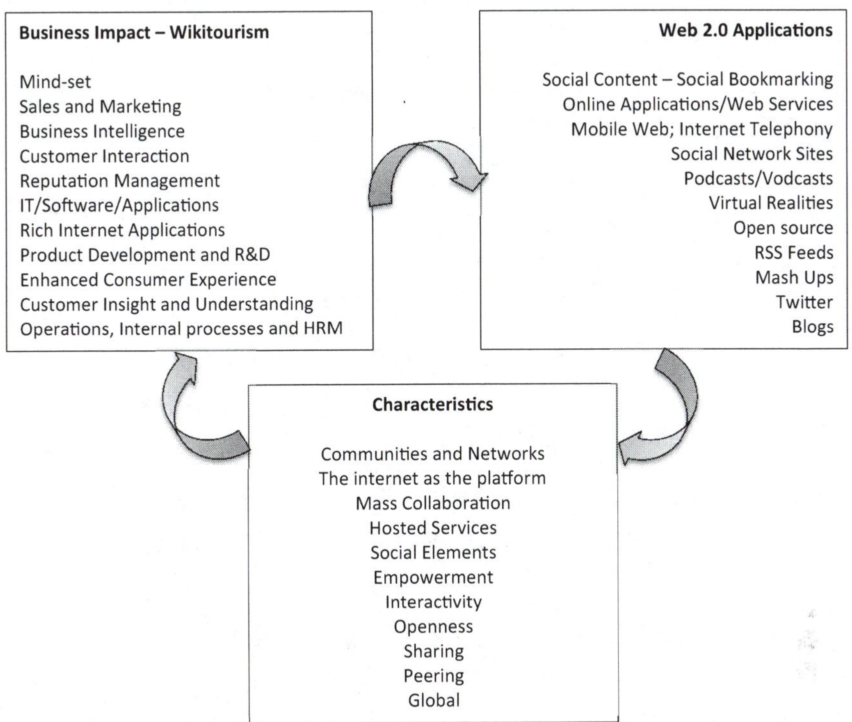

Figure 9.1 Tourism 2.0 – Social Media and Global Tourism

and Measurement Tool (see our other chapter in the book).

- Engagement and Reputation Management: the potential for proactive brand and reputation management through building active engagement and two-way dialogue with customers and online communities.
- Enhanced Customer Experience and Loyalty: improving brand loyalty through enriching the online customer experience using Rich Internet Applications such as mash-ups, podcats/vodcasts, mapping tools etc. Building strong online communities of 'high value, high growth potential, return visitors'.
- Sales/Marketing Effectiveness, Efficiency and ROI: used effectively, social media can significantly improve sales/marketing effectiveness, efficiency and ROI; especially given the declining effectiveness of more traditional forms of advertising and the 'me too' aspect of much destination marketing.
- Operations/Internal Processes: achieving cost and efficiency improvements through the use of open source software and hosted applications.

Table 9.1 Sample DMOs

Destination	International Tourist Arrivals		Official DMO Website
	2006 (000)	Share (%)	
Europe	460,835	100	-
France	79,083	17.2	http://uk.franceguide.com/
Spain	58,451	12.7	http://www.spain.info/
Italy	41,058	8.9	http://www.italiantourism.com/
UK	30,654	6.7	http://www.visitbritain.com/
Germany	23,569	5.1	http://www.germany-tourism.de/
Austria	20,261	4.4	http://www.austria.info
Russian Fed.	20,199	4.4	http://www.visitrussia.org.uk/
Turkey	18,916	4.1	http://www.goturkey.org/
Ukraine	18,936	4.1	http://www.traveltoukraine.org/
Greece	16,039	3.5	http://www.visitgreece.gr/
Poland	15,670	3.4	http://www.poland.travel/en-gb/
Portugal	11,282	2.4	http://www.visitportugal.com/
Netherlands	10,739	2.3	http://www.holland.com/global/
Hungary	9,259	2.0	http://www.hungarytourism.hu/
Croatia	8,659	1.9	http://www.croatia.hr/
Switzerland	7,863	1.7	http://www.myswitzerland.com/
Ireland	8,001	1.7	http://www.discoverireland.com/
Belgium	6,995	1.5	http://www.visitbelgium.com/
Czech Rep.	6,435	1.4	http://www.czechtourism.com/
Bulgaria	5,158	1.1	http://www.bulgariatravel.org
Norway	3,945	0.9	http://www.visitnorway.com/
England	-	-	http://www.enjoyengland.com
N. Ireland	-	-	http://discovernorthernireland.com
Scotland	-	-	http://www.visitscotland.com
Wales	-	-	http://www.visitwales.com

Measurement criteria and research approach

The key research objective was to update the 2008 benchmark evaluation of Web 2.0/social media adoption levels by leading National DMOs in Europe. This required decisions to be made concerning the sample of DMOs to be covered and the measurement/scoring criteria to be used. A second stage of the research will involve personal interviews with the DMOs covered.

The sample

To allow direct comparisons with the 2008 study, the same sample of National DMOs was evaluated comprising the 21 major country destinations in Europe in terms of international arrivals (WTO 2007). As the research was conducted in the UK, we also included the National DMOs from Scotland, England, Wales and the North of Ireland providing the final sample of 25 DMOs shown in Table 9.1.

Measurement criteria

Based on the existing literature in this area, the previous study evaluated National DMO 'Internal' and 'External' use of Web 2.0/social media; in other words, their use of 2.0/social media on their own websites and their active participation in external sites such as Facebook, Flickr, YouTube etc. Seventeen criteria were used to evaluate 'Internal' use with a further seven criteria for 'External' involvement. The unit of data collection used was a simple yes (1) or no (0) for each channel presence.

The 2010 benchmark evaluation used similar measurement criteria but with two significant updates.

- 'Channel Presence' – reflecting the growing number of social media applications now available, 29 rather than 24 criteria were used to evaluate channel presence. These are listed in Table 9.2.
- 'Engagement Profile' – the most significant update was the inclusion of criteria to evaluate the depth and level of engagement as well as channel presence. The framework used for this was based on the pioneering Engagement DB Study of Elowitz and Li (2009). This measured social media use and levels of engagement for the world's top 100 brands (see www.engagementdb.com) with the results being presented as 'social media profiles' based on channel presence and level/depth of engagement. Brands were classified into one of four main types of generic social media strategy:
  - Mavens: Brands that sustain a high level of engagement across multiple social media channels. Mavens have a robust social media strategy supported by dedicated teams. Active engagement across a range of social media channels is a key element of their overall brand management strategy.

Table 9.2 Social Media Channel Presence – Benchmark Criteria

Internal	External
Use of social media on the DMO's website	**DMO use of external social media channels**
UGC (User Generated Content)	**Social+Professional Networking Sites**
- Text and Blogs - Images - Video - Wiki Engagement rating for the above	- Facebook - LinkedIn Engagement rating for the above
User FOD (feedback or discussion)	**Microblogging**
- Forum - Ratings, reviews+feedback - Online Chat Engagement rating for the above	- Twitter Engagement rating for the above
RIA (website uses Rich Internet Applications)	**Multimedia Sharing Sites**
- Widgets - Mashups - Podcast/Vodcast Engagement rating for the above	- YouTube - Flickr Engagement rating for the above
Use of Folksonomies	**Podcasts/Audiocasts**
- Social Tagging - Social Bookmarking - Tag Cloud Engagement rating for the above	- iTunes - Apps Engagement rating for the above
Feeds (site uses In/Out Feeds to enrich content)	**Virtual Reality**
- Content Feeds IN - Content Feeds OUT Engagement rating for the above	- Second Life Engagement rating for the above
Community (website encourages networking)	**Blogs and TripAdvisor**
- Social Network Engagement rating for the above	- Blogs - TripAdvisor Engagement rating for the above
External Links (to social media channels)	**Mapping Tools**
- Links to Facebook, Twitter, YouTube, Flickr etc. Engagement rating for the above	- Google Maps or similar Engagement rating for the above
	Location Based Services
	- Foursquare/Facebook Places Engagement rating for the above
Overall Channel Score for Internal Use	**Overall Channel Score for External Use**
Total Internal Engagement Score	**Total External Engagement Score**

Source: the authors.

- Butterflies: Brands using a large number of social media channels but with lower than average engagement scores in each channel. Would probably like to become 'Mavens' but full organisational buy-in and resources to do so have not yet been achieved. Danger of spreading activities too thinly.
- Selectives: Brands that focus on a small number of channels but with high engagement scores in each one. Selectives focus on deep customer engagement in a small number of channels where it matters most. Social media initiatives at these brands tend to be lightly staffed, started by impassioned evangelists on a shoestring budget – can be a powerful beachhead for further development.
- Wallflowers: Brands using a small number of channels and with below-average engagement scores. These brands have been slow to respond to the opportunities presented by social media, currently dipping their toes in the water, cautious about the risks and uncertain about the benefits.

Scoring System

'Channel presence'

Based on a simple 1 for 'yes' and 0 for 'no', and following the EngagementDB study, the scoring method for 'Channel Presence' was as follows:

- 'High Channel Presence' – DMO is present in two-thirds or more of the available channels (i.e. 19 or more out of a total of 29 channels).
- 'Medium Channel Presence' – DMO is present in 50 per cent to two-thirds of the channels available.
- 'Low Channel Presence' – DMO uses less than 50 per cent of available channels.

'Engagement profile'

An engagement score between 0 and 5 was then allocated to each DMO for each of the 15 Web2.0/social media categories i.e. UGC, FOD, RIA, External Links, Social and Professional Networking, Multimedia Sharing Sites etc, rather than for each individual channel, as follows: low engagement 0-1, medium engagement 2-3, high engagement 4-5. Our '4Is' approach was used to benchmark engagement levels: 'Involvement' – the number of people involved in each channel e.g. Facebook 'likers', Twitter followers, YouTube viewers etc; 'Interaction' – the level of two-way dialogue as opposed to one-way broadcasting; 'Intimacy' – the brand sentiments being expressed, the balance between positive and negative sentiments; 'Influence' – e-word-of-mouth effects. These are not intangible criteria but can be measured with a very high degree of accuracy both for individual channels and in terms of the overall 'buzz' being generated about the brand across all social media channels.

Given a total of 15 engagement categories (7 'Internal' and 8 'External' i.e. the main sub-headings shown in Figure 2) the highest possible score was 75 (i.e top engagement score of 5 x 15 categories). Using a similar approach to 'Channel Presence', the scoring method for 'Engagement' was as follows:

- 'High Engagement' – DMOs with a total engagement score of 50 or more (i.e. two-thirds or more of the total score possible).
- 'Medium Engagement' – DMOs with an engagement score of 50 per cent to two-thirds of the total (i.e. 37 to 49).
- 'Low Engagement' – DMOs with an engagement score of less than 50 per cent (37 or less).

The coding guidelines and coding forms were tested through a preliminary examination of five DMOs to ensure category suitability, clarity of coding instructions and the overall reliability of the coding forms. Since it is recommended that content analysis is performed by at least two coders (Krippendorff 2004), the sites were independently evaluated by two of the current authors and one other social media expert. Intercoder reliability, which refers to the extent to which the three coders agreed on the coding of the different criteria, was calculated at 0.96, which is well above the 0.80 acceptable level (Neuendorf 2002). Following this, the few disagreements were resolved through a discussion between the three assessors. The 25 sites were evaluated in the last week of November 2010.

3. Research Findings: The Strategic Response of National DMOs to Web 2.0

Key findings from our updated 2010 benchmark evaluation are presented below. Summary 'Channel Presence' and 'Engagement' scores are shown in Table 9.3, together with an overall DMO League Table. Table 9.4 shows individual scores for each social media channel/application.

Key findings are as follows:

- Similar to our 2008 results, National DMOs in Europe continue to adopt a very cautious approach to their use of Web 2.0/social media, both in terms of 'Internal' applications and their enagagement with 'External' social media channels. Only one DMO, Visit England (www.visitengland.com) recorded a total score of two-thirds or more out of a possible 104 i.e. number of channels used + engagement score. Their nearest rival was Switzerland Tourism (www.myswitzerland.com) but with a total score of just 36. Indeed, only six DMOs scored more than 30 out of a possible 104.
- Compared to the other DMOs studied, VisitEngland were clear leaders

in their innovative use of social media on their own website. Notable features included the active encouragement of user generated content (text, images, video); visitor ratings and reviews; the use of rich Internet applications to enhance the online customer experience (widgets, mash-ups, podcasts); social bookmarking; RSS feeds; together with very clear links to external channels used. Their use of external social media channels was also impressive with a Facebook fan page of 45,500 plus 'likers' and a Twitter following of 9,000 plus. Good use was also being made of iTunes podcasts, mobile apps, an Enjoy England blog and mapping tools. YouTube, Flickr and location based services were also being used although with more limited engagement compared to the other channels.

- For the sample as a whole, the depth of engagement and number of channels used was slightly higher for 'External' social media compared to 'Internal' use on the DMOs own website. As shown in Table 9.4, the total engagement score for 'Internal' channels was 133 (or 15 per cent of the total possible) and for 'External' channels it was 212 (21 per cent of the total possible). This was a different conclusion to our 2008 study where 'Internal' use of social media exceeded 'External' use indicating that the DMOs studied had become more proactively involved in using external social media channels. However, this needs to be seen in the context of low overall engagement scores as discussed below. (Note: the total possible engagement score for 'Internal' channels was 875 i.e. number of categories (7) x number of DMOs (25) x top score for each category (5). The same calculation was used for 'External' channels. With eight categories, the top possible score was 1,000).
- In terms of 'Internal' applications, only five out of the 25 National DMOs studied encouraged user generated content on their website (text, images, videos) with only three encouraging user ratings and reviews. No DMO encouraged social networking on their website with only four using podcasts or vodcasts to enrich the online customer experience. Only eight DMOs provided the facility for social bookmarking on their site, with only five providing RSS feeds. These are surprising findings given the ease of adding these applications to a website.
- Interesting findings emerged in terms of 'External' social media use. In the previous 2008 study, only seven National DMOs had an official presence on Facebook with only six beginning to experiment with multimedia sharing sites such as YouTube and Flickr. Twitter did not exist at the time of the previous study. The 2010 study shows a significant increase in the number of National DMOs becoming involved with 'External' social media channels. As shown in Table 9.3, 21 out of the 25 National DMOs studied had an official presence on Facebook and Twitter. Twenty had an official YouTube channel with a further 12 using Flickr. While this might be seen as representing good progress since the previous study, the overall level and depth of engagement with these channels remains

limited with engagement scores of 54 for 'Social and Professional Networking', 45 for 'Microblogging and 37 for 'Multimedia Sharing' out of a possible total of 125 for each category (i.e. top possible score of 5 x number of DMOs studied 25). Reasonable use was being made of other 'External' channels such as iTunes, mobile apps and Google Maps but very limited use of virtual reality, blogs, integration with TripAdvisor or location based services.

- In terms of overall League Table positions, interesting comparisons can be made with the 2008 study. VisitEngland replaced Switzerland Tourism as the leading National DMO for their use of social media. DMOs who significantly improved their League Table positions included those from Greece, the North of Ireland, Spain, Hungary and to some extent the Netherlands. Poland, Portugal and Scotland experienced significant declines in their position.
- Based on a simple count of the number of channels used, the previous study identified three main clusters in terms of DMO Web 2.0 adoption levels. Non-Starters: DMOs with total scores between 0 and 2 representing no or very limited use of Web 2.0 technologies. Cautious Adopters: DMOs with total scores between 3 and 6 representing some basic but limited progress. Progressive Adopters: DMOs with total scores of 7 or more. Only three DMOs were classified as 'Progressive Adopters' (Switzerland, England and Poland); a further nine were 'Cautious Adopters' (Portugal, Scotland, United Kingdom, Austria, France, Germany, Ireland, Norway and Wales); with the remaining thirteen DMOs being 'Non-Starters'.
- The above results need to be seen in the context of the relative 'newness' of social media at that time. Given the rapid growth of social media over the last few years, and the greater opportunities available for DMOs, we would classify only one DMO (VisitEngland) as a 'progressive adopter' of social media based on our 2010 analysis. With only one other DMO (Switzerland) recording an overall score greater than one-third of the total possible, we would rank all other National DMOs as being very 'Cautious' or 'Non-Adopters' of social media.
- Using the EngagementDB Model, our overall classification of the 25 National DMOs studied is as follows:
  - Mavens: Only one DMO (VisitEngland) could be described as a Social Media Maven i.e. a DMO that attempts to sustain a high level of engagement across multiple social media channels.
  - Butterflies: The following DMOs would be best described as 'butterflies' i.e. brands using a large number of social media channels but with lower than average engagement scores in each channel (Switzerland, UK, Greece, Netherlands, North of Ireland, Hungary and Wales) i.e. DMOs using 10 or more channels but with a low overall engagement score.
  - Selectives: None of the DMOs surveyed could be described as a

Table 9.3 European DMO Social Media League Table

DMO	Internal Channel Presence (17)	External Channel Presence (12)	Total Channel Presence (29)	Internal Engage. Score (35)	External Engage. Score (40)	Total Engage. Score (75)	Total Score (104)
England	10	10	20	27	21	48	68
Switzerland	7	7	14	12	10	22	36
UK	4	8	12	5	15	20	32
Greece	7	6	13	9	10	19	32
Netherlands	2	9	11	6	15	21	32
N. Ireland	9	5	14	13	4	17	31
Spain	1	8	9	4	14	18	27
Hungary	4	6	10	6	11	17	27
Wales	6	4	10	8	9	17	27
Norway	3	5	8	7	11	18	26
Austria	4	5	9	6	8	14	23
Poland	4	4	8	5	9	14	22
Germany	4	6	10	5	7	12	22
France	2	7	9	4	8	12	21
Portugal	2	5	7	2	12	14	21
Ireland	0	9	9	0	12	12	21
Croatia	3	4	7	3	8	11	18
Scotland	2	5	7	3	5	8	15
Czech Rep.	1	4	5	2	8	10	15
Ukraine	2	5	7	2	4	6	13
Italy	1	4	5	1	4	5	9
Belgium	1	3	4	2	3	5	9
Turkey	0	4	4	0	4	4	8
Russia	1	1	2	1	0	1	3
Bulgaria	0	1	1	0	0	0	1
Total	**80**	**135**	**215**	**133**	**212**	**345**	**560**

Source: The authors.

Table 9.4 Individual Channel Scores

Internal (use of social media on the organisation's own website)	**No. of DMOs**	**Engagement Score**
1. UGC (website encourages user generated content)		
- Text and Blogs	5	
- Images	5	
- Video	5	
- Wiki	0	
		17
2. User FOD (feedback or discussion)		
- Forum	2	
- Ratings, reviews+feedback	3	
- Online Chat	0	
		13
3. RIA (website uses Rich Internet Applications)		
- Widgets	12	
- Mashups	9	
- Podcast/Vodcast	4	
		23
4. Folksonomies (website encourages social bookmarking, tagging)		
- Social Tagging	0	
- Social Bookmarking	8	
- Tag Cloud	1	
		20
5. Feeds (website has in/out RSS feeds to enhance content)		
- Content Feeds IN	0	
- Content Feeds OUT	5	
		12
6. Community (website has a social networking section)		
- Social Network	0	
		0
7. External Links (clear links to external social media channels used)		
- Links to Facebook, Twitter, YouTube, Flickr etc.	21	
		48
Overall Channel Score for Internal Use	80	
Total Internal Engagement Score		133

External (use of external social media channels)	**No. of DMOs**	**Engagement Score**
8. Social+Professional Networking Sites		
- Facebook	21	
- LinkedIn	15	
		54
9. Microblogging		
- Twitter	21	
		45
10. Multimedia Sharing Sites		
- YouTube	20	
- Flickr	12	
		37
11. Podcasts/Audiocasts		
- iTunes	11	
- Apps	9	
		30
12. Virtual Reality		
- Second Life	2	
		4
13. Blogs and TripAdvisor		
- Blogs	3	
- TripAdvisor	3	
		9
14. Mapping Tools		
- Google Maps or similar	10	
Engagement rating for the above		28
15. Location Based Services		
Foursquare/Facebook Places	8	
Engagement rating for the above		5
Overall Channel Score for External Use	**135**	
Total External Engagement Score		**212**

Source: The authors.

'Selective' i.e. a brand focusing on a small number of channels but with high engagement scores in each one.

- Wallflowers: The majority of DMOs studied (17 out of 25) were 'Wallflowers' i.e. brands using a small number of channels and with below-average engagement scores.

4. Discussion and Implications

Although some progress had been made since our previous study, the main conclusion of our 2010 benchmark evaluation is that the leading National DMOs in Europe are still not fully engaging with social media. Much progress still needs to be made before they are fully utilising the interactive power of Web 2.0 for building strong customer and network relationships; for engaging with and energising online communities (Li and Bernoff 2008).

The majority of National DMOs studied are 'cautious' or 'non-adopters' of Web 2.0/social media. Using the EngagementDB classification, the majority (17 out of the 25 studied) are 'wallflowers' in terms of their strategic use of social media. Good progress has been made, since the previous study, in establishing external social media channels, especially Facebook and Twitter, but the overall level and depth of engagement remains low. Only three DMOs actively encourage customer feedback, comment, ratings and reviews through their own website.

As in our previous study, the lack of progress in this area is particularly worrying given the profound impact that Web 2.0 is having on consumer behaviour and decision-making in global tourism. Travellers no longer wish to be passive recipients of destination brand messages. They are looking for a much higher level of engagement with the destination at all stages of the 'Customer Life Cycle'. This will require a major change in DMO 'mindsets' and innovative new approaches to tourism marketing, customer and network relationships. The traditional approach to destination marketing is to innovate, differentiate, market and promote, then sell. This needs to be replaced by a new model based on communities, networks, openness, peering, sharing, collaboration, customer empowerment, thinking and acting globally. Some DMOs such as VisitEngland 'get it'. The majority seen to be stuck in a social media time warp.

'Non-Starter' and 'Cautious Adopter' DMOs, in particular, will need to develop and implement effective social media strategies. Our previous research showed a high level of awareness and understanding concerning the global marketing and customer engagement potential of Web 2.0 and a high level of enthusiasm for moving forward in this area. Yet two years later, much progress still needs to be made. It would appear that the major barriers to Web 2.0/social media adoption identified in our 2008 study remain in place – internal resource constraints, organisational culture and mindset, the lack of a clear vision and strategy for 2.0, concerns about the loss of control and potential brand impact of user controlled social media. A legitimate question to ask is whether these are 'real' barriers to social media progress or senior management 'excuses' for not engaging.

Given the explosion of interest in Web 2.0/Social Media, it is not surprising that many National DMOs are beginning to 'dip their toe in the water'; experimenting with low resource, low risk social media engagement activities. These early initiatives, often started by 'social media evangelists', are very much to be encouraged. They help considerably in improving organisational knowledge and understanding of social media and provide an early indicator of what will or will not work. Hopefully, such early initiatives will firmly establish social media as a key strategic priority. However, with growing experimentation, comes the realisation that successful use of social media requires sound planning and the application of professional project management procedures to social media strategy development, implementation, management and performance measurement – 'Social Media Planning Pays'. The results of our 2008 and 2010 benchmarking studies show that few National DMOs in Europe have a clear vision or strategy for social media or an agreed implementation plan for 'getting there'.

In moving forward in this area, we would recommend the use of a Social Media Development Cycle to guide future strategy development and implementation (see Figure 9.2). This will ensure that future social media activities are fully aligned with and supportive of the overall business goals and objectives of the DMO; that Key Performance Indicators (KPIs) are agreed for monitoring and evaluating social media performance, business impact and ROI; and that all key success factors are considered, especially the organisation, people and resource aspects critical to successful strategy implementation. The Development Cycle approach is also very useful for internal and external communications – a simple framework to present social media goals, objectives, key actions and initiatives to colleagues, partners and other stakeholders.

The ten key steps in the model are summarised below:

Evaluate your social media landscape

Social Media Landscaping will help the DMO to decide the best generic social media strategy to follow in terms of the number of channels to use and depth of engagement in each channel. It will avoid the 'we must use it because it is there' syndrome. Key questions to address include: What social media applications are the most relevant for our DMO? What impact is social media having on our industry, how important has it become? How are our customers using social media? What impact is it having on customer behaviour? What online conversations are taking place relevant to our DMO; who is saying what about our brand/industry where on social media and how should we respond? A wide range of Social Media Monitoring Tools are available for monitoring the conversations taking place (see other chapter on 'Social Media Monitoring and Performance Measurement).

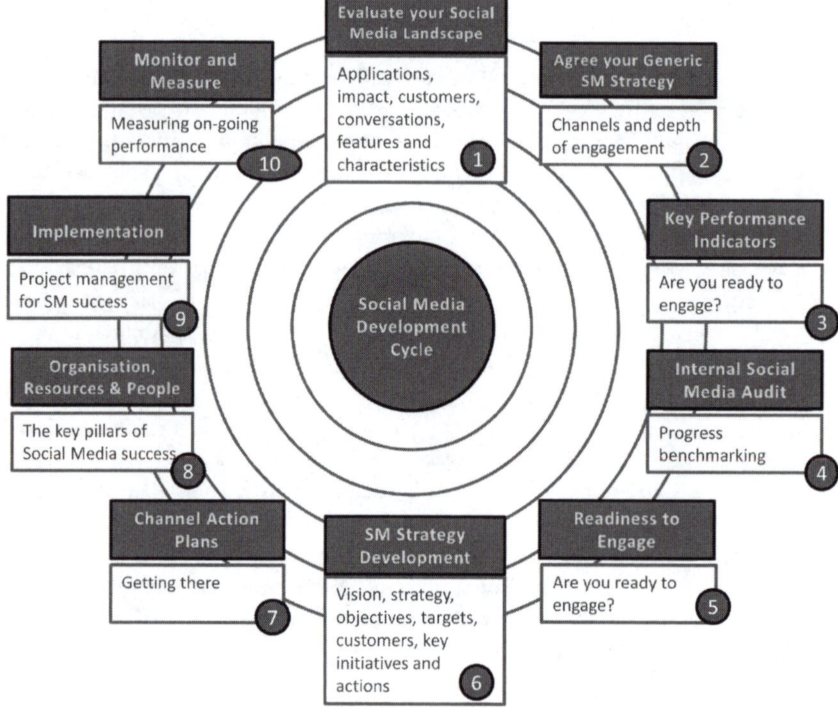

Figure 9.2 Social Media Development Cycle

What are the key features and characteristics of social media that the DMO needs to understand i.e. social media culture?

Agree the overall generic social media strategy to follow

Step 1 will allow the DMO to decide the best generic social media strategy to follow in terms of the number of channels to use and depth of engagement with each channel. Should the DMO be a 'Maven', 'Butterfly', Selective' or 'Wallflower'?

Key Performance Indicators (KPIs)

The DMO should agree the main KPIs to be used in monitoring and evaluating on-going social media performance and business impact (see our other chapter on 'Social Media Monitoring and Performance Evaluation').

Internal social media audit

The DMO should evaluate progress already made made, benchmarked against a number of important criteria including: the opportunities presented by the social media environment/landscape; the DMO's generic strategy, KPIs and industry 'best practice'. The resulting 'Gap Analysis' (i.e. the 'Strategic Gap' that exists between the 'current' and 'ideal' scenarios, between where the DMO is and where it should be) provides a very strong basis for future social media strategy development.

Your readiness to engage

The DMO should evaluate it's readiness to engage with social media; its social media strengths and weaknesses; the main barriers and obstacles to be overcome, including organisational 'mindset'.

Social media strategy development

A simplified Balanced Scorecard approach can be used for agreeing the DMO's social media vision, strategy, objectives, targets and the key initiatives and actions required for 'getting there'. The key questions to address are:

- What is the overall social media vision for our organisation?
- What are the key objectives and targets to be achieved?
- Who are your customers? Who do we need to engage with?
- What are the key Social Media Actions and Initiatives we need to take to 'get there' (including participation in 'external' social media channels)?
- What are the organisation, resource and people implications of our agreed strategy?

Channel action plans

Once the overall Social Media Strategy has been agreed, Action Plans should be developed for each priority Social Media Channel e.g. LinkedIn, Facebook, Twitter, use of 'External' Social Media 'hubs'. The Action Plan for each channel should include a clear statement of the overall objectives for that channel; the KPIs to be used; specific targets to be achieved; target customers; and the key channel actions/tasks for 'getting there'. As regards the latter, decisions need to be made in the following areas:

- Channel Set-Up.
- Design, Layout, Configuration, Profile Content, Use of Management Apps, Agree Domain.
- Integration Options.

- Web/Blog/Facebook/Twitter/YouTube/Flickr/LinkedIn/TripAdvisor.
- Content Plan.
- Tone and Style, Themes and Messages, Post Frequency, Sources of Inspiration Customers.
- Building the Community.
- Identifying, acquiring, retaining and growing your follower/fan base.
- Conversations.
- Encouraging two-way dialogue, response policy, e-word of mouth etc.
- Conversions.
- Enquiries, Sales, Visits, Recommendations.
- Performance Measurement.
- Tools, Alerts, Reports, Report Frequency.
- Organisation and People.
- Responsibilities (WHO), Commitment, Training, Project Management.

Organisation, resource and people issues

Organisation, resource and people issues are a key pillar of social media success. There are a number of critical decisions that need to be made in terms of roles and responsibilities; decision-making and control structures; the role of the Social Media Champion; resources; organisational 'mindset'; proper use policy and so on.

Implementation

Professional project management procedures should be followed at all stage of social media planning and implementation.

Performance Measurement

To ensure that social media delivers high return on investment (ROI), it is important to monitor and evaluate on-going performance benchmarked against agreed objectives, KPIs and targets. Performance evaluation should be undertaken at three main levels – individual channels, overall 'buzz' being created and business impact (see chapter on 'Social Media Monitoring and Performance Measurement').

Each step in the Social Media Development Cycle is being discussed in more detail on our Energise 2-0 Blog at www.energise2-0.com.

5. Further Research

The rapid growth of social media and the revolutionary impact it is having on global travel, tourism and hospitality is opening up many interesting areas for future research. This chapter concludes by presenting our top five areas for future research:

1. Extending the research reported here to other national, regional and city DMOs; to other sectors of the industry e.g. Visitors Atractions; and to individual tourism and hospitality businesses. This would provide a comprehensive benchmarking foundation supporting future research in a range of related topics. An annually updated global benchmarking evaluation of social media progress being made across the industry would be a very useful exercise to undertake.
2. Further research is required relating to the impact of social media on consumer behaviour in the industry.
3. The rapid emergence of a broad range of Social Media Monitoring and Measurement Tools provides a rich seam of future research possibilities.
4. More investigation should take place into the reasons for the lack of progress in this area – the major barriers and obstacles to social media adoption in global travel and tourism. This could be linked to investigations into the return on investment and business impact of social media.
5. Finally, there are interesting areas to be explored in terms of specific social media channels and their impact on the global travel, tourism and hospitality industry.

References

Aaker, D.A. 1991. *Managing Brand Equity*. New York: Free Press.

BAH (Booz Allen Hamilton) 2007. *New Online Consumer Behavior in the Middle East and Globally Demands Changes in Corporate Strategy*, Booz Allen Hamilton. Available at: http://www.boozallen.com/news/38200908?lpid=827904 [accessed: 27 January 2011].

Baker, M.J. and Cameron, E. 2008. Critical success factors in destination marketing, *Tourism and Hospitality Research*, 8(2), 79-97.

Berners Lee, T. 2006. *DeveloperWorks Interviews: Tim Berners-Lee*. IBM. Available at: http://www.ibm.com/developerworks/podcast/dwi/cm-int082206txt.html [accessed: 21 January 2011].

Blain, C., Levy, S.E. and Brent Ritchie, J.R. 2005. Destination branding: Insights and practices from destination management organizations. *Journal of Travel Research*, 43(May), 328-338.

Buhalis, D., Niininen, O. and March, R. 2007. Customer empowerment in tourism through consumer centric marketing (CCM). *Qualitative Market Research: An International Journal*, 10(3), 265-281.

Continental Research 2007. *Understanding Key Trends in Online Travel Consumer Behaviour*. EyeForTravel: Travel Distribution News, Events and Analysis.

Available at: http://www.eyefortravel.com/node/8233 [accessed: 20 January 2011].

Davey, N. 2008. *Why Change Management is Critical to Web 2.0 Success*. Available at: http://www.mycustomer.com/cgibin/item.cgi?id=133669 [accessed: 18 January 2011].

Dearstyne, B. 2007. Blogs! Mashups and Wikis: Oh, My! *Information Management Journal*, July/August, 25-33.

Douglas, A. and Mills, J.E. 2004. Staying afloat in the tropics: Applying a structural equation model approach to evaluating national tourism organization websites in the Caribbean. *Journal of Travel & Tourism Marketing*, 17(2/3), 269-293.

Eikelmann, S., Hajj, J. and Peterson, M. 2007. *Web 2.0 Profiting from the Threat*. Available at: http://www.strategybusiness.com/li/leadingideas/li00037 [accessed: 12 December 2010].

Ellion, T. 2007. *Web 2.0 and the Travel Industry: Practical Strategies for Exploiting the Social Media Revolution*. Available at: http://www.ellion.co.uk/sectors/travel/index.php [accessed: 17 December 2010].

Elowitz, B. and Li, C. 2009. *The World's Most Valuable Brands. Who's Most Engaged?* Available at: www.engagementdb.com [accessed: 30 December 2010].

Gertner, R., Berger, K. and Gertner, D. 2006. Country-dot-com: Marketing and branding destinations online. *Journal of Travel & Tourism Marketing*, 21(2/3), 105-116.

Hamill, J. and Stevenson, A. 2006. *Manage the Customer Experience and the Relationship Will Follow*. University of Strathclyde, Glasgow. Available at: http://msc.market.strath.ac.uk/BB/index.php?showtopic=1865 [accessed: 19 November 2010].

Hamill, J., Stevenson, A. and Attard, D. 2009. *Destination Marketing Organisations and Web 2.0*, ANZMAC Annual Conference. Available at: http://www.duplication.net.au/ANZMAC09/papers/ANZMAC2009-649.pdf [accessed: 18 December 2010].

Hofbauer, J., Stangl, B. and Teichmann, K. 2010, Online destination marketing: Do local DMOs consider international guidelines for their website design?, in *Information and Communication Technologies in Tourism*, edited by U. Gretzel, R. Law and M. Fuchs. Vienna: Springer Verlag, 45-57.

Högg, R., Meckel, M., Stanoevska-Slabeva, K. and Martignoni, R. 2006. *Overview of Business Models for Web 2.0 Communities: Proceedings of GeNeMe* (Dresden, Germany, September), 23-37.

Inversini, A., Cantoni, L. and Buhalis, D. 2009. Destinations' information competition and web reputation. *Information Technology & Tourism*, 11(3), 221-234.

Kotler, P. and Gertner, D. 2002. Country as brand, product, and beyond: A place marketing and brand management perspective. *Journal of Brand Management*, 9(4/5), 249-261.

Krippendorff, K. 2004. *Content Analysis: An Introduction to Its Methodology*. 2nd ed. Thousand Oaks, CA: Sage.

Li, C. and Bernoff, J. 2008. *Groundswell: Winning in a World Transformed by Social Technologies*. 1st ed. Cambridge, MA: Harvard Business School Press.

Milan, R. 2007. *Ten Things you can do in Response to Traveller Reviews*. Hotel Marketing. Available at: http://www.hotelmarketing.com/index.php/content/article/070920_10_things_you_can_do_in_response_to_traveler_reviews/ [accessed: 20 January 2011].

Morgan, N., Pritchard, A. and Pride, R. 2002. *Destination Branding*. 1st ed. Oxford: Butterworth-Heinemann.

Morgan, N., Pritchard, A. and Piggott, R. 2003. Destination branding and the role of the stakeholders: the case of New Zealand. *Journal of Vacation Marketing*. 9(3), 285.

Neuendorf, K.A. 2002. *The Content Analysis Guidebook*. Thousand Oaks, CA: Sage.

Nykamp, M. 2001. *The Customer Differential: Complete Guide to Implementing Customer Relationship Management CRM*. 1st ed. New York: AMACOM Books.

O'Connor, P. 2008. User-generated content and travel: A case study on TripAdvisor.com, in *Information and Communication Technologies in Tourism 2008*, edited by P. O'Connor, W. Höpfen and U. Gretzel. Vienna: Springer Verlag.

O'Reilly, T. 2006. *Web 2.0 Principles and Best Practices*. O'Reilly Radar. Available at: www.oreilly.com/catalog/web2report/chapter/web20_report_excerpt.pdf [accessed: 20 January 2011].

Park, Y.A. and Gretzel, U. 2007. Success factors for destination marketing websites: A qualitative meta-analysis. *Journal of Travel Research*, 46(1), 46-63.

Pike, S. 2004. *Destination Marketing Organisations*. 1st ed. Oxford: Elsevier.

Reactive. 2007. *Web 2.0 for the Tourism and Travel industry*. Reactive Media Pty Ltd. – White Paper. Available at: http://blogs.reactive.com/RequestWhitepaper.aspx [accessed: 22 January 2011].

Schegg, R., Liebrich, A., Scaglione, M. and Syed Ahmad, S.F. 2008. An exploratory field study of Web 2.0 in tourism, in *Information and Communication Technologies in Tourism 2008*, edited by P. O'Connor, W. Höpfen and U. Gretzel. Vienna: Springer Verlag, 152-163.

Schmallegger, D. and Carson, D. 2008, Blogs in tourism: Changing approaches to information exchange. *Journal of Vacation Marketing*, 14(2), 99-110.

Sigala, M. 2007. *Web 2.0 in the Tourism Industry: A New Tourism Generation and New E-business Models*. Travel Daily News. Available at: www.traveldailynews.com/pages/show_page/20554 [accessed: 12 January 2011].

Sigala, M. 2010. Web 2.0, social marketing strategies and distribution channels for city destinations: Enhancing the participatory role of travelers and exploiting their collective intelligence, in *Web Technologies: Concepts, Methodologies,*

Tools, and Applications, edited by A. Tatnall. New York: Information Science Reference.

So, A. and Morrison, M. 2003. Destination marketing organisations' website users and nonusers: A comparison of actual visits and revisit intentions. *Information Technology and Tourism*, 6(1), 129-139.

Stevenson, A. 2008. *Managing the Customer Lifecycle*. Available at: http://www.tourism2-0.co.uk/profiles/blog/show?id=2021287%3ABlogPost%3A1889 [accessed: 14 January 2011].

Tapscott, D. and Williams, A.D. 2006. *Wikinomics: How Mass Collaboration Changes Everything*. London: Atlantic Books.

Thompson, B. 2006. *Customer Experience Management: The Value of "Moments of Truth"*. CustomerThink Corp. Available at: http://www.ianbrooks.com/usefulideas/articles_whitepapers/Customer%20Experience%20Management.pdf [accessed: 12 February 2011].

Tapscott, D. 2008. *Grown Up Digital: How the Net Generation is Changing Your World.* Columbus, OH: McGraw-Hill.

Tapscott, D. and Williams, A.D. 2010. *Macrowikinomics: Rebooting Business and the World.* New York: Blackwell.

Xiang, Z. and Gretzel, U. 2010. Role of social media in online travel information search. *Tourism Management*, 31(2), 179-188.

Wang, Y. and Fesenmaier, D.R. 2006. Identifying the success factors of web-based marketing strategy: An investigation of convention and visitors bureaus in the United States. *Journal of Travel Research*, 44(2), 239-249.

WTO (World Tourism Organisation) 2007. *UNWTO Tourism Highlights 2007*. WTO Tourism Market Trends. Available at: http://www.unwto.org/facts/eng/highlights.htm [accessed: 24 January 2011].

Weber, L. 2009. *Marketing to the Social Web: How Digital Customer Communities Build Your Business.* 2nd Edition. New York: John Wiley & Sons.

Chapter 10

Arizona Meeting Planners' Use of Social Networking Media

Woojin Lee and Timothy J. Tyrrell

1. Introduction

Social networking media, also known as Web 2.0, is a new form of word-of-mouth communication (Gretzel, Kang and Lee 2008), which has a great influence on the Meeting, Incentives, Conventions and Exhibitions (MICE) industry. To date, the integration of social media into the MICE industry has been very successful as meeting planners search for innovative, low-cost ways of advertising to attendees and creating interest in events (Plummer 2010). Moreover, using the wide range of social media tools can provide huge opportunities for meeting planners to market, design, and manage events through social networking, video sharing, blogs, podcasts, social review sites, social calendaring, and social bookmarks sites (Corbin Ball Associates 2010). Today's meeting attendees and association members are seeking to interact with meeting planners by responding to blog posts, making suggestions for meeting content, engaging with speakers, and examining a variety of content (Corbin Ball Associations 2010). Accordingly, the meeting industry professionals, conference and convention organizers, and meeting and event planners are becoming increasingly skilled in using a variety of social media tools to organize the meetings, to increase audience participation, and to encourage member feedback (Blanford 2009). In fact, meeting planners benefit from social networking media when attendees share experiences and opinions that highlight the most relevant content and evaluate and compare meeting venues (Everton 2007). A survey which was recently conducted by J. Spargo & Associates, Inc. indicated that 61 per cent of meeting planners belong to Facebook, 58 per cent to LinkedIn and just 13 per cent to Twitter (Northstar Travel Media 2009).

On the other hand, since the average age of corporate meeting planners is 45.1 years and the average age of association planners is 48.7 years (The Convention Industry Council 2007), they are less likely to be comfortable with the various functions of social media than younger colleagues. Therefore, some meeting planners point out the generation gap that exists in the context of using social media, saying that:

> social media best fits the norms of Generation Y and beyond, which makes it difficult for old farts to comprehend how ingrained these resources are for those much younger who know nothing different (Hardin 2007).

However, it cannot be ignored that social media enables meeting planners to communicate more easily, quickly, and cost-effectively with suppliers, speakers, and other potential audiences while interacting with them more efficiently (Roythorne 2009). Moreover, with the US economy in recession, meeting planners are facing the problems of fewer meetings, lower attendance, budget cuts, and revenue losses (Meetingsnet 2008). As a result, meeting planners are changing their pricing models, reducing room blocks, making special deals for exhibit space, and cutting back on everything from shuttle service to food and beverages. In this environment, the effective use of social media has become essential for meeting planners. Social networks, online communities, blogs, and message boards represent important new channels to assist meeting planners' communication with markets, suppliers, and partners (Campbell 2008). Although there are numerous studies about how people are using social network sites (Boyd and Ellison 2007; Thevenot 2007; Xiang and Gretzel 2010), there are very few studies about the types of social media that have been perceived as most useful by meeting planners and the reasons why they seek to use social media. The purpose of this study is to provide an exploration of meeting planners' use of social media and the perceived usefulness of the different types of social media within the MICE industry and to examine why meeting planners use social media.

2. Literature

The value of social networking media for meeting planners

"Social networking media" can be generally defined as Internet-based applications which are created, initiated, circulated, and used by consumers in order to educate each other about products, brands, services, and issues (Xiang and Gretzel 2010). Social networking sites including Facebook, YouTube, Twitter, and Myspace enable participants to develop existing relationships, seek new relationships, and explore inspirational relationships (Boyd and Ellison 2007; Clemons, Barnett and Appadurai 2007). In the context of using the social media by associations, a survey of 325 associations conducted by *Omnipress* (Pelletier 2009) found that 80 per cent of associations using social media for meetings use some type of free social media, 35 per cent own a custom-built social media site, and 19 per cent have a social media element to their conferences. The benefits of using social media are that they can help meeting planners to expand networking and to maintain relationships with attendees and suppliers, as well as to help facilitate a competitive edge for meeting planners who are designing educational programs and obtaining instant feedback.

More importantly, it can enhance customer service and develop new business and sponsorship opportunities (Blanford 2010; Harris 2010).

Social networking media can add value both for meeting delegates and for spectators who are connected to those delegates (Meetingsnet 2008). Still, its greatest importance for the meeting planner is to produce a meeting that meets a client organization's goals (Blanchard 2005). To meet this goal, it is essential for meeting planners to not only learn and respond to attendees needs, but also to build up credibility. Social media, in general, gives meeting planners the opportunity to build up credibility when they create a blog in order to share photos from previous events, to provide vendor recommendations, or to distribute articles on event planning tips. Subsequently, the reputation obtained from the blog serves to establish the meeting planner as a trustworthy event planner (Spros 2008). It also generates new business for meeting planners who directly participate.

The variety of social networking media used by meeting planners

Social networking media includes a wide range of applications including media, content syndication, tagging, blogging, web forums, customer ratings, evaluation systems, virtual worlds, podcasting, and online videos (Xiang and Gretzel 2010). These technologies are already used by many meeting planners to find information and to relay testimonials and recommendations to support their work. It is expected that in the near future there will be an increase in the use of the "*Big 3*" social network sites – Facebook, LinkedIn, and Twitter – as tools to help facilitate attendee engagement before, during, and after an event. Particularly, Twitter will show continued growth with the application of mobile use at events. (Corbin Ball 2010). In addition, there will of course be new social media that will emerge to take a strong position within the meeting industry besides the "Big 3". The variety of social networking websites for meetings and event planners is constantly changing and as of 2010 includes (Corbin Ball Associates 2007; Hardin 2007; Lyle 2008; Meeting Planner Resources 2010):

Facebook The most popular online social community where planners can use the "event" function to build profiles for upcoming engagements that provide detailed information on an event's location, transportation options, and other requirements. Users can then invite their contacts to the event, and with the help of an RSVP status function, planners can then more accurately estimate the number of people who plan to attend. Facebook is also a very useful tool for speakers who may be willing to answer questions posted on their Facebook page after the presentation.

LinkedIn A fast-growing, business-oriented online social networking community for professionals. It can be useful for meeting planners to be able to access LinkedIn's wide network of users, also, since the planners' profile is viewable by millions of users, it can be a very efficient way to expose their business to a variety of potential customers. In addition, LinkedIn is good resource for job seekers who want to send their application to as many different employers as possible.

YouTube The popular video-sharing site where event marketers, speakers, and venues can easily and broadly distribute video clips. Meeting planners utilize these free video distribution channels as an effective way to promote an event. For example, an event speaker can post a brief video before an event to promote his or her appearance, or an attendee can post their favourite moments of an event after the fact.

Twitter A popular social media website that allows instant messages called "tweets" to be sent that answer the critical "What are you doing now?" question. Tweets can be used to promote, engage, and drive registrations for any conference or meeting. It can be used as part of an integrated marketing campaign, when used before, during, or after an event. Currently, it is important to meetings since it is primarily a mobile application.

In addition, there are several user-review sites which have been developed recently to meet meeting planners' social media needs. There are social networking sites available to meeting planners that focus on property reviews. These sites are free to meeting planners, but require registration. Visitors to these sites should be aware too that these reviews can be reported anonymously (Krantz 2008).

The followings are some examples of user-generated review sites that pertain to the MICE industry.

Elite Meetings (www.elitemeetings.com) This site features a search engine of luxury properties for meeting planners. Planners can use a "trip-advisor like" rating system to rate the properties provided by this site and to add contents. In addition, other planners are then able to share more specific information about the hotels. There are 1,281 certified properties listed on the site (Lodging Hospitality Ideas for Hotel Developers & Operators 2010).

Meetings Collaborative (www.meetingscollaborative.com) This site is focused on hotel reviews. These reviews are based on three questions: whether the reviewer was satisfied with the meeting experience; whether the reviewer would use the hotel for a future program; and whether the reviewer would recommend the hotel to colleagues. The scores are averaged for an overall rating.

MeetingUniverse.com (www.meetinguniverse.com) This site's reviews of meeting venues are particularly detailed and are based upon responses to 70 items. Overall property ratings are based on planner reviews and supplier answers to a questionnaire. Properties are awarded one to five stars, with five being best. Only people registered as planners can submit reviews and only for properties where they have held meetings of at least 50 participants in the previous 12 months (Krantz 2008).

Additionally, meeting planners have found the broad and growing variety of general internet tools to be useful in their work. Here are a few examples. Webinars are workshops using online technology as a means of communicating with key constituencies. Blogs are interactive websites that allow users to comment on content. RSS (Really Simple Syndication) lets users choose what news or information users want to receive by email, while Podcasting allows video or audio files to be downloaded and then played on a user's iPod. Finally, there are video and photo sharing sites like YouTube and Flickr and collaborative web pages such as Wikipedia (Goldstein 2008).

The different types of social networking media used before, during, and after meetings

Currently, meeting planners are adopting social networks to enhance their events and create interactive communities between attendees before, during, and after an event. The interactive communications created by social media provide a more trustworthy format of the word out about an event. For instance, social media such as Facebook, LinkedIn, and various blogs are useful for peer-ratings of sessions, speakers, and exhibits before the event (Everton 2007). Social media are also useful in pre-event market research. This usefulness can best be seen when a site such as Facebook or LinkedIn provides a meeting planner with attendee profiles and demographics for particular events (Harris 2009). The meeting planners are then more likely to engage with social media communities in the early stages of event planning by collecting ideas for keynote speakers or entertainers, by polling potential attendees about the best city for future events, or even asking for creative ideas to improve meetings, which can help ensure that an event meets the needs of attendees and exceeds expectations (Harris 2009).

During the event, live blogs and Twitter can be helpful to exchange on-going information. Without question, however, the primary social media platform used during events is Twitter. Getting attendees to log on to Twitter and allowing them to post messages on Twitter during events can give attendees a forum to discuss presentations and to continue conversations. Furthermore, it is a good way to engage people who could not attend the event by including them in the online conversation about the event (Soder 2010; Tufel 2010).

Meeting planners use social media after events for different purposes. Planners can measure audience impressions of an event using web-based surveys that have been linked to social media profiles (Carr 2009). Another way to follow up with attendees is through user-generated images and videos posted to sites such as YouTube. Flickr can also be useful in that it allows for the promotion of future events (Everton 2007).

As shown above, social networking sites can strengthen relationships among peers before, during, and after an event. More importantly, this peer-created and peer-evaluated content is regarded as more trustworthy than that provided by marketers or promotional organizations (Everton 2007).

3. Methodology

Data collection

Data were collected from members of the Arizona Sunbelt chapter of MPI (Meeting Professional International) in 2009 from June to September, using a self-administered online questionnaire. A total of 510 members received an invitation to participate in the survey, and from that group, 120 responses were received, which represents a 23.5 per cent response rate. Of 120 completed surveys, 12 incomplete responses were disregarded, resulting in 108 usable responses for this analysis.

Construct measures

All the items used to measure the constructs were adapted from prior studies with modifications for the current study. The survey included a section that asked respondents to indicate which social network sites they generally used to plan their meetings or events. There was a list of 14 social network sites, which included Webinars, text messaging, Wikis, Facebook, Linkedin, Myspace, Flickr, Twitter, YouTube, blogs, podcasts, RSS, Bebo, Second Life. These were selected from relevant meeting industry articles and interviews with meeting planners. Those who reported they had used a social network site to plan a meeting beforehand were asked to indicate which social network site they had used and to rate on a scale from 1 to 5 how useful they thought the site was. Respondents who had used social networking sites were then asked to indicate why they had used these particular sites, using a 16-point questionnaire that was derived from a meeting industry articles (Everton 2007; Pelletier 2009; Roythorne 2009). In particular, the questionnaire was designed to review how well that social networking sites allowed planners "to communicate with other planners easily and quickly", "to look for destination information", and "to get feedback from attendees after a meeting". Also, a descriptive analysis was used for this study.

4. Results

Of the 108 meeting planners who responded to the survey, 75 per cent had used social networking media to help plan meetings. The sample was more female (82.3 per cent) than male (17.7 per cent). Half (51.6 per cent) of the respondents were corporate-meeting professionals, while 38.7 per cent were association-meeting planners and 37.1 per cent were independent-meeting planners. Only 11.3 per cent were government-meeting planners. With regard to meeting-planning experience, 14.5 per cent of the respondents had over 20 years of professional meeting-planning experience, and greater than 25 per cent of the respondents showed 11-20 years of professional meeting-planning experience. The participants in the survey were asked to confirm which social networking sites they had used and to

Table 10.1 Use and Perceived Usefulness of Social Media Network Sites by Meeting Planners

Social Network Sites Used by Meeting Planners (% of Respondents)	Perceived Usefulness of Each Social Network Sites by Meeting Planners (Mean Value)
Facebook (71%)	Facebook (3.7)
LinkedIn (61%)	LinkedIn (3.1)
YouTube (60%)	YouTube (3.0)
Myspace (54%)	Blogs (2.7)
Blogs (49%)	Webinars (2.6)
Webinars (48%)	Myspace (2.4)
Twitter (46%)	Twitter (2.3)
Podcasts (40%)	Podcasts (2.1)
Wikis (33%)	Wikis (1.9)
Flickr (29%)	Flickr (1.7)
RSS (22%)	RSS (1.6)
Second Life (13%)	Second Life (1.2)
Bebo (8%)	Bebo (1.1)

rate the usefulness of each. These respondents used mostly Facebook functions (71.4 per cent), followed by LinkedIn (61.3 per cent), YouTube (60.3 per cent) and Myspace (54 per cent). Respondents rated a total of 13 social networking sites and functions typically presented on meeting-related websites such as meetingsnet.com, meetingplannerresources.org, corbinball.com, etc. (Corbin Ball Associates 2009; Meeting Planner Resources 2010; Meetingsnet 2007). The list of social networking sites included Webinars, Facebook, Wikis, LinkedIn, Myspace, Flickr, Twitter, YouTube, Blogs, Podcasts, RSS, Bebo, virtual spaces (e.g. Second life). The most commonly preferred social network sites were Facebook (29 per cent), LinkedIn (15 per cent), YouTube (13 per cent), and Twitter (11 per cent). The social networking media rated most useful were Facebook (mean=3.7), LinkedIn (mean=3.1), YouTube (mean=3.0), Blogs (mean=2.7), Webinars (mean=2.6) and Twitter (mean=2.5) (See Table 10.1 above).

The respondents were also asked to indicate why they used social media. The top three reasons were: 1) to communicate with other planners easily and quickly through chat or discussion boards (80.4 per cent); 2) to share queries, problems, solutions, and opinions with other meeting planners (70.1 per cent); and 3) to get feedback from attendees after meeting/event/convention (69.9 per cent). The complete list of reasons and percentages are given in Table 10.2.

Table 10.2 Reasons for Using Social Media Network Sites by Meeting Planners

The Reasons for Using Social Networking Sites by Meeting Planners	Frequency of Respondents (%)
To communicate with other planners easily and quickly through chat or discussion boards	80%
To share queries, problems, solutions and opinions with other meeting planners	70%
To get feedback from attendees after meeting/event/convention	70%
To discuss topics/issues that are relevant meeting industry	65%
To post announcement special activities program or entertainment/speaker line up	61%
To look for destination information (e.g., local amenities, activities)	54%
To communicate with "experts" who can help meeting planners (e.g., hotel sales manager, CVB sales manager, catering manager)	46%
To ask prospective attendees for their input on site selection or other details of the event	42%
To communicate with exhibitors	41%
To look for the right speakers	34%
To look for the right accommodations	34%
To look for the menu/catering service	32%
To get some tips for negotiating total meeting costs with sales person	31%
To look for the right meeting space information	30%
To look for audio/visual rental information	29%
To look for the transportation information	29%

5. Discussion and Conclusions

The purpose of this study was first and foremost to explore the perceived usefulness of social media as it pertains to meeting planners, and secondly to examine why meeting planners use social media.

Survey respondents indicated that they mostly used Facebook functions (71.4 per cent) followed by LinkedIn (61.3 per cent), YouTube (60.3 per cent) and Myspace (54 per cent) functions. Additionally, the respondents rated Facebook (mean=3.7) as the most useful social networking platform, followed by LinkedIn (mean=3.1), YouTube (mean=3.0), and blogs (mean=2.7). The findings of this study showed that even though they still used Myspace frequently, they did not rate it highly with regard to perceived usefulness, which makes sense since the number of Myspace users has declined of late. Among social media, LinkedIn was selected as the second most frequently used and was perceived as highly useful. When compared to other social media such as Facebook, Twitter, etc., LinkedIn is more frequently used for professional networking since it requires users to post their educational background and work experience, and thus can be regarded as a big database of resumes (Buzz2bucks 2008). Some meeting planners asserted that LinkedIn is the most efficient tool through which to meet new clients and to schedule meetings for new business opportunities, which makes this function useful throughout the meeting planning process (Buzz2bucks 2008). Another of LinkedIn's many advantages is its ability to easily control what information is disclosed.

The participants of this study were also asked to indicate why they used social media. Their top three reasons for using social media stressed the idea that effective communication has always been a critical skill for planners to have, and that now more than ever, meeting planners are able to match the interests and meet the needs of prospective customers and attendees (Brudney 2007). When compared to the top three reasons (to communicate with other planners easily and quickly through chat or discussion boards [80.4 per cent], to share the queries, problems, solutions and opinions with other meeting planners [70.1 per cent] and to get feedback from attendees after meeting/event/convention [69.9 per cent]) to the least three reasons for using the social media (to look for the right meeting space information [29.9 per cent], to look for audio/visual rental information [29 per cent] and to look for the transportation information [29 per cent]) (See Table 10.2), it indicated that the social media has greatly contribute on helping the meeting planners to enhance the interactive communication skill, rather than assisting the meeting planners to gather the information to prepare the meetings.

The increasing use of social networking media by meeting planners has been motivated both by the current economic recession and by the dynamic of behavioural adjustments. Meeting planners engage in social media to plan events with attendee-input, to market their events to a wide audience for a low price, and to foster interest in the events themselves. Professionals in the MICE industry will continue to adopt social media technologies and to integrate these technologies into traditional event planning in order to maximize their return on investment. Accordingly, the result of this study can be useful for destination management, meeting organization, and meeting suppliers who need to understand what types of social media can be adding value to their businesses.

As technology continues to improve and different types of social media outlets come and go, it will become essential for professionals in the meeting industry to have an understanding of what is available and what is trending. The careful use of social media before, during, and after events is a critical component that often determines an event's success and future vitality. In addition, it is also crucial for the meeting professional to be aware of outdated social media, current trends, and to know who the future leaders are in the business of social media. Just as

Myspace was a frontrunner a few short years ago, it is reasonable to expect that a new social media giant will emerge in the near future.

References

Blanchard, S. 2005. Meeting and convention planners. *Occupational Outlook Quarterly*, 49(3), 18-24.

Blanford, R. 2009. How to use social media for effective marketing: Tips on maximizing social networking to grow business [Online, 5 June]. Available at: http://www.suite101.com/content/how-to-use-social-media-for-effective-marketing-a122743 [accessed: 10 January 2010].

Carr, K. 2009. Organizers reap rewards of enlisting social media in event push. *Crain's Cleveland Business*, 30(13), 15.

Campbell, J. 2008. New social networks emerge for travel, meeting professionals. *Management Travel* [Online, 13 August]. Available at: http://www.management.travel/news.php?cid=travel-professionals-social-networks.Aug-08.13. [accessed: 17 May 2010].

Clemons, E.K., Barnett, S. and Appadurai A. 2007. *The Future of Advertising and the Value of Social Network Websites: Some Preliminary Examinations*: *Proceedings of the 9th International Conference on Electronic Commerce.* (Minneapolis and New York: ACM).

Corbin Ball 2010. Eleven meetings technology trends to watch for 2011. [Online: Corbin Ball's Tech Talk Blog]. Available at: http://corbinball.wordpress.com/2010/09/16/eleven-meetings-technology-trends-to-watch-for-2011/ [accessed: 17 November 2010].

Corbin Ball Associates 2007. Between you and me-the impact of social software on the meeting industry [Online: Corbin Ball Associates]. Available at: http://www.corbinball.com/articles_technology/index.cfm?fuseaction=cor_av&artID=4439 [accessed: 17 October 2010].

Corbin Ball Associates 2010. Social media – A new paradigm for meetings. [Online: Corbin Ball Associates]. Available at: http://www.corbinball.com/articles_technology/index.cfm?fuseaction=cor_av&artID=6680 [accessed: 15 October 2010].

Everton, R. 2007. How Web 2.0 creates trust for you and your events [Online, 23 October]. Available at: http://meetingsnet.com/technology/future/Creating_Trust/index.html [accessed: 10 January 2010].

Goldstein, M. 2008. Social networking. *Successful Meetings*, 57(2). 26-27.

Gretzel, U., Kang, M. and Lee, W.J. 2008. Differences in consumer-generated media adoption and use: A cross-national perspective. *Journal of Hospitality and Leisure Marketing*, 17(1-2), 99-120.

Hardin, T. 2007. The social revolution: How new media market your next meeting. *Successful Meetings* [Online, 10 September]. Available at: http://

www.mimegasite.com/mimegasite/search/article_display.jsp?vnu_content_id=1003637786 [accessed: 11 December 2009].

Harris, S. 2009. Event Profile: Tweets tweak conference marketing moves. *Meeting News* [Online, 6 August]. Available at: http://www.successfulmeetings.com/Event-Planning/Technology-Solutions/Articles/Event-Profile--Tweets-Tweak-Conference-Marketing-Moves/ [accessed: 11 November 2009].

Harris, S. 2010. Social media skepticism wanes [Online, 16 February]. Available at: http://www.successfulmeetings.com/Event-Planning/Technology-Solutions/Articles/Meetings-Social-Media-Skepticism-Wanes/ [accessed: 11 August 2010].

Stoessel. E. 2010. Elite meetings brings hotels, planners together. *Lodging Hospitality Ideas for Hotel Developers & Operators* [Online, 1 July]. Available at: http://lhonline.com/development/elite_meetings_0710/ [accessed: 15 September 2010].

Krantz, M. 2008. TripAdvisor for meetings. *Meetingsnet.com* [Online, 1 December]. Available at: http://meetingsnet.com/corporatemeetingsincentives/news/trip_advisor_meetings_1208/ [accessed: 15 September 2009].

Lyle, G. 2008. 5 awesome social networking Websites for meetings and events planning. *Certain* [Online, 10 May]. Available at: http://blog.certain.com/blog/managing-attendee-experience/0/0/5-awesome-social-networking-websites-for-meetings-and-events-planning. [accessed: 10 October 2009].

Meetings Focus 2008. High-tech solutions: Web 2.0 *Meetings Focus* [Online, 10 August] Available at: http://www.meetingsfocus.com/Webinars/take10_080827.asp. [accessed: 8 November 2009].

Meetings Net 2007. Top trends in meeting technology. Meetingsnet.com [Online, 23 July] Available at: http://meetingsnet.com/technology/future/top_tech_trends/ [accessed: 18 March 2010].

Meetings Net (2008, 1 December). Increasing attendance and revenues at association meetings during a down economy. Meetingsnet.com [Online, 1 December]. Available at: http://meetingsnet.com/associationmeetings/marketing_meetings/better_meetings_during_downturn_1208/ [accessed: 5 May 2010].

Meeting Planner Resources 2010. Generating meeting attendance by using social media. *Meeting Planner Resources, LLC* [Online, 3 May]. Available at: http://www.meetingplannerresources.org/articles/29/ [accessed: 17 June 2010].

North Star Travel Media 2009. Survey: Meeting planners use social media for networking. *Successful Meetings* [Online, 8 June]. Available at: http://meetingsreview.com/news/external/17066 [accessed: 13 July 2010].

Pelletier, S. 2009. How associations use social media for meetings. Meetingsnet.com [Online, 8 October] Available at: http://meetingsnet.com/social-media/associations_social_media1008/ [accessed: 10 September 2010].

Plummer, L. 2010. Creating booth buzz. *Tradeshow Week* [Online 15 March] Available at: http://lisaplummerwrites.com/pdf/Tradeshow%20Week-3_15_10-Creating%20Booth%20Buzz.pdf [accessed: 10 September 2010].

Soder, C. 2010. Event planning: Conference organizers embrace Twitter as conversation tool. *Crain's Cleveland Business* [Online, 29 October]. Available at: http://www.crainscleveland.com/article/20101029/FREE/310299996. [accessed: 4 November 2010].

Roythorne, P. 2009. Social Club: Are social media and Web 2.0 really affecting the way Our industry works?. Meetingsreview.com [Online, 21 April]. Available at:

http://meetingsreview.com/americas/news/2009/04/21/Are_social_media_and_Web_2.0_really_affecting_the_way_our_industry_works%3F [accessed: 4 November 2010].

Spors, K. 2008. Small business: use social media to bond with consumers. *WSJ.com* [Online, 4 August]. Available at: http://www.smsmallbiz.com/marketing/Use_Social_Media_to_Bond_With_Consumers.html [accessed: 23 September 2010].

Meetings Review 2009. Survey: meeting planners use social media for networking. Meetingsreview.com [Online, 8 June]. Available at: http://meetingsreview.com/news/2009/06/08/Survey%3A_Meeting_Planners_Use_Social_Media_for_Networking [accessed: 1 October 2010].

The Convention Industry Council 2008. 2007 Certified meeting professional report [Online, 4 February]. Available at: http://www.conventionindustry.org/CMP/docs/CIC%202007%20CMP%20Report.pdf [accessed: 28 October 2009].

Thevenot, G. 2007. Blogging as a social media. *Tourism and Hospitality Research*, 7(3/4), 282-289.

Tufel, G. 2010. Attendee's two cents. *Tradeshow Week*, 40(2), 12-20.

Xiang, Z. and Gretzel, U. 2009. Role of social media in online travel information search. *Tourism Management*, 31(2), 179-188.

Chapter 11
Web 2.0 and Pricing Transparency in Hotel Services

Evangelos Christou and Athina Nella

1. Introduction

The wide diffusion of internet usage and the evolution of web tools have constituted transparency and price comparison for many products and services feasible and easier compared to the past. This is especially the case for tourism products and mainly for travel and accommodation services and fares. As noted by O'Connor (2008), "the guest experience is becoming essentially transparent". Web 2.0 has modified the traditional B2C model of communication and has provided substantial increase to C2C communication patterns, where tourists have the opportunity to interact and comment on their previous experiences, expectations, attitudes, preferences, evaluations and post consumption experiences.

These days it is a common practice for travellers to express their views and satisfaction levels about hotels and to rate them via electronic channels such as tripadvisor.com, booking.com, virtualtourist.com, etc. Past research has shown that travel tips and hotel reviews have significant influence on a vast number of Web 2.0 users (Sigala 2007). Tourists are highly involved in the information search for tourism service purchases because of the perceived high risk factor and they are seeking ways to reduce uncertainty (Sirakaya and Woodside 2005).

Given that the intangibility of hospitality and tourism services elevates the significance of interpersonal influence (Lewis and Chambers 2000), word-of-mouth appears to constitute a particularly important source of information, even if it is spread via electronic platforms and from people who – usually – are unknown to each other. Consumers tend to rely more on consumer reviews when purchasing high involvement products (Park, Kim and Han 2007). It has been estimated that approximately 75 per cent of travellers take various online consumer reviews seriously into account as an information source when planning their trips (Gretzel and Yoo 2008).

In certain cases reviews may totally invalidate the impressions and image created by hotel site communications or advertising messages (Rocha and Victor 2010). Thus, instead of the expensive and perfectly posed photos of brochures or adverts, a customer's image of a hotel may actually be determined by comments or candid photos posted by previous guests on social network sites (O'Connor 2008). In this way, social media can act determinatively in the formation of the final hotel choice of other travellers.

A significant amount of online hotel reviews focus on value and "value for money" issues, thus leading to more "holistic" comparisons, rather than simply comparing rates through alternative booking sites. In many cases, today's travellers are keen to take control, finding and creating a great trip, rather than the cheapest trip (Schegg et al., 2008). Given that cost criteria are often examined in relation to quality thresholds and the levels of compromise a tourist is willing to accept, service, quality issues and hotel amenities can significantly influence a tourist's final selection (Sigala 2010). Even in the case of trading down, "... when consumers' first consideration is price, within the resulting consideration set consu mers next seek to minimize regret and to avoid alternatives that may be uncertain or disappointing" (Clemons and Gao 2008).

Some hotels willingly provide detailed, accurate and clear descriptions of their services and charging policies on basic and supplementary services while others deliberately omit such information. For example, details of the charges and quality of extra services, such as spa treatments, are difficult to find out in advance of a visit. Hotel reviews partly fill this gap by providing updated, indirect information regarding hotel amenities, charges and service details, which in many cases are not easily accessible otherwise. Other examples could refer to unreasonable or unexpected additional charges for internet access and parking, hotel restaurants and prices, etc. These parameters often affect the total spending of hotel customers; past research has shown that most of them wish to have a clearer picture of the overall cost rather than simply comparing room rates per night (Conrady 2007).

Recent evidence shows that online reviews are among the most important factors influencing online hotel bookings (Dickinger and Mazanec 2008; Ye et al., 2008; Ye et al., 2010). Most online review readers perceive other travellers' reviews as being more likely to provide up-to-date and reliable information compared to content posted by travel service providers (Gretzel et al., 2007). Vermeulen and Seegers (2008) propose that exposure to online reviews enhances hotels' consideration for consumers; this is because both positive and negative reviews increase consumer awareness of hotels, whereas positive reviews, in addition, improve attitudes toward hotels (Sigala et al., 2005). In simple words, a single negative online review might not cause much harm, whereas a single positive online review can have a positive effect. These effects were stronger for lesser-known hotels, while reviewer expertise was found to have only a minor, positive influence on review impact. Zehrer et al. (2010) analysed blog user reactions and concluded that a higher percentage of blog users found multiple evaluations that are congruent with one another helpful, whereas negative postings were not necessarily bad if followed by a positive counter reaction.

Another important element of online reviews is that reviewers have the opportunity to provide (or find) customized pieces of advice to specific or similar types of travellers, e.g. business travellers, family travellers, luxury travellers, students, etc. In this way, users can be exposed to customized information about important issues not only prior to their visit, but, most importantly, prior to their booking. It should not be forgotten that before the Web 2.0 era such information was scarce and it was much more difficult to find out in advance the same amount of accurate information regarding alternative hotel options.

Based on the above remarks, it can be deduced that online reviews can be a highly influential tool for consumer decision-making. This chapter focuses on the way that social media and more precisely hotel reviews assist to the transparency of hotel services. Given that room rates are easily available and comparable among different distribution channels, the next major concern for tourists should be on information concerning perceived value, value for money and additional costs that are not included in the room rate. The rationale behind this is that: a) most commonly room prices are evaluated in relation to the overall offering of the hotel and b) reviews concerning additional charges may affect substantially the total cost of selecting and staying at a hotel. The effects of increased transparency on demand and supply side issues are also examined.

2. Pricing Hotel Services

Pellinen (2003, p. 218) suggests that pricing is one of the most central management tasks for service companies. Urbany (2001) proposed that it is the most flexible element of the marketing mix, since pricing decisions can be implemented relatively quickly and at a low cost (e.g. a price cut). Pricing decisions are influenced both by internal factors (marketing goals, marketing strategy mix, cost and organization) and external ones such as the nature of the market and demand, competitors and other environmental parameters (Kotler and Armstrong 1996). Avlonitis and Indounas (2006) proposes that, pricing decisions for the services sector need to be taken from a more "holistic" approach, where apart from cost and competitive issues, emphasis should also be given to other company and environmentally related characteristics, including customers.

The development of pricing strategies is of critical importance for the hospitality industry, since it is strongly associated to many significant issues, such as hotel image, profitability and yield management. Cost-based pricing, competition-driven pricing and customer-driven pricing are the three basic hotel pricing techniques. The method of value based pricing, i.e. attempting to proactively change the customer's pay willingness by learning and leveraging the benefits pursued by the customer, is another technique which is much more profitable but more difficult to adopt (Nagle and Holden 1995). Collins and Parsa (2006) identify numerous influences on pricing decisions of hotel services, including star rating, management type, location, size and amenities. Espinet et al. (2003) suggest that town, hotel size, distance to the beach and availability of parking spaces were the main determinants of pricing for holiday hotels.

When applying yield management, pricing is typically structured around factors such as season, weekday/weekend, or the earliest/later date of purchase to the date of actual consumption of the service (Enz and Withiam 2001). In the hotel sector, yield management traditionally balances a supply of perishable room nights against demand by manipulating price and time of consumption (O'Connor and Murphy 2008). Hotels commonly use differential pricing as a revenue management tool (Kimes 2002).

The room rate strategy is regarded as one of the most important aspects of hotel marketing strategies (Pan 2007), since hotel price is one of the main influences on accommodation selection decisions (Lockyer 2005). In a highly competitive market, scientific room pricing models should consider not only operating costs but also the market environment in which the hotel operates (Gu 1997). In a recent study conducted in China, Hung et al. (2010) showed that the main attributes of hotel room rates include the number of rooms, hotel age, market conditions and number of housekeeping staff per room.

Internet has significantly changed the ways hotels distribute and, consequently, price their products. The existence of electronic distribution channels has created both opportunities and problems for revenue managers (Choi and Kimes 2002). Despite initial predictions for disintermediation, the emergence of the Internet also led to re-intermediation through the introduction of new online travel intermediaries (Buhalis and Zoge 2007). Kracht and Wang (2009) attempted to illustrate the evolving complexity of the tourism distribution systems in a temporal manner.

In many cases, online travel agencies offer better prices than the hotels' own websites. Dilemmas on price parity across channels, different pricing tactics across online channels or lowest price guarantees may also emerge. The issue of electronic distribution becomes further complicated by online channels following opaque pricing strategies (e.g. hotwire.com), where travellers book a room without knowing the name of the hotel until the payment. Revenue management applied across distribution channels (specifically online) becomes even more difficult to implement successfully (O'Connor and Frew 2002).

Price disparities among the distribution channels of hotels are also shaping consumer perceptions, who are now searching several online engines and are actively shopping around for better deals (O'Connor and Frew 2002; Murphy et al., 2006). The structure of the tourism distribution system does not only affect the available choices for consumers, but also the business models and marketing strategies adopted by the various channel participants (Pearce et al., 2004). Hotel managers are urged to choose a portfolio of distribution channels; those who successfully manage electronic distribution, add value, develop their brand, and build customer loyalty while those who fail risk losing customers to intermediaries (Sigala and Buhalis 2002).

3. The Issue of Transparency

Granados et al. (2004) proposed that the notion of transparency is regarded as consisting of three main dimensions: price, product and supplier. The authors note that price transparency supports the idea that a consumer assesses the price at which a seller and other consumers are willing to trade, which in turn determines a consumer's willingness-to-pay. Price transparency exists when information about the trading goods and transaction process are made available, such as quotes and transaction prices. A transparent pricing mechanism permits consumers to better evaluate the reservation price of sellers and other consumers, as well as supply and demand forces. Generally, the more dynamic the trading mechanism (e.g., an auction mechanism), the higher the level of price transparency (Psillakis et al., 2009).

Product transparency exists when the characteristics of the product from one or more suppliers are made available. Supplier transparency refers to the availability of information about suppliers, such as identity, inventory information, shipping costs, and on-time delivery performance. Market transparency has been defined as the level of availability and accessibility of information about products and market prices (Granados et al., 2008); transparency strategy involves design choices that influence the availability and accessibility of information about products and prices.

In the services marketing literature, Zhu (2002) defined information transparency as the degree of availability, accessibility, and visibility of information. The notion of information transparency originated from the finance literature and was mainly related to stock market regulations and banking policies. Miao and Mattila (2007) conceptualized information transparency as a transparency continuum that is a function of the degree of information sufficiency and the degree of information diagnosticity.

Buhalis and Zoge (2007) propose that the Internet has increased transparency in the marketplace. Indeed, it is widely assumed that electronic markets and internet-based selling increase price transparency and hence lower product prices. They also increase the market transparency potential in many industries and expand the possible set of strategic alternatives possessed by firms (Granados et al., 2004). Soh et al. (2006) argue that successful electronic marketplaces must provide compensatory benefits for sellers in the case of high price transparency and for buyers in the case of low price transparency.

EWom allows consumers to obtain high levels of market transparency and take on a more active role in the value chain and influence products and prices according to individual preferences (Park and Kim 2008). Moreover, eWom activity has allowed consumers to overcome most information asymmetries that characterize traditional consumer markets (Rezabakhsh et al., 2006). The issue of transparency is closely related to perceived fairness. As a concept, perceived price fairness is rooted in the theory of dual entitlement, which contends that perceptions of fairness are governed by the principle that firms are entitled to a reference profit and customers are entitled to a reference price (Kahneman et al., 1986). Consumers are expected to complain of unfairness when they encounter price changes either upward or downward while price increases are perceived to be less fair than price reductions (Kimes 2002). It has been noted that as a market becomes more familiar with revenue management practices, unfairness perceptions tend to decline over time (Kimes and Wirtz 2007; Beldona and Kwansa 2008).

Table 11.1 Transparency Parameters and their Definitions

Transparency parameters	Definition – Description	Authors
Product transparency	"availability of the characteristics of the product from one or more suppliers"	Granados et al. (2004)
Supplier transparency	"availability of information about suppliers, such as identity, inventory information, shipping costs, and on-time delivery performance"	Granados et al. (2004)
Information transparency (a)	"degree of availability, accessibility, and visibility of information"	Zhu (2002)
Information transparency (b)	"function of the degree of information sufficiency and the degree of information diagnosticity"	Miao and Mattila (2007)
Market transparency	"level of availability and accessibility of information about products and market prices"	Granados et al. (2008)
Price transparency	"availability of information about the trading goods and transaction process, such as quotes and transaction prices"	Granados et al. (2004)

4. Web 2.0 and Transparency in Hotel Services

If Web 1.0 enabled users to be directly informed about various aspects of hotel services (e.g. service quality, room rates, special offers), Web 2.0 has allowed worldwide interaction and opinion sharing for hotel services, prices, satisfaction levels and perceived value. Online hotel reviews may unveil important product and price information, thus constituting product and price transparency easier. Such reviews are considered to be more objective compared to corporate communications and increase overall transparency levels.

Web 2.0 has vastly facilitated transparency in terms of market, supplier, product, information and price. Market transparency has become a reality since there is much available and accessible information on hotel services and market prices, especially when using meta-search engines. Information transparency exists in the sense that Web 2.0 users can easily have available, accessible and sufficient information of all kinds, even from reviewers with similar needs in terms of hotel services (e.g. "We would definitely recommend for honey moon vacation").

Product transparency appears when hotel reviews describe details, characteristics and various aspects of the provided services, e.g. "poor room service options", "extremely small rooms", "rooms are in desperate need of renovation, so old furniture and lavatory", "Very poor service", The cleanliness of the hotel is unacceptable for a 5-star hotel"etc. Supplier transparency is facilitated in the sense that there are many alternative distribution channels to book a hotel and internet users have a clear picture of the total charge. Pricing transparency is also evident, since while hotel reviews may provide additional information on the pricing policies and charges of a hotel, e.g. "You have to pay for everything", "excessive rate for internet access", "The restaurant was overpriced", "ridiculously expensive".

In some cases users may read reviews combining different aspects of price and product transparency, e.g. "excessively high prices, which also did not include breakfast and internet access". Reviews expressing value for money perceptions may help users in their decision and buying process. Such examples could be reviews of the type "I would not stay here even if it was free", "Excellent value for money", "It definitely is not worth 160 euros per night!", "The hotel itself is quite average; quite expensive taking standard into consideration".

Overall, we could propose that there are two major ways that Internet facilitates price transparency in the hotel sector: a) *through the ability to compare prices through alternative* members of the distribution channel, and b) through the ability to access information on different aspects of hotel services that influence directly or indirectly the cost of a selecting and staying at a specific hotel.

The ability to compare prices through alternative members of the distribution channel

The growth of the Internet as a channel of distribution has increased customer exposure to revenue management pricing practices, and has created a shift towards complete price transparency and easy "shopping around" of hotel rates and offerings (Noone and Mattila 2009). Internet seems to influence consumers' perceptions of pricing strategies: consumers are increasingly aware of yield management practices (Sahut and Hikkerova 2009). Miao and Mattila (2007) found that consumers' price fairness perceptions and willingness-to-pay were more susceptible to the influence of externally supplied pricing information in a high rather than low transparency context. Additionally, consumers' judgemental confidence about their price perceptions was elevated in high transparency conditions.

Meta-search engines, that use a number of search engines simultaneously, or infomediaries help consumers make online price comparisons of many websites through one click, thus further facilitating price comparisons on the web (e.g. Kayak, Travelfusion, Bing Travel, FareCompare, Mobissimo, Momondo, and Skyscanner). Moreover, other websites collect historical data of prices and based on these past data can give customers forecasts on when prices may be decreasing in the future (e.g. www.farecast.com, farepredict.com). Through these websites visitors are informed whether it is advisable to book immediately or wait a few days until they make a booking. Moreover, nowadays, datavisualization has also enabled customers to compare hotels not only based on price but also on many other dimensions such as location (geo-visualization). Indisputably, nowadays it is easier to compare prices for a given hotel staying through different intermediaries. However, difficulties arouse and complexity increases when someone has to compare and select among hotels that may differ substantially, even if he is examining options of the same class standards.

The ability to access information on different aspects of hotel services that influence directly or indirectly the cost of a selecting and staying at a specific hotel

From the customer perspective, pricing goes beyond room rates to involve perceived value and value for money as well. Customer perceived value has been defined as the consumer's overall assessment of the utility of a product based on perceptions of what is received and what is given (Zeithaml 1988). As mentioned earlier in this chapter, Web 2.0 has contributed enormously to opinion and information sharing for travel issues. User-generated content is rapidly gaining traction as an input into the consumer purchase decision-making process. Hotel ratings and descriptions don't come from a single source only, for example, just from the supply side; both satisfied and unsatisfied customers can share their previous hotel experiences and rate the services they were offered. There reviews include useful information regarding core and supplementary services, charges for various amenities, service quality, staff behaviour, hotel location etc.

Tripadvisor.com, booking.com, mytravelguide.com, globalhotelreview.com, SideStep.com, travelpost.com and virtualtourist.com are some of the popular worldwide travel communities, where travellers share tips and experiences. There are millions of travel reviews available on the Web: over 40 million reviews in tripadvisor.com and 1.8 million reviews in virtualtourist.com (data from the respective websites, accessed: October 2010). These communities promise to provide users with all necessary information when planning a trip and help them take the optimal decision. In order to maintain the character of unbiased user-generated travel content and secure integrity, promotional reviews are not allowed. In many cases, members can comment on others' reviews and rate them accordingly. Users are also able to post questions in forums with high response rates (98 per cent of topics posted in the TripAdvisor forums are replied to within 24 hours) and share photos of travel experiences (5 million candid traveller hotel photos covering more than 100,000 hotels available through TripAdvisor).

Hotel reviews can provide indirect information regarding all cost aspects of selecting to stay at a particular hotel. From the tourists' perspective, when evaluating rates for alternative accommodation options, it is important to remember that they might not assess only the monetary cost expressed directly by the room rate, but also other types of costs such as time, effort and psychological costs (Christou and Kassianidis 2002). For example, when comparing two hotels of the same classification, it is interesting to compare location and distance from sights or business activities or public transport accessibility, since transportation costs and time can have a significant impact on the total spending and the overall tourism experience. Moreover, some travellers are more sensitive to the psychological cost of a selection that does not meet their expectations; being not willing to put their tourism experience in jeopardy, they seek the reassurance offered through reviews from previous hotels customers.

In certain cases, prices are thought to be indicative of quality. This is especially valid in buying decisions where there is limited access to information or there is lack of previous relevant experience. Prices for hospitality might have an impact on quality expectations, but obviously the final formation of quality expectations will depend on many other issues, such as hotel class, previous hotel experiences and brand image in the cases of global hotel brands (Christou 2010). There is also evidence that cross-cultural differences exist regarding the relationship between price and perceived quality of tourism products (e.g. Jo and Sarigollu 2007; Azim 2010).

5. Theoretical Implications

The credibility of electronic word-of-mouth has sporadically been challenged (Mack et al., 2008); however, the contemporary belief that user-generated content sites have been compromised by false reviews appears unfounded (Bray 2007; O'Connor 2010). Consumers, especially when they intend to purchase experience goods, seek to reduce their uncertainty by referring to eWom information, such as online consumer reviews (Park and Lee 2008). What is commonly accepted is that the influence of user generated content on tourism decision-making is constantly growing. Travel reviews play an important role in the trip planning process for those who actively read them, as they provide ideas, make decisions easier, add fun to the planning process and increase confidence by reducing risk and making it easier to imagine what places will be like (Gretzel and Yoo 2008).

Web 2.0 users can access rich and in most cases credible information, which increases transparency parameters (price, product, market, supplier). It is therefore proposed here that hotel reviews can have different and significant effects on hotel price perceptions and image. Positive reviews for a specific hotel may lead to the following positive outcomes on tourism behaviour:

- Overcoming choice barriers and confronting effectively initial negative attitudes.
- Enhancement and empowerment of initial positive attitudes (Sigala et al., 2005).
- Influence positively the levels of expectations for critical service parameters.

Negative comments are expected to result to the following negative effects:

- Creation of doubts and reluctances towards advertised hotel offerings.
- Eliminate a hotel from the consideration set options and avert users from

further evaluation.
- Influence negatively the levels of expectations for critical service parameters.
- Avoidance of using hotel amenities, in cases of reviews mentioning over-charges or low perceived value.

Regardless of the positive or negative character of reviews, the exposure to Web 2.0 reviews appears to help potential customers to:

- Narrow down the set of alternative accommodation options. Most users consult online reviews at the middle of the process of their trip planning in order to narrow down choices (Gretzel and Yoo 2008).
- Decrease the level of uncertainness about estimated offerings. A significant percentage of review readers also thinks that reviews increase confidence and help reduce risk by making it easier to imagine what a place will be like (Gretzel and Yoo 2008).
- Ease the procedure of the final selection. Reviews are also perceived as helping with making the decision process more efficient in that they make decisions easier because they reduce the likelihood of later regretting a decision (Gretzel and Yoo 2008). As shown in the relevant study of Gretzel and Yoo (2008) reading travel reviews also can make the planning process more enjoyable.
- Increase confidence levels for the final selection. Online reviews are used also in later stages of the planning process to confirm decisions (Gretzel and Yoo 2008).

The decision-making process is influenced by both internal (psychological) variables (e.g. attitudes, motives, beliefs) and external variables (e.g. pull factors, marketing mix). Decision-making is closely related to information search, which has been one of the most examined subjects in consumer studies (Schmidt and Spreng 1996). The external search strategy of travellers, as with any other consumer group, varies with demographic and other characteristics of the traveller (Money and Crotts 2003). Gursoy and McCleary (2004) proposed a model organizing the determinants of information search behaviour into eight categories: previous visits, involvement, intentional learning, incidental learning, familiarity, expertise, cost of internal search, and cost of external search.

It seems reasonable to hypothesize that the gravity and effect of reviews may vary depending on diverse personality and consumer behaviour characteristics, such as previous hotel experiences, frequency of review usage, cultural orientation, similarity to reviewers' characteristics etc. Gretzel and Yoo (2008) found that age differences occur across a variety of perceptions and use of online reviews. Other attributes, such as price sensitivity or budget restrictions might also influence the perceived importance of hotel reviews that involve pricing and cost parameters. The nature of decision-making (habitual, extensive or limited) for staying at a particular hotel should also affect the gravity of reviews, i.e. in a case of extensive decision-making travellers may need more views and extended advice than in the case of habitual decision-making. Sidali et al. (200) showed that the main determinants of trust in e-reviews were perceived expertness of e-reviews, credibility of the e-platform and brand familiarity.

6. Practical Implications

Dwivedi et al. (2007) proposed that with the current proliferation of blogs, message boards, and other sites of relative content, hotels are increasingly losing control over what gets written about them online. O'Connor (2010) used content analysis to identify common causes of satisfaction and dissatisfaction among reviewers on tripadvisor.com and discovered that few hotels are actively managing their reputation on the site, despite the available facility for hotels to respond to criticism, calling into question how seriously hotels are managing user-generated content. Earlier, Crotts et al. (2009), based on a review of postings on tripadvisor.com, noted that many firms assign personnel to monitor and respond to guest postings relating to their firms, to control or limit the effects of negative postings on future visits. It seems that there is still much work to do and great potential for improvement in how hotel companies could use Web 2.0 content to their own benefit.

First of all, hotels need to be more proactive, engaging in dialogue with customers to protect their brand image (Ellis-Green 2007). Hotel staff and managers should make sure that they are completely honest and clear on what they are offering to their customers and not create high expectations that do not match reality. This would mean that all of their web-site content should be absolutely reflective of the reality and that they constantly strive to meet or even surpass their class standards.

Secondly, they should make sure that they are in close touch with their customers and that they use their feedback to tackle even the slightest cause of dissatisfaction; the role of hotel staff is crucial to achieve this. It is imperative that customers' complaints are handled delicately and quickly to ensure satisfaction and positive word-of-mouth (Gursoy and McCleary 2004). Moreover, hotel customers could be asked to complete satisfaction questionnaires right after their visit, in order to provide direct feedback to hotel managers.

Thirdly, hotel owners and managers should make sure that all members of staff (front-line and back-office) are satisfied with their working conditions, since their role is crucial in service quality. Staff courteousness and their clear orientation and commitment to customer satisfaction can resolve most problems that might come up during a customer's stay.

Last, hotel managers should realize that transparency of information and prices are here to stay and, if they wish to survive in the highly competitive hospitality industry, it is imperative to use it to their best interest. Satisfied customers, who feel that perceived value was higher than what they paid, can be the best ambassadors of a hotel brand. Given the importance of Web 2.0 tools for creating electronic word-of-mouth for a hotel, it seems imperative that hotel managers systematically monitor reviews of their hotel and treat it as valuable feedback to help them identify areas needing improvement. This entails that the responsibility for review monitoring will be officially assigned to specific members of the staff.

To take it a step further, it would be useful to monitor comments regarding direct competitors, in order to identify their relative position in the market but also to imitate good practices and avoid inappropriate ones. Ideally, some of the best practices and ratings could be treated as benchmarks in an effort for continuous improvement and high customer satisfaction levels. As Litvin et al. (2008) propose, the current proliferation and widespread use of online hotel reviews is, overall, an opportunity rather than a threat to entrepreneurs and managers in the hotel industry. Those hoteliers who attempt to exploit this opportunity are expected to benefit substantially their businesses.

References

Avlonitis, G. and Indounas, K. 2006. How are prices set? An exploratory investigation in the Greek services sector. *Journal of Product & Brand Management*, 15(3), 203-213.

Azim, T.S.A. 2010. The relationship between the perception of risk and the decision making process of travel of French tourists: The case of Egypt. *Tourismos* 5(2), 29-47.

Beldona, A. and Kwansa, F. 2008. The impact of cultural orientation on perceived fairness over demand-based pricing. *International Journal of Hospitality Management*, 27(4), 594-603.

Buhalis, D. and Zoge, M. 2007. The strategic impact of the Internet on the tourism industry, in *Information and Communication Technologies in Tourism 2007*, edited by M. Sigala, L. Mich and J. Murphy. Vienna: Springer Verlag, 481-492.

Bray, J. 2007. Consumers turn the tables on revenue managers (with Metasearch 2.0). *Journal of Revenue and Pricing Management* 5(3), 324-325.

Choi, S. and Kimes, S. 2002. Electronic distribution channels' effect on hotel revenue management. *Cornell Hotel and Restaurant Administration Quarterly*, 17(1), 23-31.

Christou, E. and Kassianidis, P. 2002. Consumers perception and adoption of online buying for travel products. *Journal of Travel & Tourism Marketing*, 12(4), 93-107.

Christou, E. 2010. Investigating attitudes towards mobile commerce for travel products. *Tourism: An International Interdisciplinary Journal*, 58(1), 7-18.

Clemons, E. and Gao, G. 2008. Consumer informedness and diverse consumer purchasing behaviors: Traditional mass-market, trading down, and trading out into the long tail. *Electronic Commerce Research and Applications*, 7(1), 3-17.

Conrady, R. 2007. Travel technology in the era of Web 2.0, in *Trends and Issues in Global Tourism 2007*, edited by R. Conrady and N. Buck. Berlin and Heidelberg: Springer Verlag, 165-184.

Crotts J., Mason, P. and Davis B. 2009. Measuring Guest Satisfaction and Competitive Position in the Hospitality and Tourism Industry: An Application of Stance-Shift Analysis to Travel Blog Narratives. *Journal of Travel Research*, 48(2), 139-151.

Dickinger, A. and Mazanec, J. 2008. Consumers' preferred criteria for hotel online booking, in *Information and Communication Technologies in Tourism 2008*, edited by P. O'Connor, W. Hopken and U. Gretzel. New York: Springer Verlag, 244-254.

Dwivedi, M., Shibu T.P. and Venkatesh, U. 2007. Social software practices on the internet Implications for the hotel industry, Research in Progress. *International Journal of Contemporary Hospitality Management*, 19(5), 415-426.

Ellis-Green, C. 2007. *The Travel Marketer's Guide to Social Media and Social Networking*. McLean, VA: Hotel Sales and Marketing Association International.

Enz, C. and Withiam, G. 2001. *The 4 C Strategy for Revenue Management*. Working Paper, Center for Hospitality Research, Cornell University [Online]. Available at: http://www.hotelschool.cornell.edu/chr/i [accessed: 12 February 2011].

Espinet, J.M., Saez, M., Coenders, G. and Fluiva, M. 2003. Effect on prices of the attributes of holiday hotels: A hedonic price approach. *Tourism Economics*, 9, 165-177.

Granados, N., Gupta, A. and Kauffman, R. 2005. Transparency strategy in Internet based selling, in *Advances in the Economics of Information Systems*, edited by K. Tomak. Harrisburg, PA: Idea Group Publishing.

Granados, N., Gupta, A. and Kauffman, R. 2008. Designing online selling mechanisms: Transparency levels and prices. *Decision Support Systems*, 45(4), 729-745.

Gretzel, U. and Yoo, K-H. 2008. Use and impact of online travel reviews, in *Information and Communication Technologies in Tourism 2008*, edited by P. O'Connor, W. Hopken and U. Gretzel. Vienna: Springer Verlag, 35-46.

Gretzel, U., Yoo, K-H. and Purifoy, M. 2007. *Online Travel Review Study: Role and Impact of Online Travel Reviews. Laboratory for Intelligent Systems in Tourism.* Texas A&M University. Available at: www.tripadvisor.com/pdfs/OnlineTravelReviewReport.pdf [accessed: 12 February 2011].

Gu, Z. 1997. Proposing a room pricing for optimizing profitability. *International Journal of Hospitality Management*, 16(3), 273-277.

Gursoy, D. and McCleary K.W. 2004. An Integrative Model of Tourists' Information Search Behavior. *Annals of Tourism Research*, 31(2): 353-373.

Hung, W.T., Shang, J.K. and Wang, F.C. 2010. Pricing determinants in the hotel industry: Quantile regression analysis. *International Journal of Hospitality Management*, 29(3), 378-384.

Jo, M.S. and Sarigollu, E. 2007. Cross-cultural differences of price-perceived quality relationships. *Journal of International Consumer Marketing*, 19(4), 59-74.

Kahneman, D., Knetsch, J.L. and Thaler, R.H. 1986. Fairness as a constraint on profit seeking: Entitlements in the market. *American Economic Review*, 76(4), 728-741.

Kimes, S.E. 2002. Perceived fairness of yield management. *Cornell Hotel and Restaurant Administration Quarterly*, 35(1), 22-29.

Kimes, S.E. and Wirtz, J. 2007. The moderating role of familiarity in fairness perceptions of revenue management pricing. *Journal of Service Research*, 9(3), 229-240.

Kotler, P. and Armstrong, G. 1996. *Principles of Marketing*. Upper Saddle River, NJ: Prentice Hall.

Kracht, J. and Wang, Y. 2010. Examining the tourism distribution channel: Evolution and transformation. *International Journal of Contemporary Hospitality Management*, 22(5), 736-757.

Lewis, R.C. and Chambers, R.E. 2000. *Marketing Leadership in Hospitality: Foundations and Practices*. 3rd edition. New York: Wiley.

Litvin, S.W., Goldsmith, R.E. and Pan, B. 2008. Electronic word-of-mouth in hospitality and tourism management. *Tourism Management*, 29(3), 458-468.

Lockyer, T. 2005. The perceived importance of price as one hotel selection dimension. *Tourism Management*, 26(4), 529-537.

Mack R.W., Blose J.E. and Pan B. 2008. Believe it or not: Credibility of blogs in tourism. *Journal of Vacation Marketing*, 14(1), 133-142.

Miao, L. and Mattila, A. 2007. How and how much to reveal? The effects of price transparency on consumers' price perceptions. J*ournal of Hospitality & Tourism Research*, doi: 10.1177/1096348007302354 [accessed: 12 February 2011].

Money, B. and Crotts, J. 2003. The Effect of Uncertainty Avoidance on Information Search, Planning, and Purchases of International Travel Vacations. *Tourism Management*, 24(1), 191-202.

Murphy, J., Schegg, R. and Qiu, M. 2006. An investigation of consistent rates across Swiss hotels' direct channels. *Information Technology and Tourism*, 8(2), 105-119.

Nagle, T.T. and Holden, R.K. 1995. *The Strategy and Tactics of Pricing*. Second edition. Upper Saddle River, NJ: Prentice Hall.

Noone, B.M. and Mattila, A.S. 2009. Hotel revenue management and the Internet: The effect of price presentation strategies on customers' willingness to book. *International Journal of Hospitality Management*, 28(2), 272-279.

O'Connor, P. 2008. *User-generated Content and Travel: A Case Study on TripAdvisor.com*. Vienna: Springer Verlag.

O'Connor, P. and Frew, A.J. 2002. The future of hotel electronic distribution. *Cornell Hotel and Restaurant Administration Quarterly*, 43(3), 33-45.

O'Connor, P. 2010. Managing a Hotel's Image on TripAdvisor. *Journal of Hospitality Marketing & Management*, 19(7), 754-772.

Pan, C. 2007. Market demand variations, room capacity and optimal hotel room rates. *Hospitality Management*, 26, 748-753.

Park, D.H., Lee, J. and Han, J. 2007. The effect of online consumer reviews on consumer purchasing intention: The moderating role of involvement. *International Journal of Electronic Commerce*, 11(4), 125-148.

Pearce, D., Tan, R. and Schott, C. 2004. Tourism distribution channels in Wellington, New Zealand. *International Journal of Tourism Research*, 6(3), 397-410.

Pellinen, J. 2003. Making price decisions in tourism enterprises. *Hospitality Management*, 22, 217-235.

Psillakis, Z., Panagopoulos, A. and Kanellopoulos, D. 2009. Low cost inferential forecasting and tourism demand in accommodation industry. *Tourismos*, 4(2), 47-68.

Rezabakhsh, B., Bornemann, D., Hansen, U. and Schrader, U. 2006. Consumer power: A comparison of the old economy and the Internet economy. *Journal of Consumer Policy*, 29(1), 3-36.

Rocha, Á. and Victor, J.A. 2010. Quality of hotels websites: Proposal for the development of an assessment methodology. *Tourismos*, 5(1), 173-178.

Sahut, J-M. and Hikkerova, L. 2009. The impact of Internet on pricing strategies in the tourism industry. *Journal of Internet Banking and Commerce*, 14(1).

Schegg, R., Liebrich, A., Scaglione, M. and Ahmad, S.F.S. 2008. An exploratory field study of Web 2.0 in tourism, in *Information and Communication Technologies in Tourism 2008*, edited by P. O'Connor, W. Höpken and U. Gretzel. Vienna: Springer Verlag, 152-163.

Schmidt, J. and Spreng, R. 1996. A Proposed Model of External Consumer Information Search. *Journal of the Academy of Marketing Science*, 24(2), 246-256.

Sidali, K.L., Schulze, H. and Spiller, A. 2009. The impact of online reviews on the choice of holiday accommodations, in *Information and Communication Technologies in 2009*, edited by W. Höpken, U. Gretzel and R. Laws, Springer Verlag, 87-98.

Sigala, M. and Buhalis, D. 2002. Changing distribution channels in the travel industry-new channels, new challenges. *Information Technology & Tourism*, 5(3), 185-186.

Sigala, M. 2007. Investigating the internet's impact on interfirm relations: Evidence from the business travel management distribution chain. *Journal of Enterprise Information Management*, 20(3), 335-355.

Sigala, M. 2010. Measuring customer value in online collaborative trip planning processes. *Marketing Intelligence and Planning*, 28(4), 418-443.

Sigala, M., Jones, P., Lockwood, A. and Airey, D. 2005. Productivity in hotels: A stepwise data envelopment analysis of hotels' rooms division processes. *Service Industries Journal*, 25(1), 61-81.

Sirakaya, E. and Woodside, A. 2005. Building and testing theories of decision making by travelers. *Tourism Management*, 26(6), 815-832.

Soh, C., Markus, M.L. and Goh, K.H. 2006. Electronic marketplaces and price transparency: strategy, information technology and success. *MIS Quarterly*, 30(3), 212-223.

Urbany, J.E. 2001. Justifying profitable pricing. *Journal of Product & Brand Management*, 10(3), 141-159.

Vermeulen, I.E. and Seegers, D. 2008. Tried and tested: The impact of online hotel reviews on consumer consideration. *Tourism Management*, 30(1), 123-127.

Ye, Q., Law, R. and Gu, B. 2008. The Impact of Online User Reviews on Hotel Room Sales. *International Journal of Hospitality Management*, 28(1), 180-182.

Ye, Q., Law, R., Gu, B. and Chen, W. 2010. The influence of user-generated content on traveler behavior: An empirical investigation on the effects of e-word-of-mouth to hotel online bookings. *Computers in Human Behavior*, doi: 10.1016/j.chb.2010.04.014 [accessed: 8 February 2011].

Zehrer, A., Crotts, J. and Magnini, V. 2010. The Perceived Usefulness of Blog Postings: An Extension of the Expectancy-Disconfirmation Paradigm. *Tourism Management*, doi:10.1016/j.tourman.2010.06.013 [accessed: 12 February 2011].

Zeithaml, V.A. 1988. Consumers' perceptions of price quality and value: A means-end model and synthesis of evidence. *Journal of Marketing*, 52(July), 2-22.

Zhu, K. 2002. Information transparency in electronic marketplaces. *Electronic Markets*, 12(2), 92-99.

www.tripadvisor.com [accessed: 10 November 2010].

www.tripadvisor.com/PressCenter-c4-Fact_Sheet.html [accessed: 1 October 2010].

www.booking.com [accessed: 8 October 2010].

www.globalhotelreview.com [accessed: 3 October 2010].

www.mytravelguide.com [accessed: 11 October 2010].

www.travelpost.com [accessed: 14 October 2010].

www.virtualtourist.com [accessed: 16 October 2010].

Chapter 12

Blogs: "Re-inventing" Tourism Communication

Serena Volo

1. Introduction

The experiential nature of tourism, the dramatic evolution of digital technology and travellers' willingness to share information through this technology have given rise to multiple forms of virtual tourist communities. The rapid growth of the Web 2.0 technologies and applications and their increasing functional sophistication allow for a rich, personalized and participative co-creation of information, easily shared among all actors (and all audiences) in the virtual community (Pudliner 2007; Tussyadiah and Fesenmaier 2009). In this new technological order, the tourist becomes not only the major source of raw experiential data input and the cognitive engine that translates the experiential data into meaning, but also the control centre for its distribution and use: a true egalitarian world of information.

The functionality of Web 2.0 technology has the potential to substantially alter much of the historical role of market behaviourists, market researchers, and advertising professionals by providing alternative means for creating, interpreting and acting on information. Alternatively, this new "travellers' behaviour" data and information source might supplement the historic tourism marketing function (Mangold and Faulds 2009). Which version of these two realities actually materializes will depend on several factors, including how they are managed and what initiatives the various tourism stakeholders, firms and organizations undertake to adopt and integrate Web 2.0 technologies into their e-marketing practices. Regardless of what materializes, one thing seems certain: the study of travellers' behaviour and destination marketing practices will forever be changed.

In this chapter the nature, use and role of online travel and tourism information search will be explored and its contribution to e-marketing theories and practices, including its potential to supplant or to supplement the more traditional marketing communication functions, will be evaluated. Then Tourism British Columbia's use of social media will be analysed for its potential as a destination e-marketing vehicle and predictions made as to the future role of user generated content (UGC) in the marketing communication arena.

2. Communication in the Web 2.0 Era

The power of storytelling and word-of-mouth (WOM) communication has been recognized by marketers who often try to create "buzz" about their brands (Winer 2009; Litvin et al., 2008). Certainly, personalized testimonies are a very powerful means of information and opinion transfer about products and services. The power of word-of-mouth communication is widely recognized in the services and tourism industries, since to cope with the intangibility and the difficulty of pre-consumption evaluation most travellers undertake extensive information searches and look for advice of peers or "like-minded souls" to gain first hand recommendations (Murray 1991; Poon 1993; Fodness and Murray 1997; Sheldon 1997; Crott 1999; Lewis and Chambers 2000; Wang, Yu and Fesenmaier 2002; Chung and Buhalis 2008; Yoo and Gretzel 2011).

In today's fast-growing cyberspace, interpersonal influence has become incredibly widespread and encompasses advice from circles of friends and relatives as well as strangers. Electronic word-of-mouth (eWOM), also called "word of mouse", thanks to its timeless and borderless nature has the power to reach and engage wider audiences than traditional word-of-mouth communication. According to Litvin et al. (2008) both marketers and customers engage in eWOM, and the level of interaction and the communication scope defines a typology of eWOM channels. Electronic asynchronous media encompass emails (connecting one customer to another), websites and product reviews (one-to-many communication), and blogs and virtual communities (many-to-many type of communication). Higher levels of interaction characterize synchronous communication varying in scope from instant messaging to chat rooms, to newsgroups.

As Winer (2009) points out, while marketers are still using offline traditional marketing communication, companies' budgets are shifting towards the new digital media. Drivers of the movement towards new media encompass: the growing availability and usage of Internet, customers resistance to intrusive communication, market fragmentation, companies need to differentiate in highly competitive markets, consumers′ desire for trustworthy communication, customers' search of interaction and desire for co-creation. Indeed, with the "hypermedia environment" (Hoffman and Novak 1996) there has been a shift from the unidirectional (i.e., producers to audience) "traditional mass communication model" to a "modified mass communication model" in which customers become co-producers of communication and interact with producers, media, and, most importantly, with other customers or potential customers. In the hypermedia environment the Web 2.0 tools have allowed a re-focusing from the marketers to the customers, with customers becoming creators and communicators of content. As Sigala (2009, p. 221) stated "Web 2.0 tools have tremendously changed the way people search, find, read, gather, share, develop, and consume information, as well as on the way people communicate with each other and collaboratively create new knowledge". In this contemporary marketplace companies have witnessed a change in marketing communication paradigms, with a proliferation of social media-based conversations where customers are more interested in personalized, interactive, experience-oriented messages. Control over media consumption, ease and convenience of access are recognized as critical factors in the social media's contemporary communication paradigm (Mangold and Faulds 2009; Rashtchy et al., 2007; Vollmer and Precourt 2008). According to Mangold and Faulds (2009), in this new order of communication, managers have lost control over content and frequency of communication as social media has broadened the traditional scope of word-of-mouth. Furthermore, in the borderless social media communication space, the traditionally highly controlled frequency and content of a one-to-many (company-to-customers) communication has mutated into a freely written, always available many-to-many communication where challenges and opportunities for marketing managers are endless. Web 2.0 has contributed to users' communication empowerment and as Sigala (2009) has stated, they are considered a "tool of mass collaboration".

3. Tourism Blogs: Nature, Use and Role in Online Information Search

Definition of blogs

Blogs, short for weblogs, are free, public, web-based entries in reverse chronological order presented in a diary-style format. Rosenbloom (2004, p. 31) defined blogs as a "new form of mainstream personal communication" for information exchange and relationship building. Though definitions vary, this digital form of journaling gathers people's experiences, creating a "word of mouse" (Gelb and Sundaram 2002) characterized by: ease of access, interactivity, written format and anonymity, low set up costs and global coverage (Berthon, Pitt and Watson 1996; Dellarocas 2003). Du and Wagner (2006) identified multiple elements that make blogs valuable to users and associated their popularity with content, technology and social value, and identified – within the social value – blogs' word-of-mouth role.

Given the information-intensive nature of travel and tourism products and their difficulty of being evaluated before consumption (Halloway 2004), and tourists' desire to share their experiences, travel blogs seem to be an appropriate means to foster information exchange in the marketplace. With reference to travel blogs, Leu et al. (2005) pointed out how blogs combine text, images, videos, audios, links and a collection of tools to share authors' commentaries or news while they are travelling. In terms of communication paradigms, Litvin et al. (2008, p. 463) pointed out that blogs are interactive, but "asynchronous, channels that writers and readers access at different times", although synchronous access is a feature of blogs. Furthermore they have pointed out how blogs entail the "many-to-many communications" paradigm (Hoffman and Novak 1996) in which consumers communicate among themselves and also with the producers. Consumer-generated communication shared on the Web 2.0 is rich in "non-commercial, detailed, experiential and up-to-date information" (Yoo and Gretzel 2011) and certainly, thanks to their narrative, storytelling nature, travel blogs are unique configurations of travel and tourism content ready to be consumed.

Nature of tourism blogs

Initiated as individual online diaries, the following major types of tourism blogs have evolved (Schmallegger and Carson 2008):

- Consumer-to-consumer (C2C): this widely spread form of blogs is used to share tourism experiences and to communicate with family and friends creating electronic word-of-mouth.
- Business-to-business (B2B): these blogs are a "networking opportunity" for tourism businesses (encompassing public and private, profit and nonprofit organizations) where stakeholders can communicate "industry trends, technological developments, research findings or marketing tips".
- Business-to-consumer (B2C): also called corporate blogs, have the purpose of communicating companies' offerings and to foster relationships with customers, and their content is created in-house or by professional bloggers.
- Government-to-consumer (G2C): similar to corporate blogs in their content creation process, these blogs are created by destination marketing organizations (DMOs) to communicate with their target markets.

The tourism industry's readiness for and usage of blogs is under investigation. Recent studies have pointed out how companies and destinations should closely monitor user-generated content, focusing on identifying and satisfying the benefits users seek (e.g., information acquisition, sense of belonging, fun and enjoyment, cost and time saving) responding promptly to users' needs, providing value and community tiding activities, using content to improve services and products, and enhancing customer relationships (Parra-López et al., 2011; Sigala 2010).

Users of blogs: From lurkers to co-creators

Despite today´s great use and variety of opportunities to get involved with Web 2.0, a number of previous studies confirmed that in Web 2.0 communities "a small core of participants" creates most of the content (Preece, Nonnecke and Andrews 2004; Bishop 2007). The level of involvement or engagement in the usage of blogs, as in other consumer-generated media, depends on the level of interaction the user has with the blog content (Van Dijck 2009; Shao 2009; Yoo and Gretzel 2011). People who limit their usage of Web 2.0 application to browsing, consuming and occasionally asking questions are defined as "lurkers" (Preece, Nonnecke and Andrews 2004). According to Shao (2009), passive use includes: consuming (browsing, watching and reading) and participating (interaction is limited to content such as ranking it or extended to user-to-user communication). Active use encompasses all content producing activities from the text blog entries, to uploading pictures, videos and adding links. Individual differences in content creation and use have been identified in past studies and socio-demographic characteristics have been found to differentiate people's Web 2.0 use and creation behaviour and choices of type of Web 2.0 applications (Yoo and Gretzel 2011). In their study of personality influence on the creation of travel content in cyberspace, Yoo and Gretzel (2011) found that 83 per cent of their sample of 1682 panelists (travellers and Internet users) had never posted materials online, while half of the sample had somehow used travel-related content. Although, according to the findings, half of the sample used consumer generated media for planning purposes. Yoo and Gretzel confirmed the existence of a gap between use and creation of content, and identified lack of time and interest as the major barriers for content creation.

Tourism blogs' role in online information search

Online opinions have become more utilized in buyers' purchase decisions from entertainment to manufacturing products (Guernsey 2000; Pan, MacLaurin and Crott 2007), and an impact and time-saving effect in the decision-making process has also been acknowledged by readers of online opinions (Bickart and Schindler 2002; Hennig-Thurau and Walsh 2003). Company sponsored blog sites have been successful as they provide a "conversational human voice" (Kelleher and Miller 2006) and bloggers trust of online blogs is more than that of traditional types of media (Johnson and Kayne 2003). Weiss, Lurie and MacInnis (2008) investigated the value of information provided by "strangers" on the web and found out that providers' response speed, depth of responses, experiences and reputation relate differently to the information seeker´s goal orientation, whether it is, a decision-making or a learning orientation.

According to past research (Crotts 1999; Price and Starkov 2006; Pudliner 2007; Schmallegger and Carson 2008) blogs are likely to become a preferred travel information source that can considerably change tourism and hospitality companies' communication. Blogs published on virtual travel communities are growing in popularity due to the perceived higher credibility of consumer opinions which are seen as more authoritative word-of-mouth communications compared to traditional tourist information sources (Johnson and Kayne 2003; A.C. Nielson 2007; Chung and Buhalis 2008; Mack, Blose and Pan 2008; Schmallegger and Carson 2008).

Certainly, blog users find blog posting useful, although tourism scholars concur as to the uncertainty of the exposure to, and the usefulness and impact of eWOM on tourists' decision-making process and their ability to transform consumers' tourism experiences (Pan et al., 2007; Pudliner 2007; Xiang and Gretzel 2010; Volo 2010). Recent research has analysed blog content and blog readers' comments, their frequency, their reactions to positive and negative content and travel bloggers' level of involvement when related to the processing of advertising messages posted in blogs (Huang et al., 2010; Volo 2010; Zehrer, Crotts and Magnini 2011).

Social, functional, psychological and hedonistic benefits are the motivators for using social media in tourism planning, and a series of social and personal incentives (e.g., altruism, availability of technology, trust) have been identified as stimulators of usage, whereas debate on the costs associated with use is still open (Wang and Fesenmaier 2004; Parra-López et al., 2011; Sigala 2011; Yoo and Gretzel 2011).

4. Social Media: Supplanting or Supplementing Traditional Marketing Communication Functions?

It has been acknowledged that communication conveyed through consumer-to-consumer travel blogs is substantially different from marketing tourism communication manoeuvred by companies and destinations (e.g., Schmallegger and Carson 2008; Volo 2010). The consumer-to-consumer blogs, given the spontaneity of the commentaries and observations, allow for reporting both positive and negative experiences with tourism products and services, whereas marketer driven blog communications are biased towards the positive attributes and features of products and services (Volo 2010). In providing travel information the potential tension between the tourism industry and online consumers has been noticed by Xiang and Gretzel (2010) who have also pointed out that blogs are gaining power in distributing travel information, and they warn tourism marketers that their role could become irrelevant if they do not cope with the new social media strategies.

As past research suggests, there are two objectives that communication tries to achieve (e.g., Carlson and Zmud 1999; Daft and Lengel 1984; Weiss, Lurie and MacInnis 2008) – viz., uncertainty reduction and equivocality reduction. Therefore, consumers who lack information and want to remove ambiguity actively search for information and look for immediate feedback, and in this regard blogs are an endless source of information and communication for consumers and companies alike. The power of solicited and unsolicited organic information agents, that is word-of-mouth and word-of-mouse sources, has been recognized in past research as very powerful (Govers et al., 2007). In their study of tourism destination image formation, the authors found that covert, induced and autonomous agents (e.g., news, documentaries, books) of information were mentioned as the first most relevant source of information in destination image creation, while a travellers' own experiences and the experiences of others were the second most relevant source, and finally, overt induced information, such as tourism promotion, seemed to have very limited influence. These findings agree with past research in that they highlight customers' appreciation for personalized messages (Singh et al., 2008) and in emphasizing the persuasiveness of personal stories and experiences of other tourists (Woodside 2010).

Both blog readers and writers do feel a sense of empowerment in using this type of media, and certainly among the reasons for using social media, functional benefits (e.g., information gathering during trip planning) have been acknowledged as important motives, but virtual communities are also known to satisfy other types of needs that their users try to fulfill: These include social needs (e.g., keep in touch with known users or start new personal relationships), and psychological needs (e.g., feel part of a community of peers, escape everyday life Wang et al., 2002). Recent research has shown the multidimensionality of users' value provided by social media usage, including emotional, aesthetical and non-monetary types of value (Sigala 2010; Yoo and Gretzel 2011).

While there are no clear signs, at least not in current practice, of a full scale displacement of traditional marketing communication tourism companies and destinations must now integrate blogs and other social media into their communication strategy if they want to remain relevant to the emerging tourist mindset. The extent to which companies and destinations use corporate or governmental blogs as legitimate communication vehicles will determine the results and benefits that accrue from them. Considering what research on blog usage suggests, and current practice/use of social media, it is difficult to imagine the more traditional functions of marketing communication competing favourably with the emerging social media. Consequently, it is difficult to imagine traditional marketing functions surviving, and certainly not in their current form. The Web 2.0 platform however, will be subject to ever greater scrutiny, criticism and suspicion as it replaces the more traditional market communication channels and becomes the unchallenged leader in market communications and suffers unavoidable learning curve setbacks. Ironically, this is likely to force the traditional channels to become more customers relevant. And what we are likely to see is the traditional marketing functions supplementing the functions as taken on by the social media. How long traditional marketing functions will remain relevant, even as supplements to the new virtual order, will depend on the rate at which the public adopts the Web 2.0 as their preferred source of information, which by all indications will be sooner than later. The following example of tourism destination usage of social media represents a case of best practice, evidence of a changing communication paradigm and support of the need for more theory development on tourism 2.0.

5. Blogs and the Changing Market Communication Paradigm: The Case of HelloBC.com

Tourism British Columbia social media strategy

Tourism British Columbia (Tourism BC), the British Columbia destination marketing organization, uses the expertise of online marketing specialists and social media strategists to exploit Web 2.0 functionalities with the aim of learning from users' content and engaging them to spread viral marketing about British

Columbia (BC). These measures provide encouragement to all type of users, from pure lurkers to creators. Besides creating awareness of the BC destination in the minds of potential tourists, the social media programs are attempting to involve the local community, stakeholders and the industry in their exploitation of the media. While the full exploitation of these efforts, through the monitoring and measuring of the results are still under investigation, to date the amount of viral marketing generated from the social media programmes and strategies has been enormous. From exclusive contests sponsored by Facebook and Twitter, to photo contests via Flickr and travel games promoted by Life Points to content posted on YouTube, the social media strategists of Tourism British Columbia seem to have learned the art of "reading, responding and engaging" users. Key social media influencers are contacted to learn about them and are often involved in tourism activities designed to encourage them to communicate more about BC and its offerings. Online media strategists gather data through social media to help them understand what it is about the BC destination that makes it resonate with visitors and to help them identify market opportunities and to evaluate the potential of new products.

Tourism British Columbia blog communication

HelloBC.com, the British Columbia official tourism website, in addition to all the typical features of a destination website, has a blog that allows locals and travellers to share their experiences and hold online discussions about attractions and activities in BC. The HelloBC.com blog provides a good example of destination blogs, featuring different posting opportunities and differentiating among consumer-generated content and DMO content. The value of the blog comes from the attentive and updated selection of content made by the HelloBC social media staff and its integration with other social media. The blog contains 1922 posts distinguished in the following subsection: (1) Field Reports, (2) 2010 Olympics, (3) Podcasts, (4) Tips from Travellers, and (5) Tips from Us.

"Field Reporting for Tourism British Columbia", described as a pilot project meant to increase awareness of British Columbia tourism offerings and experiences, was hosted on YouTube.com and embedded on HelloBC.com. Field reporters were people proficient with the use of video camera and who were passionate about BC. The selected reporters were sent to all BC regions to shoot UGC style videos that were posted on YouTube.com. The program sought to create buzz and was successful since its inception. It drove online traffic to the official tourism destination website and allowed Tourism BC to gather users' statistics. Field reporters as well as other regional tourism organizations and stakeholders involved in the project were also encouraged to blog in personal blogs or in a HelloBC.com blog or any other blog platform to further enhance the benefit of social media.

The 2010 Winter Olympics was a key event on which BC was able to capitalize using social media, with 72 blogs posted on the "2010 Olympics" blog subsection between October 2009 and May 2010, of which seven contained a video and 60 contained at least one picture. The strategists of Tourism British Columbia supported and encouraged key influencers to talk about the Olympics making use of several social media and relating them to create benefits across the different media. A Twitter expert engaged followers and proposed general trip ideas and specific event related trips, and kept track of people's interest using Twitter deck. A Twitter contest was also developed for the occasion of the Pre-Olympics, and for which the prizes for the contest were tickets for the Olympics. While Tourism BC was able to triple its followers on Twitter, the winners were also solicited to blog about the Olympics and invited to be field reporters, thus becoming key influencers.

The 23 "Podcasts" posted are mostly excerpts from a radio segment on "All Points West", a CBC Victoria show, which confirms the linkages between HelloBC, the local community, stakeholders, and residents. The focus of these podcasts ranged from small, local events to places to visit.

"Tips from Travellers" (1323 blog entries) and "Tips from Us" (356 blog entries) represent the main share of HelloBC blogs. The first tip posted under the category "Tips from Us" dates back to August 2005. The first tip posted under the category, "Tips from travellers" dates back to February 2007, which is quite early in social media communication development if compared to most European DMOs websites. The style of writing of the blogs authored by the HelloBC bloggers is as informal as any traveller blog entry, which shows how HelloBC style is embedded into UGC.

Finally, in the HelloBC blog platform, blogs can be filtered by location, activity and media throughout five years of archived content. Each blog has a rating, allows for comments, has a Google Maps link to show locations, and functionality for sharing with friends through other social media, and content feeds. Integration with External Web Frameworks such as Flickr (pictures) and YouTube (video) allows bloggers to include their own multimedia content and allows for doubling the potential reach of content across social media.

Blog users' rules: What to communicate and how

A website user can choose to become a registered Tourism BC blog user and propose travel stories for consideration; these stories are subject to a selection process and Tourism BC reserves the right to accept or edit content to protect individual privacy. Instructions to providers of content to the HelloBC blogs include: be experiential, be unbiased (not promotional) in content, add your videos, include fun, and clean (no children pictures, no spam, and no profanity) and locally related content in short entries. It also kindly suggests to anyone who wants to promote products and services to use other appropriate programs, listings, and pages of the website. This important note allows for differentiating traditional promotional activities from user-generated content. Registered users can decide if they want to receive e-updates about British Columbia tourism activities and attractions, and great visibility is indeed also given to traditional marketing communication tools – e.g. travel information, brochures, etc. – and to special offers. Finally, blog user registration data is protected in accordance with the Freedom of Information and Protection of Privacy Act, and not disclosed outside of Tourism British Columbia and, significantly, bloggers can, at any time, request removal of content.

6. Conclusions and Practical Implications

Reflections on the changing communication paradigm

In this true egalitarian world of information in which consumer-generated, simultaneous and multidirectional communication has supplemented the traditional company- generated one-way communication, companies face the challenge of re-inventing their communication, tailoring it to the new media so as to be relevant in the marketplace while coping with the relative loss of control and risks associated with this democratic and global communication environment. Tourism marketing communication has mutated since the widespread deployment of Web 2.0 tools, and in order to maintain an integrated approach to communication, companies and destinations need to better understand the changing paradigm of communication and evaluate how the lessons learned in the last decade of online communication could be successfully integrated in new models of offline tourism marketing communication. That is, a shift is needed in current thinking and marketers should not apply old rules to the new social media environment but rather learn from it, understand the tourist 2.0 and apply the Web 2.0 communication paradigms to enhance the integrated marketing communication model to deliver their messages in a more interesting, innovative and effective way. In contrast to traditional media where marketers decide and manage media choice, message content, reach and frequency, and can maneuver communication in an integrated way, in social media tourism, marketers must move from the traditional online, or offline, display of their products and services to a new role of mediator and user of consumer-generated content. Certainly, the level of control ascertained by marketer's changes according to the different types of social media under consideration, while the importance of reach and frequency gets outshined by the importance of networking. Still the exploitation of social media, by which destinations and tourism enterprises can facilitate their marketing objectives, cannot be haphazard. There is much in current service marketing theory that can and should guide the development of the market communication functions within the social media context. But there are also many unknowns that must be investigated scientifically and much new theory building needed to make sense of the new communication paradigm and to make it conceptually manageable and therefore useful to tourism practice. Tourism BC usage of social media is a good "best practices" example, but more theory development is needed to define a model that can ensure social media marketing success and integrate related success measurement methods and predictions.

Practical suggestions and implications

Tourism companies' and destinations' social media, and blogs in particular, still have great need for improvement, and while the critical recommendation is to use blogs strategically, a number of suggestions can be drawn from past research and practice and from the experience and implications of the Tourism BC case:

- Use the simultaneity and multidirectional nature of blog communication.
- Use blogging throughout the company's internal and external communication.
- Use different categories of blogs to target appropriate markets on which to build on-going relationships, and provide exclusivity and individual communication when possible.
- Confront the changing communication paradigm: listen to the customers, accept their empowerment, understand their real stories, share the communication authority with them.
- Be credible, provide real information and acknowledge cases of promotion
- Share knowledge and experience with customers: market and competitive intelligence as well as insights on current trends on the marketplace will be gained.
- Humanize your messages, use the power of narratives, engage customers and understand their emotional connections to places, products, services and causes.
- Identify passionate customers who become advocates of your company.
- Encourage repeated visitation of your blog and cross-usage of social media
- Profile social media users to market them accordingly.
- Integrate your other communication tools and other social media into your blog.
- Commit to timely communication through blogs, especially for those potential tourists looking to reduce uncertainty and equivocation.

Thoughtful planning and cooperation among DMOs and tourism suppliers in the destination marketplace could allow for an integrated approach to communicating their offering and their brands to bloggers, and controlling and exploiting user generated content posted in consumer-to-consumer blogs. Furthermore, the "supply mediated blogosphere", in which DMOs and tourism companies could maintain a certain level of control, should be integrated with the "demand originated blogosphere" in which consumers freely report their tourism experiences through narratives.

Tourism experiences are well-tailored to be told in a narrative form accompanied by pictures and videos that blogs are an almost natural means of communication in today's technological world. The HelloBC blog shows that social media and blogs in particular, can be used effectively for operational as well as strategic purposes. While the new social media reality may have some of the appearance of the old "laws of the market jungle" it really is a very different "brave new reality" that can and likely will benefit both consumer and producer. In conclusion, the blogosphere is a completely new game, and all of the challenges that have confronted traditional marketing communication functions will be migrated to the virtual world, though probably in significantly mutated ways: the need for an entirely new set of metrics to track and understand the reach and effect of social marketing communications, the challenge of communication and marketing campaigns' lifespan and reach that with social media are in the hands of customers. Finally, blogs will likely become inextricably linked to, even synonymous with, brands, destinations or products. Consumers, not companies will drive the process, creating a new set of opportunities for marketing communication theory and practice development.

References

Berthon, P.F., Pitt, L. and Watson, R.T. 1996. The World Wide Web as an advertising medium: Toward an understanding of conversion efficiency. *Journal of Advertising Research*, 36(1), 43-54.

Bickart, B. and R.M. Schindler 2002. Expanding the scope of word of mouth: Consumer-to-consumer information on the Internet. *Advances in Consumer Research*, 29(1), 428-430.

Bishop, J. 2007. Increasing participation in online communities. A framework for human–computer interaction. *Computers in Human Behavior*, 23(4), 1881-1893.

Carlson, J.R. and Zmud, R.W. 1999. Channel expansion theory and the experiential nature of media richness perceptions. *Academy of Management Journal*, 42(2), 153-170.

Chung J.Y. and Buhalis, D. 2008. Information needs in online social networks. *Information Technology and Tourism*, 10(4), 267-282.

Crotts, J.C. 1999. Consumer decision-making and pre-purchase information search, in *Consumer Behavior in Travel and Tourism*, edited by A. Pizam and Y. Mansfield, Binghamton, NY: Haworth Hospitality Press, 149-168.

Daft, R.L. and Lengel, R.H. 1984. Information richness: A new approach to manager information processing and organization design, in *Research in Organization Behavior*, edited by B. Staw and L.L. Cummings. Greenwich, CT: JAI Press, 191-233.

Dellarocas, C. 2003. The digitization of word of mouth: Promise and challenges of online feedback mechanisms. *Management Science*, 49(10) 1407-1424.

Du, H. and Wagner, C. 2006. Weblog success: Exploring the role of technology. *International Journal of Human-Computer Studies*, 64(9), 789-798.

Fodness, D. and Murray, B. 1997. Tourist information search. *Annals of Tourism Research*, 24(3), 503-523.

Gelb, B.D. and Sundaram, S. 2002. Adapting to "word of mouse". *Business Horizons*, 45(4), 21-25.

Govers, R., Go, F.M. and Kumar, K. 2007. Promoting tourism destination image. *Journal of Travel Research*, 46(1), 15-23.

Guernsey, L. 2000. Suddenly, everybody's an expert on everything. *New York Times*, 3 February.

Hennig-Thurau, T. and Walsh G. 2003. Electronic Word-of-mouth: Motives for and consequences of reading customer articulations on the Internet. *International Journal of Electronic Commerce*, 8(2), 51-74.

Hoffman, D.L. and Novak T.P. 1996. Marketing in hypermedia computer-mediated environments: Conceptual foundations. *Journal of Marketing*, 60(3), 50-68.

Holloway, J.C. 2004. *Marketing for Tourism*. Harlow: Pearson Education Ltd.

http://www.hellobc.com/en-CA/HelloBCBlogs/BritishColumbia.htm [accessed: 8 February 2011].

Huang C-Y., Chou C-J. and Lin P-C. 2010. Involvement theory in constructing bloggers' intention to purchase travel products. *Tourism Management*, 31(4), 513-526.

Johnson, T. and Kayne B. 2003. Wag the blog: How reliance on traditional media and the Internet influence credibility perceptions of weblogs among blog users. *Journalism and Mass Communications Quarterly*, 11(3), 622-642.

Kelleher, T. and Miller, B.M. 2006. Organizational blogs and the human voice: Relational strategies and relational outcomes. *Journal of Computer-Mediated Communication*, 11(2), 1-12.

Leu, S., Chi, Y.P., Chang, S.C. and Shih, W.K. 2005. *BRAINS: Blog Rendering and Accessing Instantly System: Proceedings of the IEEE International Conference on Wireless and Mobile Computing, Networking and Communications* (Montreal, Canada, 22-24 August).

Lewis, R.C. and Chambers, R.E. 2000. *Marketing Leadership in Hospitality: Foundations and Practices*, 3rd Edition. New York: Wiley.

Litvin W.S., Goldsmith E.R. and Pan B. 2008. Electronic word-of-mouth in hospitality and tourism management. *Tourism Management*, 29(3), 458-468.

Mack, R.W., Blose, J. and Pan, B. 2008. Believe it or not: Credibility of blogs in tourism. *Journal of Vacation Marketing*, 14(2), 133-144.

Mangold, W.G. and Faulds, D.J. 2009. Social media: The new hybrid element of the promotion mix. *Business Horizons*, 52, 357-365.

Murray, B. 1991. A test of services marketing theory: Consumer information acquisition activities. *Journal of Marketing*, 55(1), 10-23.

Nielson, A.C. 2007. *Trust in Advertising: A Global Nielsen Consumer Report*. New York: Nielsen Media Research.

Pan, B., MacLaurin, T. and Crott, J.C. 2007. Travel blogs and the implication for destination marketing. *Journal of Travel Research*, 46(1), 35-45.

Parra-López, E., Bulchand-Gidumal, J., Gutiérrez-Taño, D. and Díaz-Armas, R. 2011. Intentions to use social media in organizing and taking vacation trips. *Computers in Human Behavior*, 27(2), 640-654.

Poon, A. 1993. *Tourism, Technology and Competitive Strategy*. Wallingford: CAB International.

Preece, J., Nonnecke, B. and Andrews, D. 2004. The top 5 reasons for lurking: Improving community experiences for everyone. *Computers in Human Behavior*, 20(2), 201-223.

Price, J. and Starkov, M. 2006. *Building a Blog Strategy in Hospitality: Grow Customer Relationships and Direct Online Revenue*. Available at: http://www.hospitalitynet.org/news/4026867.html [accessed: 12 February 2011].

Pudliner, B.A. 2007. Alternative literature and tourist experience: Travel and tourists weblogs. *Journal of Tourism and Cultural Change*, 5(1), 46-59.

Rashtchy, F., Kessler, A.M., Bieber, P.J., Shindler, N.H. and Tzeng, J.C. 2007. *The User Revolution: The New Advertising Ecosystem and the Rise of the Internet as A Mass Medium*. Minneapolis, MN: Piper Jaffray Investment Research.

Rosenbloom, A. 2004. The blogosphere. *Communication of the ACM*, 47(12), 31-33.

Schmallegger, D. and Carson, D. 2008. Blogs in tourism: Changing approaches to information exchange. *Journal of Vacation Marketing*, 14(2), 99-108.

Shao, G. 2009. Understanding the appeal of user-generated media: A uses and gratification perspective. *Internet Research*, 19(1), 7-25.

Sheldon, P.J. 1997. *Tourism Information Technology*. Wallingford: CAB International.

Sigala, M. 2009. WEB 2.0, social marketing strategies and distribution channels for city destinations: Enhancing the participatory role of travelers and exploiting their collective intelligence, in *Information Communication Technologies and City Marketing: Digital Opportunities for Cities around the World*, edited by M. Gascó-Hernández and T. Torres-Coronas. Hershey, PA: IDEA Publishing, 220-244.

Sigala, M. 2010. Measuring customer value in online collaborative trip planning processes. *Marketing Intelligence and Planning*, 28(4), 418-443.

Sigala, M. 2011. eCRM applications and trends: The use and perceptions of Greek tourism firms of social networks and intelligence. *Computers in Human Behavior*, 27(2), 655-661.

Singh, T., Veron-Jackson, L. and Cullinane, J. 2008. Blogging: A new play in your marketing game plan. *Business Horizons*, 51, 281-292.

Tussyadiah, I.P. and Fesenmaier, D.R. 2009. Mediating tourist experiences: Access to places via shared videos. *Annals of Tourism Research*, 36(1), 24-40.

Van Dijck, J. 2009. Users like you? Theorizing agency in user-generated content. *Media, Culture & Society*, 31(1), 41-58.

Vollmer, C. and Precourt, G. 2008. *Always on: Advertising, Marketing, and Media in an Era of Consumer Control*. New York: McGraw-Hill.

Volo, S. 2010. Bloggers' reported tourist experiences: Their utility as a tourism data source and their effect on prospective tourists. *Journal of Vacation Marketing*, 16(4), 297-311.

Wang, Y. and Fesenmaier, D.R. 2004. Towards understanding members' general participation in and active contribution to an online travel community. *Tourism Management*, 25(6), 709-722.

Wang, Y., Yu, Q. and Fesenmaier, D.R. 2002. Defining the virtual tourist community: implications for tourism marketing. *Tourism Management*, 23(4), 407-417.

Weiss, A., Lurie, N.H. and MacInnis D.J. 2008. Listening to strangers: Whose responses are valuable, how valuable, are they and why? *Journal of Marketing Research*, 45(4), 425-436.

Winer, R.S. 2009. New communications approaches in marketing: Issues and research directions. *Journal of Interactive Marketing*, 23(2), 108-117.

Woodside, A.G. 2010. *Case Study Research: Theory, Methods and Practice.* London: Emerald Group Publishing Limited.

Xiang, Z. and Gretzel, U. 2010. Role of social media in online travel information search. *Tourism Management*, 31(2), 179-188.

Yoo, K-H and Gretzel, U. 2011. Influence of personality on travel-related consumer-generated media creation. *Computers in Human Behavior*, 27(2), 609-621.

Zehrer, A., Crotts, J.C. and Magnini, V.P. 2011. The perceived usefulness of blog postings: An extension of the expectancy-disconfirmation paradigm. *Tourism Management*, 32(1), 106-113.

PART 3
Web 2.0: Travellers' Behaviour

Chapter 13
Introduction to Part 3

Ulrike Gretzel

1. Web 2.0 and its Implications

Web 2.0 as a technological platform, but also as a philosophy regarding control over content, provides important opportunities for information to be exchanged among travellers and between tourism marketers and travellers. Web 2.0 is ideologically as well as structurally built on the assumptions of collective intelligence. Thus, Web 2.0 is inherently social. Distributed creation, evaluation mechanisms, and opportunities to link and share create an information environment that not only supports existing information needs and search behaviours but offers new types of tourism information. Most importantly, the technologies underlying Web 2.0 enable and actively encourage new ways to engage with that information as well as with other producers and consumers of travel information.

Web 2.0 based travel information is easier to find than many types of traditional forms of tourism information and advertising available online (Xiang and Gretzel 2010). It is also perceived as more credible and useful than the information produced and distributed by tourism marketers (Gretzel and Yoo 2008; Yoo et al., 2009). In addition, consumption and creation are often interlinked, for example in the case when comments to a blog that was just read are posted or an existing travel review is rated based on its usefulness. All these factors facilitate collection and processing of tourism information and contribute to the hedonic value derived from it by making information search more personalized, active and interactive.

However, while Web 2.0 provides the technological basis for universal access and democratic ways in which information can be made available, it is the travellers who negotiate its use within particular contexts, such as availability and cost of Internet access, knowledge and skills, psychological motivators and barriers, culture, trip structures, etc. While Web 2.0 structures and particularly different social media types that emerged from it can be easily observed, very little is known about who actually takes advantage of the opportunities provided by Web 2.0 and in what ways. Consequently, there is a critical need for research on travellers' perceptions of information embedded in the Web 2.0 information landscape and their specific engagement with that information.

2. Part Overview

This part of the book is particularly concerned with social media use by travellers. As such, it not only looks at antecedents of use but also at types of use and impacts of use. In addition, it addresses the question of whether all travellers are the same when it comes to social media perceptions and use. The research it presents is situated in different geographic contexts, takes into account different theoretical frameworks, uses various methods such as structural equation modelling and network analysis, and ranges from social media use in general to specific topics such as wine tourism and agro-tourism. Despite this diversity in approaches, the part is guided by the strong underlying need to understand social media use so that changes in travellers' information search and decision-making can be anticipated and explained.

Chapter 14 written by Parra-López, Gutiérrez-Taño, Díaz-Armas and Bulchand-Gidumal specifically looks at influences on travellers' intentions to use social media, recognizing that motivations are important but that skills and access are also needed. Their discussion on technological developments further stresses the importance of recognizing changing skill requirements and access opportunities. Yoo and Gretzel in Chapter 15 then look at use patterns, impacts of use and characteristics of travel-related social media users and creators. They find that significant differences exist among social media types in terms of their usage and that social media creators are a minority with specific demographic characteristics. In Chapter 16, Khal, Mehmet, Fevzi and Anil examine travellers' attitudes regarding the use of social networks, and their findings provide interesting conclusions regarding the potential use of this specific Web 2.0 application for travel marketing purposes.

Vrana, Zafiropoulos and Vagianos examine blog communication patterns in Chapter 17, analysing how bloggers link to each other and what types of topics the most influential bloggers include. Their work particularly addresses how structural properties of the social media landscape have important influences on what content will be most likely found by travellers. In Chapter 18, Sidali, Fuchs and Spiller investigate how trust in social media is constructed and whether greater trust leads to greater influence on decision-making. They also test whether these relationships differ among different groups of travellers, in this case agro-tourists and non-agro tourists.

Overall, the results of these studies stress the growing importance of social media and their increasing influence on travel decisions. They also point to phenomena that are not yet completely understood and require more research, such as what aspects of social media contents increase trust and thus heighten influence on decisions and how motivations, opportunities and access differ for different social media types and thus lead to diverse usage patterns. Chapter 16 reminds us that social media are social and, therefore, social perspectives that investigate relationships are needed in analysing them.

A strong message that can certainly be taken away from this part is that social media are used by travellers to inform and enrich their travel experiences. They are not a fad but rather a new reality that has important implications for the informational landscape of tourism as well as the language of tourism (Dann 1996). They are also not just another information source in the already long list of tourism information sources but rather represent a completely new way for travellers to consume, process and share information.

References

Dann, G.M.S. 1996. *The Language of Tourism: A Sociolinguistic Perspective*. Wallingford, CT: CAB International.

Gretzel, U. and Yoo, K-H. 2008. Use and Impact of Online Travel Reviews. *Information and Communication Technologies in Tourism 2008*, edited by P. O'Connor, W. Höpken and U. Gretzel. Vienna: Springer Verlag, 35-46.

Xiang, Z. and Gretzel, U. 2010. Role of social media in online travel information search. *Tourism Management*, 31(2), 179-188.

Yoo, K-H., Lee, Y-J., Gretzel, U. and D.R. Fesenmaier 2009. Trust in Travel-Related Consumer Generated Media, in *Information and Communication Technologies in Tourism 2009*. Vienna: Springer Verlag, 49-60.

Chapter 14
Travellers 2.0: Motivation, Opportunity and Ability to Use Social Media

Eduardo Parra-López, Desiderio Gutiérrez-Taño, Ricardo J. Díaz-Armas and Jacques Bulchand-Gidumal

1. Introduction

The increasingly widespread use of information and communication technologies and social media has triggered major changes in tourist behaviour in terms of the organisation of travel, the actual travel and post-travel behaviour. These changes are altering travellers' decision-making processes. Consumers consult, listen to and participate in web-based conversations concerning holiday travel (Cox, Burgess, Sellito and Buultjens 2007). In view of the impact these collaborative behaviours have on tourists' decisions concerning the choice of travel elements (destination, accommodation, activities, restaurants, etc.) an understanding of the antecedents to the use and adoption of social media by tourists before, during and after travel is of crucial importance for destination managers and tourism businesses (Sigala and Marinidis 2009; Yoo and Gretzel 2008b).

The present chapter discusses the behaviours and profile of the new traveller as regards the organisation and execution of holiday travel, as well as his/her post-travel behaviours. It sets out the results of research conducted to analyse the extent to which motivation, opportunity and ability (MOA) are determining factors in intentions to use social media to organise holiday travel and during the holiday itself. Finally, the chapter draws a number of conclusions and notes some future trends with respect to traveller 2.0 behaviour.

2. Background on Travellers 2.0

Technology use by travellers 2.0

Travellers 2.0 look to the web to obtain information on holiday travel, share experiences, buy travel-related services etc, purposes for which they utilise a variety of devices (PCs, smartphones, tablets, etc.). As a result, photo-sharing tools, videos, blogging, microblogging, maps, geo-referencing, travel communities, etc. (Flickr, YouTube, Blogger, Twitter, Google Maps, Foursquare, TripAdvisor) are acquiring increasing popularity for travel-related consultations or as a means of contributing experiences and recommendations (Chung and Buhalis 2008). The main uses of technology by travellers 2.0 are as follows:

- *Information searches*: The bulk of technology use by travellers 2.0 is related to searches for information on the different products and services to be used during a trip (U.S. Travel Association 2009). Searches are conducted using alphanumerical search engines or more advanced augmented reality systems and are performed before (for organisational purposes or to seek information on services booked), during, and after the travel.
- *Information posting:* The chief characteristic of the traveller 2.0 is content generation (*user-generated content*), which may take the form of a simple rating, more extensive comments or graphic documentation (photos, videos).
  - *Travel pictures:* through photos or videos, with a growing tendency for the images to be shared as soon as they are obtained.
  - *Comments:* via simple rating mechanisms or fuller reviews of the product or service received, the tourist rates everything consumed during the trip. As the possibilities for giving such ratings at the actual time of consumption increase, their numbers will grow exponentially.

ITCs of travellers 2.0

Travellers 2.0 use an extensive range of technologies and devices simultaneously when organising holiday travel and during the actual holiday and can therefore said to be multi-device travellers. ICT used include the following:

- *Laptops*: A number of simultaneous trends in recent years – falling laptop prices, extended battery life (Gookin 2008), the availability of a wide range of suitably-weighted devices to cater for all needs, and, lastly, increased free WiFi availability or access to reasonably-priced user connections (3G) – have led a growing number of users to travel with their laptops. In the space of just two years (2007-2009), ownership of devices of this type has risen by 10 per cent (U.S. Travel Association 2009). Also deserving mention in this regard is the emergence of netbooks, low-cost and limited-capacity laptops that can be used for the Internet access and to download camera photos, etc. (Thompson 2009).
- *PDAs*: For a time, these devices were considered to be relatively useful in terms of their contribution but with the emergence of increasingly powerful smartphones they have gradually disappeared (Charlesworth 2009).
- *Smartphones*: Evolved from the mobile phone and PDA (Charlesworth 2009), these devices are set to become the main traveller 2.0 device. A single piece of equipment which can be used for calls and texting, as well as to take and share photos and videos, update user profiles on social media,

rate products and services during the holiday and connect to the Internet to obtain information on products and services.

- *Tablets*: This segment is currently undergoing redefinition as a result of the emergence of devices consisting solely of a 7-10 inch display which offer the advantage that they can be used in situations where a laptop is less convenient. In addition, they tend to be lighter than laptops and have a longer battery life. Consequently, tablets are set to become an increasingly important tool for the traveller 2.0 user.
- *Cameras*: Cameras have always been tourists' favourite gadget. 76 per cent of the Internet-using travellers in the United States own a camera, the figure remaining unchanged between 2007 and 2009 (U.S. Travel Association 2009). Cameras are now beginning to include options that facilitate social media use behaviour. Recent developments include geopositioning, which enables the photo to be geotagged when uploaded on the web, and connectivity, which enables a photo to be printed or shared directly from the camera without the need for any additional equipment.
- *Games, video games*: In general, video games do not increase the possibilities for travellers 2.0, although mobile video games allow tourists to connect up and use them on the move. Oh et al. (2009) found that more than 40 per cent of tourists use their mobile phone for games.
- *E-books*: Devices of this type offer increasing real-time the Internet connection possibilities, transforming current travel guides into much richer and more interactive formats that allow tourists to access up-to-date and collaborative information in which they too can participate by rating products and services consumed.
- *Mobile broadband*: According to ITU (2010), in 2010 mobile broadband will be used by 15 per cent of the population, a high figure if it is recalled that the concept only appeared in 2004-2005 and that the figure was approximately 8 per cent in 2008. The trend therefore is towards more and more travellers with high communications capabilities.

Barriers to technology use

The following are the main barriers faced by tourists in their use of the aforementioned technologies:

- *Price*: Despite the ever-increasing communication possibilities noted above, it is not uncommon for a tourist to visit another country and find himself in an area where free access is unavailable. Mobile broadband (3G) is still unaffordable for most travellers in such situations, particularly in the case of inter-continental travel (Kenteris et al., 2010).
- *Distrust*: Users generally perceive that public exposure on the web can represent a loss of privacy, which is not always viewed positively by travellers 2.0 (Govani and Pashley 2005; Gross and Acquisti 2005).

- *Complex environment*: Although the effort associated with social media use was not generally perceived as an obstacle to predisposition to use (Parra-López et al., 2010), some factors nonetheless constitute a barrier: excessively long/complicated registration processes or uncertainty as regards the appropriate site to post user generated content.

Future trends

In this section, we will outline some of the technologies of the future which, in our opinion, will impact significantly on the possibilities of travellers 2.0:

- *Geolocation*: This is one of the three scenarios envisaged by Schmidt-Belz et al. (2003). Although services that utilise geolocation already exist, the trend can be expected to grow in the years to come years as smartphone use becomes more widespread.
- *Better connectivity possibilities*: Recent years have seen an increase in the number of free WiFi networks. Indeed, the availability of wireless connectivity is currently the amenity most appreciated by tourists (J.D. Power and Associates 2010). This trend will become more pronounced with the generalisation of technologies such as WiMAX, LTE, broadband mobile networks, etc. Some operators already offer data roaming as part of their data tariffs.
- *Wireless energy*: One of the major trends for the coming 5-10 years, this is set to impact heavily on the tourism sector given that a current problem encountered when taking a gadget of any kind on a trip is the short battery life and the need for a different charger for each type of device. This trend will be complemented by longer-life batteries based on new materials that multiply their capacity.
- *Personalisation*: Various systems on both the demand and supply sides seek to tailor provision to specific user needs. As Web 3.0 (also known as semantic web) develops, services of this type will grow.
- *Frame-of-mind recommendations*: Technological systems initially provided general recommendations based on the products and services earning the highest ratings (e.g. TripAdvisor). These systems have gradually been refined and are now capable of tailoring the recommendation to the user given that they know some of the latter's tastes (e.g. FilmAffinity). Systems are now being developed that can not only adapt to the user's general characteristics but can detect the frame of mind depending on various circumstances (day of the week, time of day, latest status updates on social networks, etc.). Based on these, a recommendation tailored specifically to the particular moment can be made (e.g. Rockola) (Teichmann and Zins 2009).
- *Augmented Reality (AR)*: Augmented reality is a direct or indirect vision of the real, physical world in which the elements are enriched by ICT-

generated information: information overlays with museum details, access to the museum ticket purchase facility, estimated distances to a given location, etc. As a result, augmented reality technology is viewed as offering extensive possibilities for the tourism sector (Kansa and Wilde 2008). A study by Juniper Research (Holden 2009) estimates that the AR market will generate revenue in excess of 500 million euros in 2014, primarily from payment application downloads and, in particular, from advertising.

Traveller 2.0 behaviour

Given the nature of tourism and its products and services, information is vital to tourists during planning, booking and the actual experience. It retains this importance after the travel has ended and tourists wish to pass the experience on to their social environment. Technology in general, and Internet technology specifically, fosters and drives the creation and dissemination of tourism information. Additionally, it is now possible to combine online and offline channels in the holiday decision-making and purchase process. The online channel is acquiring an increasingly central role given that it facilitates links between channels and technological media on the web (Steinbauer and Werthner 2007; Dolnicar, Laesser and Matus 2009). This change helps the new tourism consumer be better informed/trained, acquire independence from information generated by the tourism firm and involve himself to a greater extent in the selection and purchase process.

New web-based technologies play an important role in the three stages of the purchase process: pre-consumption, consumption and post-consumption. In the *pre-consumption stage* the tourist looks for the information needed to plan the holiday, forms expectations, weighs up alternatives, and compares and selects what interests him/her most. Once the supplier is notified of the services and products chosen, the *consumption* of the tourist experience takes place and here the tourist connects to the web to find detailed information on a specific activity or resource, add to information he/she has already obtained or contract new services. Lastly, in the *post-consumption* stage, the tourist shares his/her experience and documentation, reliving moments from the holiday. Moreover, depending on the tourist's use of the technologies and proficiency in Web 2.0, this communication activity will have greater impact on other potential tourists.

Tourists increasingly turn to the Internet as a key information source for planning and carrying out their trip (Cai, Feng and Breiter 2004). Gretzel and Yoo (2008a) state that online, collaborative information plays an increasingly prominent role in decision-making. Information generated by tourists who are already inter-connected on Web 2.0 is considerably impacting the decisions of other Internet users. Indeed, according to Chung and Buhalis (2008), it is the most influential factor in the choice of a tourism destination.

More tourists are turning to the web and the tourism industry needs to realise that its consumers are being influenced by web spaces where conversations on the experiences marketed by the industry take place (Litvin, Goldsmith and Pan

2008). In terms of the technologies most widely used during travel (Tnooz 2010), mobile maps (56 per cent US, 63 per cent non-US) lead the way, followed by social networks (38 per cent and 64 per cent respectively), virtual/3D tours (30 per cent and 27 per cent) and blogs (32 per cent and 22 per cent). The specific technologies most frequently cited in the study by Tnooz (2010) are Facebook, Flickr, search engines and GPS applications.

Another specific consequence of this technological change and use of different tools is that tourists not only seek information to help with travel decisions but also derive enjoyment from interaction with others. They engage in online social relationships, enjoy materials posted by others people or create their own materials (Chung and Buhalis 2008).

Important in this respect are travel reviews or stories, which are not merely a source of ideas for the tourists who read them but bring an element of fun to the travel planning process (Gretzel and Yoo 2008b) and provide enjoyment prior to the travel experience. The tourist can have fun while at the same time forming more realistic and reliable expectations of the destination or location to be visited.

With the growth of Web 2.0 and the spread of social communication media and user-generated content (opinions, ratings, photos and videos), travel consumer decisions are clearly being affected by these new concepts (O'Connor 2008). A survey by Gretzel and Yoo (2008) found that 97.7 per cent of the Internet users who travel said they read other travellers' comments during the travel planning process. This situation is causing a major change in tourist behaviour and in the way users seek, rate, evaluate, buy and consume products and services on the web.

The Internet has become a space where consumers can share their experiences with others, read others' opinions, in order to help fellow consumers take better decisions (O'Connor 2008). Information is essential to travellers and the Internet allows them to find travel-related information without the need for intermediaries. Thanks to this growth, travellers are increasingly becoming co-producers and distributors, who should work in cooperation with tourism services and products. They generate content in blogs, podcasts, wikis, mash-ups and maps to share their travel experiences with other people, they comment on aspects that have surpassed or fallen short of their expectations, on the advantages and disadvantages of tourism products and services, all of which should be taken up and managed by tourism organisations.

Through social networks travellers engage in direct contact with other travellers with similar interests in a destination. They generate more readily accessible information that facilitates the evaluation of travel alternatives during decision-making on the web. In this way, the Internet user-generated content brings security to online travellers in travel planning and purchase processes.

Motivations for travellers' usage of social media

One of the great advantages of Web 2.0 is that it affords travellers the opportunity to post comments, leading to a situation unobserved until now: visitors become

Table 14.1 Motivations for Social Media Engagement by Tourists: Literature Review

Authors	Motivations
Hennig-Thurau Gwinner and Walsh and Gremler (2004)	Venting negative feelings; platform assistance; concern for other consumers; extra-version and positive self-enhancement; social benefits; economic incentives; helping the company and advice seeking
Ardichvili, Page, and Wentling (2003); Bonacich and Schneider (1992); Osterloh and Frey (2000)	Community citizenship
Kellock (1998) and Wasko and Faraj (2000)	Reciprocity
Constant, Sproull, and Kiesler (1996)	Moral obligations
Wasko and Faraj (2000)	Self-interest
Daugherty et al. (2008)	Ego-defensive and social
Chung and Buhalis (2008)	Acquire information, social-psychological motives and for hedonic benefits
Yoo and Gretzel (2008a)	Intrinsic and positive motives: enjoyment and positive self-improvement, concern for other consumers, desire to assist the company, as opposed to revenge
Other Studies	
Wang and Fesenmaier (2004a, 2004b)	General study on motivations for participation in travel communities
Parra-López, Gutiérrez-Taño, Bulchand-Gidumal, Díaz-Armas (2010)	General study on motivations for participation in travel communities and the importance of the social costs and benefits

producers of information (active prosumers; Toffler 1970). They are acquiring an increasingly important role and firms must realise the need to involve them in content creation. At the same time, they become transmitters of such content. This phenomenon, known as "consumer generated media" (CGM), enables customer value to be enhanced and customer intelligence to be exploited (Sigala 2009).

Notwithstanding the growing popularity of CGM, the scientific literature shows that only a small number of users are capable and motivated to create on-line content (iProspect 2007; Daugherty, Eastin and Bright 2008; Nonnecke and Preece 1999; Preece et al., 2004) and that a considerable proportion of on-line users merely consumes information penned by others (Connolly and Thorn 1990; iProspect 2007; Nonnecke and Preece 1999; Preece et al., 2004). The big challenge therefore is how to secure active participation by visitors (Bishop 2007).

From the above preliminary considerations and the findings of the literature, a number of motivations can be discerned as regards the participation in social media by tourists (Daugherty et al., 2008; Hennig-Thurau, Gwinner, Walsh and Gremler 2004; Kim and Schrier 2007) (Table 14.1).

Less attention has been paid to other motivational factors such as the barriers faced by tourists in using social media, as discussed by Preece et al. (2004), Nonnecke and Preece (1999), and by Ardichvili et al. (2003), who examine the barriers to on-line participation in knowledge exchange in virtual communities.[1] In a similar vein, Mason (1999) suggested that people lurk in virtual environments out of feelings of incompetence.[2] Lastly, with respect to motivational barriers to content creation, Gretzel, Yoo, and Purifoy (2007) highlight time constraints as one of the primary reasons for non-contribution, followed by lack of interest, lack of confidence and laziness.[3]

3. Researching Motivation, Opportunity and Ability in Traveller 2.0 Use of Social Media

This section summarises research carried out to analyse the extent to which motivation, opportunity and ability (MOA) are determining factors in intentions to use social media to organise holiday travel and during the holiday itself.

Theoretical framework and hypothesis development

The MOA model, first proposed by MacInnis and Jaworski (1989), posits that individuals process information based on their underlying motives, opportunities and abilities. The model includes four key elements. Firstly, as the variable dependent it considers the intentions to use social media to organise holiday travel and during the actual holiday. Secondly, it posits that these intentions are influenced by motivation, which in turn is mediated by the (functional, social and hedonic) benefits of use. Thirdly, it posits that intentions are affected by opportunities for use. Lastly, the model suggests that user ability facilitates and encourages usage.

1 This work is important for the results as it stresses the relevance of specific themes and content in virtual communities.

2 Any analysis of motivational barriers to participation in virtual communities must necessarily include the works by Nonnecke (2000) and Katz (1998), which offer interesting content on the motivations that lead tourists to participate in travel communities.

3 Similarly, Chalkiti and Sigala (2008) also found that time was an important barrier to participation in virtual communities for Greek tourism professionals.

Intentions to use social media in vacation trips

The nature of the prospects of use has been analysed by a series of elements suggested by previous relevant works (Dasgupta et al., 2002; Wang et al., 2002; Wang and Fesenmaier 2004a). The first element to be considered is the tourists' perception of how the travellers' contributions about their vacation experiences are going to evolve: commenting on social networks, uploading photos and videos and evaluating the trip. Similarly, the tourist's own intention to increase his/her use of the tools is also considered a variable of the prospect of use. The final element considered is the intention of recommending and encouraging friends and family to use these technologies.

Motivation

Motivation is commonly considered a force that drives individuals towards their goals. In the MOA approach motivation comprises the disposition, willingness, interest and desire to participate in a particular behaviour. Extended to our context here, motivation refers to the desire of tourists to use social media to organise their holiday travel and during the actual holiday and is a factor that positively influences their intentions (H1). Individual motivation to use social media is determined by the perceived benefits of said media. In this case, the functional benefits (H2a), social benefits (H2b) and the enjoyment perceived in using the media (H2c) have been considered as antecedents of motivation.

Opportunity

Opportunity refers to the availability of time and existence of favourable conditions that make the action possible. In this particular case, opportunity arises when the tourist is not conditioned by time constraints in his/her desire to use social media. Opportunity as perceived by users is encouraged if interference of any kind (excessive information, slow download speed etc.) that impedes the interaction goal is removed (H3).

Ability

Ability is synonymous with skills and competences and reflects individuals' beliefs concerning their own ability in terms of performance and results achievement (Hong et al., 2002). Applied to the context analysed here, it denotes individuals' perception of their abilities and skills with respect to social technologies, their knowledge of collaborative tools and websites and their proficiency in using them. This perception has a significant effect on social media use behaviour (Bigne et al., 2010) (H4).

Research method and data analysis

The research instrument utilised to obtain the necessary information was a self-administered survey conducted with a population sample from the Canary Islands meeting the requirements of being regular the Internet users and having taken a holiday during the previous year. The data were collected during the month of May 2009 and a broad sample of 404 respondents was used.

The structure of the sample by gender was 53 per cent males and 47 per cent females, and by age, 13.3 per cent of the respondents were aged from 18 to 25; 23.9 per cent from 25 to 35, 38.8 per cent from 35 to 45, and 23.9 per cent above 45. All members of the sample had access to and habitually used the Internet, both at home (97 per cent) and at work (92.8 per cent).

The data analysis method chosen was structural equations, using the Partial Least Squares (PLS) technique (Fornell and Cha 1994). The factorial loads for all the items are above 0.707, the composite reliability (CR) above 0.8 in all cases and the average variance extracted (AVE) for each indicator construct is above 0.5. Consequently, the measurement model fulfils the prerequisites (Fornell and Larcker 1981; Chin 1998; Nunnally 1978) (Table 14.2).

4. Results

The explained variance (50.3 per cent) of the latent variable "Intentions to use" demonstrates adequate predictive power (Figure 14.1). With regard to the hypotheses regarding the antecedents of motivation proposed in the model, the results obtained were as follows:

- Hypothesis H2c, which posited a positive direct relationship between the perceived functional benefits and motivation for using social media to organise holiday travel and during the actual travel, is confirmed (β=.328, $p<.05$).
- Hypothesis 2c, concerning the positive relationship between perceived hedonic benefits and motivation, is confirmed (β=.207, $p<.05$).
- Conversely, Hypothesis 2b is not confirmed and consequently a positive relationship cannot be said to exist between the perceived social benefits and motivation (β=.191, non-significant).

With regard to the hypotheses concerning the direct relationships with "Intentions to use", the results were as follows:

- Hypothesis 1, which posited the existence of a positive relationship between motivation and the intentions to use social media, is confirmed (β=.486, $p<.001$).
- Hypothesis 4, which posited the existence of a positive relationship between

Table 14.2 Properties of the Constructs

Construct	Item	Loading	AVE	CR
Functional Benefit	Social media tools enable me to keep up to date with the tourist sites.	0.899	0.743	0.896
	Social media tools give me the possibility to exchange information about tourist sites.	0.844		
	Social media tools permit me to save costs.	0.841		
Social Benefit	Social media tools enable me to stay in contact with others who share the same interests.	0.878	0.740	0.894
	My personal relationships with people with similar motivations on the trip increase.	0.895		
	Social media tools provide me with a strong feeling of belonging to a group.	0.804		
Hedonic Benefit	The use of social media tools is both pleasing and fun.	0.869	0.747	0.855
	I am proud of participating with opinions and sharing tourist experiences.	0.860		
Motivations	I always share with friends and colleagues what I know and discover about places to visit.	0.811	0.670	0.910
	I like sharing my experiences and knowledge.	0.831		
	My experiences and comments about trips may be of interest to others.	0.804		
	I use the contributions of others and I feel an obligation to contribute as well.	0.801		
	I'm able to communicate my tourist experiences to others.	0.845		
Opportunity	I have access to the technology needed to access these social media tools (computer, broadband)	0.807	0.547	0.828
	*Contributing opinions on travel websites often involves processes that are too complicated.	0.756		
	*There are so many travel websites that I find it difficult to know where to go.	0.707		
	*The personal effort and time I need to find trip-related information of interest is excessive.	0.683		
Ability	I am a person with technological skills; I like to be up to date with them.	0.801	0.666	0.889
	I know sites and tools for sharing my travel tales experiences.	0.813		
	I find that these social media tools for sharing on the Internet experiences about travel are easy to use.	0.838		
	It's easy to learn these social media tools.	0.812		
Intentions to use	I think that more and more people will use these social media tools.	0.813	0.751	0.900
	I am sure that I will use these tools again to organise and develop vacation trips	0.895		
	In the future, I will encourage my friends to use and contribute in these social media tools.	0.890		

Note: *Recoded (inverse scale).

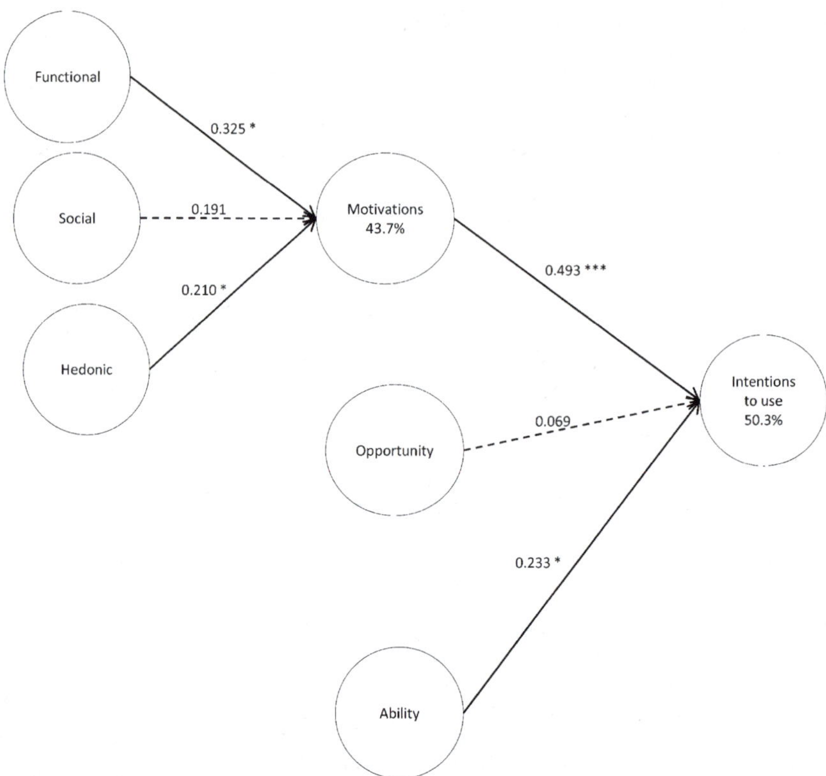

Figure 14.1 Causal Relations Estimated in the Structural Model

Note: Significance: *** p <.001 level; ** p <.01 level; * p <.05 level.

ability and intentions to use, is also confirmed (β=.233, p<.05).

- However, hypothesis 3, which posited the existence of a positive relationship between opportunity and intentions to use, is not confirmed (β=.084, non-significant).

Discussion

The results of the analysis undertaken indicate the importance of motivation and ability in accounting for intentions to use social media. However, opportunity is not found to be a factor. The greatest impact is seen in the case of motivation, namely, the disposition, willingness, interest and desire to participate. Said motivation is affected by the functional and hedonic benefits perceived by users. However, it is not influenced by the social benefits.

Accordingly, the main conclusion to be drawn by anyone interested in promoting and fostering the use of collaborative technology tools for the organisation and execution of holiday travel is the need to increase the user benefits: better knowledge of destinations, cost savings, and fun derived from the use of the tools. The study also indicates that the skills and competences of users stimulate their intention to use social media.

Managers of tourism firms and destination policy makers should concentrate in identifying the clients' needs for information in the social media so that they can respond actively and favour the perception of functional benefits. Thus, it is necessary to "listen" constantly to the tourists' contributions in the social media in order to participate and respond immediately to suggestions, needs and queries, thus increasing the perception of functional utility. This will favour the tourists' use of these tools in relation to the product or service offered by the firm or destination.

Moreover, if the Internet community managers identify and expand the online conversations that take place about their product, the perception of functional utility increases. In that respect, community managers must identify the resources, and the groups and communities interested in their type of product since, if participation related to that product increases, its presence and the knowledge about it increases, with possible direct impact on the generation of sales and/or interest in visiting it.

The results of this study also suggest that the community managers should recognise and be thankful for the tourists' participation in terms of contributions (photos, videos, comments, etc.), about their products. That recognition entails the perception of psychological and hedonic benefits and, therefore, the participation and the evaluation of their products will increase.

5. Conclusions: Traveller 2.0 Trends

Behaviours of tourists who make extensive use of the Internet and ICTs (information and communications technologies) have changed radically in recent years and are significantly impacting the tourism sector, basically in two ways. On the one hand, from the content point of view, travellers 2.0 are co-creators of content: they comment on the hotels where they stay, they give ideas on new activities to do, they engage with other travellers and design new experiences, etc. All of these influence the decisions of other travellers, thus changing significantly the consumption patterns in the sector.

On the other hand, from the technology point of view, new devices (such as smartphones, tablets etc.), technologies (maps, geotagging etc.), and connectivity (WiFi, 3G networks, etc.) facilitate such behaviours before, during and after travel. The use of ICTs during travel has acquired greater potential in recent years and affords travellers a higher level of satisfaction in the travel experience and allows them to use social media at the same time.

Trends in the development of these technologies will lead to greater use by travellers as well as increasing their impact. These circumstances have triggered important changes in the holiday industry. Due to this, tourism organisations must monitor and participate in the conversation to influence decision-making by tourists and to generate an appropriate image on the Internet.

References

Ardichvili, A., Page, V. and Wentling, T. 2003. Motivation and barriers to participation in virtual knowledge-sharing communities of practice. *Journal of Knowledge Management*, 7(1), 64-77.

Bigné, E., Hernández, B., Ruiz, C. and Andreu, L. 2010. How motivation, opportunity and ability can drive online airline ticket purchases. *Journal of Air Transport Management*, 16(6), 346-349.

Bishop, J. 2007. Increasing participation in online communities: A framework for human–computer interaction. *Computers in Human Behavior*, 23, 1881-1893.

Bonacich, P. and Schneider, S. 1992. *Communication Networks and Collective Action*. Oxford: Pergamon Press.

Cai, L.A., Feng, R. and Breiter, D. 2004. Tourist purchase decision involvement and Information preferences. *Journal of Vacation Marketing*, 10(2), 138-148.

Charlesworth, A. 2009. *The Ascent of Smartphone. Engineering and Technology*, 14 February-27 February 2009. Available at: http://ieeexplore.ieee.org/stamp/stamp.jsp?tp=andarnumber=4913985 [accessed: 26 October 2010].

Chin, W.W. 1998. Issues and opinion on structure equation modelling. *MIS Quarterly*, 22(1), 7-16.

Chung, J.Y. and Buhalis, D. 2008. *A Study of Online Travel Community and Web 2.0: Factors affecting Participation and Attitude*. Proceedings ENTER2008, Vienna: Springer Verlag, 267-278.

Chung, J.Y. and Buhalis, D. 2008. Web 2.0: A Study of Online Travel Community, in *Information and Communication Technologies in Tourism 2008*, edited by P. O'Connor, W. Höpken and U. Gretzel. Vienna: Springer Verlag, 70-81.

Connolly, T. and Thorn, B.K. 1990. *Discretionary Databases: Theory, Data, and Implications*. Newbury Park, CA: Sage Publications.

Constant, D., Sproull, L. and Kiesler, S. 1996. The kindness of strangers: On the usefulness of weak ties for technical advice. *Organization Science*, 7, 119-135.

Cox, C., Burgess, S., Sellitto, C. and Buultjens, J. 2007. Consumer-generated Web-based Tourism Marketing, Sustainable Tourism Cooperative Research Center (STCRC), Gold Coast Campus. Griffith University, Australia.

Dasgupta, S., Granger, M. and McGarry, N. 2002. User acceptance of E-collaborative technology: An extension of the technology acceptance model. *Group Decision and Negotiation*, 11, 87-100.

Daugherty, T., Eastin, M.S. and Bright, L. 2008. Exploring consumer motivations for creating user-generated content. *Journal of Interactive Advertising*, 8(2). Available at: http://www.jiad.org/article101 [accessed: November 2010).

Dolnicar, S., Laesser, C. and Matus, K. 2009. Online versus paper: Format effects in tourism surveys. *Journal of Travel Research*, 47(1), 21-24.

Fornell, C. and Cha, J. 1994. Partial Least Squares, in A*dvanced Methods of Marketing Research*, edited by R.P. Bagozzi. Cambridge, MA: Blackwell, 52-78.

Fornell, C. and Larcker, D.F. 1981. Evaluating structural equation models with unobservable variables and measurement error. *Journal of Marketing Research*, 18, 39-50.

Gookin, D. 2008. *Laptops For Dummies*. Hoboken, NJ: Wiley Publishing, Inc.

Govani, T. and Pashley, H. 2005. Student awareness of the privacy implications when using Facebook. Unpublished manuscript. Available at: http://lorrie.cranor.org/courses/fa05/tubzhlp.pdf [accessed: 10 March 2010].

Gretzel, U., Yoo, K-H. and Purifoy, M. 2007. *Online Travel Review Study: The Role and Impact of Online Travel Reviews.* College Station, TX: Laboratory for Intelligent Systems in Tourism.

Gretzel, U. and Yoo, K-H. 2008. Use and impact of online travel reviews, in *Information and Communication Technologies in Tourism 2008*, edited by P. O'Connor, W. Höpken and U. Gretzel. Vienna: Springer Verlag, 35-46.

Gross, R. and Acquisti, A. 2005. Information revelation and privacy in online social networks (The Facebook case). Alexandria, VA: ACM Press.

Hennig-Thurau, T., Gwinner, K.P., Walsh, G. and Gremler, D.D. 2004. Electronic word-of-mouth via consumer-opinion platforms: What motivates consumers to articulate themselves on the Internet? *Journal of Interactive Marketing*, 18(1), 38-52.

Holden, W. 2009. Mobile Augmented Reality: Forecasts, Applications and Opportunity Appraisal 2009-2014. Juniper Research, Nov. 2009. Available at: http://www.juniperresearch.com/reports/mobile_augmented_reality [accessed: 26 October 2010].

Hong, W., Wong, W., Thong, J. and Tam, K. 2002. Determinants of user acceptance of digital libraries: An empirical examination of individual differences and system characteristics. *Journal of Management Information Systems*, 18(3), 97-124.

iProspect. 2007. iProspect social networking user behaviour study. Available at: http://www.iprospect.com/premiumPDFs/survey_2007_searchmarketersocialnetworking.pdf [accessed: 8 November 2010].

ITU. 2010: ICT Indicators Database. Available at: http://www.itu.int/ITU-D/ict/statistics/ [accessed: 26 October 2010].

J.D. Power and Associates. 2010: 2010 North America Hotel Guest Satisfaction Index Study. Available at: http://businesscenter.jdpower.com/JDPAContent/CorpComm/News/content/Releases/pdf/2010137-nahg.pdf [accessed: 26 October 2010].

Kansa, E.C. and Wilde, E. 2008. Tourism, Peer Production, and Location-Based Service Design. *2008 IEEE International Conference on Services Computing*.

Kellock, P. 1998. *The Economies of Online Cooperation: Gifts and Public Goods in Computer Communities*. London: Routledge.

Kenteris, M., Gavalas, D. and Economou, D. 2011. Mytilene e-guide: A multiplatform mobile application tourist guide exemplar. *Multimedia Tools and Applications*, 52, 241–262.

Kim, E. and Schrier, T. 2007. A *Content Analysis of Hotel Customer's Post-purchase Online Evaluations*. Conference paper presented at The 2007 Las Vegas International Hospitality and Convention Summit, Las Vegas, Nevada, USA.

Litvin, S.W., Goldsmith, R.E. and Pan, B. 2008. Electronic word-of-mouth in hospitality and tourism management. *Tourism Management*, 29(3), 458-468.

MacInnis, D.J. and Jaworski, B.J., 1989. Information processing from advertisements: toward an integrative framework. *Journal of Marketing*, 53, 1-23.

Mason, B. 1999. Issues in virtual ethnography, in *Workshop on Ethnographic Studies in Real and Virtual Environments: Inhabited Information Spaces and Connected Communities*, edited by Kathy Buckner. Edinburgh: Queen Margaret College, 61-69.

Nonnecke, B. and Preece, J. 1999. Shedding light on lurkers in online communities, in *Workshop on Ethnographic Studies in Real and Virtual Environments: Inhabited Information Spaces and Connected Communities*, edited by Kathy Buckner. Edinburgh: Queen Margaret College, 123-128.

Nunnally, J. 1978. *Psychometric Theory*. New York: McGraw-Hill.

O'Connor, P. 2008. Generated content and travel: A case study on Trip Advisor, in *Information and Communication Technologies in Tourism 2008*, edited by P. O'Connor, W. Höpken and U. Gretzel. New York: Springer Verlag.

Oh, S., Lehto, X.Y. and Park, J. 2009. Travelers' Intent to Use Mobile Technologies as a Function of Effort and Performance Expectancy. *Journal of Hospitality Marketing and Management*, 18(8), 765-781.

Osterloh, M. and Frey, B.S. 2000. Motivation, knowledge transfer, and organizational forms. *Organization Science*, 11(5), 538-550.

Parra-López, E., Bulchand-Gidumal, J., Gutiérrez-Taño, D. and Díaz-Armas, R. 2011. Intentions to use social media in organizing and taking vacation trips. *Computers in Human Behavior*, 27(2), 640–654.

Preece, J., Nonnecke, B. and Andrews, D. 2004. The top 5 reasons for lurking: Improving community experiences for everyone. *Computers in Human Behavior*, 20(2), 201-223.

Schmidt-Belz B., Laamanen H. and Poslad S.Z. 2003. Location-based Mobile Tourist Services – First User Experiences, in *Information and Communication Technologies in Tourism 2003*, edited by A. Frew. Vienna: Springer Verlag, 115-123.

Sigala, M. and Marinidis, D. 2009. Exploring the transformation of tourism firms' operations and business models through the use of web map services, in The *European and Mediterranean Conference on Information Systems 2009 (EMCIS 2009)*, Founded and organised by the Information Systems Evaluation and Integration Group, Brunel University, UK and Izmir, Turkey, 13-14.

Sigala, M. 2007. *Web 2.0 in the Tourism Industry: A New Tourism Generation and New E-business Models*. Available at: www.traveldailynews.com/pages/print/20554 [accessed: 24 October 2010].

Sigala, M. 2009. E-service quality and Web 2.0: Expanding quality models to include customer participation and intercustomer support. *The Service Industries Journal*, 29(10), 1341-1358.

Steinbauer, A. and Werthner, H. 2007. Consumer Behavior in e-Tourism, in *Information and Communication Technologies in Tourism 2007*, edited by M. Sigala, L. Mich and J. Murphy. Vienna: Springer Verlag, 65-76.

Teichmann, K. and Zins, A. 2009. Planning and Exploratory Buying Behavior, in *Handbook of Tourist Behavior: Theory and Practice*, edited by M. Kozak and A. Decrop. New York and Oxon: Routledge, 83-95.

Thompson, C. 2009. *The Netbook Effect: How Cheap Little Laptops Hit the Big Time*. Wired Magazine, March 2009. Available at: http://www.wired.com/gadgets/wireless/magazine/17-03/mf_netbooks [accessed: 26 October 2010].

Tnooz. 2010. *How Travellers Use Technology to Search, Book and Play when Away*. Available at: http://www.tnooz.com/2010/08/12/news/survey-how-travellers-use-technology-to-search-book-and-play-when-away/ [accessed: 26 October 2010].

Toffler, A. 1970. *Future Shock*. New York: Bantam Books.

US Travel Association. 2009. *Travelers' Use of the Internet, 2009 Edition*. Available at: http://travel.utah.gov/publications/newsletters/files/2010_01_21/Travelers%20Use%20of%20the%20Internet%20-%202009.pdf [accessed: 26 October 2010).

Wang, Y., Yu, Q. and Fesenmaier, D. 2002. Defining the virtual tourist community: Implications for tourism marketing. *Tourism Management*, 23(4), 407-417.

Wang, Y. and Fesenmaier, D.R. 2004a. Modelling participation in an Online Travel Community. *Journal of Travel Research*, 42(3), 261-270.

Wang, Y. and Fesenmaier, D.R. 2004b. Towards Understanding the Needs and Motivations for Contributing to an Online Travel Community: An Integrated Model, *Tourism Management*, 25, 709-722.

Wasko, M.M. and Faraj, S. 2000. It is what one does: Why people participate and help others in electronic communities of practice. *Journal of Strategic Information Systems*, 9, 155-173.

Wu, C-R., Chang, C-W. and Lin, H-L. 2007. An organizational performance measurement model based on AHP sensitivity analysis. *International Journal of Business Performance Management*, 9, 77-91.

Yoo, K-H. and Gretzel, A. 2008a. The influence of perceived credibility on preferences for recommender systems as sources of advice. *Journal of Information Technology and Tourism*, 10(2), 133-146.

Yoo, K-H. and Gretzel, U. 2008b. Understanding differences between online travel review writers and non-writers, in *Proceedings of the 13th Annual Graduate Education and Student Research Conference in Hospitality and Tourism*, edited by T. Hara. Orlando, FL, 3-5 January 2008, 21-29.

Chapter 15
Use and Creation of Social Media by Travellers

Kyung-Hyan Yoo and Ulrike Gretzel

1. Introduction

In 2006, *TIME* magazine assigned the title of Person of the Year to "You", the modern online users who create and control information. Since then, these online users have been increasingly empowered by the emergence of a plethora of social media applications that support the creation and use of social media. The growing availability and popularity of these applications have transformed the way people communicate, make decisions, socialize, learn, entertain themselves, interact with each other, or even do their shopping (Constantinides and Fountain 2008). Not surprisingly, these impacts can also be identified with relation to consumer behaviour in travel and tourism.

Given the experiential nature of tourism, the information created by other travellers is even more important and influential in travellers' information search and decision-making processes. Growing numbers of travellers search and consume travel information created by other travellers for their travel planning and share their experience after returning from trips (Cox, Burgess, Sellitto and Buultjens 2009). According to a recent report, more than 80 per cent of leisure travel buyers were influenced by various types of user-generated contents including videos, reviews and blogs in the context of travel purchase decisions (PhoCusWright 2008). Similarly, other studies found that 40 per cent of online travel planners consider user-generated contents in their travel decision (JupiterResearch 2008) and 23 per cent of US Internet users' vacation decisions are influenced by social media (Ad-ology Research 2009). In addition, a study by Brown (2009) found that more than one-quarter of US Internet users who followed brands on social networks followed a travel brand. Further, more than half of travel marketers indicated that they continue to invest heavily in social media despite the economic downturn (eMarketer 2009a). Clearly, social media have taken on an important role in shaping the attitudes and behaviours of travel consumers as well as travel and tourism marketers.

Recognizing the growing importance of social media, recent academic tourism publications increasingly discuss social media trends in tourism (e.g. Pan, MacLaurin and Crotts 2007; Sigala 2008; O'Connor 2008; Tussyadiah and Fesenmaier 2008; Cox et al., 2009; Xiang and Gretzel 2009; Yoo and Gretzel

2010; Volo 2010). While current findings provide some important insights for understanding social media in tourism, there is still a lack of studies that have empirically investigated how social media are used and created by travellers. Further, the rapid changes in the social media field create a need for more theoretically grounded research that can describe and explain new consumer behaviours beyond a specific social media application. Consequently, this chapter seeks to provide an examination of online social media use and creation by travellers that focuses on main issues related to creation and use. For that purpose, this chapter will first review relevant studies that examined social media use and creation. Then, based on the findings of two national surveys on travellers' social media use conducted in the United States in 2008 and 2010, this chapter will provide empirical findings addressing the following issues: 1) patterns of use; 2) impacts on trip planning and decision-making; and, 3) characteristics of travel-related social media users and creators. Finally, this chapter will conclude with a discussion of the opportunities and challenges that exist for travel practitioners as well as researchers given the investigated characteristics and behaviours of travel-related social media users and content creators.

2. Theoretical Foundations

Social media foundations

Web 2.0 is considered to be a new version of the World Wide Web that changed the ways end-users engage with the Web (Kaplan and Haenlein 2010; O'Reilly 2005). The fundamental principle of Web 2.0 is that online users add value by generating contents through various application tools including blogs, wikis and social networks (Chaffey et al., 2009; Parise and Guinan 2008; O'Reilly 2005). While many use the terms social media and Web 2.0 interchangeably, these concepts are closely related but different. Web 2.0 is considered as the platform for the evolution of social media. Social media refer to "a group of Internet-based applications that build on the ideological and technological foundations of Web 2.0, and that allow the creation and exchange of User-Generated Content" (Kaplan and Haenlein 2010: 61). This includes a number of different applications which allow online users to "post", "tag", "digg", or "blog", and so forth, on the Internet (Xiang and Gretzel 2009).

Various forms of social media currently exist and new sites appear online every day. According to Constantinides and Fountain (2008), there are five main categories of social media, which include blogs, social networks, content communities, forums/bulletin boards and content aggregators. Kaplan and Haenlein (2010) classified social media into six types based on the degree of social presence/media richness and the degree of self presentation/disclosure. Their classification of social media includes blogs, social networking sites (e.g., Facebook), virtual social worlds (e.g.,

Second Life), collaborative projects (e.g., wikipedia), content communities (e.g., You Tube) and virtual game worlds (e.g., World of Warcraft).

Using these various types of social media, a growing number of online users becomes increasingly involved in various online activities. According to Shao (2009), online individuals deal with social media in three ways: consuming, participating and producing contents online. The findings of previous studies (Nonnecke and Preece 2001; Shao 2009; Tedjamulia et al., 2005; Van Dijck 2009) indicated that a majority of online users just consumes the contents posted by others. Some engage in user-to-user interactions and user-to-content interactions, such as ranking the content and posting comments, but do not create online contents. Only a small number of users creates online contents including text, images, audio and video. These studies suggested that the three activities may represent a path of gradual involvement with social media. People begin their relationship with social media as consumers or lurkers but gradually evolve to the next stage of participating and then finally come to produce CGM contents. Similarly, Forrester (2007) developed "Social Technographics", which categorized social computing behaviours into a ladder with six levels of participation. The study found that 13 per cent of US online adults are "Creators" who publish contents to their social media sites while 19 per cent are "Critics" who comment on social media sites and also post ratings and reviews. Some users are "Collectors" (15 per cent) who use RSS or tag web pages or "Joiners" (19 per cent) who simply join and use social networking sites. A good percentage of online users are found to be "Spectators" (33 per cent) who consume social media contents generated by other peers or "Inactives" (52 per cent) who are not involved in any of these activities.

Social media in tourism

In tourism, Web 2.0 also referred to as "Travel 2.0" describes a new interactive approach to travel technologies (PhoCusWright 2006). Travel 2.0 applications include content syndication, mash-ups, AJAX, tagging, wikis, web forums/message boards, customer ratings systems, virtual worlds, podcasting, blogs and online videos (Schmallegger and Carson 2008). Among these various types of social media used by travellers, travel blogs have received a lot of research attention (Braun-LaTour, Grinley and Loftus 2006; Douglas and Mills 2006; Karlsson 2006; Lee, Yoo and Gretzel 2009; Lin and Huang 2006; Mack, Blose and Pan 2008; Pan et al., 2007; Pudliner 2007; Schmallegger and Carson 2008; Thevenot 2007; Tussyadiah and Fesenmaier 2008; Volo 2010; Wenger 2008). Travel blogs were identified not just as a good platform that can communicate travel experiences outside of the narratives of tourism marketers (Pudliner 2007) but also an effective tool for promotion, product distribution, management as well as research (Schmallegger and Carson 2008; Volo 2010). The trustworthiness of blogs to travellers (Mack, Blose and Pan 2008) and the cultural differences in terms of social media use and impacts (Lee, Yoo and Gretzel 2009; Volo 2010) were also discussed. Other important forms of travel social media are online travel reviews and communities. The popularity and impacts of travel reviews have been investigated in previous studies (Gretzel and Yoo 2008; O'Connor 2008; Vermeulen and Seegers 2009; Yoo et al., 2009). Online travel communities have the longest tradition as online venues for travellers to engage in travel storytelling, to find or share information, and also to support travel planning (Arsal, Backman and Baldwin 2008; Chung and Buhalis 2008; Kim, Lee and Hiemstra 2004; Wang and Fesenmaier 2004a, Wang, Yu and Fesenmaier 2001). In addition, other multimedia forms of travel social media such as videos, photo sharing and podcasting are increasingly used by travellers to portray their tourism experiences (Tussyadiah and Fesenmaier 2009; Xie and Liew 2008).

With these various social media applications, more and more online travel content is created by travellers and serves as an important information source for trip planners as well as tourism practitioners (Carrera et al., 2008; Gretzel et al., 2009; Litvin, Goldsmith and Pan 2008; Pan, MacLaurin and Crotts 2007; Xiang and Gretzel 2009; Yoo and Gretzel 2008a). According to a recent report by eMarketer (2010), three out of the top ten online travel information sources used by US adults were social media sites. Social media contents are extremely search engine friendly (Gretzel 2006), thus the contents are easily accessible to travellers (Xiang and Gretzel 2009). Further, recent advances in mobile technologies and rising ownerships of smart phones mean travellers can easily access social media during their travel. According to a recent report by the Pew Research Center (2010), more than half (52 per cent) of Americans own laptops, 85 per cent own cell phones and the number of tablet computer users is rapidly growing as well. The US smart phone users now amount to more than 45 million (ComScore 2010) and, importantly, the smart phone has become one of the most important devices for travellers (Charlesworth 2009). Using their mobile technologies, travellers actively access social media in the course of their travel for information searches, posting of accounts of their experiences, as well as networking. A report by Tnooz (2010) found that social networks technology is one of the most widely used technologies during travel (38 per cent in the US and 64 per cent outside of the US.) It is obvious that social media provide a fertile venue for travellers to create and share their travel experiences and also take on an important role in tourist information search and decision-making. Thus this suggests the needs of better understanding on social media users and creators and what factors contribute to their social media engagement.

Users and creators of social media

Online users deal with social media in a number of different ways. As discussed earlier, social media users were classified into different categories based on their social media participation (Forrester 2007; Nonnecke and Preece 2001; Shao 2009; Tedjamulia et al., 2005; Van Dijck 2009). Previous studies identified a number of different factors that influence social media involvement behaviours. Forrester Research (2007) suggests that online users' social media engagements differ by their primary life motivation, the types of social media sites used and even the type of PC ownership. Trust has also been addressed as an important factor that influences social media use and creation (Nielsenwire 2009; Yoo et al., 2009). A higher level of trust leads to a higher level of social media engagement (Burgess et al., 2009; Yoo, Lee and Gretzel 2007). In addition, the personality of users has been found to be influential in determining social media behaviours (Acar and Polonsky 2007; Jeng and Teng 2008; Ross et al., 2009; Yoo and Gretzel 2010). Although the results are somewhat inconsistent, existing research suggests positive influences of openness, extraversion, agreeableness and conscientiousness on social media creation motivations and behaviours, while negative relationships were suggested for neurotic individuals. A good number of studies also indicated influences of individuals' socio-demographic characteristics such as age, gender, education and income on social media activities. For most types of social media, younger users were found to be more active users and creators (Jones and Fox 2009; Lenhart et al., 2007; Verna 2009) while US bloggers tend to be mostly 25 or older males (Technorati 2010). Male adults are more active social media creators than female adults while females tend to dominate when users are limited to preteens, teens and college students (Verna 2009). The US social media user is found to be more likely college educated, full-time employed and dominantly white (eMarketer 2009b). Further, levels of education and income of social media users differ by type of social media. The users of LinkedIn tend to be more educated, have higher income and are more likely full-time employed while Facebook and Myspace users tend to have lower incomes and are more likely students.

In terms of travel-related social media use and creation, a number of previous studies have investigated the determinants of social media engagement behaviours. Wang and Fesenmaier (2004b) suggested that travellers engage in online travel communities for functional, social, psychological and hedonic benefits. Similarly Chung and Buhalis (2008) found that travellers get involved in virtual communities for information, social-psychological and hedonic benefits. The study by Yoo and Gretzel (2008a) found that travel review writers who contribute to TripAdvisor are mostly motivated by intrinsic motives of enjoyment, concerns for other travellers or the desire to help the company while only some are motivated by the opportunity for venting. Recent findings (Parra-Lopez et al., 2010), indicate that travellers more likely intend to use social media when they perceive greater benefits and greater altruism, availability, individual predisposition or trust. However, it was also found that costs related to the use of social media like effort, privacy concerns or difficulty to use do not significantly affect intentions to use social media. In addition, travellers' gender and income level (Yoo and Gretzel 2008a), nationality (Gretzel, Kang and Lee 2008) culture (Lee, Yoo and Gretzel 2009), membership in a generational cohort (Yoo and Gretzel 2009) and their involvement in trip planning (Yoo and Gretzel 2008b), as well as their personality (Yoo and Gretzel 2010) have been identified as factors influencing travellers' social media use and creation behaviours, suggesting that travellers' personal characteristics are important factors to be taken into account when trying to understand engagement with social media. Looking specifically at travel social media creation, travel social media creators tend to be young (Yoo and Gretzel 2009), male, and have higher incomes and greater internet skills (Yoo and Gretzel 2008c). They are also more likely frequent travellers as well as highly involved in trip planning (Yoo and Gretzel 2008b). In addition, being part of a collectivist culture was found to increase the likelihood to produce blog contents targeting a general public, while individualistic values lead to the creation of contents that reflect personal experiences and serve the purpose of documentation and ego-enhancement (Lee et al., 2009). Further, travel photo posting was found to be a prominent activity for younger generations while boomers and seniors are not likely to post photos online (Yoo and Gretzel 2009).

While these studies suggest a number of factors and characteristics regarding travel social media users and creators, the findings are rather fragmented since most findings are limited to certain social media types or specific individual characteristics. Further, previously identified profiles for social media users and creators should be updated given the growing popularity of social media. Thus, this chapter seeks to close this knowledge gap by providing the findings of two recent US national surveys on travellers' social media engagement.

3. Methodology

Two online surveys representative of the general US population were conducted with the support of the National Laboratory for Tourism and eCommerce and the U.S. Travel Association. The first online survey was conducted in July 2008. A total of 59,186 members of a commercial online research panel residing in the United States were invited to participate in the survey. No additional incentives beyond the rewards provided by the panel company were offered. A total of 3,109 panellists responded to the survey invitation but only 2,671 indicated they were active Internet users. Further, of those Internet users, 1,682 had travelled for pleasure within 12 months prior to the study. These online travellers form the actual sample for the 2008 study.

In 2010 a similar study was conducted. This time a total of 2,046 panellists responded to the survey invitation but only 1,810 indicated they were active Internet users. Further, of those Internet users, 1,221 had travelled for pleasure within 12 months prior to the study. These online travellers form the actual sample for the 2010 study. The two samples obtained are comparable in terms of demographics, but with the 2010 sample being slightly more male and younger. Some adjustments were made to the 2010 questionnaire to reflect the emergence of new social media such as Twitter.

4. Findings

Patterns of use

Xiang and Gretzel (2009) provide evidence that travellers are likely to find social media related sites during their online information search queries. However, it is not clear whether travellers actively seek out social media sites

Table 15.1 Websites Used for Planning Overnight Pleasure Trips

Website Type Used	2008 (% of online travellers)	2010 (% of online travellers)
Online Travel Agency/ Auction	52.4	43.1
Search Engine	48.6	51.1
Service Provider	46.0	35.3
Tour Operator	4.8	5.2
Full Service Travel Agency	7.2	7.3
Destination	24.8	23.0
Travel-Related Blogs/ Communities	8.6	5.7
Travel Price Comparison	12.1	10.8
Travel Sales/Special Websites	7.7	5.9
Photo/Video Sharing	N/A	4.6
Social Networking	N/A	8.1

when planning overnight pleasure trips. The two surveys asked travellers to indicate which websites they used during their online travel planning efforts. The Results (Table 15.1) show that online travel agency and auction sites (Expedia, Travelocity, Priceline, etc.), general search engines (Google, Yahoo!, etc.) and service provider websites (airlines, hotels, rental cars, etc.) are most prominently used in online travel searches. However, pure social media sites like blogs and communities as well as photo/video sharing sites and social networking sites are also used in the context of online travel planning. The results are pretty stable over time, except for online travel agencies and service providers losing ground in 2010.

When asked whether they used contents/media created by other travellers, about half of the respondents indicated that they did and this result was almost exactly the same for both years (Table 15.2). The high percentage of people stating that they use social media but lower percentages of users of pure social media sites suggests that social media embedded in travel websites such as online travel agency and destination sites are important.

In terms of types of social media used, travel reviews are the most prominent form (Table 15.3). Photos posted by others are also frequently used as input in travel planning processes. Audio files/podcasts and tweets are only used by a minority of online travellers who use social media. The difference between 2008

Table 15.2 Use of Travel-Related Consumer-Generated Media

Did you read comments/ materials posted online by other travellers in the course of planning your most recent overnight pleasure trip?	2008 (% of online travellers)	2010 (% of online travellers)
Yes	50.5	49.2

Table 15.3 Types of Social Media Used

Type of Social Media	2008 (% of social media users)	2010 (% of social media users)
Travel Reviews	80.5	71.8
Tweets	N/A	6.9
Photos	50.6	54.9
Videos	14.2	23.9
Blogs	21.8	21.7
Comments on Blogs	23.6	25.6
Postings in Discussion Forums	22.4	21.9
Audio files/Podcasts	3.8	4.6

and 2010 in terms of videos could be to some extent due to the significant gender influence on video use and the slightly higher male ratio in the 2010 sample.

Analyses were also conducted to see whether specific types of social media were connected to broad overall social media use. Table 15.4 shows that of those who use social media for travel, many only use one or two types, while some use three. However, there is also a small portion of online travellers who use social media very broadly.

The number of social media types used was then linked to the specific forms of social media. The results (Table 15.5) show that of those who use just one type, most use travel reviews, followed by photos. Looking at when specific types reach at least 50 per cent penetration, tweets and videos are connected only with the broadest levels of use while podcasts are still not widely used even by those who use five or more social media types for travel planning.

Impact on travel planning

One of the most important questions to answer is whether social media actually influence travellers' decisions. Table 15.6 shows that a considerable percentage

Table 15.4 Number of Social Media Types Used

Number of Social Media Types Used	2008 (% of social media users)	2010 (% of social media users)
1	38.8	39.3
2	29.0	23.9
3	17.3	18.0
4	8.5	9.8
5 or more	6.5	9.2

Table 15.5 Social Media Use Scope

	Number of Social Media Types Used									
Social Media Type	**1**		**2**		**3**		**4**		**5 or more**	
	2008	**2010**	**2008**	**2010**	**2008**	**2010**	**2008**	**2010**	**2008**	**2010**
Travel Reviews	73.0	54.7	85.1	79.1	85.6	85.5	90.2	82.2	100	95.7
Tweets	-	1.1	-	1.8	-	6.0	-	17.8	-	60.2
Photos	12.4	20.4	70.1	65.5	77.9	80.7	74.5	82.2	100	98.3
Videos	2.1	6.6	6.3	10.0	23.1	38.6	39.2	44.4	77.8	82.4
Blogs	3.9	3.3	12.1	11.8	30.8	21.7	68.6	57.8	92.6	95.7
Blog comments	3.9	8.3	11.5	13.6	42.3	31.3	68.6	60.0	94.4	89.8
Discussion forum postings	3.9	5.5	14.9	15.5	39.4	32.5	52.9	53.3	87.0	83.6
Audio/ podcasts	0.9	0.0	0.0	2.7	1.0	3.6	5.9	2.2	48.1	44.4

of online travellers who use social media perceives at least some impact on their decision-making. The greatest impact is felt with respect to where to stay, which is not surprising given the dominance of travel reviews, which most often are written regarding hotels. However, activities and restaurant choices are also very much

Table 15.6 Influence of Social Media Use on Travel Decisions

Travel Decision	2008 (% of social media users)	2010 (% of social media users)
Where to go	57.2	68.8
How to go there	52.5	59.5
When to go	51.5	61.4
What to do	75.2	76.6
Where to stay overnight	81.0	81.8
Where to eat	68.3	76.6
Where to shop	56.2	65.1

influenced. In general, greater impacts were perceived by the social media users in the 2010 study compared to the 2008 respondents.

Impacts were also measured with respect to certain travel information search behaviours. About half of those who use social media for travel planning indicated that the use changed their information search behaviours (Table 15.7). In general, these influences were even higher in 2010. The most influenced aspects of travel information search are the amount of time spent on advance planning, the number of information sources used, and the amount of print-outs taken on the trip. In all cases, social media use tended to increase these facets of travel planning.

Characteristics of users and creators

While half of online travellers are social media users, only about 20 per cent of online travellers have ever posted travel-related contents online (Table 15.8). When looking at social media users, the percentage increases but is still rather low, indicating that a majority of social media users solely consume contents. Thus, it is important to not only understand who uses social media but also to analyse who the content creators are.

As far as the socio-demographic characteristics of social media users are concerned, there were no gender differences between users and non-users. However, there were significant differences in terms of age, with social media users being younger than non-users. Social media users are also less likely divorced/separated/widowed than non-users and are more likely employed full-time. No significant differences exist regarding education level and income. Social media users are also more likely Hispanic or Asian in ethnic origin than non-users.

Comparing those who create travel-related social media to those online travellers who do not, again no significant gender differences can be found but age differences do emerge with younger online travellers being more likely social media creators. In addition, social media creators are more likely single and again

Table 15.7 Influence of Social Media on Travel Information Search

Travel Information Search Behaviour	2008 (% of social media users)	2010 (% of social media users)
Number of destinations considered	44	45.9
Amount of time spent on advance planning	49.5	55.8
Number of information sources used	55.3	56.5
Use of ads (TV, radio, press) for travel ideas	41.5	45.9
Stops at visitor information centres	43.6	47.2
Likelihood of buying travel guidebooks/maps	45.9	48.4
Number of travel brochures ordered	45.3	48.6
Amount of print-outs taken on trips	52.2	52.1

Table 15.8 Travel-Related Social Media Creators

Have you ever posted travel related comments/materials online?	2008 (% of online travellers)	2008 (% of social media users)	2010 (% of online travellers)	2010 (% of social media users)
Yes	17.0	27.0	21.9	37.2

more likely employed full-time. Similar to social media users, no significant differences in terms of education and income emerged. Regarding ethnic origin, social media creators are more likely Asian.

5. Summary and Discussion

Social media are not used by all online travellers for travel planning but by a substantial number of them. The findings related to usage patterns show that although new social media constantly emerge, the patterns were pretty stable from 2008 to 2010. Also, the results clearly indicate that social media used for travel planning are not equal. Some appeal to a broad group of travellers while others are only used by those who use social media extensively. Online travellers not only use social media, the information derived from them has a considerable impact on travel decisions, most notably where to stay, what to do and where to eat. Social media use also changes information search behaviours in that it leads to more time spent planning, more information sources used and more print-outs taken on the trip for at least half of the social media users. Thus, interestingly, social media use expands information search and use instead of providing efficiencies.

While many online travellers use social media for their travel planning, only a small portion actively contributes contents. From a practical point of view, it is very important to understand who these users are and even more essential to examine by whom social media contents are created. The findings show that age, marital status, employment status and ethnic origin are important drivers of both travel social media use and creation.

The findings mostly confirm what the existing literature has found: social media are important information sources for travellers and influence travel planning and decision-making. However, the results presented in this chapter suggest that while overall social media use statistics are useful to understand global patterns, great differences exist among the various types of social media. These differences have so far not received sufficient attention. Further, the research confirmed that social media users and social media creators differ from the general population of online travellers in terms of demographic characteristics. This means that market insights derived from social media contents do not necessarily reflect general opinions.

This chapter provided an American perspective on social media use and creation in tourism. However, its general approach in terms of conceptualizing use and influence provides an overall framework that is applicable to other contexts. It showed that there are degrees in use linked to types of social media. It further illustrated that social media are not just another information source but rather fundamentally change travel planning for those who use them. At the same time, it has to be recognized that social media use has not completely replaced other forms of online travel information search but rather speaks to a certain group of travellers.

References

Acar, A.S. and Polonsky, M. 2007. Online social networks and insights into marketing communications. *Journal of Internet Commerce*, 6(4), 55-72.

Adology Research 2009. *Travel & Vacation Services-Summer 2009*. Available at: http://www.ad-ology.com/ [accessed: 12 November 2010].

Arsal, I., Backman, S. and Baldwin, E. 2008. Influence of an Online Travel Community on Travel Decisions, in *Information and Communication Technologies in Tourism 2008,* edited by P. O'Connor, W. Höpken and U. Gretzel. Vienna: Springer Verlag, 82-93.

Braun-LaTour, K.A., Grinley, M.J. and Loftus, E.F. 2006. Tourist memory distortion. *Journal of Travel Research*, 44(4), 360-367.

Brown, M. 2009. *AdReaction 2009: Brands + Consumers + Social Media.* Available at: http://www.millwardbrown.com/Home.aspx [accessed: 1 November 2010].

Burgess, S., Sellitto, C., Cox, C. and Buultjens, J. 2009. Trust perceptions of online travel information by different content creators: Some social and legal implications. *Information Systems Frontiers*. Available at: http://www.springerlink.com/content/042534467t55m0t5/ [accessed: 28 August 2009].

Carrera, P., Chiu, C-Y., Pratipwattanawong, P., Chienwattanasuk, S., Ahmad, S.F.S. and Murphy, J. 2008. My Space, My Friends, My Customers, in *Information and Communication Technologies in Tourism 2008*, edited by P. O'Connor, W. Höpken and U. Gretzel. Vienna: Springer Verlag, 94-105.

Chaffey, D., Ellis-Chadwick, F., Mayer, R. and Johnston, K. 2009. *Internet Marketing: Strategy, Implementation and Practice* (4th Edition). Upper Saddle River, NJ: Prentice Hall.

Charlesworth, A. 2009. The ascent of smartphone. *Engineering & Technology*, 4(3), 32-33.

Chung, J.Y. and Buhalis, D. 2008. WEB 2.0: A study of online travel community, in *Information and Communication Technologies in Tourism 2008,* edited by P. O'Connor, W. Höpken and U. Gretzel. Vienna: Springer Verlag, 70-81.

ComScore 2010. *comScore Reports February 2010 U.S. Mobile Subscriber Market Share.* Available at: http://www.comscore.com/Press_Events/Press_Releases/2010/4/comScore_Reports_February_2010_U.S._Mobile_Subscriber_Market_Share [accessed: 1 November 2010].

Cox, C., Burgess, S., Sellitto, C. and Buultjens, J. 2009. The role of user-generated content in tourists' travel planning behavior. *Journal of Hospitality Marketing and Management*, 18(8), 743-764.

Constantinides, E. and Fountain, S.J. 2008. Web 2.0: Conceptual foundations and marketing issues. *Journal of Direct, Data and Digital Marketing Practice*, 9(3), 231-244.

Douglas, A. and Mills, J. 2006. Logging Brand Personality Online: Content Analysis of Middle Eastern and North African Destinations, in *Information and Communication Technologies in Tourism 2006*, edited by M. Hitz, M. Sigala and J. Murphy. Vienna: Springer Verlag, 345.

eMarketer 2009a. *Online Leisure Travel: Six Post-recession Trends.* Available at: http://www.emarketer.com [accessed: 5 November 2010].

eMarketer 2009b. *Demographic Profile of US Social Network Users, by Network*, May 2009. Available at: http://www.emarketer.com [accessed: August 2009].

eMarketer 2010. *Types of Online Sources Used to Research Travelers*, June 2010. Available at: http://www.eMarketer.com [accessed: 20 September 2010].

Forrester 2007. *Forrester's New Social Technographics Report*. Available at: http://www.forrester.com [accessed: 5 November 2010]

Gretzel, U. 2006. Consumer generated content – trends and implications for branding. *e-Review of Tourism Research*, 4(3), 9-11.

Gretzel, U., Kang, M. and Lee, W. 2008. Differences in Consumer-Generated Media Adoption and Use: A Cross-National Perspective. *Journal of Hospitality Marketing and Management*, 17(1/2), 99-120.

Gretzel, U., Lee, Y-J., Tussyadiah, I. and D.R. Fesenmaier 2009. Recounting Tourism Experiences: The Role of New Media. *International Conference on Tourist Experiences: Meanings, Motivations, Behaviours*, 1-4 April 2009, Preston, UK.

Gretzel, U. and Yoo, K-H. 2008. Use and Impact of Online Travel Reviews. *Information and Communication Technologies in Tourism 2008*, edited by P. O'Connor, W. Höpken and U. Gretzel. Vienna: Springer Verlag, 35-46.

Jeng, S-P. and Teng, C-I. 2008. Personality and motivations for playing online games. *Social Behavior and Personality*, 36(8), 1053-1060.

Jupiter Research 2008. *US Online Travel Consumer Survey, 2008*. Available at: http://www.jupiterresearch.com/bin/item.pl/home/ [accessed: 20 November 2010].

Jones, S. and Fox, S. 2009. Generations Online in 2009. Pew Internet & American Life Project. Available at: http://www.pewinternet.org/Reports/2009/Generations-Online-in-2009.aspx

Kaplan, A.M. and Haenlein, M. 2010. Users of the world, unite! The challenges and opportunities of Social Media. *Business Horizons*, 53, 59-68.

Karlsson, L. 2006. The Diary Weblog and the Travelling Tales of Diasporic Tourists. *Journal of Intercultural Studies*, 27(3), 299-312.

Kim, W.G., Lee, C. and Hiemstra, S.J. 2004. Effects of an online virtual community on customer loyalty and travel product purchases. *Tourism Management*, 25, 343-355.

Lee, Y., Yoo, K-H. and Gretzel, U. 2009. Social Identity Formation Through Blogging: Comparison of U.S. and Korean travel blogs. *Proceedings of the 14th Annual Graduate Student Research Conference in Hospitality and Tourism*. Las Vegas.

Lenhart, A., Madden, M., Macgill, A.R. and Smith, A. 2007. *Teens and Social Media.* Pew Internet & American Life Project. Available at: http://www.pewinternet.org/Reports/2007/Teens-and-Social-Media.aspx [accessed: 5 May 2008].

Lin, Y-S. and Huang, J-Y. 2006. Internet blogs as a tourism marketing medium: A case study. *Journal of Business Research*, 59, 1201-1205.

Litvin, S.W., Goldsmith, R.E. and Pan, B. 2008. Electronic word-of-mouth in hospitality and tourism management. *Tourism Management*, 29(3), 458-468.

Mack, R.W., Blose, J.E. and Pan, B. 2008. Believe it or not: Credibility of blogs in tourism. *Journal of Vacation Marketing*, 14(2), 133-144.

Nielsenwire 2009. *Global Advertising: Consumers Trust Real Friends and Virtual Strangers the Most.* Available at: http://blog.nielsen.com/nielsenwire/consumer/global-advertisingconsumers-trust-real-friends-and-virtual-strangers-the-most/ [accessed: 25 April 2010].

Nonnecke, B. and Preece, J. 2001. *Why Lurkers Lurk.* Proceeding of Seventh Americas Conference on Information Systems, Boston.

O'Connor, P. 2008. User-Generated Content and travel: A case study on TripAdvisor.com, in *Information and Communication Technologies in Tourism*

2008, edited by P. O'Connor, W. Höpken and U. Gretzel. Vienna: Springer Verlag, 47-58.

O'Reilly, T. 2005. *What is Web 2.0. Design Patterns and Business Models for the Next Generation of Software*. Available at: http://oreilly.com/web2/archive/what-is-web-20.html [accessed: 10 November 2009].

Pan, B., MacLaurin, T. and Crotts, J.C. 2007. Travel Blogs and the Implications for Destination Marketing. *Journal of Travel Research*, 46, 35-45.

Parra-Lopez, E., Bulchand-Gidumal, J., Gutierrez-Tano, D. and Díaz-Armas, R. 2010. Intentions to use social media in organizing and taking vacation trips. Computers in Human Behavior, Available at: www.elsevier.com/locate/comphumbeh [accessed: 20 November 2010].

Parise, S. and Guinan, P.J. 2008. Marketing Using Web 2.0. *Proceedings of the 41st Hawaii International Conference on System Sciences.*

Pew Research Center's Internet & American Life Project 2010. Gadget Ownership. Available at: http://pewresearch.org/pubs/1763/americans-and-their-gadgets-technology-devices

PhoCusWright 2006. *Travel 2.0, Web 2.0, Services and Silver Bullets*. Available at: www.phocuswright.com [accessed: 20 November 2010].

PhoCusWright 2008. *The PhoCusWright Consumer Travel Trends Survey Tenth Edition*. Available at: www.phocuswright.com [accessed: 23 June 2009].

Pudliner, B.A. 2007. Alternative Literature and Tourist Experience: Travel and Tourist Weblogs. *Journal of Tourism and Cultural Change*, 5(1), 46-59.

Ross, C., Orr, E.S., Sisic, M., Arseneault, J.M., Simmering, M.G. and Orr, R.R. 2009. Personality and motivations associated with Facebook use. *Computers in Human Behavior*, 25, 578-586.

Schmallegger, D. and Carson, D. 2008. Blogs in tourism: Changing approaches to information exchange. *Journal of Vacation Marketing*, 14(2), 99-110.

Shao, G. 2009. Understanding the appeal of user-generated media: A uses and gratification perspective. *Internet Research*, 19(1), 7-25.

Sigala, M. 2008. WEB 2.0, social marketing strategies and distribution channels for city destinations: Enhancing the participatory role of travelers and exploiting their collective intelligence, in *Information Communication Technologies and City Marketing: Digital Opportunities for Cities around the World,* edited by M. Gascó-Hernández and T. Torres-Coronas. Hershey, PA: Information Science Publishing.

Technorati 2010. *State of the Blogosphere, 2010*. Available at: http://technorati.com/blogging/article/who-bloggers-brands-and-consumers-day/ [accessed: 10 November 2010].

Tedjamulia, S.J.J., Olsen, D.R., Dean, D.L. and Albrecht, C.C. 2005. Motivating Content Contributions to Online Communities: Toward a More Comprehensive Theory, in *Proceedings of the 38th Hawaii International Conference on System Sciences (HICSS).*

Thevenot, G. 2007. Blogging as social media. *Tourism and Hospitality Research*, 7, 287-289.

Time December, 2006. *Time's Person of the Year: You.* Available at: http://www.time.com [accessed: 10 November 2010].

Tnooz 2010. *How Travellers Use Technology to Search, Book and Play when Away.* Available at: http://www.tnooz.com/2010/08/12/news/survey-how-travellers-use-technology-to-search-book-and-play-when-away/[accessed: 23 June 2009]

Tussyadiah, I.P. and D.R. Fesenmaier 2008. Marketing Places through First-Person Stories: An Analysis of Pennsylvania Roadtripper Blog. *Journal of Travel & Tourism Marketing*, 25(3-4): 299-311.

Tussyadiah, I.P. and D.R. Fesenmaier 2009. Mediating Tourists Experiences – Access to Places via Shared Videos. *Annals of Tourism Research*, 36(1), 24-40.

Van Dijck, J. 2009. Users like you? Theorizing agency in user-generated content. *Media, Culture & Society*, 31(1), 41-58.

Verna, P. 2009. *User-Generated Content: More Popular than Profitable?* eMarketer. Available at: http://www.emarketer.com [accessed: 30 June 2009].

Vermeulen, I.E. and Seegers, D. 2009. Tried and tested: The impact of online hotel reviews on consumer considerations. *Tourism Management*, 30(1), 123-127.

Volo, S. 2010. Bloggers' reported tourist experiences: Their utility as a tourism data source and their effect on prospective tourists. *Journal of Vacation Marketing*, 16(4), 297-311.

Wang, Y. and Fesenmaier, D.R. 2004a. Modeling participation in an Online Travel Community. *Journal of Travel Research*, 42(3), 261-270.

Wang, Y. and Fesenmaier, D.R. 2004b. Towards understanding members' general participation in and active contribution to an online travel community. *Tourism Management*, 25(6), 709-722.

Wang, Y., Yu, Q. and Fesenmaier, D.R. 2001. Defining Virtual Tourism Community, in *Information and Communication Technologies in Tourism* 2001, edited by P. Sheldon, K. Wöber and D.R. Fesenmaier. Vienna: Springer Verlag, 262-271.

Wenger, A. 2008. Analysis of travel bloggers' characteristics and their communication about Austria as a tourism destination. *Journal of Vacation Marketing*, 14(2), 169-176.

Xiang, Z. and Gretzel, U. 2009. Role of social media in online travel information search, *Tourism Management*, 31(2), 179-188.

Xie, F. and Liew, A.A. 2008. Podcasting and tourism: An exploratory study of types, approaches and content. *Journal of Information Technology & Tourism*, 10(2), 173-180.

Yoo, K-H. and Gretzel, U. 2008a. What motivates consumers to write online travel reviews? *Information Technology & Tourism*, 10(4), 283-295.

Yoo, K-H. and Gretzel, U. 2008b. The Influence of Involvement on Use and Impact of Online Travel Reviews. *Hospitality Information Technology Association (HITA) Conference*, Austin, TX, 15-16 June 2008.

Yoo, K-H. and Gretzel, U. 2008c. Understanding Differences Between Online Travel Review Writers and Non-Writers, in *Proceedings of the 13th Annual*

Graduate Education and Student Research, edited by T. Hara. Conference in Hospitality and Tourism, Orlando, FL, 3-5 January 2008, 21-29.

Yoo, K-H. and Gretzel, U. 2009. Generational Differences in CGM Perceptions and Use for Travel Planning. *Proceedings of the 40th Annual Conference of the Travel and Tourism Research Association*, Honolulu, HI.

Yoo, K-H. and Gretzel, U. 2010. Influence of personality on travel-related consumer-generated media creation. *Computers in Human Behavior*. Available at: www.elsevier.com/locate/comphumbeh [accessed: 27 November 2010].

Yoo, K-H., Lee, K.S. and Gretzel, U. 2007. The role of Source Characteristics in eWOM: What Makes Online Travel Reviewers Credible and Likeable?, in *Information and Communication Technologies in Tourism 2007*, edited by M. Sigala, L. Mich, J. Murphy and A. Frew. Edinburgh: Axon Imprint, 23-34.

Yoo, K-H., Lee, Y-J., Gretzel, U. and Fesenmaier, D.R. 2009. Trust in Travel-Related Consumer Generated Media, in *Information and Communication Technologies in Tourism 2009*, edited by W. Höpken, U. Gretzel and R. Law. Vienna: Springer Verlag, 49-60.

Chapter 16
Users' Attitudes Toward Online Social Networks in Travel

Khaldoon "Khal" Nusair, Mehmet Erdem, Fevzi Okumus and Anil Bilgihan

1. Introduction

Over the last 12 years the Internet has completely transformed how travel is bought and sold. With the advancements of Internet technologies, increasing numbers of travellers are using the Internet to seek destination information and to conduct transactions online. According to the Travel Industry Association of America (TIA 2005), 67 per cent of US travellers have used the Internet to search for information on destinations or check prices or schedules. In addition, 41 per cent of US travellers have booked at least some aspects of their trips via the medium (Litvin, Goldsmith and Pan 2008). However, the emphasis in the online experience began to shift from selling, searching, and consuming to creating, connecting and exchanging (Quinby 2010).

Throughout the last few years, the overall trend in travel businesses worldwide has been the adoption of new e-marketing strategies that utilize the ever-advancing Internet technology applications available today. One of the foremost technology applications used in travel business promotion has been the use of online social networking (OSN) websites. Boyd and Ellison (2007) define OSN as Internet applications that allow users to form connections with companies or other users that would not have been formed otherwise. While consumers find emotional and practical benefits in participating in online discussions, these conversations tend to have profound commercial implications (Riegner 2007).

Social networking focuses on building online communities of people who share interests and activities, or who are interested in exploring the interests and activities of others. It includes the ability to browse, search, and invite friends to interact, share reviews, comments, blog entries, discussions, events, videos, ratings, music and more. OSN sites typically allow users to create a "profile" and to exchange public or private messages and list other users or groups they are connected to in some way. Content of social media sites may include text, images, video or any other media.

Recently we have witnessed an expansion of Online Social Networks (OSNs) into travel. Thus, before and during vacation trips, travellers use the Online Social

Networks to obtain information about the trips and to share their experiences related to the trip. Research has shown that 88 per cent of leisure travellers reported being influenced by online travel reviews (Steinbrink 2008). Gretzel and Yoo (2008) found that travel review readers seek information from virtual travel communities, travel guidebook sites, and travel distribution sites. They found travellers to be concerned with cleanliness, hotel location, hotel guest room size, staff, hotel facilities and breakfast (Stringam and Gerdes 2010). Overall, the role of OSN websites, such as Twitter remains an evolving and often elusive opportunity for travel marketers (Quinby 2010).

As OSNs are becoming more popular, researchers have begun to observe its usefulness as marketing tools. The growth and impact of the OSNs on travel cannot be underestimated. Users of social network sites chat about travel experiences on Myspace, YouTube, Facebook, and blogs. It requires monitoring of customers' reviews in order to defend their online reputation. OSNs help businesses to create, to learn about competitors, and to intercept potential prospects (Mahajan 2009). Additionally, e-word-of-mouth through OSNs will inevitably change the structure of travel information, the accessibility of travel information, and subsequently travellers' knowledge and perception of various travel products (Litvin et al., 2008). With respect to online social networks like Facebook, Twitter, and Myspace, there has been some research focusing on travellers, but most studies have been rather limited in scope. The purpose of this study is twofold: (1) to examine the primary OSNs that are used for travel purposes; (2) to examine users' perceived experience and attitude towards the use of OSNs.

2. Literature Review

Online social networks

Different types of OSNs include not only the most popular sites like Facebook, Twitter, and Myspace, but also include wikis, blogs, message boards, podcasts, and vlogs (Thevenot 2007). OSNs allow users to create profiles, invite friends, send emails and instant messages, and post video, photo, audio, and blog content. OSNs can be divided by the application usage and type. Kaplan and Haenlein (2009) suggest that there are six major forms of social networks: collaborative projects, blogs, content communities, social networking sites, virtual game worlds, and virtual social words. These six forms identify a more general categorization of the social network applications while Chul, Miller, and Roberts (2009) categorize social network technologies into five categories that are based on more of a managerial perspective. These five categories include broad collaboration, broad communication, collective estimation, metadata creation, and social graphing. Overall, OSNs include a wide range of new technological applications such as media and content syndication, mash-ups, AJAX, tagging, wiki, web forums and message boards, customer ratings, podcasting, blogs, and online videos (Schmallegger and Carson 2008).

An increasing number of travellers are using the OSNs for travel decisions (Vermeulen and Seegers 2009). According to a recent survey, more than 74 per cent of travellers use the comments of other consumers when planning trips for pleasure (Gretzel and Yoo 2008). Contemporary travellers benefit from the Internet to acquire travel related information, share their experiences/opinions/reviews for hotels, resorts, inns, vacations, travel packages, vacation packages, travel guides to reduce their risk before purchase (Xiang and Gretzel 2010). Travellers reviews have a significant impact on business performance, with a 10 per cent increase in traveller review ratings boosting online bookings by more than five per cent (Ye, Law, Gu, and Chen 2010). It is estimated that the online reviews influence more than US$10 billion in online travel purchases every year (Compete 2007).

According to Xiang and Gretzel (2010), the top five OSNs in travel are: Tripadvsisor, Virtualtouris, Igougo, Mytravel, and Yelp. Online Social Network websites about destinations, hotels and tourism have become important sources of information for travellers (Pan, MacLaurin, and Crotts 2007). The main reason for using OSN is the benefits (social, functional and psychological and hedonic) that the user can get (Parra-López, Bulchand-Gidumal, Gutiérrez-Taño, Díaz-Armas 2010). Social benefit is linked to the level of participation in the use of social media when planning vacation trips (Chung and Buhalis 2008). In addition, Wang and Fesenmaier (2004) considered the psychological and hedonic benefits as important factors for users to involve in social networks.

Most popular online social networks

Not all OSN sites or blogs specialize in travel, but some present social discussions and postings about travel experiences by all types of travellers including businesses, families, and groups. This section will focus on leading social network technologies that have been used in travel: Facebook, Myspace, Twitter, Flickr, and TripAdvisor.

1. Facebook Facebook was created in early 2004 by Mark Zuckerberg, Dustin Moskovitz, Chris Hughes, and Eduardo Saverin. Facebook is considered the largest social network with over 350 million users. The median age of a Facebook user is 26 (Morgan 2009). For the week ending 30 January 2010, visits to Facebook accounted for 49.23 per cent of the overall number of visits to all of the top twenty social networking websites combined. The Trips application, a social travel application built on Facebook Platform, enables Facebook users to share their travel plans and to make new friends while travelling. Trips application is a powerful tool that helps users to plan trips and sharing travel experiences. Users can search for other users who have similar travel interests and discover who will be travelling or has travelled to the destination of their interest (Grant-Braham 2007).

2. Twitter Twitter is the most recent OSN that has evolved in a short amount of time. Twitter, founded on 21 March 2006, is a form of microblogging that limits users to posts with 140 characters or less. Twitter accounted for 1.12 per cent of the overall social networking site visits (Experian Hitwise 2010). The median age of a user of this social network is 31 years old (Morgan 2009). In February 2009, it was ranked as the third most popular social network site in terms of the number of users, with 55 million visitors generated by 6 million visitors (Kazeniac 2009). Twitter has become a popular method for tracking and directing the consumer's attention to travel related products and services (World Tourism 2009).

3. Myspace Myspace was launched in mid 2003 in Santa Monica, California by Tom Anderson. A recent study by Experian Hitwise stated that Myspace earned 16.36 per cent of the overall visits to social networking sites. Young users (in their teens and 20s) are most prevalent on Myspace (Caverlee and Webb 2008). Myspace is growing fast in use and popularity among travellers who want to document and share travel related experiences (Gretzel 2006).

4. Flickr Flickr can also be categorized as a content community in which users do not have to create a profile to view content. Flickr was developed by Ludicorp in 2004 and later purchased by Yahoo in 2005. Flickr emerged as a rich media sharing site allows millions of travellers to share their travel experiences through pictures. Flickr has over two billion pictures stored and over forty million visitors each month (Flickr.com).

5. TripAdvisor TripAdvisor was established in 2000 and since then has become a major travel information site. TripAdvisor has over twenty million unique visitors each month (ComScore 2009). TripAdvisor features more than 10,000,000 traveller reviews which have been used members to plan nearly 17,000,000 trips within one week. A study by Gretzel et al. (2007) found that looking at other tourists' comments and travel blogs was the most popular online activity on TripAdvisor. Collaborative projects are the creation of many end-users who can add, remove, and change content. Travel businesses should be aware of the impact that collaborative projects can have on their businesses because of the increasing trend toward becoming a main source of information for end-users (Kaplan and Haenlein 2009). TripAdvisor is the world's largest travel information and advice site with over five million unbiased reviews covering 220,000 hotels and attractions worldwide.

Online social network websites and word-of-mouth

Word-of-mouth (WOM) communication is perceived to be reliable, creditable, and trustworthy (Shiffman and Kanuk 1995). According to recent research, marketers spent more than $1.5 billion in WOM initiatives in 2008, and the amount is expected to rise to $3 billion in 2013 (PQ Media 2009). WOM in the context of OSN websites is of interest to scholars and practitioners because of the extraordinary growth, popularity, and influence of such networks. Firms are intentionally pushing for consumer-to-consumer communications through WOM communications (Kozinets, de Valck, Wojinicki and Wilner 2010). Users of OSN sites interact for information related to travel and thus those applications are essential to spread positive WOM. A recent study denotes that people appear to trust unbiased views from users outside their immediate social network, such as online reviews (Duanna, Gub, and Whinstion 2008). Moreover, the Internet developed rapidly as an information medium for tourists and a platform for tourism organizations to represent themselves (Dickinger and Bauernfeind 2009). Web 2.0 presented new applications changing the users' communication on a social basis. As a result, electronic-word-of-mouth (eWOM) became an uprising trend for consumers. In some instances, eWOM is a way of sharing insider information before deciding to engage business with a firm. Jansen, Zhang, Sobel, and Chowdury (2009) brought to light that 19 per cent of the postings on Twitter contain a brand name for a product or service. Of these postings, more than half of them were positive; however, 33 per cent were unfavourable to the company, or product.

Online social network websites and users' attitude

An investigation into the attitude of users toward OSN websites will have practical and theoretical implications. Attitude is defined as the degree to which the individual favours the behaviour being examined (Ajzen 1991). Ajzen and Fishbein (1980) demonstrate that attitudes toward an object influence intentions and ultimately influence behaviour and use of the object. Literature highlights that attitude towards technology is one of the most common construct variables for technology adoption and acceptance (Fetscherin and Lattemann 2008). The increased usage of OSNs in travel makes it important to develop an understanding of users and attitudes toward these sites. User's perceptions about OSN sites usage may be developed while they participate. The intrinsic motivation such as enjoyment is a significant antecedent of attitude toward using OSNs (Hsu and Lin 2008). Gangadharbtla (2008) reports that Internet self-efficacy, need to belong, and collective self-esteem have positive effects on attitudes toward OSNs. Tourism is an information-intense industry (Sheldon 1997; Werthner and Klein 1999); therefore, it is critical to understand changes in technologies and consumer behaviour that impact the distribution and accessibility of travel-related information (Xiang and Gretzel 2010). In technology usage contexts, cognitive dissonance theory (CDT) implies that users' pre-usage cognitions (e.g., attitude) are typically based on second-hand information, such as vendor claims, communicated via interpersonal or mass media channels. Over time, as users gain first-hand experience with technology usage, they evaluate the extent to which their initial cognition is consonant or dissonant with their actual experience, and revise their cognition and/or behaviour to achieve greater consonance (Bhattacherjee and Premkumar

2004). Social networking sites offer a space in which people can satisfy the need to belong to that particular community by using services provided by the site.

3. Methodology

Profile of the participants of the study:

During the months of May-August 2010, 20,000 emails have been sent to random sample residing in the US who have an email address through rent-a-list.com company's database and have used online social networks for travel related purposes. Subjects were asked questions related to online social network sites (e.g. their favourite site, their preferred method to access the site, purpose of using the site, etc.). In total, 2578 respondents clicked on the link for the questionnaire in the invitation email. After removing the incomplete responses, 538 questionnaires were left for data analysis.

Descriptive data was collected to define the profile of respondents. The gender profile of respondents was similar to previous studies where majority of OSN users are female. In this study the gap was larger than other similar studies where 68 per cent were female while 32 per cent were male. Several media reports over the last few years have indicated that females tend to spend more time on Social Network websites than men. In addition, the majority of respondents were Caucasian (68 per cent) while the remaining 32 per cent included Native Americans (1 per cent), Asian/Pacific Islanders (5 per cent), African Americans (13 per cent), Hispanics (6 per cent) and other races (7 per cent). The socioeconomic status of the sample revealed that the majority have some college education (35 per cent) and an annual household income of less than $50,000 (56 per cent). About 20 per cent have a 4-year college degree and 12 per cent have graduate education. 40 per cent of the participants are employed full-time while 23 per cent are employed part-time. A significant portion of the respondents, 37 per cent reported that they are currently not working. Interestingly, 51 per cent of the respondents are between 35 and 54 years of age, while 7 per cent are less than 24 and 5 per cent are between 65 and 74 years of age. Forty-seven per cent are married, while the rest are single (18 per cent), divorced/separated (16 per cent), widowed (4 per cent) or unmarried couples living together (15 per cent). It should be noted that the use of an on-line survey and panel company involves the use of large e-mail databases and may introduce certain limitations and biases into the sampling procedures. Therefore, the profile provided may be somewhat similar but not identical with that of the average social media user in the US. Overall, the OSN user that was most represented in this study can be described as a Caucasian female, who was between 35 and 54 years of age, married, employed full time with less than $50,000 annual household income and with some college education. The descriptive statistics provide clues as to the type of user who spent time using social networks. In order to better understand

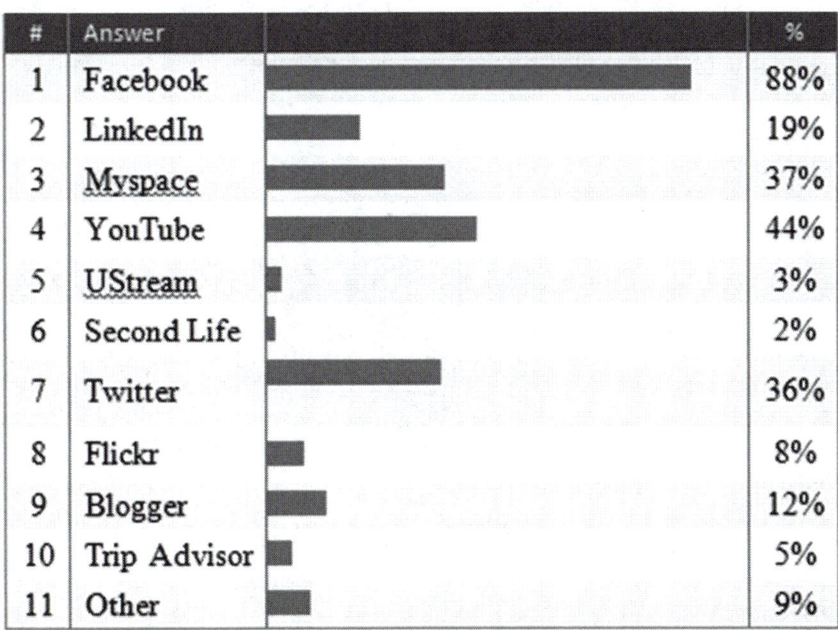

#	Answer	%
1	Facebook	88%
2	LinkedIn	19%
3	Myspace	37%
4	YouTube	44%
5	UStream	3%
6	Second Life	2%
7	Twitter	36%
8	Flickr	8%
9	Blogger	12%
10	Trip Advisor	5%
11	Other	9%

Figure 16.1 Reported Usage for Social Networking and UCG Websites

usage and preferences, further questions were included. These are discussed in the following section.

Usage and Preferences for Social Networking Websites

There are numerous OSNs as well as user generated content sites. It is important to capture the preferences of users to identify sites that address the ever evolving needs and expectations of OSN users. The participants surveyed indicated using a variety of social networking and user generated content (UGC) websites. The most popular social networking website in travel appears to be Facebook, which is used by 88 per cent of the respondents. This result confirms the increased popularity of Facebook over the past few years. YouTube, a user generated content site, ranks second in terms of usage (44 per cent), followed by Myspace (37 per cent) and Twitter (36 per cent). Less than 10 per cent of the respondents have indicated usage of other social networking websites such as Friendster, tagged, myYearbook and PeopleString (See Figure 16.1). It should be noted that these preferences are likely to differ based on geographic representation of respondents across the world. The reported usage of OSNs in this study is similar to past US based consumer studies reported in the news media. Facebook's dominance in this market, so far, seems to be inevitable at least for the foreseeable future. The "connecting power" of Facebook seems to be making this particular network the most appealing for almost everyone across the board.

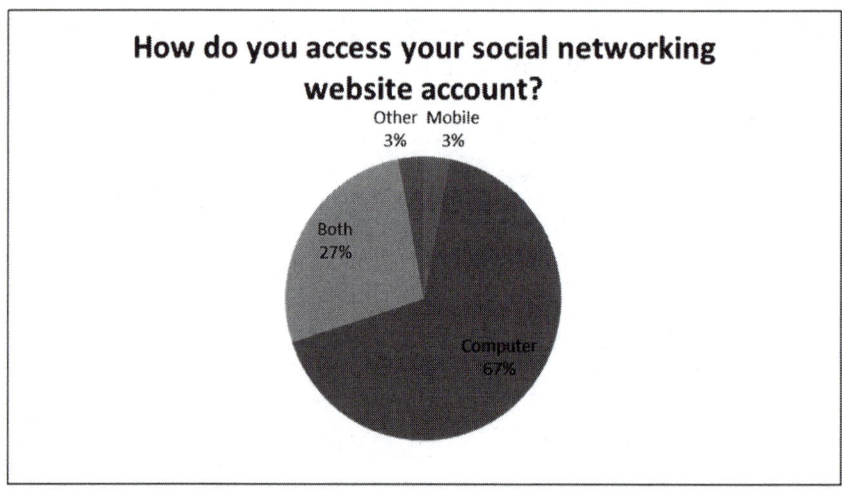

Figure 16.2 How Users Access Social Networking Websites

The respondents were also asked to select their favourite OSN site for travel related purposes. Seventy-two per cent of the respondents indicated that Facebook is their favourite social networking website for travel related purposes. YouTube ranked second (12 per cent). Only 4 per cent have indicated Myspace as their favourite, and only 1 per cent has indicated TripAdvisor as their preferred website. About 5 per cent have indicated other websites as their favourite. These results contradict with some of the news reports and trade journal articles where TripAdvisor is defined as the leading choice of social network site for travel related purposes. Indeed, TripAdvisor provides rich user generated content. However, Facebook increasingly offers travel related applications and the results indicate that these applications fulfill the need for travel related social networking.

Reported Method of Access to Social Networking Websites

The method of access to social networks is just as important as the preferences for such networks. Users are able to access social network sites via a variety of ways. In order to determine the direction of preference in access to these sites, respondents were asked to indicate what devices they primarily use to log onto their social network accounts. Sixty-seven per cent of the respondents indicated that they access their accounts mainly through the computer. In spite of the steady increase in popularity and usage of smart mobile devices, which now host social networking website applications, only 3 per cent indicated that they access their accounts through mobile devices. However, it should be noted that 27 per cent indicated they access their accounts through both the computer and mobile devices (See Figure 16.2). These numbers are highly likely to change as smart phone usage increases amongst the US population.

#	Answer		%
1	Less than 50		36%
2	51 to 100		23%
3	101 to 150		7%
4	151 to 200		11%
5	201 to 250		6%
6	251 to 300		3%
7	More than 300		13%
	Total		100%

Figure 16.3 Number of Contacts Per User

#	Answer		%
1	1-2 months		10%
2	3-4 months		5%
3	5-6 months		7%
4	7-12 months		12%
5	1-2 years		30%
6	3-4 years		21%
7	5 -6 years		8%
8	7 or more years		8%
	Total		100%

Figure 16.4 Time Duration for Using Online Social Networks

Social Circles on Social Networking Websites

Peer-pressure to join in is true for OSN sites and it is also believed that the popularity of social media networking spreads through word-of-mouth among friends. In order to determine any potential patterns between personal social circle of respondents and their social network sites, the respondents were asked the following questions: "What percentage of your personal circle uses social networking websites?". 61 per cent have indicated that more than 50 per cent

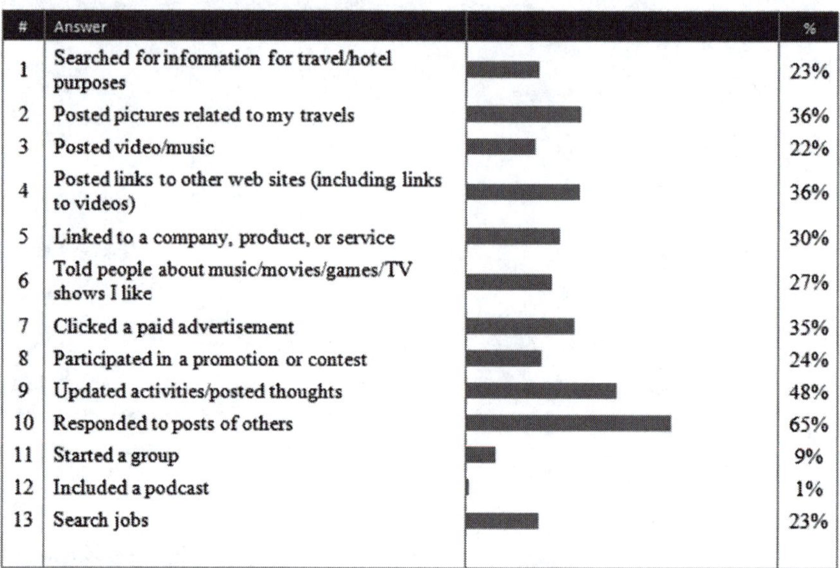

#	Answer		%
1	Searched for infomation for travel/hotel purposes		23%
2	Posted pictures related to my travels		36%
3	Posted video/music		22%
4	Posted links to other web sites (including links to videos)		36%
5	Linked to a company, product, or service		30%
6	Told people about music/movies/games/TV shows I like		27%
7	Clicked a paid advertisement		35%
8	Participated in a promotion or contest		24%
9	Updated activities/posted thoughts		48%
10	Responded to posts of others		65%
11	Started a group		9%
12	Included a podcast		1%
13	Search jobs		23%

Figure 16.5 Activities Engaged in When Using Online Social Network Sites

of their personal circle uses OSN websites. This includes 20 per cent (which represents the majority of the surveyed participants) indicating that more than 90 per cent of their personal circle uses social networking websites. Seven per cent indicated that less than 10 per cent of their personal circle uses social networking. A smaller portion of the surveyed participants (4 per cent) indicated that 20-29 per cent of their personal circle uses OSN websites.

When asked "how many contacts/friends do you have on your favourite social networking website?", 36 per cent of respondents indicated that they have less than 50 contacts on their favourite social networking website. Twenty-three per cent reported to have between 51 and 100 contacts while 13 per cent have indicated that they have more than 300 contacts on their favourite social networking website (see Figure 16.3 below). The number of contacts can be indicator for the increased potential exposure to ideas, stories, and applications related to travel behaviour.

Frequency of Access to Social Networking Websites

Frequency of access to OSN websites could be related to exposure to travel related information and communication. Thus, the respondents of the study were asked about the frequency of access to the social networks. The frequency analysis of the responses indicated that 57 per cent of the participants check their OSN websites 1 to 5 times per day, while 21 per cent check the websites 1 to 5 times per week and 10 per cent check their websites one to five times per month. Despite reports that

#	Answer		%
1	I look for restaurants information		21%
2	I look for hotels information		20%
3	I look for destinations information		18%
4	I look for bars/nights information		6%

Figure 16.6 Information Sought by Users of Online Social Network Sites

social networking websites are addictive, only 4 per cent of the surveyed participants check the websites 5 to 10 times per day. Nevertheless, almost 60 per cent of the respondents access their preferred choice of social network daily. It is important to continue to monitor this information for future studies and identify changes in patterns of access. In addition, 43 per cent have indicated that they spend less than an hour each day on the social networking websites, while five per cent have indicated that they spend more than five hours on the respective websites per day. The amount of time 'invested' in social network can be attributed to many factors such as users' perception of social networks as a commitment, escape, and so on.

In order to get a better perspective of the experience and exposure of respondents to social networking sites, the respondents were also asked about their length of membership to social network sites. Less than 40 per cent of the respondents have been using such sites for over three years. About one third of the survey participants have been using such websites for 1 to 2 years, and 34 per cent have been using social network websites for one year or less (See Figure 16.4). These reported numbers are likely to change as social network trends evolve and its influence on different generations of users change.

Common Activities Engaged on Social Network Sites

One of the objectives of the research study was to determine the range of typical activities users of social network sites engage in. The choice for activities can be an indicator for the way travel information is gathered. The participants have indicated that they have engaged in activities such as responding to posts of others (65 per cent), updating activities/posting thoughts (48 per cent), posting pictures related to travels (36 per cent), posting links to other websites (36 per cent), viewing paid advertisements (35 per cent), and searching for jobs (23 per cent). Other self reported uses (7 per cent) of these websites included contacting old friends, playing games, chatting, and sharing information (See Figure 16.5). These responses clearly indicate a level of trust amongst the users' "circle of friends".

When asked about the types of content read in the past few months, 52 per cent have indicated that they read blogs on the social networking websites, and 50 per cent have indicated that they read forum/message boards and online news feeds on the social networking websites. This is very helpful for marketing purposes.

Interesting content can easily generate a following and influence travel related decisions.

Role of Social Network Sites

Some practitioners believe that OSN sites are very influential in making purchasing decisions. For example, there are many news reports that point out to the growing popularity of TripAdvisor among travellers when making purchasing decisions. Twenty-one per cent of our respondents have indicated that they do use the websites to look for information on restaurants, while 20 per cent have indicated that they look up information on hotels and 18 per cent have indicated that they look up information on destinations (see Figure 16.6). Again, it should be noted that Facebook, not TripAdvisor, was the main choice for many users when seeking such information.

Perceived Experience and Attitudes Towards the Use of Online Social Networks

What about the perceived experience and attitudes of respondents towards social networks? Perceived quality of experience could influence users' attitudes and likelihood of usage of social networks. When asked about these issues, the participants of the survey agreed that they have fun and enjoy using the social networking websites. They have strongly indicated their intent to use the social networking websites over the next one month, and even over the next one year. The participants have indicated that they would rather use the social networking websites than not use them at all. In spite of their positive feelings for the websites, the participants do not strongly consider that stopping the use of the social networking websites would be a personal sacrifice, nor do they have the anxiety that something will be lost if they stop using the social networking websites. They also do not strongly consider that a lack of available alternatives would be a serious consequence of stopping the use of their favourite social networking websites. The above mentioned set of responses could indicate the need for future research on loyalty to social networks. Lack of loyalty to such sites could have major implications if another attractive and influential trend becomes available.

Overall, a majority of the participants feel strongly that the social networking websites are useful, fun to use, interesting and enjoyable. A majority of respondents have expressed their liking for and satisfaction with Social Network Sites. However, while the participants have indicated that they recommend the websites to their friends, they do not necessarily promote the websites by telling people positive things about them. This could yet be another question about the loyalty of the users to their respective social network sites. In addition, it appears that the websites are used more for socialization, self-expression, and communication, and less for information on new destinations, restaurants and hotels. This does not, however, diminish the potential of influence interactions with others may have on users' travel related decisions.

4. Conclusions

It is inevitable that Facebook and other social media websites will play a growing role in travel related behaviour and decisions. From the results of this 2010 study, it is apparent that the growth in online travellers' use of social networks to share their travel experiences is on the rise. The results of this study reveal that Facebook (88 per cent), YouTube (44 per cent), Myspace (37 per cent), and Twitter (36 per cent) are the most used social networks for travel related planning and information search. These social media sites are increasingly becoming a very important source for travellers for getting travel advice and suggestions. The trends identified in this study indicate an increased amount of trust and dependence in social networks when it comes to seeking travel related information. Utilizing the reviews and comments of others can make a trip an exciting experience. According to a study by World Travel Market (2010), 28 per cent of those who used social media consulted forums and chat rooms, where peers discussed their personal experiences with various destinations. Consequently, tourism destinations should consider promoting their products via these social media sites. For instance, destinations should create a Facebook page and encourage user generated content. Furthermore, distributing destination news via Twitter tweets can increase users' awareness. One must consider that high volume posting may change a user's attitude towards the destination and may encourage the user to terminate the social network relationship. On the other hand, a shy presence on a social networking site will not benefit the destination, nor will it increase awareness. Furthermore, unrelated postings may confuse the tourist and defeat the purpose of the destination's OSN.

In this study, 30 per cent of respondents indicated that they assess their accounts via mobile devices (27 per cent both mobile and computer, and 3 per cent mobile only). There is a great potential for marketers to boost the percentage of mobile users to access the OSNs. Indeed, a range of mobile communities have been established that focus especially on mobile communication and interaction possibilities. According to Tasch and Brakel (2004), mobile communities differ in several aspects from the traditional online communities. Mobile communities can be ubiquitously accessed through mobile devices without time and place constraints. One could safely assume that the use of mobile access to OSNs will increase as the smart phone usage rises amongst US consumers. Mobile devices that combine social and local services through programs like Facebook Places will gain significant traction over standalone location-based services. As user adoption increases and mobile-specific features such as check-ins (e.g. Facebook Places, FourSquare) are rolled out, mobile OSN will present significant marketing opportunities for destinations seeking to engage an audience in contexts and environments. Furthermore as the mobile data speed increases, handsets and social networks continue to improve their mobile offerings. Given the trend lines, destinations must consider that mobile will drive the future of social networking. Savvy destinations will take advantage of this new opportunity and contrive fresh strategies to deliver relevant messages and tools tailored specifically for this channel. Location awareness will be a key feature of OSNs by allowing tourists to broadcast their location to everyone on their social network. Due to the unbiased information shared in online social networks based related to travel experiences; many travellers tend to look for restaurant information, hotel information, and destination information. Creating a unique social network that allows participants to create a profile and share opinions, feelings, stories, photos, and the like can easily be a source of competitive advantage. More and more consumers search for online reviews, read tweets, blogs, friend feeds, before making decisions. As a result, electronic-word-of-mouth is becoming more and more important, and destinations find a new interest in reputation management.

A social networking site that is easily accessible, straightforward, and appealing enables participants to be engaged in unique ways (Aggarwal 2008). In this study, more than 50 per cent of users check their OSN sites 1 to 5 times per day. This supports the significant role technology plays in the activities and daily life of Internet users of social networking sites. Therefore, to maintain its competitive edge, social networking website must develop appropriate marketing strategies that help build customer relationships, customer satisfaction, trust, and perhaps most importantly loyalty.

It is important for destinations to take advantage of and promote their products via OSN. Destinations can create and upload custom Facebook pages and customize the tabs to tailor their specific offerings (e.g., event pages, destination specific items such as meetings and conferences, things to do, promotions, etc.). Survey findings indicated that a majority (44 per cent) of respondents use YouTube. Organizations should create and promote search optimized videos about the destination and local attractions. Findings point out that 36 per cent of respondents posted pictures related to their travels; organizations should therefore consider creating an account on photo sharing sites, such as Flickr or Picassa, and give hyperlinks to these websites in order to encourage user posting. Organizations should also integrate and cross-link their OSNs, to maximize user-generated content and awareness.

5. Practical Implications

Social networking websites are significant sources for contemporary travellers for getting travel advice and suggestions. Travellers started to use these websites in order to review products and services, and to support or criticize organizations for the quality of their offerings (Chung and Buhalis 2008). However, as Sigala (2011) brought to light that tourism firms were slow to adopt these tools. The trends identified in this study suggest firms and destinations to exploit user generated content. It is recommended that firms and destinations can increase users' awareness however it should be also noted that high volume posting may change a user's attitude towards the destination/firm and may encourage the user to terminate the social network relationship. Mobile OSNs are increasingly gaining popularity and they present significant marketing opportunities for destinations seeking to engage an audience in contexts and environments. It is advised that destinations, hospitality firms and tourism organizations should recognize and appreciate user participation in terms of contributions to the OSN, and it is suggested to send thank you notes to the customers' positive comments and reviews. In the same vein, negative comments should be identified and responded promptly. Every comment should be taken seriously, in addition, a quick response should be provided. This demonstrates future travellers that the property/destination's image is more reliable than comments that have not been answered to online queries. Travellers should find a wealth of information on a range of travel related topics on OSNs; they can gain a strong sense of community and have many opportunities and mediums to share their experiences and interact with other members. Keeping relationships through discussion boards and creating a sense of belonging to a community of like-minded people is important for OSNs. Furthermore, OSNs should devote resources to ensure that customer needs such as involvement, entertainment, information and identification are met (Wang and Fesenmaier 2004). Educating employees with a formal training program on the risks and benefits of social media is also important for organizations. Sigala (2010) suggested that in order to enhance the adoption and the usage of geocollaborative portals (e.g. Yahoo! Trip Planner), designers should develop and include tools and system functionality that relate to technological, social, emotional, and task-organizational factors, it is advised to destinations/organizations to concentrate on those areas.

Travellers are actively involved in providing customer service support, consequently, organizations might consider adopting data mining techniques in order to identify the trends. Similarly, data mining tools might be used for competitive analysis by gathering reviews of competitors. Organizations should also integrate and cross-link their OSNs, to maximize user-generated content and awareness. Lastly, it is proposed that organizations should consider promoting events, building a community, driving web traffic and generating leads of new travellers by adopting OSNs. Allowing people to participate in polls and contribute to travel tips is also advised. With global travellers spending more time on OSNs, destinations should see this as an opportunity to use these sites for customer service, sales, marketing, and networking.

References

Aggarwal, B. 2008. Interview with Matt Cutts from Google regarding best practices for promoting hotels online. *Hotel Online*. March.

Ajzen, I. 1991. The theory of planned behavior. *Organizational Behavior and Human Decision Processes*, 50(2), 179-211.

Ajzen, I., Fishbein, M. and Heilbroner, R.L. 1980. *Understanding Attitudes and Predicting Social Behavior*, 278. Englewood Cliffs, NJ: Prentice Hall.

Bhattacherjee, A. and Premkumar, G. 2004. Understanding changes in belief and attitude toward information technology usage: A theoretical model and longitudinal test. *MIS Quarterly*, 28(2), 229-254.

Boyd, D. and Ellison, N. 2007. Social network sites: Definition, history, and scholarship. *Journal of Computer-Mediated Communication*, 13(1).

Caverlee, J. and Webb, S. 2008. A large-scale study of Myspace: Observations and implications for online social networks. *Proceedings of ICWSM.*

Chul, M., Miller, A. and Roberts, R. 2009. Six Ways to Make Web 2.0 Work. *McKinsey on Business Technology (Summer 2009)*, 16.

Chung, J. and Buhalis, D. 2008. A study of online travel community and Web 2.0: factors affecting participation and attitude, in *Proceedings ENTER2008*. Innsbruck: Springer Verlag Wien, 267-278.

Compete, Inc. 2007. *Consumer Generated Content: Learning from Travel Innovations* [Online]. Available at: https://media.competein.com/med/uploads/files/traveltrends_consumer_generated_travel_content.html. [accessed: 20 December 2010].

ComScore. 2009. Total U.S. Online Video Market. *Video Matrix (U.S)* [online]. Available at: http://www.marketingcharts.com/interactive/Facebook-twitter-grow-more-than-100-11943/ [accessed: 3 October 2010].

Dickinger, A. and Bauernfeind, U. 2009. An Analysis of Corporate E-mail Communication as Part of Airlines' Service Recovery Strategy. *Journal of Travel & Tourism Marketing*, 26(2), 156-168. doi:10.1080/10548400902864651.

Duana, W., Gub, B. and Whinston, A.B. 2008. Do online reviews matter?: An empirical investigation of panel data. *Decision Support Systems*, 45(3), 1007-1016.

Experian Hitwise. 2010. Top 20 Sites & Engines. *Main Data Center* [online]. Available at: http://www.hitwise.com/us/resources/data-center [accessed: 1 September 2010].

Fetscherin, M. and Lattemann, C. 2008. User acceptance of virtual worlds. *Journal of Electronic Commerce Research*, 9(3), 231-242.

Gangadharbatla, H. 2008. Facebook me: Collective self-esteem, need to belong, and internet self-efficacy as predictors of the iGeneration's attitudes toward social networking sites. *Journal of Interactive Advertising*, 8(2), 1-28.

Grant-Braham, G. 2007. Silver surfers become largest on online group. *Hospitality in Focus*, 1-5.

Gretzel, U. 2006. Consumer generated content – trends and implications for branding. *E-Review of Tourism Research*, 4(3), 9-11.

Gretzel, U. and Yoo, K-H. 2008. Use and Impact of Online Travel Reviews. *Information and Communication Technologies in Tourism: Proceedings of the International Information and Communication Technologies in Tourism Conference Austria, 2008*. New York: Springer Verlag, 35-46.

Gretzel U, Yoo, K-H. and Purifoy, M. 2007. *Online Travel Review Study: Role and Impact of Online Travel Reviews*. Laboratory for Intelligent Systems in Tourism, Texas A&M University. Available at www.tripadvisor.com/pdfs/OnlineTravelReviewReport.pdf [accessed: 17 October 2010].

Hsu, C. and Lin, J. 2008. Acceptance of blog usage: The roles of technology acceptance, social influence and knowledge sharing motivation. *Information & Management*, 45, 65-74.

Jansen, B.J., Zhang, M., Sobel, K. and Chowdury, A. 2009. Twitter power: Tweets as electronic word of mouth. *Journal of the American Society for Information Science and Technology*, 60(10), 1-20.

Kaplan, A. and Haenlein, M. 2009. Users of the world, unite! The challenges and opportunities of Social Media. *Business Horizons* (2010) 53, 59-68.

Kazeniac, A. 2009. Social networks: Facebook takes over top spot, Twitter climbs. Available at: http://blog.compete.com/2009/02/09/facebook-myspace-twitter-social-network/ [accessed: 28 November 2011].

Kozinets, R., de Valck, K., Wojinicki, A. and Wilner, S. 2010. Networked Narratives: Understanding Word-of-mouth marketing in online communities. *Journal of Marketing*, 74, 71-89.

Litvin, S., Goldsmith, R. and Pan, B. 2008. Electronic word-of-mouth in hospitality and tourism management. *Tourism Management*, 29(3), 458-468.

Mahajan, P. 2009. Use of social networking in a linguistically and culturally rich India. *The International Information & Library Review*, 41(3), 129-136.

Morgan, J. 2009, 5 March. *Twitter Demographics*. Available at: http://www.socialmediatoday.com/SMC/78505 [accessed: 13 September 2010].

Pan, B., MacLaurin, T. and Crotts, J. 2007. Travel blogs and the implications for destination marketing. *Journal of Travel Research*, 46(1), 35-45.

Parra-López, E., Bulchand-Gidumal, J., Gutierrez-Tano, D. and Díaz-Armas, R. 2011. Intentions to use social media in organizing and taking vacation trips. *Computers in Human Behavior*, 27(2), 640-654.

PQ Media. 2009. *Exclusive PQ Media Research: Despite Worst Recession in Decades, Brands Increased Spending on Word-of-mouth Marketing 14.2% to 1.5 billion in 2008* [online]. Available at: http://www.pqmedia.com/about-press-20090729-wommf.html [accessed: 18 January 2011].

Quinby, D. 2010. PhoCusWright's Social Media in Travel: Traffic & Activity. *PhoCusWright Report: Global Edition*, 1-27.

Riegner, C. 2007. Word of Mouth on the Web: The Impact of Web 2.0 on Consumer Purchase Decisions. *Journal of Advertising Research*, 436-447.

Schmallegger, D. and Carson, D. 2008. Blogs in tourism: Changing approaches to information exchange. *Journal of Vacation Marketing*, 14(2), 99-110.

Sigala, M. 2010. Measuring customer value in online collaborative trip planning processes. *Marketing Intelligence & Planning*, 28(4), 418-443.

Sigala, M. 2011. eCRM 2.0 applications and trends: The use and perceptions of Greek tourism firms of social networks and intelligence. *Computers in Human Behavior*, 27(2), 655-661.

Sheldon, P.J. 1997. *Tourism Information Technology*: Cab International New York.

Shiffman, L. and Kanuk, L. 1995. *Consumer Behavior*, 9th ed. Upper Saddle River, NJ: Prentice Hall.

Steinbrink, S. 2008. *The PhoCusWright Business Travel Trends Survey*. Third Edition. Sherman, CT: PhoCusWright Inc.

Stringam, B. and Gerdes, J. 2010. Are Pictures Worth a Thousand Words? Success Factors for Hotel Website Design. *Journal of Hospitality and Tourism Technology*, 1(1) , 30-49.

Tasch, A. and Brakel, O. 2004. Location Based Community Services. New Services for a new Type of Web Communities, *Proceedings of the IADIS Conference on Web-Based Communities*, Lisbon, Portugal, 24-26 March.

Thevenot, G. 2007. Blogging as a social media. *Tourism and Hospitality Research*, 7(3/4), 1467-3584.

TIA. 2005. *Executive Summaries-travelers' Use of the Internet, 2004 ed.* [online]. Available at: http://www.tia.org/researchpubs/executive_summaries_travelers_use.htmlS. [accessed: 15 October 2010].

Vermeulen, I. and Seegers, D. 2009. Tried and tested: The impact of online hotel reviews on consumer consideration. *Tourism Management*, 30(1), 123-127.

Wang, Y. and Fesenmaier, D. 2004. Modeling Participation in an Online Travel Community. *Journal of Travel Research*, 42(3), 261-270.

Werthner, H. and Klein, S. 1999. *Information Technology and Tourism: A Challenging Relationship*. Vienna: Springer Verlag.

World Tourism. 2009. *17 Ways You Can Use Twitter: A Guide for Beginners Marketers and Business Owners* [online]. Available at: http://www.world-tourism-news.eu/news/a17-ways-you-can-use-twitter-a-guide-for-beginners-marketers-and-business-owners/ [accessed: 20 October 2010].

Xiang, Z. and Gretzel, U. 2010. Role of social media in online travel information search. *Tourism Management*, 31(2), 179-188.

Ye, Q., Law, R., Gu, B. and Chen, W. 2010. The influence of user-generated content on traveler behavior: An empirical investigation on the effects of e-word-of-mouth to hotel online bookings. *Computers in Human Behavior*, 27(2), 634-639.

Chapter 17

An Exploration of Wine Blog Communication Patterns

Vasiliki Vrana, Kostas Zafiropoulos and Dimitrios Vagianos

1. Introduction

Blogs belong to the new generation of Web 2.0 technology that facilitates content and media syndication, and person-to-person interactivity (Ng and Matanda 2009; Sigala 2007). In the last few years blogs have been growing in popularity as they are an innovation in personal publishing, and have become a key part of current online culture (Hsu and Lin 2008; Marlow 2004). The increased collaboration they offer has developed collective wisdom on the Internet (Agarwal and Liu 2008) and has tremendous impact on the profile, expectations and decision-making behaviour of Internet users, on the way consumers use the Internet, and on e-business models that businesses need to develop and/or adapt (Sigala 2007).

Blogging in the wine industry is widespread and several different types of wine blogs with different purposes exist. Thach (2009: 144) defined wine blogs as:

> Interactive websites in which a blogger writes wine reviews and informational or opinion pieces about wine, and encourages readers to type their responses to the blog so that others may read and respond as well.

Wineries, marketers and retailers, wine writers, wine businesses, or everyday consumers establish their wine blogs to share their passion for wine, provide wine news, review wines and provide ratings, promote and sell wine and wine related products and finally to share their wine-travel experiences (Thach 2009; Zafiropoulos et al., 2010). In the "complete list of wine blogs" Yarrow (2010) recorded 882 wine blogs, the majority written in English (607) but also in German (35), Dutch (4), Italian (41), French (39) Japanese (2), Chinese (5) Spanish (22), Portuguese (11), Hungarian (2), Norwegian (2), Indonesian (1) and Slovak (1). In the list there are Winery Blogs (67) and Wine Podcasts (43) too. According to Thach (2010) nine major types of wine blogs exist: "review of wines", "wine and food", "wine education", "Winemaking and Viticulture", "Specific Region", "Wine and Culture", "Winery Blog" ,"Wine Business" and "Other".

Blogs are a form of social hypertext, functioning as a one-to-one mapping between a network of web pages and a network of people, facilitating in that way members' social interactions and providing conversation (Chin and Chignell

2007; Nardi et al., 2004; Herring et al., 2005). From interlinking between them blog communities emerge (Efimova and Hendrick 2005; Efimova et al., 2005).

> The discovery of information networks among websites or among site producers through the analysis of link counts and patterns, and exploration into motivations or contexts for linking, has been a key issue in this social science literature. (Park and Jankofski 2008: 62)

This chapter investigates conversational patterns between wine blogs. It studies incoming links between bloggers through blogrolls. A "blogroll" is a list of blogs that many bloggers maintain. The blogroll occupies a permanent position on the blog's home page and is the list of blogs that the blogger frequently reads or especially admires and thus offers links to these blogs. Blogrolls evolved early in the development of blogs and serve as a navigation tool for blog readers to find other blogs with similar interests (Marlow 2004). Commenting on this Drezner and Farell (2004: 7) wrote:

> Blogrolls provide an excellent means of situating a blogger's interests and preferences within the blogosphere. Bloggers are likely to use their blogrolls to link other blogs that have shared interests.

Blogrolls are also great traffic driving tools.

> With each blogroll that your blog is listed on, comes the possibility that readers of that blog will click on your link and visit your blog. (Available at: http:// weblogs.about.com /od/partsofablog /qt/ WhatIsa Blogroll.htm)

The chapter proposes a methodology for locating central, influential wine blogs and studies these blogs' content. Snowball sampling is used starting from the Top 100 Wine Blogs of "The Wine Blog Search Engine", to locate the blogs. Blogs along with their incoming links are recorded. Next, a statistical analysis locates central or popular blogs and content analysis investigates possible connections network centrality with content.

2. Background

The wine industry

Wine has been a European product for many centuries. France, Italy, Germany, Spain, Greece, Portugal, Moldova, Romania, Bulgaria and Hungary are the most important wine producers. Nowadays, more than three-quarters of the volume of world wine production, consumption and trade involves Europe (Anderson et al., 2001). The European Union (EU 27) occupies a leading position on the world wine market, produces 60.0 per cent of wine and accounts for 55.4 per cent of wine imports and 72.8 per cent of exports (Lazanyi 2008). The rest involves New World countries settled by Europeans: California, Australia, Argentina, Chile, New Zealand, South Africa, and Uruguay. Wine production and consumption are increasing in these countries and are beginning to challenge the European dominance in international markets (Anderson et al., 2001; Lazanyi 2008).

The average world wine production for the period 1971-1975 was 313.1 Mhl and it was increasing progressively until 1985. The 1986-1990 period, was characterized by a sharp drop in world wine production compared to that of the early 1980s followed by a five-year period where this trend continued and even accelerated. Since 1995, the trend has reversed despite occasionally unfavourable climate conditions. World wine production in 2007 stood at 265.9 Mhl, lower than the average of the previous five-year period (OIV 2007).

Regarding worldwide consumption of wine from the beginning of the 1980s to the mid-1990s, world wine consumption lagged. During this period, however, the trend started to reverse and the world consumption stopped falling and slowly started to rise. 2007 showed an increase of 5.2 million hectoliters in world consumption, which followed a 5.6 million hectoliters increase between 2005 and 2006. This change therefore confirms the above-mentioned trend. The tendency towards reduction in world consumption experienced during the 1980s and 1990s has concerned almost exclusively table wines, whereas higher quality wines have seen their market share increasing progressively. In the European Union (EU), the proportion of quality wine consumption within total wine consumption increased from 30 per cent in 1986 to 46 per cent in 2006 (European Commission 2008). This resulted in the establishment of a growing investment market for fine wines and increased the number of wine auctions around the world. Auction houses have expanded their presence to new geographical regions outside Europe and the United States to reach new customers, especially in Asia and the worldwide turnover from some 90 million USD in 2003 increased to more than 276 million USD in 2008 at major auction houses (Masset and Weisskopf 2010).

Wine is also a resource that generates a flow of tourists interested in discovering the source of the product, vineyards, wineries and the ways of production, wine festivals and wine shows (Asero and Patti 2009; Hall and Macionis 1998) and provides competitive advantage to regions with a grape and wine industry and business for wineries and other related products such as restaurants and the food sector in general (Getz 1998; Di Gregorio and Licari 2006).

> Wine tourism can be defined as visitation to vineyards, wineries, wine festivals and wine shows for which grape wine tasting and/or experiencing the attributes of a grape wine region are the prime motivating factors for visitors. (Hall et al., 1993: 6)

Even though the volume of wine tourism has increased and competitive positioning of wine tourism regions has become a strategic issue (Asero and Patti 2009; Di

Gregorio and Licari 2006; Williams 2001) little is known about the complexity of the wine tourism product and the manner in which it is marketed and managed (Carmichael 2005; Hall et al., 2000).

Blogs and the wine industry

Blogs are not only employed in personal environments but also in organizations and enterprises (Kolbitsch and Maueur 2006) and as they are growing in popularity, businesses and organizations are looking for ways to exploit them. An organizational or corporate blog is a means of communication between organization/corporate and its public and enables an industry to interact meaningfully with their potential customers (Jüch and Stobbe 2005; Kosonen et al., 2007; Lu and Hsiao 2007). In this vein, some wineries have already established their own blogs. Stormhoek Vineyards, a small winery in South Africa, tripled its sales in two years by using a wiki and blogs to create groups for wine tasting parties (Lai and Turban 2008).

Blogs have the power of the impartial information and e-word-of-mouth that is diffusing online like a virus (Sigala 2007). Bloggers provide more authentic information, gained through personal experience (Sharda and Ponnada 2007) and trust one another. Kozinets (2002) wrote on this, that people who interact in spaces like blogs over a long period of time, trust the opinions of the other users and take them into consideration when making a purchase decision. There are certain product categories on the web which require more information for people to make a purchase; therefore, recommendations on the web are very helpful. Products not so widely popular and expensive products are successfully recommended products (Leskovec et al., 2007). Wine fits this category suggesting wine blogs may be useful for some consumers to make wine selections (Thach 2010). This has important implications in the wine industry, as blog reviews of wine influence buying patterns and can sell a product or not. Thach (2010: 2) mentioned:

> Wine blogs are not monitored and there are no official guidelines or rules regarding what can be published – therefore, there are many diverse opinions about wines and wine brands. Because of this some bloggers may write either positive or negative reviews about wine that can help or hinder wine sales.

Tourism products fit this category also as they can hardly be evaluated prior to their consumption (Rabanser and Ricci 2005) and depend on accurate and reliable information (Kaldis et al., 2003) thus elevating the importance of interpersonal influence (Lewis and Chambers 2000).

> As information is the lifeblood of tourism, the use and diffusion of Web 2.0 technologies have a substantial impact on both tourism demand and supply. (Sigala 2009: 221)

The discussions, information exchange and collaboration taking place in wine blogs provide value for wine tourists' trip planning. O'Neill et al. (2002) studied wine tourism in Australia, and found that visitors' recommendations boost wine sales when vacationing opinion leaders told of their experiences.

3. Methodology of Research

This research used the "Wine Blog Search Engine", and records the Top 100 Wine Blogs. It used snowball sampling starting with the top 100 wine blogs (http://alawine.com/wine-blog-rankings.html). Snowball sampling is a common sampling method for locating blogs, since it emphasizes the community characteristics of the blogs because it takes account their actual inter-linkage properties. Wine blog ratings in the Top 100 list are standardized composite scores based on multiple relative link popularity rankings from three top search engines and Technorati, as well as Google page rank scores. Top 100 blogs served as starting points and through their blogrolls new blogs are found. Next, blogrolls of these newly found blogs were used to locate new blogs etc. The procedure resulted in a record of 1230 wine blogs. Sampling took place during June-July 2010.

Along with the blogs, the incoming links among them were recorded. The reason for recording incoming links from blogrolls to other blogs is to observe and record formal interconnections between blogs. These interconnections take the form of suggestions to potential users. Users may benefit from navigating through incoming links and visit blogs that are considered familiar, important or relevant by other blogs. Thus suggested blogs are granted a certain degree of worth and value.

Incoming links are represented by a graph showing the social network of wine blogs. This network is associated with a 1230 x 1230 binary non-symmetric adjacency matrix (connection matrix). In this matrix if blog I links to blog J then 1 is placed at the cell (i, j), otherwise 0 is placed in this cell. It should be made clear that although the number of incoming links is the main variable of the analysis, it is not by itself sufficient to represent the whole network of the recorded blogs. This is the reason for forming the adjacency matrix. Consequently the variables for the analysis are now 1230, a number which is equal to the columns of the adjacency matrix. Each column in the matrix represents the way that a blog is linked by any of the 1,230 blogs.

This chapter adopts a statistical approach for studying networks, although other graph theoretic approaches also exist such as finding components or cliques. These graph theoretic notions are used in the study of social networks to locate actors who interact with each other. The statistical approach followed in this chapter, in particular multidimensional scaling and cluster analysis, is the preferred method because the aim is to find groups of blogs with these properties: 1) within these groups the blogs need not be interconnected but rather 2) they can constitute cores in the sense that if a blog links some blogs within the core groups, it is likely that it links the other blogs within the core group as well. This means that blogs in the particular groups may be considered to be of the same family or sharing common properties. In this sense, clustering algorithms applied on the original adjacency matrix are considered suitable for locating these groups.

The proposed method was originally introduced by Vrana and Zafiropoulos (2010) for locating core traveler groups. Zafiropoulos et al. (2010) applied this framework to analyse Top 100 wine blogs. The present chapter expands their work. By finding such central groups, one can explore how bloggers are organized and easily follow how conversation proceeds. It is important to locate such groups in order to see how wine blogs are organized, which blogs are considered important and which are the characteristics that make them popular in relation to their content.

This particular framework uses Multidimensional Scaling (MDS) primarily as a data reduction technique and also to quantify the original binary data. The method reproduces the original data and map them on a fewer dimensions space while the effort is to keep intact the distances among the original data on the new reproduced data. "Stress" is a measure of goodness of fit between distances of original data and distances of the reproduced data. Better fit is assumed when stress is close to zero. Two step clustering uses the quantified data from MDS to produce clusters of blogs with similar properties. Some of the clusters that are produced by two step clustering gather the largest number of incoming links. If this happens then they should be considered as central conversational or focal points. Two step cluster analysis is useful for large data sets when no prior knowledge of the number of cluster exists. For two step cluster analysis Log-likelihood distance measure and Schwarz's Bayesian Criterion (BIC) were used. The optimal number of clusters is found when BIC presents its greater change.

4. Findings

An MDS solution producing two dimensions is suitable for the analysis since it has a very good goodness of fit index (Stress=0.06). Two dimensions are suitable for the analysis since the original data distances are fairly maintained (stress=0.06), while data can easily represented on the two dimensional space. Two step cluster analysis results in the formation of two clusters according to BIC (Table 17.1). Cluster 1 consists of only 43 wine blogs, or 3.5 per cent of the recorded clusters. The cluster contains a very small minority of central and popular blogs since the average percentage of incoming links of the blogs within the cluster is 7.76 per cent. This means that the average blog in Cluster 1 gets incoming links from 7.76 per cent of the 1230 blogs. In contradiction, Cluster 2 contains all the remaining 1187 blogs and has an average percentage of incoming links which is less than one (0.63). Further, the standard deviation of the percentage of incoming links for this cluster is 0.83. Thus, the majority of blogs within Cluster 2 do not differ much regarding incoming links. Considering these two characteristics of the clusters, namely their volume on the one hand and their percentage of incoming

Table 17.1 Clusters of Wine Blogs

Clusters	Number of blogs	Average percentage of incoming links	Standard deviation of percentage of incoming links
Cluster 1	43	7.76	4.37
Cluster 2	1187	0.63	0.83
Total	1230	0.89	1.79

links on the other, the property of skewness emerges. Cluster 2 contains the vast majority of wine blogs on the one hand, but these blogs are unpopular in the sense of getting few incoming links, on the other. Cluster 2 contains all the peripheral – non central – blogs, since they do not have many incoming links. In contrast, Cluster 1 contains very few but very popular blogs. Cluster 1 may serve, within the framework introduced in this research, as a blogs communication core. Analysis of such core groups is the purpose of this research.

Blogs belonging to Cluster 1 can be described as being "Authority" blogs in a Search Engine Optimization sense because they can serve as efficient means of navigation. Users who are looking for relevant information can be directed to these blogs, which are regarded favourable or important by other blogs, and economize both time and unnecessary information. On the other hand, practitioners and marketers could locate these authority blog groups and find out about the interests of the users and next approaching them with information or commercial offerings.

Investigating common properties of central blogs

The particular 43 wine blogs constitute a core in the social network of the 1230 recorded blogs. Because of the way they are formed, i.e. using incoming links and performing cluster analysis, this means in general that if a blog links to a blog of a specific cluster, it is likely that it links to other blogs within the cluster. It is for this reason plausible to argue that blogs within a cluster are considered homogeneous regarding certain properties that they may share. So it is interesting to investigate what these common properties might be. If such properties are discovered through the present research this would not necessarily prove the hypothesis that sharing common characteristics or properties is the reason for the formation of the core or central cluster. It would however provide a strong indication the hypothesis holds. Further future research could justify this hypothesis.

Content analysis is used for the discovery of common properties and characteristics of the blogs using the NVIVO 8 Content Analysis software tool. The data content is chosen to be the written content included in the 43 wine blogs in the central cluster. For each blog, the following features were recorded in the content body:

1. The main title of the blog along with a summarized description. This description is usually given underneath the title, from the blog logo or it can be copied from the Blog script (it is usually a description that appears as a title on the upper part of the browser window when visiting a page).
2. The "about" part of each blog (when applicable) where the scope of the blog is given, the motivation of the founder to create it etc. Usually there is also information concerning the author, such as his/her interests, academic background, gender or place of origin.
3. The main part of this analysis, the posts of the Wine blogs, including the title of each post, its main body followed by its comments. Obviously this content can be huge. Additionally, it is dynamic due to the nature of a blog itself. For this reason the analysis has unavoidably involved sampling, in order to form the final content body from the corpus. In order to remove subjectivity of the analysis, the sample size was decided according to the following: all posts from a certain period of time were collected where this time window was specified in a way that includes:
   - content that qualitatively includes most of the posts that deal with the scope that a certain blog serves. The post topics were found mostly to recur after a certain period of time and usually no new topics are discovered after a while.
   - approximately the same data amount in terms of media content units from all blogs.
   - In frequently updated blogs this period of time can be a month whereas in less frequently updated blogs we may have to examine posts from eight or nine months. It all has to do with the rate the blogger updates his/her content.
4. Other features such as the existence of a sponsor, advertisements or awards in the blog.

For the study, the units of the media content were decided to be words or phrases. Synonyms or small phrases were grouped together for the purpose of this investigation. This analysis looked for specific areas of interest where usually discussions are occurring among the several blogs through their posts/comments. It further investigated the rate at which discussions relevant to each of these areas of interest occur in all 43 blogs of the identified cluster. Taking into consideration previous research on wine blogs' content (Thach 2010), the analysis identified 20 main areas of interest relevant to "wine" that source material may belong to. These areas of interest (named topics from now on) are presented in Table 17.2.

Table 17.2 indicates some common properties that appear to exist in the blogs forming the cluster, regarding their content. Wine reviews are the main common topic. Wine dining, wine publications, wine tasting, and restaurant review are discussed by more than half of the blogs in the cluster, while the first nine topics in Table 17.2 have high occurrence rate. Further, a new application of cluster analysis using as variables the 20 topics (where value 1 is applicable if a blog

Table 17.2 Discussion Topics describing Cluster Blogs' Content

Topic	Description	% of central blogs where discussion about topic occurs
Wine reviews	Reviewing wines, rating or ranking	76.7
Wine dining	Food that best "pairs" with specific wines	60.5
Wine publications	Any form of published wine reference such as sites, magazine newspapers and other social media but not books	55.8
Wine tasting	The process of wine tasting	51.2
Restaurant review	Reviewing wine bars, restaurants serving food and wine	51.2
Wine news	News relevant to wine industry/market/consumption	46.5
Wine making	The process of wine making, references to Wineries	44.4
Wine event	Wine conferences, congress, festivals	41.9
Wine tourism	Travelling that involves wine (e.g. tasting)	41.9
Geoponic	Climate conditions, treading, geoponic factors that affect the vintage, the treading and the wine making process	30.2
Cheap wines	References to good value-for-money wines, usually under a certain low price	27.9
Wine education	The process of teaching winemaking, wine tasting etc	25.6
Images	Photos/images that involve wine making vineyard etc.	23.3
Wine marketing	References to wine business, promotion, sales etc.	23.3
Wine packaging	Boxes, bottle and label design	20.9
Book reviews	Reviewing books about wines	18.6
Culture and wine	Culture references around wine	16.3
Wine commentary	Interviews of distinguished wine reviewers, comments around wine generally	14.0
Recommendations	Recommendation mainly suggesting certain types of wine, when/how to enjoy wines etc.	11.6
Wine serving	Suggestions of how to best serve wine	7.0

discusses a topic and 0 if not), suggests that wine reviews, wine dining, wine publications, wine tasting, restaurant reviews, wine news, wine events, and wine tourism are common discussion topics in the central blogs. This means that if for example central blogs discuss wine reviews, it is likely to discuss nearly all the other issues of the list as well. In conclusion, it can be argued that wine reviews,

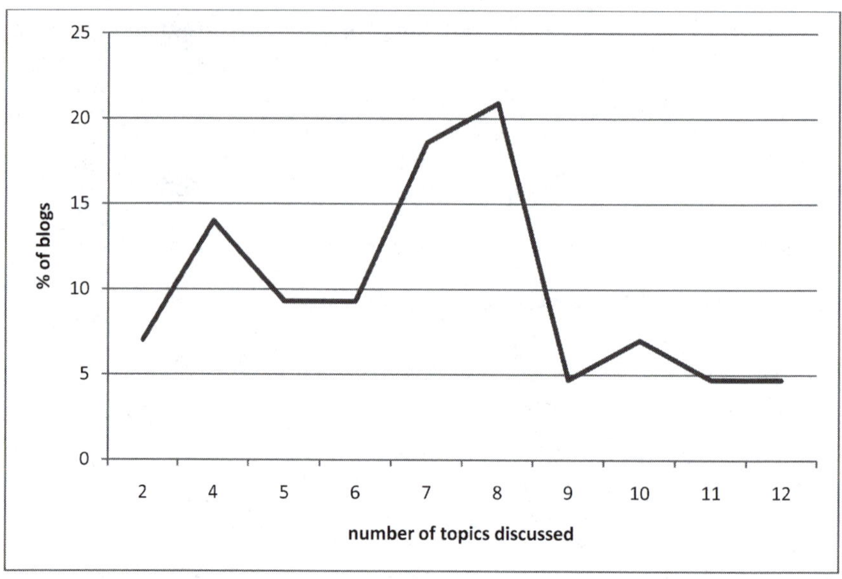

Figure 17.1 Frequency of Discussed Topics within Central Blogs

wine dining, wine publications, wine tasting, restaurant reviews, wine news, wine events, and wine tourism are all popular topics and they occur jointly in central blogs. This finding is associated and supported by the findings of Figure 17.1, which indicates the relevance percentage of the content of the blogs of Cluster1. It can be seen in Figure 17.1 that any blog in the cluster covers at least 2 topics of the 20 selected where the mean number of the topics covered is 6.88 or 34.4 per cent of the total topics. Additionally, any topic appears to have a chance to be covered in at least 5 blogs where the mean number of blogs in which it is covered is 14.8 or 34.4 per cent of the total.

Central blogs are clustered in terms of incoming links, but they may also be considered to form a cluster in terms of their content. Findings do not provide a proof of this argument but rather an indication. Further and broader research is needed in order to establish a possible link between cluster formation regarding incoming links and common properties within cluster's blogs.

5. Conclusion

This research demonstrated a framework for studying central wine blogs. The reasoning for this is that hyperlinks between blogs can provide the means to locate the most popular and informative blogs because they can be considered to be the bloggers' proposals or recommendation to other bloggers. This chapter proposes a methodology for locating linkage patterns and describes how blogs are networked, forming in this way central groups of wine blogs. Only a minority (3.5 per cent) of the wine blogs are really involved in networking, while the average interlinking is low. However, there exists one central blog cluster, which can be located by using the proposed method. Bloggers appreciate this cluster possibly because blogs within it have common content characteristics. Content analysis of central cluster blogs provides an indication that maybe an association exists between clustering according to social networking properties on the one hand and common content of the blogs on the other.

It is common for central blogs to be reached by others who navigate through a series of incoming links that lead to them. In this fashion, it is probable that these blogs have the potential to address many visitors and therefore it is probable that they have a bigger impact on the provision of information. Locating these blogs is important and useful for both researchers and practitioners, since one can easily locate them and be informed and analyse discussions of the most influential blogs. This might be very useful particularly for small unknown wineries and regions. In this vein less known wineries' blogs may contact one of the large 'focal point' blogs, to publicize their wines and regions interested in wine tourism may contact these blogs in order to attract visitors. Also knowing what the most popular discussion topics are, certain promotion strategies could be applied.

This research presents some limitations. First, blogs are recorded using a starting point of one particular website. Although this website specializes in wine blogs and snowball sampling takes account of community characteristics of the blogs, other search engines could be considered as well. Second, focusing on the central blogs leaves the vast majority of the sample out of the analysis. This does not allow making statements regarding the uniqueness of the core blogs. This would be a very interesting project for future research, but the main objective of this research is to locate and analyse only the central or core blog groups. A new study could make comparisons between blogs in the core groups and those not belonging to the core groups, revealing in this way the unique properties of blogs within core groups.

References

Agarwal, N. and Liu, H. 2008. Blogosphere: Research Issues, Tools, and Applications. *SIGKDD Explorations*, 10(1), 18-31.

Anderson, K., Norman, D. and Wittwer, G. 2001. *Globalization and the World's Wine Markets: Overview* [Online: Centre for International Economic Studies and School of Economics University of Adelaide. Discussion Paper 014]. Available at: www.adelaide.edu.au /cies/ papers/0143.pdf [accessed: 12 May 2010].

Asero, V. and Patti, S. 2009. *From Wine Production to Wine Tourism Experience: The Case of Italy* [Online: American Association of wine economists. AAWE working Paper no 52 Economics]. Available at: www.wine-economics.org/workingpapers/AAWE_WP52.pdf [accessed: 4 October 2010].

Chin, A. and Chignell, M. 2007. Identifying communities in blogs: Roles for social network analysis and survey instruments. *International Journal Web Based Communities*, 3(3), 345-363.

Carmichael, B. 2005. Understanding the Wine Tourism Experience for Winery Visitors in the Niagara Region, Ontario, Canada. *Tourism Geographies*, 7(2), 185-204.

Di Gregorio, D. and Licari, E. 2006. *Rural Development and Wine Tourism in Southern Italy*. 46th Congress on European Regional Science Association 30 August-3 September, Volos, Greece. Available at: http://www-sre.wu-wien.ac.at/ersa/ersaconfs/ ersa06/papers/626.pdf [accessed: 29 March 2009].

Drezner, D. and Farrell, H. 2004. *The Power and Politics of Blogs*. Annual Meeting of the American Political Science Association, Washington, DC. Available at: http://www.utsc.utoronto.ca/~farrell/blogpaperfinal.pdf [accessed: 31 March 2008].

Efimova, L. and Hendrick, S. 2005. *In Search for a Virtual Settlement: An Exploration of Weblog Community Boundaries* [Online]. Available at: https://doc.novay.nl/dsweb /Get/ Document-46041 [accessed: 12 May 2010].

Efimova, L., Hendrick, S. and Anjewierden, A. 2005. *Finding "the Life between Buildings": An Approach for Defining a Weblog Community*. AOIR Internet Research 6.0: Internet Generations, Chicago. Available at: http://peach.mie.utoronto.ca/~achin/Publications/achin_IJWBC07.pdf [accessed: 20 August 2009].

European Commission 2008 [Online]. Available at: http://europa.eu.int/comm/agriculture/markets/wine/index es.htm.

Getz, D. 1998. Wine tourism: Global overview and perspectives on its development, in *Wine Tourism-Perfect Partners, Proceedings of the First Australian Wine Tourism Conference*, edited by Dowling, R. and Carlsen, J., Canberra: Bureau of Tourism Research.

Herring, C., Kouper, I., Paolillo, J., Scheidt, L-A., Tyworth, M., Welsch, P., Wright, E. and Yu, N. 2005. *Conversations in the Blogosphere: An Analysis "From the Bottom Up"*, Proceedings of the Thirty-Eighth Hawai'i International Conference on System Sciences (HICSS-38). Los Alamitos.

Hall, C.M., Cambourne, B., Macionis, N. and Johnson, G. 1993. Wine Tourism and Network Development in Australia and New Zealand. Review, Establishment and Prospects. *International Journal of Wine Marketing*, 9(2), 5-31.

Hall, C.M. and Macionis, N. 1998. Wine tourism in Australia and New Zealand, in *Tourism and Recreation in Rural Areas*, edited by R.W. Butler, C.M. Hall and J.M. Jenkins. New York: John Wiley & Sons, 267-298.

Hall, C.M., Sharples, L., Cambourne, B. and Macionis, N. 2000. *Wine Tourism Around the World*. Oxford: Butterworth Heinemann.

Hsu, C-L. and Lin, C-C. 2008. Acceptance of blog usage: The roles of technology acceptance, social influence and knowledge sharing motivation. *Information and Management*, 45(1), 65-74.

Jüch, C. and Stobbe, A. 2005. Blogs: The new magic formula for corporate communications? Economics. Digital economy and structural change. *Deutsche Bank Research*, 53. Available at: http://www.dbresearch.com/PROD/DBR_INTERNET_EN-PROD/PROD0000000000190745.pdf [accessed: 1 May 2009].

Kaldis, K., Boccorh, R. and Buhalis. D. 2003. Technology Enabled Distribution of Hotels. An Investigation of the Hotel Sector in Athens, Greece. *Information and Communication Technologies in Tourism in 2003*. Vienna: Springer Verlag, 280-287.

Kolbitsch, J. and Maurer H. 2006. The Transformation of the Web: How Emerging Communities Shape the Information We Consume. *Journal of Universal Computer Science*, 12(2), 187-213.

Kozinets, R.V. 2002. The field behind the screen: Using netnography for marketing research in online communities. *Journal of Marketing Research*, 39, 61-72.

Lai, L.S.L. and Turban, E. 2008. Groups Formation and Operations in the Web 2.0 Environment and Social Networks. *Group Decis Negot*, 17, 387-402.

Lazanyi, J. 2008. Trends in wine production and trade. *Applied Studies in Agribusiness and Commerce*, 2(1-2), 137-146.

Leskovec, J., Adamic, L.A. and Huberman, B. 2007. The dynamics of viral marketing. *ACM Transactions on the Web*, 1(1).

Lewis, R.C. and Chambers, R.E. 2000. *Marketing Leadership in Hospitality, Foundations and Practices*, 3rd ed. New York: Wiley.

Lu, H-P. and Hsiao, K-L. 2007. Understanding intention to continuously share information on weblogs. *Internet Research*, 17(4), 345-361.

Marlow, C. 2004. *Audience, Structure and Authority in the Weblog Community*. 54th Annual Conference of the International Communication Association, Available at: http://www.researchmethods.org/ICA2004.pdf [accessed: 1 May 2009].

Masset P. and Weisskopf, J-P. 2010. *Raise your Glass: Wine Investment and the Financial Crisis*. [Online, American Association of wine economists. AAWE working Paper, no. 57 Economics. Available at: www.wine-economics.org/workingpapers/AAWE_WP57.pdf [accessed: 4 October 2010].

Nardi, B. Schiano, D. and Gumbrecht, M. 2004. *Blogging as Social Activity, or, Would You Let 900 Million People Read Your Diary?*, Proceedings of the 2004 ACM Conference on Computer Supported Cooperative Work, New York, USA, 222-231.

Ng, J-Y. and Matanda, M. 2009. *The Role of Citizenship Behavior in E-service Quality Delivery in Blog Retailing*, ANZMAC 2009, 30 November-2 December, Melbourne. Australia. Available at: www.duplication.net.au/ANZMAC09/papers/ANZMAC2009-562.pdf [accessed: 30 September 2010].

OIV, 2007. *World Vitivinicultural Statistics 2007 – Structure of the World Vitivinicultural Industry 2007* [Online International Organization of Vine and Wine]. Available at: http://news.reseauconcept.net/images/oiv_uk/Client/Statistiques_commentaires_annexes_2007_EN.pdf [accessed: 3 September 2010].

O'Neill, M., Palmer, A. and Charters, S. 2002. Wine production as a service experience – the effects of service quality on wine sales. *The Journal of Services Marketing*, 16(4), 342-362.

Rabanser, U. and Ricci, F. 2005. Recommender Systems: Do They Have a Viable Business Model in E-Tourism?, in *Information and Communication Technologies in Tourism in 2005*. Vienna: Springer Verlag, 160-171.

Sharda, N. and Ponnada, M. 2007. Tourism Blog Visualizer for better tour planning. *Journal of Vacation Marketing*, 14(2), 157-167.

Sigala, M. 2007. WEB 2.0 in the tourism industry: A new tourism generation and new e-business models, *Ecoclub*, 90, 5-8.

Sigala, M. 2009. WEB 2.0, social marketing strategies and distribution channels for city destinations: Enhancing the participatory role of travelers and exploiting their collective intelligence, in *Information Communication Technologies and City Marketing: Digital Opportunities for Cities around the World*, edited by M. Gascó-Hernández and T. Torres-Coronas. Hershey, PA: IDEA Publishing, 220-244.

Thach, L. 2009. Wine 2.0: The Next Phase of Wine Marketing? Exploring US Winery Adoption of Wine 2.0 Components. *Journal of Wine Research*, 20(2), 143-157.

Thach, L. 2010. *Wine Blogs: Expressing Diverse Wine Opinions in a New Realm of Online Wine Relationship Marketing*. 5th International Academy of Wine Business Research Conference, 8-10 February 2010 Auckland (NZ), Available at: http://academyofwinebusiness.com/wp-content/uploads/2010/04/Thach-Wine-Blogs.pdf [accessed: 18 September 2010].

Williams P. 2001. The Evolving Images of Wine Tourism Destination. *Tourism Recreational Research*, 26(2), 3-10.

Yarrow, A. 2010. *The Complete List of Wine Blogs*. Available at: www.vinography.com [accessed: 1 November 2010].

Vrana, V. and Zafiropoulos, K. 2010. Locating Central Travelers' Groups in Travel Blogs' Social Networks. *Journal of Enterprise Information Management*, 23(5), 595-609.

Zafiropoulos, K., Vrana, V. and Vagianos, D. 2010. *Conversation Authorities among Popular Wine Blogs*. EuroCHRIE, Passion for Hospitality Excellence, Amsterdam 25th-28th October.

Chapter 18
The Effect of E-Reviews on Consumer Behaviour: An Exploratory Study on Agro-Tourism

Katia L. Sidali, Matthias Fuchs and Achim Spiller

1. Background and Introduction

The advancement of information technology has caused substantial repercussions in almost all global markets (De Valck, van Bruggen and Wierenga 2009), thereby leading to a "renegotiation of the relationships between companies and consumers" (Kucuk and Krishnamurthy 2007). Web 2.0, i.e., a varied range of Internet-mediated communication tools, such as blogs, wikis, chat rooms, interactive websites, etc., has particularly empowered customers as they may signal and disseminate information about their consumption experiences to other like-minded people. One of those branches where Web 2.0 technologies have changed market dynamics most profoundly is travel and tourism. On the supply side, the provision of freely accessible authoring tools has allowed the transition from rather static to dynamic tourism websites (Fuchs and Höpken 2011). On the demand side, travel and destination information increasingly consists of user generated content, often also referred to as electronic word-of-mouth (eWOM) (Litvin, Goldsmith and Pan 2008). Particular types of eWOM are online or e-reviews that collect and display online product evaluations (often) anonymously posted on the web by peers.

The study at hand focuses on the significance of e-reviews in special-interest tourism, i.e. farm tourism or agro-tourism which comprises all tourism and recreation activities connected with farms (Phillip, Hunter and Blackstock 2010; Przezbórska 2003). Mostly in the form of small and medium-sized enterprises (SME), farm operators in Germany currently amount to 25,000 (BMELV 2006). Similar to other countries, they typically suffer from shortages of tourism-related business knowledge (Huang 2006), which in turn leads to entrepreneurial restrictions with regard to innovations, product development and strategic planning (Veeck, Che and Veeck 2006). Against this background it is not surprising that only few suppliers have so far implemented e-reviews to improve the marketing effectiveness of their facilities (Sidali 2009) and still the majority of farm tourism operators ignore the benefits of adopting Web 2.0 applications (Huang 2006). Nevertheless, studies focusing on international hotel chains could show that e-reviews have become trustworthy sources of information (Schmeißer

2010; Yoo et al., 2009). Furthermore, scholars suggest that Web 2.0 technologies display positive effects on booking behaviour (Xiang and Gretzel 2010; Fuchs, Scholochow and Höpken 2009; Pan, MacLaurin and Crotts 2007).

Unfortunately, similar studies for farm tourism are lacking. In addition, sector specific demand studies on tourist behaviour are often outdated. As a consequence, it is difficult to infer whether farm guests show a different behaviour towards Web 2.0 tools than other tourist segments (Lüdke 2001). However, this information is necessary for upcoming investment decisions regarding, for instance, the upgrade of websites with e-review applications.

Thus, our study tests a consumer behaviour model on the base of survey data gathered by 216 respondents from Germany. The purposes of this analysis are threefold: (a) to explore the determinants that make anonymously-posted e-reviews be perceived as trustworthy (b) to assess the impact of trust in e-reviews on consumers' decisions to book accommodation and (c) to test whether there are significant differences between agro-tourists and non agro-tourists.

2. Theoretical Framework

Trust in e-reviews

As a result of the service character and the spatial distance between supply and demand, travel and tourism industries show large degrees of information asymmetries. This implies that customers cannot precisely assess a product's quality before purchasing it (Clerides, Nearchou and Pashardes 2004), thereby causing considerable market inefficiencies (Akerlof 1970).

Trust is considered to be an effective mechanism to sustain information equilibrium, because it reduces consumption risks and transaction costs (Ebert 2006). Accordingly, hotel rating systems stem from the endeavour to signal the potential customer highest quality of the hotel's value proposition. Similar mechanisms which rectify information asymmetries in tourism markets are e-reviews, which are also considered to be highly trustworthy information sources (Gretzel 2007; Hennig-Thurau 2005).

According to the literature some characteristics appear to be quite stable cognitive antecedents of trust. More precisely, Raimondo (2000) and Moorman, Deshpandé and Zaltman (1993) identified '*competence*' (also referred to as 'expertness and dynamism') and '*integrity*' (i.e. credibility, morality, reliability) as significant predictors of trust. Whereas the competence dimension identifies a consumer's belief that his or her counterpart has the required expertise to make a judgement about the matter in question (Raimondo 2000; Ebert 2006), integrity refers to the perceived similarity between trustor and trustee (Coulter and Coulter 2002). Regarding the former dimension, the literature on e-reviews emphasizes its importance, although to different extents: in her study on the impact of online travel reviews, Gretzel (2007) identifies perceived expertness of the author as a significant motivating dimension to read e-reviews, whereas Vermeulen and Seegers (2009) state that its role in increasing the formation of (i.e. positive) attitudes towards (reviewed) hotels is limited. Finally, the dimension of integrity refers to source credibility which, according to Giffin (1967), plays a crucial role in the formation of interpersonal trust along the communication process. In our study this dimension refers to the virtual place where e-reviews are posted. According to Hennig-Thurau (2005), virtual environments controlled by third parties, such as travel opinion platforms, are perceived as being highly credible and, thereby, the e-reviews posted on them. Based on previous research, the following hypotheses have been derived: the higher the perceived expertness of an e-review (H1), and the higher the general credibility of the e-platform (H2), the higher the trust in this e-review.

The literature regarding trust and its antecedents also identifies affective dimensions, such as '*benevolence*' (i.e., goodwill, responsiveness) and '*brand familiarity*'. The former is described as a consumer's perception that the other person acts to the best of his or her knowledge and in the interest of the consumer (Coulter and Coulter 2002). Findings from Gretzel (2007) support the significance of this dimension in the context of online-reviews. Accordingly, hypothesis H3 assumes that the friendlier the style of an e-review, the higher the trust in this e-review.

Brand familiarity is often considered a precondition of trust (Luhmann 1979). However, the findings of previous studies differ in terms of the direction of the relationship between this construct and trust as well as eWOM. For example, Sundaram and Webster (1999) show that brand familiarity has a moderating effect on the impact of WOM on brand evaluations, while Gefen (2000) found that brand familiarity builds trust (in that brand).

Based on the above discussion, we think that, if a consumer is already familiar with certain (e.g. hotel) brands, the latter will be considered more trustworthy compared to an anonymously-posted online review (cf. Luhmann 1979; Gefen 2000). This is reflected by hypothesis H4, assuming that the higher the reader's familiarity with a brand, the less trusted the e-review.

Accommodation choice

In the same way as offline WOM is supposed to affect consumers' purchase behaviour (Arndt 1967), it is finally hypothesized that trustworthy e-reviews influence consumers' booking behaviour. More precisely, as stated by hypothesis H5, one would expect that the higher the trust in e-reviews, the more likely the reader is to book the accommodation.

Proposed difference among farm and non-farm tourists

As mentioned, literature focusing on the demand side of German farm tourism is rather incomplete and shows contradictory data, so that it is difficult to discern a consistent picture of farm guests' online behaviour. Although there is some

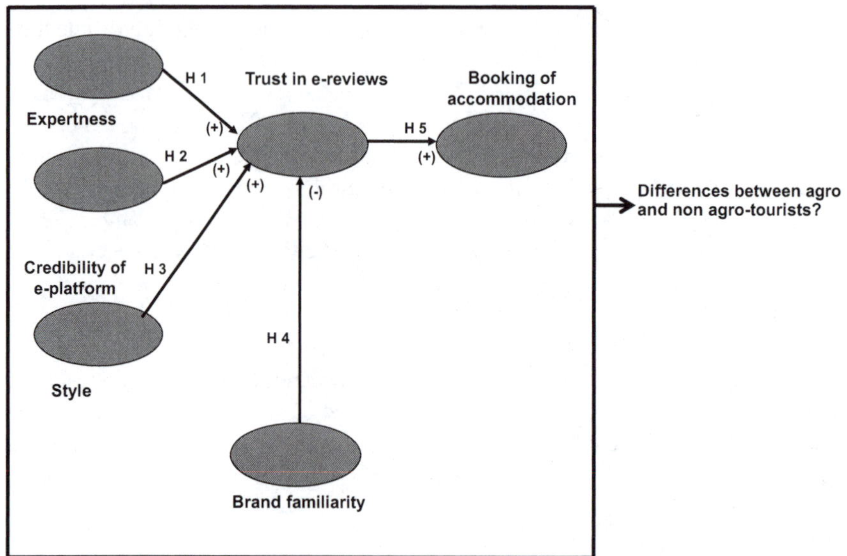

Figure 18.1 Theoretical Framework

evidence that personal recommendation plays the most important role in choosing a farm holiday (Lüdke 2001; Lender 1997), the online behaviour of farm guests is still almost unknown. Nevertheless, some recent studies report that the use of the Internet has gathered momentum in agro-tourism over the last eight years, both for information searching and booking activities (BMELV 2008; FUR 2007). Nevertheless, according to a report by the German government, Internet affinity of farm guests still scores extremely low (BMELV 2009). Therefore, we will test, through group comparisons, whether the relationships between the above mentioned model constructs differ between farm and non-farm tourists. To sum up, Figure 18.1 presents a graphical representation of the theoretical model to be tested.

3. Empirical Assessment

Determinants of trust in e-reviews and impact on choice of accommodation

Data was collected in several German cities[1] via self-administered questionnaires during May 2008. Data collection took place in the context of an academic marketing research project during which students were recruited as interviewers. Random sampling techniques were not used because of financial and time

1 Berlin, Göttingen, Hamburg, Munich.

restraints, thus, convenience sampling was employed (cf., Huang 2006). The final number of questionnaires obtained was 216.

The questionnaire incorporated a set of items regarding information search behaviour, two measurement components concerning 'trust in e-reviews' and 'consumption behaviour' (i.e., choice of accommodation) as well as a set of socio demographic characteristics. Furthermore, in order to discern the perceived popularity of e-platforms, the questionnaire included a list of travel-related platforms; thus, respondents could indicate their degree of familiarity with e-platforms.[2]

Since there are no established scales of trust in e-reviews in the field of farm tourism available, new ones were developed based on the mentioned literature. More specifically, we formulated six items for 'trust in e-reviews' and one item for 'credibility of e-platform' based on Raimondo (2000). The items for 'perceived expertness' and 'style' of the e-review were constructed based on the findings of Gretzel (2007). Finally, we formulated two items for 'brand familiarity' based on the results of Gefen (2000). Moreover, these items were cross-validated by domain experts who delivered valuable feedback about readability and their collocation with the categories discussed above (i.e., expert validity, cf. Henning-Thurau 2005). Finally, a pre-test was conducted which led to slight modifications of some statements.[3]

In order to examine the dimensionality of the item set, confirmatory factor analysis (CFA) was performed. CFA is typically used to find out whether a set of data is compatible with a pre-specified factor structure and to see whether the factor structure among various sub-samples is stable (Hair et al., 2006; Grunert et al., 1997). As hypothesized, the achieved number of factors with an Eigenvalue greater than one was five: trust in e-review, two cognitive determinants of trust (i.e., 'expertness' and 'credibility of e-platform') and two affective determinants of trust in e-review (i.e., 'style' and 'brand familiarity').

Subsequently, these successfully validated measurement constructs were included in a linear structural equation model (SEM) to which a variable of consumer behaviour (i.e., 'choice of accommodation') was added as dependent variable (Reisinger and Turner 1999). The latter consists of an index derived from a two-stage approach. Firstly, respondents were asked to choose an accommodation promoted by different sources of information (i.e., e-reviews, conventional hotel rating system, review in a travel guide and recommendation of a travel agency). Secondly, based on these answers we built an index that measures the probability of choosing an accommodation promoted by an e-review using a scale ranging

2 The list of travel e-platforms contained: hotelinfodienst.de, myhotelcheck.de, lastminute.de, travel24.com, virtualtourist.com, TravelScout24.de, TripAdvisor.de, LonelyPlanet.de, Start.de, discounttravel.de, Expedia.de, Hotel.de, Holidaycheck.de, hotelinfos24.de, priceline.de.

3 According to Henning-Thurau (2005), a similar process of item generation is common in the literature and may be interpreted as a hint for criterion validity.

from 5 (i.e. very high probability) to 1 (i.e. very low probability). Due to a rather small sample size, data is analysed by the SmartPLS 2.01 software and by applying a bootstrapping method.[4]

Multi-group comparisons (MGC)

In order to test whether differences between respondents with previous experience in agro-tourism and all other respondents (i.e., no previous experience with agro-tourism) exist, the sample was split and the model was run for three groups: the overall sample (n = 216), the two sub-samples i.e., individuals with prior agro-tourism experience at least once (n=50), and individuals without any prior agro-tourism experience (n=166).

We conducted an MGC of PLS models by applying the following procedure: after having tested the goodness of fit of every model for the three groups, we assessed measurement invariance for each model in the samples (cf., Chin and Dibbern 2010; Dibbern and Chin 2005). Accordingly, we checked for group differences with respect to (a) constructs (i.e., loading estimates of each construct) and (b) effects (i.e., path estimators) (Eberl 2010).

The goodness-of-fit of the measurement models for the groups was checked via several tests in order to assure indicator and construct reliability as well as construct validity (Hair et al., 2006). With respect to factor invariance, literature distinguishes between several threshold values in accordance with the model's compatibility level: from minimal comparability to weak identity. The latter identifies "samples [which] can differ in the level of endorsement of the various items, while everything else – their complete meaning structure, including item reliability – is the same" (Grunert et al., 1997).

Concerning the differences in effects, the goodness-of-fit of the structural models is assessed by means of a) R^2 values as well as b) the direction and c) the magnitude of the path coefficients (Dibbern and Chin 2005). Finally, structural invariance is analysed by means of pair-wise t-tests performed between groups (i.e. agro-tourists versus non agro-tourists). In this way we tested the significance of any differences among the sub-samples.[5]

A minimal number or the absence of significant differences between groups ensures structural invariance (cf., Eberl 2010). Hence, if path coefficients in two data-sets are not significantly different, one could conclude that the strength of the influence between the two constructs involved can be generalized (ibid.).

---

4 This re-sampling procedure is employed in order to obtain the pooled standard errors upon which the t-tests are based (Dibbern and Chin 2005).

5 The approximated t-test statistic is derived from a variation of Chin's (Eberl 2010) formula (Available at: www.smartpls.com, accessed: 2 May 2010): t = (path1-path2)/((SE12+SE22)0.5).

4. Results

Sample description

Respondents were on average 39 years old. At 53 per cent, women were slightly overrepresented. As far as tourist behaviour is concerned, the average number of holidays per year was one to two, and the average vacation length was one to two weeks. Interestingly, previous experience with reading e-reviews is relatively low: 40 per cent of respondents have never read e-reviews before, followed by 40 per cent who only sporadically did so (i.e., 'rarely to sometimes'). Only 20 per cent read e-reviews on a regular basis. Even lower experience levels emerged for posting e-reviews: 29.5 per cent of respondents have articulated themselves on the web once, followed by 13 per cent who rarely to sometimes do so, and only 1.5 per cent who do so 'often to very often'. Thus, almost 56 per cent have not had previous experience of posting e-reviews. This result surely reflects the fact that in Germany online travel platforms are used fairly infrequently which is further corroborated by the fact that only 3 out of 10 online travel platforms were recognized by the respondents.

From the analysis of the two sub-samples of agro-tourists and non agro-tourists, interesting differences emerged regarding their frequency of taking a holiday, which was measured by a 5-point Likert-type scale, ranging from (0) never to (4) more than three times. The findings show that agro-tourists travelled more frequently during the 12 months prior to the study than non agro-tourists (i.e., 2.38 versus 1.89 times, respectively). Respondents belonging to the group of agro-tourists probably take this type of vacation as a second or third holiday per year. Another difference between the two groups concerns the frequency of posting e-reviews. The latter was measured by means of a 5-point Likert-type scale ranging from never (-2) to always (+2). Interestingly again, agro-tourists score higher in their experience of posting e-reviews than non agro-tourists (-1.75 versus -2.14, respectively) showing an even higher propensity to post e-reviews than the sample average (i.e., -2.06). Hence, agro-tourists seem to be more likely to articulate their opinions and assessments on the web, probably as a result of their high travel frequency and experience.

The measurement model in the overall sample and in the sub-samples

As mentioned above, CFA was conducted for both the overall sample and the two sub-groups. Table 18.1 provides an overview of the loading coefficients obtained. Moreover, several measures of fit are displayed: indicator reliability and loading values were analysed using T-tests (Hair et al., 2006). Significance tests were conducted using a bootstrap routine with 700 re-samples. Construct reliability and convergence validity were tested by means of the composite reliability (CR) and the average variance extracted (AVE) (Hair et al., 2006). Whereas for the former the literature estimates a threshold of either 0.7 (Dibbern and Chin 2005) or 0.6 (Bagozzi and Yi 1988), it is expected that the AVE should not be lower than 0.5

Table 18.1 Results of CFA of the Overall Sample and the two Sub-samples

Constructs[1]	Overall sample (n=216)				Agro-tourists (n=50)				Non agro-tourists (n=166)			
	r	t	CR	AVE	r	t	CR	AVE	r	t	CR	AVE
Brand familiarity			0.79	0.66			0.43	0.44			0.82	0.70
Brand 1	0.918	15.724			0.966	6.702			0.911	6.043		
Brand 2	0.730	4.4642			0.600	2.182			0.757	3.021		
Style of review			0.83	0.70			0.84	0.73			0.82	0.69
Style 1	0.826	12.569			0.874	17.131			0.789	6.371		
Style 2	0.857	17.337			0.821	14.247			0.874	8.643		
Perceived Expertness			0.81	0.52			0.81	0.53			0.83	0.56
Expert 1	0.598	8.620			0.609	8.938			0.589	6.467		
Expert 2	0.720	16.434			0.761	21.3761			0.691	11.102		
Expert 3	0.830	32.574			0.823	32.1509			0.836	15.477		
Expert 4	0.800	26.662			0.818	26.577			0.781	11.703		
Credibility of e-platform[2]	-	-	-	-	-	-	-	-	-	-	-	-
Trust in e-review			0.87	0.49			0.85	0.46			0.60	0.57
Trust 1	0.817	32.621			0.851	47.614			0.790	15.187		
Trust 2	0.819	31.816			0.835	42.340			0.826	15.672		
Trust 3	0.852	43.767			0.872	48.700			0.843	17.336		
Trust 4	0.653	14.757			0.554	9.891			0.723	12.556		
Trust 5	0.654	13.261			0.676	14.077			0.643	9.755		
Trust 6	0.609	10.548			0.566	10.964			0.644	13.294		
Accommodation choice[2]	-	-	-	-	-	-	-	-	-	-	-	-

Note: [1] Five point rating scale. IR=Indicator Reliability. AVE=Average Variance Extracted. CR=Composite Reliability [2] = tests not possible for one-item constructs Trust 1= Before booking a hotel I read other e-users' experiences; Trust 2=E-reviews help me to make the right buying decision; Trust 3=In comparison to catalogues I trust e-reviews more; Trust 4=I think that e-reviews are trustworthy; Trust 5=If a hotel is promoted by tourists, I am more willing to book it; Trust 6=To me positive e-reviews are very important; Expert=The number of posted e-reviews is very important to me; Expert 2 = I trust e-reviews written by people who travel a lot; Expert 3 =The more detailed an e-review the more I trust it; Expert 4=I only trust e-reviews which have received high ratings; Style 1=I trust more e-reviews written in a friendly manner; Style 2=I especially trust e-reviews posted by people similar to me; Brand 1=If a hotel is well known reviews by others are not very important; Brand 2=If a hotel has a high rating reviews by others are not very important; Credibility 1=Travel opinion platforms are trustworthy to me.

Table 18.2 Path Values and Goodness of Fit for Endogenous Constructs

Values of path coeff. for endogenous constructs	**Overall sample (n=216)**	**Agro-tourists (n=50)**	**Non agro-tourists (n=166)**
	Sample mean path coeff. **T-Value**	Sample mean path coeff. **T-Value**	Sample mean path coeff. **T-Value**
Brand familiarity -> Trust in review	-0.203 4.094	-0.123 0.969	-0.206 3.810
Perceived expertness of review -> Trust in review	0.498 9.263	0.430 4.345	0.514 9.211
Style of review -> Trust in review	0.127 2.376	0.069 0.681	0.132 2.403
Credibility of e-platforms -> Trust in review	0.337 7.012	0.479 4.692	0.297 5.900
Trust in review -> Choice	0.301 4.956	0.489 5.164	0.228 3.420
	R2-Value	**R2-Value**	**R2-Value**
Trust in e-review	61.4%	66.2%	60.8%
Accommodation choice	8.9%	23.9%	5.2%

Note: Significant values are shown in bold. Significance at 0.001 level = 2 tailed t-test t > 3.291; Significance at 0.01 level = 2 tailed t-test t > 2.576; Significance at 0.05 level = 2 tailed t-test t> 1.960.

(Homburg and Giering 1996). Table 18.1 displays scale reliabilities for the three samples. Although the matrices of loading coefficients are not fully identical, all scales display reliability and validity values above or only slightly below the desirable criteria. Moreover, although items' reliabilities differ slightly between the sub-samples, loadings show similar patterns, thus, the constructs can be considered as fully comparable among groups.

Table 18.2 displays all path coefficients and related significance levels. The R^2 values related to the construct 'Trust in e-review' are satisfactory, both in the overall sample (61.4 per cent) and in the two tourist typologies of farm and non-farm guests (66.2 per cent and 60.8 per cent, respectively). Concerning 'accommodation choice', the lowest R^2 value emerged for the sub-sample of non agro-tourists (R^2 = 5.2 per cent), whereas a relatively higher one was achieved for the more homogenous sub-group of agro-tourists (R^2 = 23.9 per cent).

The SEM results are, first of all, discussed by analysing the path coefficients in the overall sample. Interestingly, 'perceived expertness' emerged as the strongest component of 'trust in e-review' (0.498), twice as strong as 'brand familiarity' which, as hypothesized, displays a negative influence on trust in e-reviews

(-0.203). Furthermore, 'credibility of the e-platform' has a highly significant influence on 'trust in e-reviews' (0.337). By contrast, a relatively low influence is displayed by a 'friendly style' (0.127). As expected, 'trust in e-reviews' displays a significant influence on 'choice of accommodation' (0.301). Thus, H1 to H5 could not be rejected. Based on these findings, our model demonstrates that perceived 'expertness' of the e-review and 'credibility of the e-platform' are 'central cues' of trust in e-reviews. This suggests that, especially in highly competitive markets such as travel and tourism, managers should choose highly customized e-platforms that offer online-users several possibilities to infer the competence of peers, for instance, by assessing the ranking of each recommendation, by ordering the reviews according to the market segments (i.e., reviews of single parent travellers, of wellness tourists), etc. This would not only reinforce the 'perceived expertness' of the content of e-reviews, but would also increase the traffic on the travel site, thus further enhancing the credibility of the latter. In addition, our results demonstrate that the style of an online-review as well as brand familiarity may only be interpreted as "peripheral cues" since their impact on trust in e-reviews is much lower compared to the "cognitive" antecedents of trust.

With respect to MGC, perceived 'expertness' and 'credibility of the e-platform' emerged as core determinants of the latent variable 'trust in e-reviews' for all three groups. Moreover, with respect to the overall sample and the group of non agro-tourists, all independent variables display a significant influence on the latent variables (i.e., 'trust in e-review' and 'choice of accommodation').

By contrast, within the group of agro-tourists only the path values of perceived 'expertness' and 'credibility of the online-platform' are significant, thus implying that only these factors determine trust formation. Moreover, the impact of 'trust in e-reviews' in relation to 'choice of accommodation' is relatively strong within this sub-sample (R^2 = 23.9 per cent) although weak among non agro-tourists (R^2 = 5.2 per cent). These results clearly suggest that among farm tourists the evaluation of product experience attributes by online users is extremely important when booking an accommodation. As a managerial implication, farm operators need to effectively monitor online reviews posted on travel platforms and take advantage of them in order to develop a product differentiation strategy (Xiang and Gretzel 2010).

Testing for significant differences between agro-tourists and non agro-tourists

Since the structural model in each group has an acceptable goodness-of-fit, group differences can be compared. To this end, pair-wise t-tests were conducted. If path coefficients in two groups are not significantly different, the strength of the influence between two measured constructs may be generalized (Eberl 2010). As shown by Table 18.3 there are no significant differences between the two sub-samples concerning perceived 'expertness' of e-reviews, implying structural equivalence between these groups concerning this determinant of trust in e-reviews (ibid.). By contrast, differences emerged with respect to 'credibility of e-platforms' and 'choice of accommodation'. More precisely, for the sub-sample of agro-tourists

Table 18.3 Differences in Path Estimators between the two Sub-groups

Differences of path coefficients of subsample of non agro-tourists to subsample of...	**...agro-tourists**
	Difference of sample mean path coeff. **T-Value**
Brand familiarity -> Trust in review	-0.084 -0.666
Perceived expertness of review -> Trust in review	0.084 0.738
Style of review -> Trust in review	0.0633 0.787
Credibility of e-platforms -> Trust in review	-0.813 **1.657**
Trust in review -> Choice of accommodation	-0.2608 **2.356**

Note: Significant values are shown in bold. Significance at 0.001 level=2 tailed t-test t > 3.291; Significance at 0.01 level=2 tailed t-test t > 2.576; Significance at 0.05 level=2 tailed t-test t > 1.960 Significance at 0.10 level=2-tailed t test t > 1.65.

'credibility of the e-platform' as well as 'trust in e-reviews' have a significantly stronger influence on the respective latent variable (i.e., 'trust in e-reviews' and 'choice of accommodation').

Obviously, agro-tourists seem to be particularly sensitive towards Web 2.0-based information exchanged via e-review applications (Sidali 2009). For agro-tourism managers this clearly implies a most accurate choice of Web 2.0 platforms in terms of overall coherence and with respect to particular sensitive topics. Prominent examples for Web 2.0 applications are community sites (e.g., LonelyPlanet), review sites (e.g., TripAdvisor), blogs and blog aggregators (e.g., blogspot.com), social networking sites (e.g., Facebook) and media sharing sites (e.g., YouTube, Flickr) (Xiang and Gretzel 2010). The idea of placing a farm's address on a platform designed only for the farm tourism sector could be very useful for setting up farm tourism communities. Reports of best practice corroborate this assumption: farm tourism operators in Italy recently started to promote their facilities by using online travel platforms, such as www.agriturismo.it, that not only host farms' addresses and product descriptions but also include online-reviews continuously posted by farm guests (Sidali 2009).

5. Conclusions and Outlook

In the course of the last decade travel and tourism has undergone a dramatic change of strategic goals associated with Internet-based technologies (Fuchs and Höpken 2008: 253). Moreover, on the demand side the frontiers between web users and editors have blurred (Fuchs and Höpken 2011). Finally, the ease of exchanging huge amounts of information via the Internet has led to better informed consumers. Hence, the Internet has become the 'social network' which is continuously empowering the customers (Xiang and Gretzel 2010; Kim, Lee and Hiemstra 2004).

The study at hand has identified the drivers behind trust formation in e-reviews and its impact on consumption behaviour by narrowing the scope of research to special-interest tourism, i.e., farm tourism or agro-tourism. The empirical findings reveal that promotion of agro-tourism should afford more consideration to e-reviews as the impact of third-party endorsement on consumption decision is particularly high among agro-tourists.

For farm tourism operators this means that once 'online presence' is established, several advantages can be achieved. Not only customers but particularly niche-operators will benefit from the 'common knowledge base' created by Web 2.0 technologies: the established information base gives the company valuable customer feedback. Furthermore, the decision to let consumers review value-creation processes signals the company's willingness to reduce information asymmetries between supply and demand, thus, positively affecting its reputation.

This study has certain limitations that should be considered. Firstly, the convenience sample employed implies that the empirical results may not be fully representative (Huang 2006). Furthermore, the dependent variable included in the SEM was built by just replicating the Web environment, thereby asking respondents to compare among different sources of information. Surely, although applied technical measures for construct reliability and validity proved to be successful, this procedure could be the reason for an eventual evaluation bias (Brown, Broderick and Lee 2007), particularly also since respondents showed a scarce level of knowledge of both e-reviews and e-platforms.

However, all in all, the findings of this study generally tend to confirm the fact that the German farm tourism sector is an economic branch that is still evolving and that the usage of new information and communication technologies will offer excellent opportunities to establish innovative and strong relationships not only among agro-tourists, but also between farmers and agro-tourists which in turn, will further develop and increase the base of loyal customers.

References

Akerlof, G.A. 1970. The market for "lemons": Quality uncertainty and the market mechanism. *Quarterly Journal of Economics*, 84, 488-500.

Arndt, J. 1967. Role of product-related conversations in the diffusion of a new product. *Journal of Marketing Research*, 4, 291-295.

Bagozzi, R.P. and Yi, Y. 1988. On the evaluation of structural equation models. *Journal of the Academy of Marketing Science*, 16(1), 74-94.

BMELV (Bundesministerium für Ernährung, Landwirtschaft und Verbraucherschutz), 2009. *Urlaub auf dem Bauernhof/Urlaub auf dem Lande.* Bonn: BMELV.

BMELV (Bundesministerium für Ernährung, Landwirtschaft und Verbraucherschutz), 2008. *Expertise Urlaub auf dem Bauernhof/Lande.* Bonn: BMELV.

BMELV (Bundesministerium für Ernährung, Landwirtschaft und Verbraucherschutz), 2006. *Urlaub auf dem Bauernhof/Urlaub auf dem Lande.* Bonn: BMELV.

Brown, J., Broderick, A.J. and Lee, N. 2007. Word of mouth communication within online communities: Conceptualizing the online social network. *Journal of Interactive Marketing*, 21, 2-20.

Chin, W.W. and Dibbern, J. 2010. An introduction to a permutation based procedure for multi-group PLS analysis. Results of tests of differences on simulated data and a cross-cultural analysis of the sourcing of information system services between Germany and the USA, in *Handbook of Partial Least Squares*, edited by V.E. Vinzi et al. Berlin: Springer Verlag, 171-193.

Clerides, S., Nearchou, P. and Pashardes, P. 2004. *Intermediaries as Quality Assessors in Markets with Asymmetric Information: From UK Package Tourism* [Online]. Available at: http://www.aueb.gr/deos/seminars/Clerides2-12-04.pdf [accessed: 24 May 2010].

Coulter, K.S. and Coulter, R.A. 2002. Determinants of trust in a service provider: the moderating role of length of relationship. *Journal of Services Marketing*, 16(1), 35-50.

De Valck, K., van Bruggen, G.H. and Wierenga, B. 2009. Virtual communities: A marketing perspective. *Decision Support Systems*, 47(3), 185-203.

Dibbern, J. and Chin, W.W. 2005. Multi-Group Comparison: Testing a PLS Model on the Sourcing of Application Software Services across Germany and the U.S.A. Using a Permutation Based Algorithm, in *Manual of PLS-path Modelling*, edited by F. Bliemel, Stuttgart: Schäffer-Poeschel.

Eberl, M. 2010. An application of PLS in multi-group analysis. The need for differentiated corporate-level marketing in the mobile communications industry, in *Handbook of Partial Least Squares*, edited by V.E. Vinzi et al. Berlin: Springer Verlag, 487-514.

Ebert, T. 2006. Operationalisation of trust in business networks dealing with complex products and food products, in *Trust and Risk in Business Networks*, edited by M. Fritz et al. Bonn: University ILB.

Fuchs, M. and Höpken, W. 2008. Structural and behavioural changes on account of new information and communication technologies in tourism, in *Change Management in Tourism*, edited by G. Bierling. Berlin: Schmidt, 247-262.

Fuchs, M. and Höpken, W. 2011. E-Business horizons in the tourism industry: Challenges for research and practice, in *Food, Agri-Culture and Tourism,* edited by K.L. Sidali et al. Berlin: Springer Verlag.

Fuchs, M., Scholochow, C. and Höpken, W. 2009. e-Business adoption, use and value creation – an Austrian hotel study, *Information Technology & Tourism*, 11(4), 267-284.

FUR (Forschungsgemeinschaft Urlaub und Reisen) 2007. *Kurzfassung Reiseanalyse RA 2007*. Kiel.

Gefen, D. 2000. E-commerce: The role of familiarity and trust. *The International Journal of Management Science*, 28, 725-737.

Giffin, K. 1967. The contribution of studies of source credibility to a theory of interpersonal trust in the communication process. *Psychological Bulletin*, 68(2), 104-120.

Gretzel, U. 2007. *Online Travel Review Study: Role and Impact of Online Travel Reviews* [online]. Available at: http://www.tripadvisor.com/ pdfs/Online Travel Review Report.pdf [accessed: 2 May 2008].

Grunert, K.G., Brunsø, K. et al., 1997. *Food-related Lifestyle: Development of a Cross-culturally Valid Instrument for Market Surveillance* [Online]. Available at: http://research.asb.dk/fbspretrieve/88/wp12.pdf [accessed: 19 May 2010].

Hair, J.F., Anderson, R.E., Tatham, R.L. and Black, W.C. 2006. *Multivariate Data Analysis*. Upper Saddle River, NJ: Pearson/Prentice Hall.

Hennig-Thurau, T. 2005. "Word-of-Mouse": Why consumers listen to each other on the Internet, in *Jahrbuch der Absatz- und Verbrauchsforschung*, edited by GfK Nürnberg. Berlin: Duncker & Humblot, 52-75.

Homburg, C. and Giering, A. 1996. Konzeptualisierung und Operationalisierung komplexer Konstrukte – Ein Leitfaden für die Marketingforschung. *Marketing – Zeitschrift für Forschung und Praxis*, 18(1), 5-24.

Huang, L. 2006. Rural tourism revitalization of the leisure farm industry by implementing an e-commerce strategy. *Journal of Vacation Marketing*, 12(3), 232-245.

Kim, W.G., Lee, C. and Hiemstra, S.J. 2004. Effects of an online virtual community on customer loyalty and travel products purchases. *Tourism Management*, 25(2), 343-355.

Kucuk, S.U. and Krishnamurthy, S. 2007. An analysis of consumer power on the Internet. *Technovation: The International Journal of Technological Innovation*, 27(1/2), 47-56.

Lender, P. 1997. *Der Markt für Urlaub auf dem Bauernhof in Schleswig-Holstein*, Dissertation, University of Kiel.

Litvin, S.W., Goldsmith, R.E. and Pan, B. 2008. Electronic word-of-mouth in hospitality and tourism management. *Tourism Management*, 29(3), 458-468.

Lüdke, M. 2001. *Nutzung des Internet als Marketinginstrument für landwirtschaftliche Unternehmen: Ansatzpunkte für einen Online-Marketing-Mix landwirtschaftlicher Direktvermarkter sowie Anbieter von Urlaub auf dem Bauernhof*. Aachen: Shaker.

Luhmann, N. 1979. *Trust and Power*. Chichester: Wiley.

Moorman, C., Deshpandé, R. and Zaltman, G. 1993. Factors affecting trust in market research relationships. *Journal of Marketing*, 57, 81-101.

Pan, B., MacLaurin, T. and Crotts, J.C. 2007. Travel blogs and the implications for destination making. *Journal of Travel Research*, 46(1), 35-45.

Phillip, S., Hunter, C. and Blackstock, K. 2010. A typology for defining agritourism. *Tourism Management*, 31(6), 754-758.

Przezbórska, L. 2003. Relationships between rural tourism and agrarian restructuring in a transitional economy: The case of Poland, in *New Directions in Rural Tourism*, edited by D. Hall et al. Aldershot: Ashgate, 203-222.

Raimondo, M.A. 2000. The measurement of trust in marketing studies: A review of models and methodologies. Paper presented at the 16th IMP-conference, Bath, UK.

Reisinger, Y. and Turner, L. 1999. Structural equation modelling with LISREL: Application in tourism. *Tourism Management*, 20(2), 71-88.

Schmeißer, D.R. 2010. Kundenbewertungen in der eTouristik – Segen oder Fluch?: Psychologie der Reiseentscheidung im Social Web, in *Social Web im Tourismus*, edited by D. Amersdorffer et al. Berlin: Springer Verlag, 41-56.

Sidali, K.L. 2009. *Farm Tourism: A Cross-country Empirical Study in Germany and Italy*. Dissertation [Online]. Available at: http://amsdottorato.cib.unibo.it/2248/. University of Bologna.

Sundaram, D.S. and Webster, C. 1999. The role of brand familiarity on the impact of word-of-mouth communication on brand evaluations. *Advances in Consumer Research*, 26, 664-670.

Veeck, G., Che, D. and Veeck, A. 2006. America's changing farmscape: A study of agricultural tourism in Michigan. *The Professional Geographer*, 58(3), 235-248.

Vermeulen, I.E. and Seegers, D. 2009. Tried and tested: The impact of online hotel reviews on consumer consideration. *Tourism Management*, 30(1), 123-127.

Xiang, Z. and Gretzel, U. 2010. Role of social media in online travel information search. *Tourism Management*, 31(2), 179-188.

Yoo, K-H., Lee, Y-J., Gretzel, U. and D.R. Fesenmaier 2009. Trust in travel-related consumer generated media, in *Information and Communication Technologies in Tourism*, edited by W. Höpken et al. Vienna: Springer Verlag, 49-60.

PART 4
Web 2.0: Knowledge Management and Market Research

Chapter 19
Introduction to Part 4

Marianna Sigala

1. Exploiting Web 2.0 for Knowledge Management and Market Research

In the information society, knowledge represents the major asset of a tourism firm enabling it to survive as well as to achieve a competitive advantage. The advances and tools of Web 2.0 represent a very interactive platform not only for storing and searching, but also for creating and disseminating information and knowledge. In this vein, more and more companies are trying to exploit Web 2.0 for identifying new ways to cultivate and support knowledge sharing and creation with their customers, suppliers and many other partners (Wagner and Bolloju 2005; Christou 2003, 2010). Moreover, many firms are also exploring ways to utilise Web 2.0 tools (such as social networks, blogs and wikis) for creating and supporting a knowledge sharing culture and infrastructure amongst their employees and project groups (Chalkiti and Sigala 2008).

Nevertheless, Web 2.0 exploitation for knowledge management (KM) practices possesses several implications and challenges for tourism firms such as: how to identify, collect and evaluate the value of UGC and social intelligence on Web 2.0? how to analyse and interpret such knowledge for informationalising their business decision-making? how to create an open culture of knowledge sharing and creation within their firm and business networks? what are the risks and costs of adopting such an open knowledge sharing strategy supported by Web 2.0? It is evident that factors facilitating and/or inhibiting firms exploiting Web 2.0 for knowledge management may refer to (Liu et al., 2007): technological factors (e.g. functionalities of information systems; technical security issues; easy of use of the platform); organisational factors (e.g. knowledge sharing culture and values; creation and maintenance of communities of practice; trust and transparency); managerial factors (e.g. management commitment and support; incentives for knowledge management); and individual (employee, customer etc.) factors (e.g. personal values, capabilities and motivation).

2. Overview of the Part

This part of the book aims to answer and provide more insight into the above mentioned issues. Chapter 20 is written by Marianna Sigala and Kalotina Chalkiti and investigates the role of Information and Communication Technologies (ICT) and specifically, Web 2.0 for supporting KM processes. The chapter reviews the related literature in order to identify and analyse the different levels of technology supported KM practices adopted by firms. The chapter also demonstrates how Web 2.0 advances transform KM to a new phase by migrating KM from a technology-centric to a people-centric approach by supporting conversational and collaborative KM processes. The chapter also provides and discusses empirical data investigating the type of Web 2.0 usage of Greek tourism firms for supporting their KM processes. The findings provide useful information about the adoption stage of KM 2.0 from Greek tourism firms as well as several practical implications to tourism professionals for enhancing their Web 2.0 enabled KM.

Chapter 21 is written by John C. Crotts, Boyd H. Davis, and Peyton R. Mason demonstrates the use of quantitative, computer-supported coding methods for analysing qualitative data from tourism blogs by adopting a linguistics approach. The findings and practical implications of the chapter help researchers to consider the possibilities of the source of data, avoid pitfalls, and encourage refinements and extensions of the research related methods.

Chapter 22 is written by Alan Stevenson and Jim Hamill and it summarises the current 'state-of-the art' thinking on Social Media Monitoring (SMM) by using a practical case example of city destinations. The chapter provides an overview of what the current suite of tools can deliver, the implications for travel, tourism and hospitality businesses and the practical advice in developing an SMM strategy. The case example presents top level results of an SMM exercise covering the top ten city destinations worldwide, together with a more detailed analysis of two cities (London and New York). The chapter concludes by presenting a '6Is' framework for measuring social media performance and business impact. The framework has direct practical relevance to tourism and related businesses and could also be used as a basis for future research in this area.

References

Chalkiti, K. and Sigala, M. 2008. Information Sharing and Knowledge Creation in online forums: The case of the Greek online forum "DIALOGOI". *Current Issues in Tourism*, 11(5), 381-406.

Christou, E. 2003. Guest loyalty likelihood in relation to hotels' corporate image and reputation: A study of three countries in Europe. *Journal of Hospitality & Leisure Marketing*, 10, 85-99.

Christou, E. 2010. Investigating attitudes towards mobile commerce for travel products. *Tourism: An International Interdisciplinary Journal*, 58, 7-18.

Liu, X. Magjuka, R.J. Bonk, C.J. and Seung-Jee, L. 2007. Does sense of community matter? An examination of participants' perceptions of building learning communities in online courses. *Quarterly Review of Distance Education*, 8, 9-24.

Wagner, C. and Bolloju, N. 2005. Supporting knowledge management in organizations with conversational technologies: Discussion forums, weblogs, and wikis. *Journal of Database Management*, 16, 1-8.

Chapter 20
Knowledge Management and Web 2.0: Preliminary Findings from the Greek Tourism Industry

Marianna Sigala and Kalotina Chalkiti

1. Introduction

Nowadays, knowledge is widely recognised as one of the most crucial competitive assets substantially supporting and fostering an enterprise's adaptation, survival and outstanding performance (Bohn 1994; Boisot 1998; Mertins et al., 2000; O'Dell and Grayson 1998). This is because by being mainly tacit (intangible) and embedded in organisational structures and cultures, knowledge cannot be easily copied and substituted and so, it creates business value in a unique, inimitable and non-transferable way. As information is the lifeblood of tourism, tourism organisations are not excluded from this knowledge revolution (Poon 1993; Sigala and Chalkiti 2007).

However, previous studies investigating KM in tourism have placed an increased importance on intra-firm KM, overlooking the need to also engage in knowledge exchange and creation with stakeholders beyond the borders of the firm (Bouncken 2002). On the other hand, in a highly interconnected and dynamic world, technology advances and specifically, Web 2.0 advances empower tourism firms to cultivate and expand their knowledge sharing practices with their customers, suppliers, various partners and other stakeholders (Chalkiti and Sigala 2008). Indeed, Young (2008) predicted that by 2013 social networking will be a decent substitute for KM applications. Nowadays, KM is evolving to a new phase that places collective intelligence at its core and promotes its use by accelerating its distribution. Although tourism research has emphasised and explored the ways in which the collective intelligence of Web 2.0 can be used for CRM, new service development, marketing and reputation management strategies (e.g. O'Connor 2010; Pan et al., 2007; Sigala 2011, 2008), there is a lack of research investigating whether and how tourism firms exploit Web 2.0 for enriching and expanding their KM practices.

The aim of this chapter is to first analyse how Web 2.0 enhances and transforms KM practices and then to investigate how Greek tourism firms exploit Web 2.0 tools for supporting their KM. The chapter starts by identifying the KM processes and then debating the role and limitations of ICT for supporting these

KM processes. The chapter continues by analysing the transformative power of Web 2.0 that migrates KM from a technology-centric to a people-centric approach that overcomes the conventional approaches to ICT-driven KM by supporting conversational and collaborative KM processes. The literature has shown that different types of technology exploitation reflect different levels of technology supported KM practices. Consequently, a questionnaire measuring the different types of Web 2.0 usage for KM was developed and used to collect data from Greek tourism firms. The preliminary findings of a large-scale national survey provide interesting information about the level of adoption of Web 2.0 by Greek tourism firms and the chapter concludes with several practical implications for addressing the KM gaps of the Web 2.0 exploitation.

2. Knowledge Management Processes

Knowledge management (KM) is a structured approach to addressing the core processes of creating, codifying, using, measuring and retaining knowledge while leveraging it to compete in turbulent business markets (Tobin 1998; Rowley 2000). Research has focused on the role and beneficial impact of KM in supporting different business processes and functions. For example, developing management processes to build and maintain good quality customer relations, thus enhancing customer lifetime value; enhancing the performance of supply chains and fostering organisational learning and continuous improvement (Boisot 1998; Mertins et al., 2000; Ruhanen and Cooper 2003; Sigala 2011, 2008; Sigala and Chalkiti 2007).

Knowledge is generally categorised into explicit knowledge that can be easily encoded, stored and transmitted (von Krogh 1998), and tacit knowledge that is normally developed from action and experience, and shared through highly interactive communication (Zack 1999). Knowledge is created through an intertwining of the various forms of knowledge (tacit, explicit, individual and collective) expressed by a knowledge spiral (Nonaka et al., 2000) that shows the iterative conversation from tacit to explicit knowledge through four modes: socialisation, externalisation, combination and internalisation. The literature does not provide any standard and holistic KM framework (Jennex 2005; Ponis et al., 2009), but the existing numerous and fragmented KM frameworks comprise the following five generic KM processes: acquisition, generation/creation, codification, storing, sharing/transfer and utilisation/application of knowledge. Many authors (e.g. Davenport and Prusak 1998; von Krogh 1998) place a greater emphasis on the knowledge creation processes that create and accumulate intellectual capital. This is because knowledge creation can mobilise and refresh the KM spiral processes with additional and updated knowledge, while the accumulated knowledge enhances the absorptive capacity of actors that in turn empowers them to better assimilate and produce further knowledge. Equally, many researchers have argued that knowledge sharing processes are also an essential part of effective KM (Bock and Kim 2002; Markus 2001; Wasko and Faraj 2005), because knowledge sharing lies at the core of continuous improvement processes, and is quintessential in terms of transforming an individual's process improvements into actual learning. In this vein, knowledge sharing is an essential component of knowledge creation activities (Davenport and Prusak 1998). Knowledge sharing is the process by which an individual imparts his or her expertise, insight, or understanding to another individual so that the recipient may potentially acquire and use the knowledge to perform his or her task(s) better. However, knowledge sharing involves knowledge exchange activities between individuals, groups and communities of practices (Wasko and Faraj 2005).

3. The Role, Levels and Limitations of ICT-driven KM Processes

Technology is widely recognised (e.g. Nonaka and Takeuchi 1995) as a crucial factor that can boost knowledge creation processes by mobilizing and converting knowledge. Nowadays, the internet represents the most successful open information distribution mechanism enabling people to network for sharing, debating, (co)-creating knowledge and learning from each other (Chalkiti and Sigala 2008; Karger and Quan 2005; Wagner and Bolloju 2005).

The role of Information and Communication Technologies (ICT) in intra-organisational KM has received extensive research attention (Kankannalli et al., 2003; Rhodes et al., 2008; Robert 2009; Yang and Wu 2008). Traditionally, ICT are viewed as a collection of technological capabilities and tools (e.g. e-mail, intranets, databases, forums etc.) that capture and store knowledge (Grover and Davenport 2001) in order to enable firms to manage, retrieve, disseminate and process information (Swan et al., 2000). Several authors have analysed the role of ICT in facilitating all the previously identified KM processes. For example, Jackson (2000) defined KM within the context of information systems (IS) to have functions that facilitate and enhance the collection, organisation, refining, analysis, and dissemination of all forms of knowledge. Zack (1999) described the ICT-driven KM as a process aiming to create and disseminate knowledge within firms that includes activities such as knowledge retrieval, refinement, indexing, distribution, and representation. Rosenberg (2001) proposed a KM pyramid model that includes three layers of ICT-driven KM processes. The lowest level represents technology enabled document management supporting information storage and distribution. The second layer represents KM processes of information creation, sharing, and management, where people actually store information in the ICT, create new content, and enrich knowledge databases for further online retrievals. The third layer refers to the entrepreneurial wisdom, which expresses the affordances of ICT to empower people to create organisational know-how. Jackson (2000) supported Zack's (1999) arguments that ICT can enable higher order KM and creation processes, by arguing that ICT enable multidimensional KM processes that create knowledge value that is not the same thing as data or information. Zack's (1999) KM pyramid model is also important, because it enables firms to identify their stage/level of ICT exploitation for supporting and enhancing KM processes.

The increasing importance of ICT for KM is attributed to the business need to make KM more independent from human resources in order to protect organisational knowledge from challenging factors such as staff turnover, power challenges affecting knowledge sharing and knowledge hoarding (Connelly and Kelloway 2000; Walsham 2001). However, despite the great theoretical emphasis on ICT capabilities to support KM, the impact of ICTs is questionable (Thomas 2005), while some studies have also shown the inability of ICT to successfully support KM processes (Butler 2003; Schultze and Boland 2000). Reasons contributing to the lack of success of ICTs to support KM processes relate to issues inherited to the ICT's capabilities required to support the KM processes and to the factors of the external environment mediating the role of ICTs to support KM processes. Analytically, these issues are summarised as the following: the epistemological challenges and debates concerning the nature of knowledge and the subsequent conventional approach of ICTs towards KM that treats knowledge as a commodity; the disregard of the social and cultural aspects of knowledge (e.g. power); and the unstable contemporary workforce where staff turnover, labour mobility and flexible labour utilisation strategies have casualised the workforce.

Concerning the epistemological challenges, some researchers believe that knowledge is an object that can be stored and shared because of its explicit nature (Nonaka 1994), while others argue that it is always tacit (Polanyi 1966) and consequently cannot be captured via ICT. Depending on the view, the role and importance of ICT differs. Researchers in favour of the distinct tacit and explicit dichotomy claim that ICT are excellent ways of capturing, storing and transferring knowledge. This represents the conventional approach of ICT-enabled KM (Swan et al., 2000; Swan and Scarbrough 2001) that treats knowledge as a commodity and adopts an information processing epistemology (Roos and von Krogh 1996), whereby knowledge and information are perceived as synonymous (Terrett 1998) and learning is an individual rather than a group activity (Currie and Kerrin 2004). However, based on this approach, an important limitation of ICTs to support KM focuses on the former's ability to only capture and process data and information, not knowledge (Butler 2003; McGee and Prusak 1993). Consequently, ICT are unable to support cognitive and decision-making processes (Boland et al., 1994), which in turn corroborate the ICT's narrow focus on the construction of knowledge. Indeed, ICT consider the construction of knowledge as a functionalist activity and disregard 'the socially constructed, distributed, and embedded nature of knowledge and the process by which it changes' (Pentland 1995: 2), which is a major limitation as Nonaka and Tageuki (1995) emphasised that the social dimension is key to the whole knowledge creation process.

On the other hand, researchers believing in only the tacit nature of knowledge argue that ICT are unsuccessful because they disregard the socio-cultural context of knowledge (Leonard and Sensiper 1998; Tsoukas and Vladimirou 2001). For example, ICT appear to support the externalisation and recording of explicit knowledge, while disregarding the tacit components of knowledge and their pivotal role (Walsham 2001). Studies have also shown that human resources are critical in supporting KM processes, knowledge cannot be separated from its socio-cultural context, and thus, ICT can only offer ways to support employees' actions (Edvinsson 2000; Hull 2000; Scarbrough 2003). Hence, it is recommended that ICTs are perceived as being able to complement other factors enabling knowledge sharing, rather than presenting the solution to knowledge sharing problems. Also, acknowledging the socio-cultural aspect of knowledge and how these characteristics influence KM, businesses may benefit from finding ways to encourage social interactions by creating distinct areas in workplaces such as communal coffee machines or water coolers (Brown and Duguid 1991). This is because ICTs are great facilitators of data and information sharing but 'can never substitute for the rich interactivity, communication and learning that is inherent in dialogue. Knowledge is primarily a function and consequence of the meeting and interaction of minds' (Fahey and Prusak 1998: 273). Indeed, as ICTs cannot entirely replace the social cues in face-to-face interactions, this may explain why researchers argue against the overreliance on ICT to potentially replace human interaction activities (Connelly and Kelloway 2008).

Overall, ICTs are limited in supporting KM processes, because they have traditionally discounted the human-centred view of knowledge – that of knowledge being tacit and co-constructed through interactions by individuals. Since the socio-cultural aspects of knowledge have been disregarded, the effectiveness and role of ICT to support KM has been minimal (McDermott 1999; O'Dell and Grayson 1998).

4. Web 2.0 and KM 2.0

Web 2.0 appears to address many of the limitations of the conventional ICT-driven KM, as Web 2.0 considers the human and social aspects of knowledge. By changing the way people search, share and create knowledge, Web 2.0 advances have enabled technology-supported KM to move from a technology-centric highlighting the information processing and centralised aspects of ICT to a people-centric approach that enhances and emphasises the conversational and collaborative-based KM processes. As a result research talks about KM 2.0 (McKinsey 2007) which is characterised by the need to discover and participate in social networks/communities of knowledge and enable them to acquire, co-create and share collective intelligence.

Web 2.0 empowers individuals to take an active role in knowledge co-construction by providing and debating content with others through a conversational and collaborative approach (Jonassen 2000). For example, discussion forums, wikis, and weblogs, are conversational technologies enable knowledge creation and sharing through a process of discussion with questions and answers (discussion forum), collaborative editing (wikis), or through a process of storytelling (weblogs) (Wagner and Bolloju 2005). In this vein, Web 2.0 expands the cognitive and knowledge creation abilities of an individual by enabling him/her to process knowledge beyond his/her own inner mental processes and to consider the contextual and social aspects of this knowledge. Conversations in Web 2.0 are recognised as a useful medium for knowledge exchange and extraction (Nishida 2002) and address the social dimension of KM processes (Nonaka and Tageuki 1995) that have been ignored by the conventional ICT-driven KM.

Several authors have analysed how different Web 2.0 tools enable people to create and share knowledge. For example, Yu et al. (2010) discussed how blogs enhance knowledge sharing amongst professionals, because blogs support both the codification of knowledge (e.g. through tags and the profiling information of knowledge creators) and the interpersonal communication and conversations. Ullrich et al. (2008), Bateman et al. (2007) Seldow (2006) and Hayman (2007) have analysed how (social) tagging can support knowledge creation and dissemination by enabling processes such as information filtering, categorisation, recalling and negotiation and linking of meanings. However, Jonassen (2000) has effectively summarised how individuals' participation in Web 2.0 can support all types of KM processes and ultimately, contribute to a collaborative construction of knowledge, as follows:

- Using Web 2.0 as a knowledge repository (e.g. uploading public resources in YouTube.com, blogs), which enables information transmission.
- Pseudo-collaborating with others when using the personally suggested resources by Web 2.0 tools that the latter derive from collecting and analysing the personal data of others (e.g. links, preferences etc.).
- Selecting, collecting and sharing information through RSS, e-mail alerts etc.
- Selecting and sharing information in social networks of common interests (e.g. profile updating in Facebook).
- Decision- and judgement-making by evaluating online resources (e.g. voting, liking resources in Facebook).
- Categorisation and generation of resources through (personal or public) tagging (e.g. bookmark sharing and social/collaborative searching). This higher order cognitive process contributes to the construction of meta-knowledge which is shared and compared with others (e.g. learning and creating knowledge from others' judgements/categorisations).
- Collaborative edition of knowledge (e.g. wikis) which also creates relations with others.
- Negotiation of means, which is an essential element of the collaborative construction of knowledge, through online conversations [e.g. in (micro) blogs] that enable information comprehension, feedback, reflection and contributions.

Similar to Rosenberg's (2001) pyramid of ICT-supported KM, the above-mentioned types of Web 2.0 participation demonstrate that, depending on the type and level

Table 20.1 Knowledge Conversion Circles enabled by Web 2.0

FROM / TO	Tacit Knowledge	Explicit knowledge
Tacit Knowledge	**Socialisation** participate in online discussions/forums and social networks update profile and distribute information in social networks	**Externalisation** users placing tags to their bookmarks, to their documents; users posting comments to online discussions
Explicit knowledge	**Internationalisation** sense-making and learning-by-doing processes (e.g. participate in simulations on virtual words); passive learning by reading others' comments and online discussions; keeping notes of what it was read; writing reflections of reading/ discussions	**Combination** users building a collective knowledge; users uploading information on a social network or a wiki

Source: adapted from Nonaka et al., 2000.

of use of Web 2.0, individuals and social networks enable and foster different levels/stages of Web 2.0 KM processes. The lowest levels will represent Web 2.0 usage for solely storing, categorising, sharing and distributing information, higher levels will represent usage of Web 2.0 for discussing, synthesising and negotiating knowledge, while the highest level will refer to Web 2.0 exploitation for co-creating knowledge.

Studies have also shown how Web 2.0 can support all four circles of knowledge conversion processes according to Nonaka's spiral model (e.g. Wagner and Bolloju 2005). Table 20.1 provides several examples on how individuals can use Web 2.0 to support such knowledge conversions. Consequently, conversational and collaborative KM is argued to yield benefits at numerous stages of the KM process beginning with knowledge creation and ending with knowledge use and refinement (Wagner and Bolloju 2005).

Research has also shown that Web 2.0 enhances not only the functional (information processing), but also the socio-affective aspects of KM activities (Liu et al., 2007; Rovai 2002). For example, wikispaces and blogs allow contribution, but also relationship-building amongst individuals (Jonassen 2000), while tagging enables the formation of social networks (Ullrich et al., 2008). Thus, Web 2.0-enabled KM processes instil a participatory, more democratic and collaborative approach to KM that supports a dynamic, conversational and flexible creation and renewal of knowledge (Avrami 2006; Lee and Lam 2007) and

Table 20.2 Participants' Profile

What is your age group?	**Number of responses (N= 94)**	**% of responses (N=94)**
19-30 years	18	19%
31-40 years	43	46%
41-50 years	20	21%
51-60 years	11	12%
> 60 years	2	2%
Total	**94**	100%
What is your highest education achievement?	**Number of responses (N= 94)**	**% of responses (N=94)**
High-school	5	5%
Vocational education	6	6%
Undergraduate degree	35	37%
Postgraduate degree	42	45%
PhD	6	6%
Total	**94**	**100%**
How many years have you worked in tourism?	**Number of responses (N= 94)**	**% of responses (N=94)**
< 5 years	25	27%
6 -10 years	23	24%
11-20 years	28	30%
21-30 years	11	12%
> 30 years	7	7%
Total	**94**	**100%**
What is your gender?	**Number of responses (N= 94)**	**% of responses (N=94)**
Male	50	53%
Female	44	47%
Total	**94**	**100%**
Years of using the WorldWideWeb	**Number of responses (N= 94)**	**% of responses (N=94)**
1-3 years	2	2%
3-6 years	14	15%
> 6 years	78	83%
Total	**94**	**100%**
Type of professional activity	**Number of responses (N= 94)**	**% of responses (N=94)**
Sole trader	37	41%
Employee	55	59%
Total	**94**	**100%**

In which tourism sector are you employed?	**Number of responses (N=94)**	**% of responses (N=94)**
Hotel	33	35%
Restaurant	4	4%
Travel agency	13	14%
MICE	4	4%
Transport	4	4%
Cultural organisations, leisure	4	4%
Destination management organisation	9	10%
Public tourism organisation	15	16%
Other (consultants)	3	3%
Other (education)	5	5%
Total	**94**	**100%**
What is the size of the business you work for?	**Number of responses (N= 94)**	**% of responses (N=94)**
1-10 employees	44	47%
11-20 employees	7	7%
21-50 employees	13	14%
> 50 employees	30	32%
Total	**94**	**100%**
Where is your business located?	**Number of responses (N= 94)**	**% of responses (N=94)**
Peninsular (urban)	46	49%
Peninsular (rural)	15	16%
Insular (urban)	16	17%
Insular (rural)	17	18%
Total	94	100%
In which department do you work?	**Number of responses (N= 94)**	**% of responses (N=94)**
Marketing	25	27%
Operations	30	32%
Finance	8	8.5%
Human resources	5	5.3%
General manager	19	20%
Other (international relations)	2	2.1%
Other (education)	5	5.3%
Total	**94**	**100%**

overcomes the common pitfalls of ICT-driven KM whereby knowledge hoarding and saturation were frequent drawbacks and the processing of knowledge was in the hands of technology engineers (McDermott 1999).

5. Research Methodology

The aims of this chapter are twofold: a) investigate the role and use of Web 2.0 for supporting and enhancing KM practices; and b) explore the level of Web 2.0 exploitation for KM by Greek tourism firms. The related literature was reviewed and subsequently a research instrument was designed for collecting information about the different ways in which tourism professionals use Web 2.0 for KM purposes. A large-scale national web-based survey was undertaken from November 2010 to January 2011 by distributing the questionnaire through various means: a) press releases and a banner promoting the online questionnaire on traveldailynews.gr (the latter represents the most known and largest professional portal in the Greek tourism industry featuring more thousands subscribers and visitors in each website on a daily basis), b) press release to online and offline media (e.g. Melody radio station, Greek Travel Pages, GTP) and c) e-mail targeting members of the eBusiness group in tourism of the Greek Networking and Research, www.grnet.gr).

One hundred and thirty six responses were received until 12 January 2011. Forty-two were incomplete and excluded. Ninety-four usable responses were used for this research and the preliminary findings are presented below.

6. Analysis and Discussion of the Findings

Respondents' profile

The 94 respondents reflect a good and varied profile of tourism professionals in Greece (Table 20.2). Respondents represent young and mature professionals (65 per cent were under 40 years old), have received tertiary education (88 per cent) and were male (53 per cent). The majority of respondents worked for hotels (35 per cent), travel agencies (14 per cent) and public tourism organisations (10 per cent), but also the remaining 41 per cent were employed in several sectors such as the MICE, transport, cultural, education and other sectors. Respondents also represent a good balance of sole traders (41 per cent) and employees (59 per cent) of both small (54 per cent with fewer than 20 employees) and large businesses (46 per cent with more than 21 employees), working mainly in operations and marketing positions (59 per cent), while a significant 20 per cent also represents general management staff. Respondents' profiles also reflects a good balance of professionals with varied experience in the tourism industry (respondents' working experience in tourism varies equally from one to over 30 years). Although most respondents are located in peninsular urban locations (49 per cent), other

Table 20.3 Participants' Frequency and Reasons of using Social Media

How frequently and for what reason do you use at least one social media?	Usage for social purposes (e.g. contact friends) (99%)		Usage for personal purposes (e.g. entertainment, education) (98%)		Usage for professional purposes (e.g. search for information) (96%)	
	Number of responses	**% of responses (N = 70)**	**Number of responses**	**% of responses (N = 64)**	**Number of responses**	**% of responses (N = 72)**
Every day	42	60%	31	48%	33	46%
Once a week	7	10%	12	19%	9	13%
2-3 times a week	13	19%	10	16%	10	14%
2-3 times a month	4	5%	3	5%	9	13%
Rarely	3	4%	7	11%	8	11%
Never	1	1%	1	2%	3	4%
	70	**100%**	**64**	**100%**	**72**	**100%**

respondents almost equally represent residents of other areas. Finally, respondents' use and experience of the internet is quite good (i.e. 83 per cent have been using the WWW for more than six years).

Purposes and frequency levels of Web 2.0 usage

The majority of the participants (80 per cent) used at least one type of social media, while only 20 per cent of respondents claimed not to use any type of social media. This reflects a high adoption rate of Web 2.0 by tourism professionals, which is also followed by high frequency usage levels of Web 2.0 (Table 20.3). Analytically, findings reveal that nearly all respondents use Web 2.0 for all three major purposes; although the use of Web 2.0 for social purposes had the lead (99 per cent), personal purposes followed (98 per cent) and less respondents (96 per cent) used Web 2.0 for professional purposes. Hence, it is evident that most Web 2.0 users are already aware and are exploiting the benefits of technology not only for social/personal, but also for professional purposes. Findings also illustrate that Web 2.0 has become part of the respondents' agenda, since more than half of the respondents use Web 2.0 every day or once a week. The latter is true for all three types/purposes of Web 2.0 usage, although findings reveal again that the use of Web 2.0 for social purposes is the highest, followed by Web 2.0 for personal reasons and then, for professional purposes. This is not surprising

Table 20.4 Activities of Web 2.0 Users for Professional Purposes (% of Adopters/Users per Activity)

Please indicate the frequency you use Web 2.0 for each of the following reasons	% of Web 2.0 users that use Web 2.0 for each reason	Rarely				Very Frequently	
		1	2	3	4	5	6
Search and collect professional information (N=62)	89%	7 (13%)	7 (13%)	7 (13%)	12 (22%)	4 (7%)	25 (45%)
Search and read information (N=57)	93%	3 (6%)	10 (19%)	7 (13%)	8 (15%)	10 (19%)	19 (36%)
Create and store information in Web 2.0 applications for personal use (e.g. store contacts on Facebook) (N=60)	92%	11 (20%)	6 (11%)	11 (20%)	10 (18%)	13 (24%)	9 (16%)
Upload and store information in Web 2.0 applications for public use (e.g. Upload useful links on Facebook) (N=55)	87%	10 (21%)	4 (8%)	8 (17%)	12 (25%)	9 (19%)	12 (25%)
Disseminate information (e.g. disseminate through professional lists or social networks) (N=60)	88%	7 (13%)	9 (17%)	6 (11%)	8 (15%)	18 (34%)	12 (23%)
Participate in electronic discussions to share and create new information (N=56)	89%	10 (20%)	11 (22%)	13 (26%)	8 (32%)	7 (28%)	7 (28%)
Create and refresh personal profile and status in social networks (N=57)	96%	9 (16%)	8 (15%)	11 (20%)	12 (22%)	8 (15%)	9 (16%)
Search and participate in professional social networks by creating a professional personal profile (N=54)	91%	7 (14%)	12 (24%)	7 (14%)	13 (27%)	9 (18%)	6 (12%)
Search for experts (N=52%)	81%	12 (29%)	7 (17%)	12 (29%)	5 (12%)	12 (29%)	4 (10%)
Meet new people (N=5)	80%	1 (25%)	1 (25%)	1 (25%)	0 (0%)	1 (25%)	1 (25%)

Table 20.5 Types of Information Managed through Web 2.0

Type of information managed through Web 2.0	% of Web 2.0 users managing each type of information	Rarely				Very Frequently	
		1	2	3	4	5	6
Competitors (N=59)	85%	11 (22%)	9 (18%)	7 (14%)	8 (16%)	7 (14%)	8 (16%)
Customers-demand (N=65)	91%	8 (14%)	6 (10%)	10 (17%)	12 (20%)	4 (7%)	19 (32%)
Suppliers (N=53)	83%	10 (23%)	7 (16%)	10 (23%)	8 (18%)	1 (2%)	8 (18%)
Legal framework, government decisions about tourism (N=56)	88%	12 (24%)	8 (16%)	9 (18%)	5 (10%)	4 (8%)	11 (22%)
Political, economic, technological and socio-cultural environment (N=57)	91%	6 (12%)	6 (12%)	11 (21%)	11 (21%)	7 (13%)	11 (21%)
Human resource management (N=51)	80%	8 (20%)	6 (15%)	7 (17%)	7 (17%)	9 (22%)	4 (10%)
Collaborators (N=56)	89%	8 (16%)	6 (12%)	7 (14%)	6 (12%)	14 (28%)	9 (18%)
Operations management (N=52)	83%	4 (9%)	4 (9%)	15 (35%)	8 (19%)	7 (16%)	5 (12%)
Other (information about the future of tourism, N=1)	100%	0 (0%)	0 (0%)	0 (0%)	0 (0%)	0 (0%)	0 (0%)

when considering previous findings showing that social pressures and the need to communicate/find friends is the number one reason motivating people to join and use Web 2.0 tools (e.g. Parra-Lopez et al., 2011). This study confirms this, while it also indicates that the exploitation of Web 2.0 for professional reasons follows and it may be adopted only after people have adopted and are familiarised with the functionality and benefits of Web 2.0 for social/personal purposes. Future studies are however required to confirm the latter.

To better understand the type of use of Web 2.0 for professional purposes, the survey also explored and gathered data about the specific activities performed by Web 2.0 users (Table 20.4). A great majority of respondents (more than 80 per cent) used Web 2.0 for all listed types of activities. However, findings reveal that the most popular activity in Web 2.0 (adopted by 96 per cent of Web 2.0 users) is to "create and refresh personal profile and status in social networks", which was closely followed by: "search and read information" (93 per cent); "create and store information in Web 2.0 applications for personal use" (92 per cent) and "Search and participate in professional social networks by creating a professional profile" (91 per cent). This finding demonstrates that the most important activity (and so, reason) for using Web 2.0 for professional purposes is for finding and joining social networks in order to search, read and store information for personal usage. Such a finding highlights the major benefit of Web 2.0 as an important and heavily used source of professional knowledge. However, the findings also demonstrate the lower usage of Web 2.0 for more advanced knowledge processes than knowledge searching/reading, such as the sharing and discussion of knowledge with others for creating (meta)- and/or new knowledge. This is supported by the fact that fewer Web 2.0 users reported using technology tools for activities such as: "search and collect professional information" (89 per cent), "participate in electronic discussions to share and create new information" (89 per cent), "disseminate information" (88 per cent) and "upload and store information in Web 2.0 applications for public use" (87 per cent). In other words, the majority of Web 2.0 users exploit Web 2.0 tools for supporting their internal KM processes rather than for enhancing and facilitating their external KM processes by collaborating, understanding and debating the perspectives of other professionals. This is further supported by the fact that activities such as "search for experts" (80 per cent) and "meet new people" (80 per cent) were reported to be conducted by the smallest percentage of Web 2.0 users. In addition, findings regarding the frequency of Web 2.0 for each activity also support the previous conclusions, since activities demonstrating an internal use of Web 2.0 tend to be conducted more frequently than the activities referring to an external use of Web 2.0.

In other words, according to the Li and Bernoff's (2008) typology of Web 2.0 users, Greek tourism professionals can be categorised as follows regarding their use of Web 2.0 for professional purposes: the majority of them represent joiners of social communities, which they mainly exploit for searching, storing and collecting information (collectors) and substantially fewer use social networks for distributing (distributors), debating (critics) and creating (creators) new information. This gap in terms of Web 2.0 exploitation for KM purposes reflects a weakness, but also a potential opportunity for Greek tourism professionals. Therefore, it is suggested that in general, Greek tourism professionals should stop being solely passive consumers of online content, and in contrast, they should start exploiting Web 2.0 for becoming more active contributors and creators of knowledge in social networks.

As most respondents used Web 2.0 mainly for information collection it is also interesting to investigate the type of information that Web 2.0 users manage through Web 2.0. Survey data about this issue are provided in Table 20.5. A very high percentage of Web 2.0 users (more than 80 per cent) exploit Web 2.0 for identifying and learning information about all types of issues listed by the survey. However, based on findings regarding the respondents' percentages of Web 2.0 use (and frequency of Web 2.0 usage for managing each information type), the type of information that is mainly managed by Web 2.0 refers to information about: customer-demand, the PESTEL (Political, Economical, Societal, Technological, Environmental, Legal) factors as well as the collaborators. Fewer Web 2.0 users exploit Web 2.0 for searching and learning about competitors (85 per cent), suppliers (83 per cent), operations (83 per cent) and HRM (80 per cent). This finding is not surprising when considering that the tourism industry is the most volatile and vulnerable industry affected by many PESTEL factors and for which every professional needs to stay informed and alerted about their dynamic changes. In addition, the findings also reveal that the greatest majority of Web 2.0 users exploit Web 2.0 for managing information that is external to the firm (e.g. collaborators, environment, customer-demand). On the other hand, significantly fewer respondents exploit Web 2.0 for managing information related to internal issues such as HRM and operations. This represents a weakness of the Web 2.0-supported KM processes of tourism professionals, but it may also reflect a lack of awareness and/or of an existence of Web 2.0 applications that professionals can use for purposes such as organisational learning, organisational networking, internal communication and knowledge exchanging.

7. Conclusions and Future Research

Web 2.0 changes the way people search, share and create information. In this vein, Web 2.0 applications enable the migration of KM practices from a technology-centric to a people-centric approach by supporting conversational and collaborative KM processes. This chapter investigated the role of Web 2.0 for supporting and enhancing KM processes by reviewing the related literature, as well as collecting primary data from Greek tourism professionals in order to explore their type and level of Web 2.0 exploitation for KM purposes. Although findings revealed a high level of Web 2.0 for KM practices, Greek professionals tended to use Web 2.0 for internal KM processes such as searching, storing and collecting information rather than external KM processes such as sharing, discussing and creating knowledge with others. In this vein, Greek professionals demonstrate a low level of Web 2.0 use for KM processes which is a weakness but also a future opportunity for them. Findings also revealed that the majority of respondents exploit Web 2.0 for managing information that is external rather than internal to the firm. In this vein, it is suggested that future research should be conducted in order to investigate the following issues: factors motivating and/or inhibiting tourism professionals to exploit Web 2.0 for higher level KM processes as well as for internal KM practices. Factors such as organisational trust, management commitment, risk/threat of losing corporate information, and professionals' skills are supposed to influence the type and level of Web 2.0 exploitation for KM. However, future research should investigate both their level of influence as well as the strategies that firms need to adopt in order to eliminate their negative impact.

References

Bateman, S. Brooks, C. McCalla, G. and Brusilovsky, P. 2007. *Applying Collaborative Tagging to E-Learning: Proceedings. of 16th International World Wide Web Conference* (Banff, Alberta, Canada, 8-12 May).

Bock, G.W. and Kim, Y.G. 2002. Breaking the myths of rewards: An exploratory study of attitudes about knowledge sharing. *Information Resources Management Journal*, 15(2), 14-21.

Bohn, R.E. 1994. Measuring and managing technological knowledge. *Sloan Management Review*, 36(1), 61-73.

Boisot, M.H. 1998. *Knowledge Assets: Securing Competitive Advantage in the Information Economy*. New York, NY: Oxford University Press.

Bouncken, R. 2002. Knowledge management for quality improvement in hotels, in *Knowledge Management in Hospitality and Tourism*, edited by R. Bouncken and P. Sungsoo. New York, NY: The Haworth Hospitality Press, 25-59.

Brown, J.S. and Duguid, P. 1991. Organizational Learning and Communities of Practice. *California Management Review*, 40(3), 112-132.

Butler, T. 2003. From Data to Knowledge and Back Again: Understanding the Limitations of KMS. *Knowledge and Process Management: The Journal of Corporate Transformation*, 10(4), 144-155.

Chalkiti, K. and Sigala, M. 2008. Information Sharing and Knowledge Creation in online forums: The case of the Greek online forum "DIALOGOI". *Current Issues in Tourism*, 11(5), 381-406.

Connelly, C.E. and Kelloway, E.K. 2003. Predictors of employees' perceptions of knowledge sharing culture. *Leadership & Organization Development Journal*, 24(5), 294-301.

Currie, G. and Kerrin, M. 2003. HRM & Knowledge Management Enhancing Shared Learning in a Pharmaceutical Company. *International Journal of Human Resource Management*, 14(6), 1027-1045.

Davenport, T. and Prusak, L. 1998. *Working Knowledge: How Organizations Manage What They Know*. Boston, MA: Harvard Business School Press.

Edvinsson, L. 2000. Some perspectives on intangibles and intellectual capital. *Journal of Intellectual Capital*, 1(1), 12-16.

Fahey, L. and Prusak, L. 1998. The eleven deadliest sins of knowledge management. *California Management Review*, 40, 265-277.

Grover, V. and Davenport, T.H. 2001. General perspectives on knowledge management: Fostering a research agenda? *Journal of Management Information Systems*, 18(1), 5-21.

Hayman, S. 2007. Folksonomies and Tagging: New development in social bookmarking. *Education Services Australia* [Online]. Available at: http://www.educationau.edu.au/jahia/webdav/site/myjahiasite/shared/papers/arkhayman.pdf [accessed: 15 December 2010].

Hull, R. 2000. Knowledge Management and the Conduct of Expert Labour, in *Managing Knowledge: Critical Investigations of Work and Learning*, edited by C. Pritchard, R. Hull, M. Chumer and H. Willmott. Basingstoke: Palgrave Macmillan.

Jackson, C. 2000. Process to Product: Creating tools for knowledge management, in *Knowledge Management and Business Model Innovation*, edited by Y. Malhotra. Hershey, PA: Idea Group Publishing, 402-412.

Jackson, P. and Klobas, J. 2008. Building knowledge in projects: A practical application of social constructivism to information systems development. *International Journal of Project Management*, 26(3), 304-315.

Jennex, M.E. 2005. What is knowledge management? *International Journal of Knowledge Management*, 1(4), i–iv.

Jonassen, D. 2000. *Theoretical Foundations of Learning Environments.* Mahwah, NJ: Lawrence Erlbaum.

Kankanhalli, A., Tan, B.C.Y. and Wei, K.K. 2005. Contributing knowledge to electronic knowledge repositories: An empirical investigation. *MIS Quarterly*, 29(1), 113-143.

Karger, D.R. and Quan, D. 2005. What would it mean to blog on the semantic web? *Web Semantics: Science, Services and Agents on the World Wide Web*, 147-157.

Krogh, G.V. 1998. Care in knowledge creation. *California Management Review*, 40(3), 133-153.

Leonard D. and Sensiper, S. 1998. The role of tacit knowledge in group innovation. *California Management Review*, 40, 112-132.

Liu, X., Magjuka, R.J., Bonk, C.J. and Seung-Jee, L. 2007. Does sense of community matter? An examination of participants' perceptions of building learning communities in online courses. *Quarterly Review of Distance Education*, 8(1), 9-24.

Markus, M.L. 2001. Towards a theory of knowledge reuse: Types of knowledge reuse situations and factors in reuse success? *Journal of Management Information Systems*, 18(1), 57-93.

McDermott, R. and O'Dell, C. 2001. Overcoming cultural barriers to sharing knowledge. *Journal of Knowledge Management*, 5, 76-85.

McGee, J. and Prusak, L. 1993. *Managing Information Strategically*. New York: John Wiley & Sons.

McKinsey 2007. *How Businesses are Using Web 2.0.* McKinsey Global Survey. Available at: http://www.finextra.com/Finextra-downloads//featuredocs/hobu07.pdf [accessed: 15 December 2010].

Mertins, K., Heisig, P. and Vorbeck, J. 2000. *KM Best Practices in Europe*. Berlin and Heidelberg: Springer Verlag.

Nishida, T. 1999. Facilitating community knowledge evolution by talking virtualized egos: *Proceedings of the HCI International '99 (the 8th International Conference on Human-Computer Interaction) on Human-Computer Interaction: Communication, Cooperation, and Application Design (Germany)*, 2, 437-441.

Nonaka, I. and Takeuchi, H. 1995. *The Knowledge-Creating Company.* New York: Oxford University Press.

Nonaka, I., Toyama, R. and Nagata, A. 2000. A firm as a knowledge-creating entity: A new perspective on the theory of the firm. *Industrial and Corporate Change*, 9(1), 1-20.

O'Connor, P. 2010. Managing a Hotel's Image on TripAdvisor. *Journal of Hospitality Marketing & Management*, 19(7), 754-772.

O'Dell, C. and Grayson, C.J. 1998. *If Only We Knew What We Know*. New York: The Free Press.

Pan, B. MacLaurin, T. and Crott, J.C. 2007. Travel blogs and the implication for destination marketing. *Journal of Travel Research*, 46(1), 35-45.

Parra-Lopez, E. Bulchand-Gidumal, J. Gutiererez-Tano and Diaz-Amas, R. 2011. Intentions to use social media in organizing and taking vacation trips. *Computers in Human Behaviour*, 27, 640-654.

Pentland, B.T. 1995. Information Systems and Organizational Learning: The Social Epistemology of Organizational Knowledge Systems. *Accounting, Management and Information Technology*, 5, 1-21.

Ponis, S., Vagenas, G. and Koronis, E. 2009. Exploring the Knowledge Management Landscape, in *Cultural Implications of Knowledge Sharing, Management and Transfer: Identifying Competitive Advantage*, edited by D. Harorimana. Hershey, PA: IGI Global, 1-25.

Poon, A. 1993. *Tourism, Technology and Competitive Strategies*. Wallingford: CAB International.

Rhodes, J., Hung, R., Lok, P., Lien, B., and Wu, C., 2008. Factors influencing organisational knowledge transfer: Implication for corporate performance. *Journal of Knowledge Management*, 12, 84-100.

Robert, C. 2009. Annotation for knowledge sharing in a collaborative environment. *Journal of Knowledge Management*, 13, 111-119.

Roos, J. and von Krogh, G. 1996. The Epistemological Challenge: Managing Knowledge and Intellectual Capital. *European Management Journal*, 14(4), 333-337.

Rosenberg, M.J. 2001. *E-Learning: Strategies for Delivering Knowledge in the Digital Age.* NY: McGraw Hill Publishing.

Rowley, G. and Purcell, K. 2001. As cooks go, she went: Is labour churn inevitable? *Hospitality Management*, 20(2), 163-185.

Rowley, J. 2000. From learning organisation to knowledge entrepreneur. *Journal of Knowledge Management*, 4(1), 7-15.

Ruhanen, L. and Cooper, C. 2003. Developing a Knowledge Management Approach to Tourism Research. *TedQual*, 6(1), 13.

Scarbrough, H. 2003. Knowledge management, HRM and the innovation process. *International Journal of Manpower*, 24(5), 501-516.

Scarbrough, H. and Swan, J. 2001. Explaining the diffusion of knowledge management: The role of fashion. *British Journal of Management*, 12, 3-12.

Schultze, U. and Boland, R.J. 2000. Knowledge management technology and the reproduction of knowledge work practices. *Journal of Strategic Information Systems*, 9(2-3), 193-212.

Seldow, A. 2006. Social Tagging in K-12 Education: Folksonomies for Student Folk. *Harvard Graduate School of Education* [Online]. Available at: http://mrseldow.gradeweb.com/custom/Social_tagging_in_K12_Education_Seldow_4_3_06.pdf [accessed: 15 December 2010].

Sigala, M. 2008. *Web 2.0 tools Empowering Consumer Participation in New Product Development: Findings and Implications in the Tourism Industry: Proceedings of the Annual International Council for Hotel, Restaurant and Institutional Education, (I-CHRIE) Convention "Welcoming a New Era to Hospitality Education"* (Atlanta, Georgia, USA: 30 July-2 August 2008).

Sigala, M. 2011. eCRM 2.0 applications and trends: The use and perceptions of Greek tourism firms of social networks and intelligence. *Computers in Human Behavior*, 27, 655-661.

Sigala, M. and Chalkiti, K. 2007. Improving performance through tacit knowledge externalization and utilization: Preliminary findings from Greek hotels. *International Journal of Productivity & Performance Management*, 56(5-6), 456-483.

Swan, J. and Scarbrough, H. 2001. Knowledge Management: Concepts and Controversies. *Journal of Management Studies*, 38(7), 913-921.

Swan, J., Newell, S. and Robertson, M. 2000. Limits of IT-driven Knowledge Management Initiatives for Interactive Innovation Processes: Towards a Community-Based Approach: Proceedings of the 3rd Hawaii International Conference on System Sciences (Island of Maui, 4-7 January).

Thomas, H. 2005. ICT and Lean Management: Will They Ever Get Along? *International Journal of Digital Economics*, 59, 53-75.

Tobin, D.R. 1998. Networking your knowledge. *Management Review*, 46-48.

Tsoukas, H. and Vladimirou, E. 2001. What is organisational knowledge? *Journal of Management Studies*, 38(7), 973-993.

Ullrich, C., Kerstin, B., Heng, L., Xiaohong, T., Liping, S. and Ruimin, S. 2008. *Why Web 2.0 is Good for Learning and for Research: Principles and Prototypes: Proceedings of the 17th International World Wide Web Conference* (Beijing, China, 21-25 April).

Wagner, C. and Bolloju, N. 2005. Supporting knowledge management in organizations with conversational technologies: Discussion forums, weblogs, and wikis. *Journal of Database Management*, 16(2), 1-8.

Walsham, G. 2001. Knowledge Management: The Benefits and Limitations of Computer Systems. *European Management Journal*, 19(6), 599-608.

Wasko, M.M. and Faraj, S. 2005. Why should I share? Examining social capital and knowledge.

Yang, H. and Wu, T. 2008. Knowledge sharing in an organisation. *Technological Forecasting & Social Change*, 75, 1128-1156.

Young, O. 2008. Global enterprise Web 2.0 market forecast: 2007-2013. Forrester Research.

Yu, T.K., Lu, L.C. and Liu, T.F. 2010. Exploring factors that influence knowledge sharing behavior via weblogs. *Computers in Human Behaviour*, 26, 32-41.

Zack, M.H. 1999. Managing codified knowledge. *Sloan Management Review*, 40(4), Summer, 45-58.

Chapter 21

Analysing Blog Content for Competitive Advantage: Lessons Learned in the Application of Software Aided Linguistics Analysis

John C. Crotts, Boyd H. Davis and Peyton R. Mason

1. Background

Today most people turn first to the internet not only to research the possibilities on where to vacation, stay, and what to do and see, it is also a place where word-of-mouth has evolved to the next level where consumers are making recommendations to each other. In fact, according to a recent survey 73 per cent of the surveyed were online the day before (Pew Internet and American Life Project 2008).

Travel reviews, found on such sites as TripAdvisor.com, Raveable.com, and TripWolf.com, as well as blogs and microblogs such as Facebook, Flickr, and Twitter, act as a community where consumers connect and become involved with one another. Within these Web 2.0 communities, there are two basic behavioural orientations, one of information search and the other of social interaction (Kurashima, Tezuka and Tanaka 2005). It is the sphere of social interaction where a blogger posts evaluations, or reacts to others with subsequent postings, that provides a rich source of marketing intelligence information.

The motivation to post an evaluation on a travel blog stems from a common enjoyment in sharing valuable information (Bronner and de Hoog 2011; Smith, et al., 2007) and is typically tied to the writer's confidence (Wesson and Pulford 2009). Today consumers generally accept eWOM as more credible than marketer communication (Allsop, Bassett and Hoskins 2007; Gunter, Campbell, Touri, and Gibson 2009; Pan, MacLaurin, and Crotts 2007). Now when a person seeks advice or information, it goes beyond family, friends, and face-to-face contacts and extends to the web where it includes eWOM too.

As market researchers, the closest we can get to gaining a full and complete understanding of our customers is by listening to what they say to others about us, and how they say it. People instinctively make their words work for them. Their words fall into patterns. These patterns can be measured to discover underlying attitudes and emotions: what we call people's *stance.*

Making sense of what is meaningful and motivating out of the enormous volume of online postings is like drinking from a fire hose. Researchers who wish to avail themselves of the data are faced with the problem of how to cull this verbosity of comments on their research topic. Several companies will analyse such data for a fee (e.g., BuzzMetrics, Open Calais, ScoutNet, Visible Technologies). However, their methods are proprietary, raising questions as to the reliability and validity of their results.

Over the years, we have applied various combinations of methods to analysing blog postings to answer fundamental questions from clients. Crotts, Mason and Davis (2009) focused on identifying one hotel company's strengths and weaknesses in each of four competitive environments; while Crotts and Mason (2010) explored the impact of critical incidents on consumer loyalty and repeat intent on behalf of a hotel industry's supplier. In addition, we have been given the opportunity – though unsuccessful – to propose better ways to optimize a travel blog's database for its users through web analytics. What we have learned from these experiences has afforded us the opportunities to test theory in ways that before proved beyond the reach of our academic research (Crotts and Magnini 2011; Zehrer, Magnini and Crotts 2011; Magnini, Crotts, and Zehrer 2011). We believe the future of this line of web analytic research is quite promising.

The remainder of this chapter is organized as follows. First, we will discuss issues related to accessing travel blog data from legal and methodological standpoints. Second, we will explore issues related to detection of false and misleading blog postings in an attempt to limit or mitigate their potential influence on a research project's results. Third, we will compare and contrast two software-aided methods to analyse qualitative data. Lastly, we will discuss what the future may look like in monitoring in real time shifts in consumer sentiment.

2. Accessing Data

Today all the leading travel blogs place restrictions on how their website's contents can be used. Researchers would be wise to carefully review each travel blog's terms and restrictions before extracting their data for research purposes. Travel blogs such as TripAdvisor are designed "to assist customers in gathering travel information, posting opinions of travel related issues, engaging in interactive travel forums and for no other purposes". The company is owned by the online travel agency Expedia; it can justify the cost of developing and maintaining such a free service through the 20 to 30 per cent commissions paid by hotels derived from reservations made by means of click-throughs from TripAdvisor.

Activities prohibited by the leading travel blogs are the use of a website or its contents for any commercial purpose; and accessing its contents using any blog scrapers or any manual process for any purpose without their express written permission. With this said we have, to date, always been given permission to access a travel blog's data when we clearly state our research is for academic purposes only. However, the permission to assess the data always comes with the restriction that blog-scrapers will not be used, relegating the data collecting process to the tedious and time-consuming task of copying and pasting. This is an understandable restriction given that commercially available blog-scraping software, or spiders, can potentially bog down the performance of a website while in use. They can also be easily detected and blocked by a travel blog's systems manager.

We have also learned that most travel blogs have entered into relationships with market research firms who are granted access to the data for commercial purposes. Avalonreport.com was the first to reach such an agreement, producing under a subscription price for hotels what can be thought of a dashboard summary of what recent guests are saying about their specific properties on the leading blogs. Quickly following were alternatives by chatterguard.com, .revinate.com, and tnooz.com. We believe these arrangements are good for the lodging industry in that they not only influence companies to improve their service standards, but also provide hotel managers a convenient means in which to monitor the blogosphere. However, researchers attempting to access the same data for commercial purposes will find their requests denied, relegating their options to unregulated blogosphere that can be identified at Google's blog index.

Issues of Deceptive Blog Postings

Virtually all the managers and executives we come into contact with, both love and loathe travel blogs. They love it when customers say nice things about them, and loathe it when they do not. However, everyone considers it is plausible that evaluations are being posted on blogs that are untrue or deceptive. Though managed travel blogs take precautions to limit deception, deceptive postings are possible (Yoo and Gretzel 2008) and have been identified as far from rare in interpersonal communications (Vrij 2000) to online dating services (Hancock Curry, Goorha and Woodworth 2005).

Deception is defined as the deliberate attempt by one party to create a belief in others that the communicator knows is untrue (Burgoon, Blair, Qin, and Nunamaker 2003). To illustrate, it is conceivable that some managers may deliberately attempt to counter a negative but truthful evaluation by a recent guest with a deceptive positive one that they post in an attempt to counter the negative publicity. It is also not far-fetched to assume that a dubious manager may attempt to malign their competition by posting a negative evaluation posing as a recent guest. Assuming the above to be possible, the questions evoked are: to what degree does deception occur in travel blogs and to what degree do such occurrences corrupt the overall results in one's research? Hence, all researchers must judge prior to their data analysis whether it is important to control the potential of false or deceptive blog postings being captured in the dataset that could influence the study's results.

The roots of today's text analysis methods to detect the presence of deception go back to the earliest days of psychology. Freud's (1901) work focused on identifying a person's linguistic mistakes that reveal their hidden intentions. His enduring popularity is partially attributable to his assertion that subconscious thoughts, emotions, and experiences drive an individual's behaviour and can be revealed through Freudian slips in their use of language. According to Tausczik and Pennebaker (2010), the words a person uses in daily life reflect what he or she is paying attention to, but also what he or she is thinking about, trying to avoid, feeling, and attempting to organize and analyse in the world around them. In such analysis, trained raters read the transcripts of subjects' narratives and tag words or phrases that represent the dimension (e.g. honest, deceptive) being studied.

Beginning in the late 1970s researchers began pioneering software to make the corpus analysis more efficient and objective (Davis and Mason 2010). Linguistic Inquiry and Word Count (LIWC) by Pennebaker and Francis (1996) is the software we have used. The current 2009 software package, in its eighth version, is based on methods and algorithms, which the authors make transparent in the literature, and has generally performed well in tests of validity (Tausczik and Pennebaker 2010). LIWC is designed for studying the emotional, cognitive, and structural components present in people's verbal and written speech, and was originally developed as part of an exploratory study of language and disclosure. The software uses weighted factors scores to identify the individual cases or narratives low in agency that are then scrutinized linguistically for cues or markers of deception, thereby eliminating those cases deemed to be warranted. Nevertheless, no method to detect deception should be considered anywhere close to perfection. Like lie detectors that monitor subjects' heart rates, blood pressure, etc., they should be considered probabilistic systems where cues of deception are identified in language that can produce false positives (negatives).

A number of researchers have attempted through experimental designs to identify language features in written messages that signal the presence of deception (Yoo and Gretzel 2008; Zhou and Sung 2008; Hancock, Curry, Goorha and Woodworth 2005; Zhou, Burgoon, Nunamaker and Twitchell 2004; Burgoon, et al., 2003). Comparing messages containing lies with those that are honest, attempts to identify the language features unique to each. Newman, Pennebaker, Berry and Richards (2003), in a series of controlled experiments, found that participants who were deceptive used far fewer first person singular words like *I* and *my* in their narratives. The lack of these words is often cited as a marker of deception where the deceiver is experiencing guilt over their actions (Newman et al., 2003; Vrij 2000).

Similarly the method known as stance-shift analysis scrutinizes related language features they call *agency* by analysing whether the speaker takes personal responsibility for his/her opinions (Crotts et al., 2009; Lord, Davis and Mason 2008; Davis and Mason 2010).

This analysis detects when a person wants to emphasis a point in the flow of a conversation by shifting the way he/she is expressing his/her thoughts. A stance-shift may identify agency in the form of personalization, strong opinion, increased rationale, or expression of affect/emotion.

4. Quantitative Methods for Analysing Qualitative Data

The Stance-Shift Analysis method represents an extended approach to analysing large qualitative datasets (Davis and Mason 2010; Crotts, et. al. 2009). It involves a three step process aided by software where: 1) qualitative collected data is parsed, tagged and coded through using corpus-based software packages; 2) the coded data is analysed for underlying patterns of language use which index attitudes and opinions; these patterns are what we call dimensions of stance; and 3) these stance dimensions are scaled and analysed quantitatively through proprietary software. More specifically, narratives are coded for stance-shift analysis language features that identify shifts in the manner in which the authors are expressing themselves (Mason, Davis and Bosley 2005). These shifts of stance identify when the speaker moves into narrative sections that exhibit strong opinions, justifications, expressions of affect, and agency. Those sections that are statistically significant (1-standard deviation), relative to the blog author's mean for the full posting, are of particular interest. In these sections, the writer signals an ability or predilection to make choices, and suggests or displays personalized intentions, which are then selected for semantic analyses.

The importance of this approach is in its ability to detect the subtleties of people's feelings as expressed in their language. It works by spotlighting the complexities of participants' responses through computational analysis of their words and language features as they move from topic to topic. People have multiple reasons for how they say what they say, and they may not be aware of all of them. By examining the ways in which word patterns reflect stances, we can draw inferences more skillfully. Data collected from the online universe does not just look or feel different, it *is* different. People are still doing and saying what they did before Web 2.0, but often use a different syntax and lexicon when posting to these forums. People change their language use, or modify their ways of cooperating, and sometimes even change their names. However, people's inner motivations do not really change. They keep the same style they use when they talk. In the online universe, just like face-to-face contact, style can be scaled to measure group solidarity or cohesion; and style can be scaled to measure consumer perceptions of a brand or service.

We have described and demonstrated three methods to analyse such data recently (Capriello, Mason, Davis and Crotts 2011). They are the manual method of coding content, corpus-based semantic analysis, and stance-shift analysis. Given the sheer volume of the data available, the manual coding method – though useful – will, we believe, remain regulated to limited exploratory analysis and the test of theory. Industry is fixated on real-time monitoring. A fully automated process analysis of narrative contents, once developed, will be in high demand.

Table 21.1 Language Features in Transcribed Language (Output Table from a Corpus-Based Software Package)

Semantic Category	Frequency	%
Parts of buildings	1395	2.27
Residence	1032	1.68
Pronouns	6005	9.79
Judgement of appearance: Beautiful	822	1.34
Stationary	623	1.02
Furniture and household fittings	597	0.97
Food	691	1.13

However, to date, such a capability is difficult to achieve because of the complexity of language; words must be disambiguated and language features identified.

As mentioned, various corpus-based analytic software packages have recently emerged as a partial alternative to on-the-fly analysis. These reduce the time and effort necessary through automating essentially manual coding with limited human intervention, typically for annotation of each word keyed to its part of speech, as used for major desktop dictionaries, or its semantic category, based on words that are used similarly. An example of semantic categories is drawn from 200 guest narratives from TripAdvisor.com describing their stays in hotels located in downtown Atlanta, GA (See Table 21.1).

In this dataset, a total of 61,354 words were categorized by the software into one of 233 semantic categories and subcategories. The method provides a reliable and efficient way to identify the most frequently mentioned themes in the evaluative narratives. The word phrases in the most frequently mentioned categories can subsequently be reviewed by researchers for sentiment (e.g., positive, negative) and greater detail. In addition the words in each category can be potentially clustered, showing not only their sub-groupings but their relationship between customer's likes and dislikes (Pan, Crotts and Rashid 2009).

The following example (See Table 21.2) is an excerpt from the results of a stance-shift analysis applied to the same dataset we used for the corpus-based analysis previously discussed. This analysis distilled into five pages what had been 187 printed pages of guests' experiences, by identifying the most salient comments. Stance-shift analysis eliminates those comment sections of the narrative that tend to be informational and exhibit a low degree of social connection.

The above postings were placed in categories that came from what people are saying about different aspects of a resort. These are the actual words from high stance sections of the travellers' comments, though the statements have

Table 21.2 Data Extracted from Online Postings

Attribute	Delights	Disappointments
Decor	No comments.	Carpet in hallways faded and stained. The decor is in keeping with the newer look of sleek and not fussy...I like a little more old world charm myself.
Location	It is in the perfect location, The resort is in great location Great location Its best attribute is that it is located on the corner.	View was adequate, but mostly just rooftops.
Reservation/ Check-in	Extremely friendly fast check-in and staff.	The … agent also told me in no uncertain terms that the "third party online agent" bookings do not receive the same priority as direct reservations when it comes to specific room. Requests such as non-smoking, size of bed, etc. All in all it was a very snobby response that really turned me off…
Staff	Doormen were very professional The staff was more than gracious "Loved it! The people make the stay memorable". What made our stay really special were the people – from the front desk, who gave us an early check in, to the elevator operators who couldn't have been more wonderful, to the concierge.	Elegant, white-gloved elevator operators friendly, but drenched in heavy perfume which is stifling when going to top floors. When we heard all the noise we called the operator to inquire what it was – it sounded like bulldozers going back and forth above our heads and we didn't realize it was a party space.
Concierge	What made our stay really special were the people – from the front desk ... to the concierge.	Went to concierge desk with supporting documentation and airline tickets. regarding explicit request and we were curtly waved away.
Service	Service was top notch service is what make a top notch hotel, and this was the best service I've received, anywhere.	No negative comments.
Room	The rooms were spotless and everything worked fine. The sheets in the room were clean and pressed. We were in a standard room, which was plenty spacious room to move around. Traditional decor, but nice enough. Very comfy beds, and plenty of big towels, toiletries, etc.	Shower pressure is fine for an old hotel. Room carpet and furniture shabby but clean. The bed and room were small but wonderful and so quiet. The room was very spacious (overlooking park), not very quiet – there was all the time an AC machine working noisily.

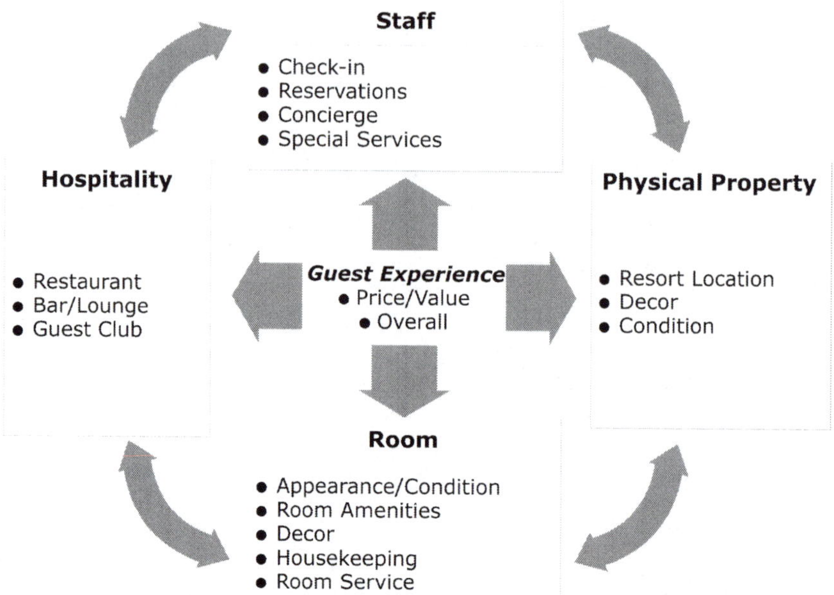

Figure 21.1 Comments Self-categorized and Summarized in an Actionable Manner

been shortened. Briefly, we started the analysis to identify the most important stance segments of the comments and the categorization emerged out of how the travellers' discussed their experience; it was not predetermined by us (See Figure 21.1).

The postings are coded for the 24 language features or parts-of-speech; these features are counted and weighted for importance. Where the high scores indicate the traveller is expressing a high degree of stance. It is the high scores (1-standard deviation) that represent what we call a stance-shift occurs. The shift indicates a change in how the traveller is responding to his or her topic. This change of emphasis signals a shift from presentation of information to increased social involvement. The heightened involvement manifests itself as opinions, rationales, affect and personalization for action.

Patterns of stance in electronic-word-of-mouth (eWOM) identify the salient aspects of the guests' vacation experiences. Stance patterns fall naturally into categories that can summarize a large number of postings in a useable fashion. To further enhance the usefulness of the stance-shift analysis these results then can be placed into a visual format (See Figure 21.2). For this example, we prepared a competitive market overview in which the disappointments were subtracted from the delights.

Why go through all the trouble of mining travel blogs? We contend that understanding what guests are saying can be a great boost to marketers by

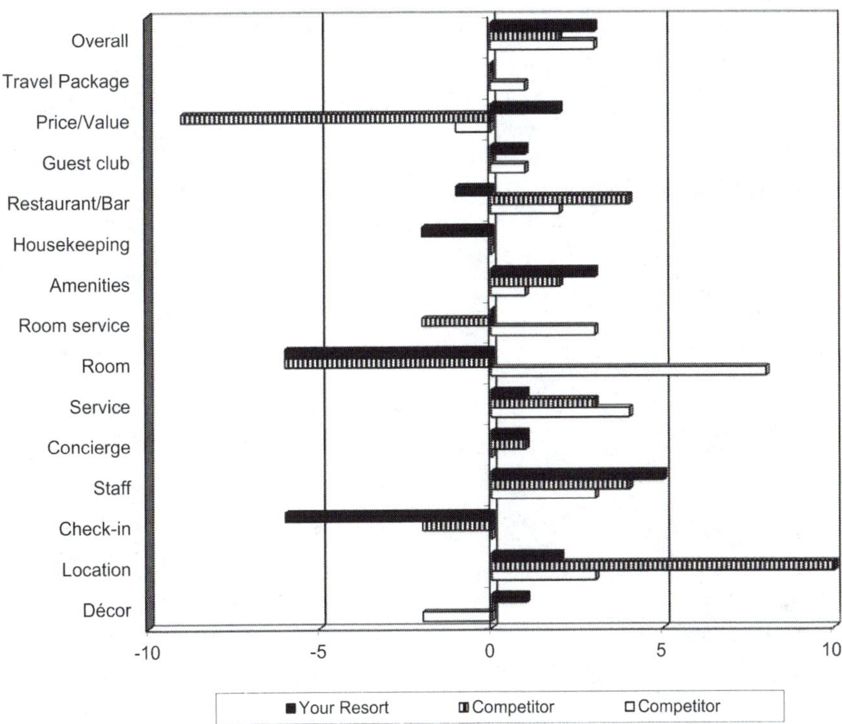

Figure 21.2 Competitive Market View: Vacationers' Disappointments and Delights

allowing them to be more confident in their branding, positioning, and segmenting decisions. In addition, managers learn first-hand what drives guest satisfaction and how to measure up to their competition.

5. Conclusions and What the Future May Look Like

Listening to our clients describe their needs, it is clear that real time fully automated systems are needed that can efficiently and reliably track not only what customers are saying on travel blogs, but also how they are saying it. Corpus-based software and stance-shift analysis are a start, but still require the time and effort of trained researchers to interpret the results. Once a fully automated system is achieved, companies will have data ideally suited to monitor and make real time adjustments in their efforts designed not only to react to changes in consumer sentiment across each of the social media, but to influence it as well. Companies are experimenting with ways to optimize their positions on all forms of social media (e.g., blogs, tweets etc.) and what they need is a means to identify each strategy's effectiveness to influence change in consumer sentiment. Each strategy has a beginning and ending date as well as a cost that can be spread across all dates of a campaign's implementation. A means of assessing quantifiably the consumer buzz – if you will – on a daily, weekly or monthly basis could be included in the marketing mix models used to determine the effect marketing, including the social media, has on its sales. Moreover, companies are also experimenting in ways to influence what consumer's say about them on the social media. A fully automated system would be of immediate value to firms in assessing the effect of their marketing on a company's position in the blogosphere marketplace.

References

Allsop, D., Bassett, B. and Hoskins, J. 2007. Word-of-mouth Research: Principles and applications. *Journal of Advertising Research*, 47(4), 398-411.

Bronner, F. and de Hoog, R. 2011. Vacationers' eWOM: Who posts and why, where and what. *Journal of Travel Research*, 50(1).

Burgoon, J., Blair, J.P., Qin, T., Nunamaker, J. and Jay F. 2003. Detecting deception through linguistic analysis. *Lecture Notes in Computer Science*, 2665(2003), 91-101.

Crotts, J. and Magnini, V. 2011. The customer delight construct: Is surprise essential? *Annals of Tourism Research*, 38(2).

Crotts, J., Mason, P. and Davis, B. 2009. Measuring guest satisfaction and competitive position in the hospitality and tourism industry. An application of stance-shift analysis to travel blog narratives. *Journal of Travel Research*, 48(3), 139-151.

Crotts, J. and Mason, P. 2010. An analysis of travel blogs to determine the frequency of pests and their impact on guest loyalty: An extension of stance-shift analysis. *ASEAN Journal of Hospitality and Tourism*, 9(2), 2-24.

Crotts, J., Mason, P. and Davis, B. 2009. Measuring guest satisfaction and competitive position: An application of stance shift analysis of blog narratives. *Journal of Travel Research*, 48(3), 139-151.

Davis, B. and Mason, P. 2010. Stance shift analysis, in *Interviewing in Criminal,* edited by V. Lord and A. Cowan. *Justice*. Sudbury, MA: Jones & Bartlett, 273-281.

Freud, S. 1901. *Die Psychopathologie des Alltagslebens*. Frankfurt: Fischer.

Gunter, B., Campbell, V., Touri, M. and Gibson, R. 2009. Blog, news and credibility. *New Information Perspectives*, 61(2), 185-204.

Hancock, J., Curry, L., Goorha, S. and Woodworth, M. 2005. Automated linguistic analysis of deceptive and truthful synchronous computer-mediated communication. *Proceedings of the 38th Annual Hawaii International Conference on System Sciences.*

Kurashima, T., Tezuka, T. and Tanaka, K. 2005. *Blog Map of Experiences: Extracting and Geographically Mapping Visitor Experiences from Urban Blogs*. Lecture Notes in Computer Science 3693. Vienna: Springer Verlag, 379-396.

Lord, V., Davis, B. and Mason, P. 2008. Stance-shifting in language used by sex offenders: Five case studies of assignment of responsibility. *Psychology, Crime and Law*, 14(4), 357-379.

Magnini, V., Crotts, J. and Zehrer, A. 2010. Identifying drivers of customer delight through travel blog analysis. *Journal of Travel Research*, 49(2), 153-164.

Mason, P., Davis, B. and Bosley, B. 2005. Stance analysis: when people talk in online focus groups, in *E-Marketing Vol. II*, edited by S. Krishnamurthy. Hershey, PA: Idea Group, Inc.

Newman, M., Pennebaker, J., Berry, D. and Richards, J. 2003. Lying words: Predicting deception through linguistics styles. *Personality and Social Psychology Bulletin*, 29(4), 665-675.

Pan, B., Crotts, J. and Raschid, A 2008. A survey method for identifying key drivers of customer delight. *International Journal of Contemporary Hospitality Management*, 20(4), 462-470.

Pan, B., McLauren T. and Crotts, J. 2007. Travel blogs and their implications for destination marketing. *Journal of Travel Research*, 46(1), 35-47.

Pennebaker, J. and Francis, M. 1996. Cognitive, emotional, and language processes in disclosure. *Cognition and Emotion*, 10(6), 601-626.

Pew Internet and American Life Project. 2008. *Internet Usage Overtime Survey*. March 2000-May 2008.

Rayson, P., Berridge, D. and Francis, B. 2004. Extending the Cochran rule for the comparison of word frequencies between corpora. *7es Journées internationales d'Analyse statistique des Données Textuelles*.

Rayson, P. and Garside, R. 2000. *Comparing Corpora Using Frequency Profiling*. Proceedings of the Workshop on Comparing Corpora – Volume 9. Hong Kong: 9 October.

Rayson, P., Berridge, D., Francis, B. 2004. Extending the Cochran rule for the comparison of word frequencies between corpora. *Journées internationales d'Analyse statistique des Données Textuelles*, 7(1), 1-12.

Smith, T., Coyle, J., Lightfoot, E. and Scott, A. 2007. Reconsidering models of influence: The relationship between consumer social networks and word-of-mouth effectiveness. *Journal of Advertising Research*, 47(4), 387-396.

Tausczik, Y. and Pennebaker, J. 2010. The psychological meaning of words: LIWC and computerized text analysis methods. *Journal of Language and Social Psychology*, 29(1), 24-54.

Vrij, A. 2000. *Detecting Lies and Deceit: The Psychology of Lying and the Implications for Professional Practice*, John Wiley & Sons, Chichester: England.

Wesson, C. and Pulford, B. 2009. Verbal expressions of confidence and doubt. *Psychological Reports*, 105(1), 151-160.

Yoo, K-H. and Gretzel, U. 2008. Detection of deceptive hotel reviews: Influences of length and type of reviews. *Proceedings of the 14th Annual Graduate Student Research Conference in Hospitality and Tourism*. Las Vegas, 4-6 January 2009.

Zehrer, A., Crotts, J. and Magnini, V. 2011. Perceived usefulness of blog postings: An extension of the expectancy disconfirmation paradigm. *Tourism Management*, 32(1), 106-113.

Zhou, L., Burgoon, J., Nunamaker, J. and Twitchell, D. 2004. Automated linguistics based cues for detecting deception in text-based asynchronous computer-mediated communication. *Group Decision and Negotiation*, 13(1), 81-106.

Zhou, L. and Sung, Y-W. 2008. Cues to deception in online Chinese groups. *Proceedings of the 41st Hawaii International Conference on System Sciences.*

Chapter 22

Social Media Monitoring: A Practical Case Example of City Destinations

Alan Stevenson and Jim Hamill

1. Introduction

One of the major Web trends over the last few years has been the emergence of a wide range of Social Media Monitoring (SMM) tools. Used effectively, these tools can deliver two main business benefits to travel, tourism and hospitality organisations. First, by monitoring online brand conversations, SMM tools can deliver real-time actionable insight leading to more effective online brand reputation management. Second, by monitoring the overall 'buzz' being created about a brand, the use of SMM tools has become essential to measuring social media performance, business impact and return on investment.

Given the growing importance of these tools, it is essential that tourism and related businesses understand the rationale and potential benefits from Social Media Monitoring; the range of tools available; their relative features, functions and limitations. It is important that organisations apply these tools 'strategically', closely linked to agreed social media objectives, targets and key performance indicators.

Using a practical case example of city destinations, this chapter summarises current 'state-of-the art' thinking on Social Media Monitoring. The chapter presents an overview of what the current suite of tools can deliver; implications for travel, tourism and hospitality businesses; and practical advice in developing an SMM strategy. The case example presents top level results of an SMM exercise covering the top 10 city destinations worldwide, together with a more detailed analysis of two cities (London and New York), and is used to highlight the following:

- Explain how Social Media Monitoring tools can be applied; their key features, functions and limitations.
- Identify key criteria tourism organisations should be monitoring as part of an agreed social media performance measurement strategy.
- Best-practice in the use of SMM tools.
- The business case for investing in an SMM solution.
- Future implications for suppliers of these tools and researchers within this area.

The chapter concludes by presenting a '6Is' framework for measuring social media performance and business impact. The framework has direct practical relevance to tourism and related businesses and could also be used as a basis for future research in this area.

2. Social Media Monitoring Tools Explained

As a class of software application, Social Media Monitoring (SMM) tools are a relatively new and innovative development. While there are important differences between the various tools, the common feature is that they facilitate monitoring and analysis of online brand conversations across multiple social media channels. SMM tools index relevant information across different social media platforms on a daily or more frequent basis, provide a mechanism for users to search or interrogate this information (by keyword, date parameter, and so on) and return relevant results which can form the basis of further analysis and data visualisation. In essence, they provide a vehicle for monitoring 'who is saying what about your brand, where online and the overall sentiments (positive/negative) being expressed'. SMM Tools have become essential to a well planned and coordinated brand reputation and social media perfomance management strategy.

There are over 200 different SMM tools available, ranging from very sophisticated but expensive solutions to no or very low cost tools which can often provide a 'good enough' service for small tourism and hospitality businesses.

The most sophisticated (and most expensive) tools include Radian6, Sysomos Heartbeat, Alterian SM2, BuzzTracker and Infegy Social Radar amongst others. These allow businesses to monitor and evaluate the following:

- The 'river of news': all the information pertaining to a business, industry, product or competition.
- The volume of relevant mentions.
- Topic trends: peaks and troughs over a period relating to specific events, marketing campaigns or potential reputation issues.
- Details of what is being discussed, displayed as a 'tag cloud of most frequently mentioned key words or phrases.
- Results categorised by the mention medium e.g. tweet, blog post, forum post, news item, video or image.
- Key influencers i.e. channels and individuals with the greatest potential for generating viral, eword-of-mouth effects.
- The overall brand sentiment (positive/negative) being expressed.
- Language variants – some tools support analysis in 10 or more languages.
- Real-time updates through email alerts or RSS (Really Simple Syndication) feeds.
- The opportunity to develop 'actionable insights' from the data presented.

SMM tools need not be expensive. There are a range of free or low cost tools that provide some of the aforementioned features but with less in-depth presentation and analysis of results. For many tourism businesses, especially SMEs, these free or low cost tools provide a 'good enough' level of insight and functionality. Examples include Google Alerts, Social Mention, Trackur, Topsy, Viralheat, Blogscope and others.

3. Theoretical Background

The two main uses of SMM tools for travel, tourism and hospitality organisations are to:

- Deliver actionable customer insights from online brand conversations, especially customer-to-customer conversations.
- Monitor on-going social media performance and business impact.

Based on the above, four main strands of the existing literature are relevant to this chapter – the general literature on customer management/CRM; the emerging literature on eCRM and, more recently, eCRM in a Web 2.0 environment; social media performance measurement, business impact and return on investment (ROI); and the literature on destination branding and reputation management.

A very large and extensive number of studies have been published on the topic of customer management/CRM. Recent papers by Kevork and Vrechopoulos (2009); Richards and Jones (2008); Sanad, Fidler and McBride (2010); Frow and Payne (2007); Holger and Hoyer (2010); and Egan and Harker (2005) provide good overviews of the literature in this area. Papers by Liao, Chen and Deng (2010); Kim and Hawamdeh (2008); Peters and Pressey (2010); Payne, Storbacka and Frow (2008) synthesise the emerging literature on customer insight management; with the new topic of CRM 2.0 being covered in papers by Band (2008) and Förster (2010). Sigala (2011) presents a useful summary of emerging thinking relating to eCRM in a Web 2.0 environment. The author argues that Web 2.0 provides numerous opportunities for better eCRM through active listening and monitoring of customer-to-customer conversations taking place across a range of social media platforms. Given the growing number of online customer conversations taking place, success in this area obviously depends on robust monitoring software – the topic of this chapter.

A recent blog post by the authors of this chapter provides a concise summary of emerging thinking in terms of social media performance measurement and business impact, with a particular focus on Key Performance Measures and Social Media Analytics (Hamill and Stevenson 2010). Our own '6Is' approach is briefly summarised in the recommendations section.

Finally, a very large volume of literature exists on destination branding and reputation management; for example, see Buhalis (2000); Dinnie (2004); Fan

(2006); Gertner, Berger and Gertner (2006); Gnoth (1998); Govers, Go and Kumar (2007); Gugjonsson (2005); Hankinson (2001); Hosany, Ekinci and Uysal (2005); Kahn (2006); Lebedenko (2001); O'Shaughnessy and O'Shaughnessy (2000); Papadopoulos (2004); Parkerson and Saunders (2004). Very little has been written, however, concerning the revolutionary impact of Web 2.0 on destination branding. Two areas worthy of future investigation would be the impact of customer empowerment (Buhalis, Nininen and March 2007) on destination branding and the declining effectiveness of traditional sales and marketing practices in a social media era.

4. Case Example: City Destinations

To illustrate the range of issues involved in effective SMM, the remainder of this chapter presents a practical case example of a social media monitoring exercise covering the top 10 most visited cities worldwide, based on published visitor numbers from 2009 (WTO 2010). A top level analysis is presented covering Paris, London, Singapore, Kuala Lumpur, Hong Kong, New York, Bangkok, Istanbul, Dubai and Shanghai, together with a more detailed analysis of London and New York. The period covered is the 12 months from 1 December 2009 to 30 November 2010.

Key steps

There are three key steps involved in running an effective SMM analysis:

- Step 1: Agree the main research questions

It is critical to choose a set of research questions that the analysis should answer. The questions will vary from one organisation to another but will usually be strongly influenced by the organisation's core strategy and business objectives. In the case example below, research questions have been created that combine the key capabilities of SMM Tools (for performance measurement and conversation monitoring) alongside the desire to produce destination specific actionable insights. Six core research issues were addressed:

- Number – the total number of mentions/conversations for each destination over the 12 month period covered – a good proxy measure for online brand 'buzz'.
- Where? – the most important channels where relevant conversations are taking place.
- Influencers – who are the key influencers, where do they 'hang out' and what level of influence do they have?
- What? – the topics and issues being discussed.

  - Sentiments – the balance between positive and negative brand sentiments being expressed.
  - Actionable Insights – the 'calls-to-action' delivered by the data analysis.

- Step 2: Create a set of key phrases

It is important to find the right set of key phrases that will produce voluminous results whilst reducing the level of irrelevant mentions. Keyword construction can be a time-consuming task and involve a level of trial and error. The task can be broken into the following constituent parts:

  - The Root Search Phrase to be used. For the purpose of the case example, a narrow root search phrase was used – "Visit Paris", "Visit Shanghai"; "Visited Paris", "Visited Shanghai" etc. This results in a smaller number but more relevant results compared to a more generic root search such as destination name only. A number of alternative but related root searches could have been used e.g. "Visiting Paris", "Visiting Shanghai". The level of relevant information returned can be increased through additional root search phrases.
  - The Focus Search Phrase – this is useful in determining additional context for each of our roots. For example, "Visiting Paris" + "Eco-Tourism" would return only those mentions where the key phrase Eco-Tourism is also present.
  - The Language Variants – a key consideration in (a) and (b) is use of language. Key phrases can be augmented with language specific root and focus search phrases. It is important to involve a language expert in both the keyword construction and the analysis. Language variants are not included within the case example which has been conducted solely in the English language.
  - "Not" Phrases – in order to deliver more meaningful results, it is important to create a list of key phrases in order to exclude certain mentions from the results when present. For example, "Apple records" might want to exclude mentions of "Apple laptops" from their 'river of news'.

- Step 3: Choose the tool and run the analysis

As one of the main aims of this chapter was to evaluate what the current suite of SMM tools can deliver, it was important to use one of the more 'sophisticated' tools. For the purposes of the case example, we used the SMM tool SocialRadar from Infegy. According to the company's website (www.infegy.com/socialradar.php), Social Radar is the most robust SMM tool available (it is also one of the most expensive) covering over 4 billion social media posts collected over three years of historic data. It is claimed that its 'web crawler' minimises the ampount of spam picked up – an issue of growing importance in social media monitoring (see final section of the chapter). While the other tools listed above would have provided a similar analysis, the use of Socail Radar allows us to evaluate the results delivered by one of the most expensive tools available.

The key phrases were inputted into the specialist functions within SocialRadar. The software then interrogates its database of indexed blog posts and comments, video and image sites, Twitter feeds, discussion forums, news articles etc. for relevant mentions. Results are then delivered covering the six key questions listed previously – How many mentions? Where? Influencers? What is being discussed? Sentiments being expressed? Actionable insights?

5. Results

This section presents summary results of our SMM Analysis for the ten city destinations, together with a more detailed discussion of the results for London and New York. Due to time and space limitations, only top level results are presented. The software does allow a much deeper micro-level analysis and insight than can be presented in the chapter. Although restricted to top level results, the case example does highlight the power and usefulness of SMM tools but also the current limitations and weaknesses of existing software in some areas.

The presentation of findings follows the six main research questions listed earlier.

Number of mentions

The number of mentions (conversations) about a destination can be used as a first estimate of the level of online 'buzz' being created about the brand. On-going monitoring of this 'buzz' should be a key element of a destination's social media performance measurement strategy.

For the 12-month period covered in the case example, Table 22.1 shows the total number of mentions for each city for the key phrases 'visit' and 'visited'. Key points to note are as follows:

- The city with the highest level of online 'buzz' is London with 15,171 mentions, followed by New York (11,476) and Paris (9,591). The number of mentions for other cities was significantly lower, especially for Kuala Lumpur, Istanbul, Bangkok and Shanghai. The fact that the analysis was conducted only in English may have been a contributing factor in the low rankings of some of these cities.
- Despite the fact that narrow search terms were used, it is clear that a very large number of online conversations are taking place for the top ranked cities. This provides the Destination Management Organisation (DMO) and local tourism businesses in these cities with a major opportunity for

Table 22.1 Social Media Mentions by Top 10 Visited Cities

City	Total Mentions	Visitor Rank	Mention Rank
London	15,171	9	1
New York	11,476	5	2
Paris	9,591	10	3
Singapore	5,562	8	4
Dubai	3,113	2	5
Hong Kong	3,036	6	6
Shanghai	2,064	1	7
Bangkok	1928	4	8
Istanbul	1101	3	9
Kuala Lumpur	398	7	10

Note: Visitor Rank based on visitor numbers 2009 using WTO 2010 statistics; Mention Rank based on the total number of social media 'mentions' for each city over the period covered.

Source: The authors.

online engagement with existing and potential customers (marketing as a conversation); developing deep customer insight through online feedback, comment and review; and for real-time brand reputation management. This will require an allocation of resource, time and effort to ongoing social media monitoring and performance measurement. The low rankings achieved by other cities may indicate that a more proactive social media strategy is required to generate online 'buzz'.

- Interesting findings emerge when comparing Social Media Mentions with Visitor Number Rankings (Table 22.1). London significantly outperforms New York in terms of Mention Rank compared to their respective Visitor Number Rankings of 9 and 5 respectively. Paris significantly over-performs in terms of Mention Rank (third) compared to its 10th position in terms of visitor numbers. The Mention Ranks of London, New York, Paris and Singapore are higher than their Visitor Rank. The converse is true of Dubai, Shanghai, Bangkok, Istanbul and Kuala Lumpar.
- The Number 1 Mention Rank of London is very interesting to note given that VisitEngland is the leading national DMO in Europe for their proactive

use of social media – see our other chapter in this book. The evidence presented here suggests that there may be a strong positive correlation between social media engagement and social media performance. A more detailed analysis of the data would be required to confirm this.

Where?

As stated above, it takes time, effort and resource for a DMO or tourism business to develop and implement an effective SMM strategy. As a consequence, it is important to target limited resources to the most important social media channels and high influence posts i.e. channels where most of the relevant conversations are taking place and the posts with the highest online influence (potential for e-word-of-mouth effects). This section discusses channel importance with 5.3 covering the key question of influence.

SMM Tools can indicate the top sources or channels where relevant conversations are taking place. This would require a more detailed analysis of all posts covering all ten cities and is 'out-of-scope' of this chapter. For illustrative purposes, a more detailed analysis was undertaken of 1,000 individual post sources for two cities, London and New York (500 sources each).

More than half the sources for each city (279 for London and 322 for New York) were classified as 'low value' i.e. the source contributed less than two posts over the period and provided an influence score of less than 10. A weakness of Social Radar is that it does not provide a detailed description of how 'influence' is measured apart from a generic statement that it comprises a combination of readership, user-base, followers and authority. An 'influence' score of 10 or less would be considered very low. Posts in this group are, therefore, excluded from further analysis. Channel/source distribution of the remaining posts is shown in Table 22.2 with some interesting comparisons between the two cities, especially the very high importance of blog posts for New York (50 per cent of total posts) compared to London (29 per cent) and the greater importance of website posts for the latter. This may reflect the more rapid uptake of blogging in the US during the period covered.

A major issue with Table 22.2 is the under-representation of social and professional networking sites. This highlights a major technical limitation of many SMM tools, namely sites that refuse access to the software. Facebook and Linkedin are notable examples of network sites that are "closed" to most Social Media Monitoring tools. From an analyst's perspective this means that no tool can provide all the information needed – further manual searches across social networks are required to augment any SMM tool analysis. The requirement for additional work or manual review is a recurring theme with SMM tools. With over 600 million people worldwide using Facebook, legitimate questions can be asked concerning how comprehensive is the coverage provided by most SMM tools.

Table 22.2 Mentions by Channel Source

	London		New York	
	No. of Mentions	**% of Total Mentions**	**No of Mentions**	**% of Total Mentions**
Blog	64	29	89	50
Website	81	37	40	22
News	37	17	26	15
Images	19	9	6	3
Spam	8	4	6	3
Forum	0	0	5	3
Articles	3	0	2	1
Directory	0	0	1	1
Network	0	0	1	1
Twitter	6	3	1	1
Video	3	1	1	1
Total	**221**	**100**	**178**	**100**

Source: The authors.

Influence and influencers

Identifying influencers and online brand advocates should be a key element of a well planned social media marketing strategy. Influencers and advocates can help to build positive, e-word-of-mouth brand impact.

Finding key influencers and brand advocates would be a tedious task without SMM tools as it would involve reviewing the source of each mention, determining their followers, forum size, blog readership and the number of relevant posts over a long period. Even although not clearly defined or explained (see above), one of the major strengths of SMM tools is that they provide an estimated score for post influence based on a combination of readership, user-base, followers and authority. To illustrate this further, Table 22.3 shows key influencers for the two cities examined in more detail, London and New York. Only blog sources with two or more relevant posts and an influence score of 10 or more are shown.

Key points to note from Table 22.3 are as follows:

- For London, there are 15 blogs with an influence score of 10 or more and for New York 18. However, it is clear that there are major variations in relative influence with scores ranging from 1,910 to 18 for London and 974 to 16 for New York.

Table 22.3 High Influence Blogs

Source	Influence Score	Category
London		
London Relocation Blog	30	Accommodation
Hotel Review Blog	132	Accommodation
Josie-Mary	18	Craft
The Tight Tan Slacks of Dezso Ban	36	Fitness
The Pleasure Monger	49	Food
Gossip Blender	1910	Lifestyle
Nothing To Do With Arbroath	222	Lifestyle
Mass Hole Mommy	154	Lifestyle
Brockley Central	110	London Life
The London Word	48	London Life
KillerHipHop.com	216	Music
The wonderful world of Carminelitta	21	Music
World Of Nokia	79	Technology
Suzy Guese	83	Travel
Booking Advisor Official Blog Empty Kingdom: You are Here,	82	Travel
New York		
We are Everywhere	308	Art
Democralypse Now	974	Comedy
The Dream Lounge	28	Consultancy
Coercs	57	Electronics
Daily Blender	126	Food
The Eaten Path	67	Food
Fresh Local and Best	48	Food
Being Brazen	152	Lifestyle
tried to live forever every day of the year	65	Lifestyle
swinkler.info	16	Music
Arms Control Wonk	364	Politics
Florida Scuba Diving	100	Scuba Diving
Concrete Elbow by Steve Tignor	89	Tennis
The Wimbledon Blog	23	Tennis
Arthur Frommer Online	192	Travel
Booking Advisor Official Blog	82	Travel
NYU Local	621	University
Tim Stout	24	Writing

Note: Social Radar does not fully define how it measures 'Influence'. The data shown is a composite measure based on a combination of readership, user-base, followers and authority. The higher the score, the more influential is the blog. Only sources with an influence score of 10 or more are shown.

Source: The authors.

- As might be expected, travel and accommodation blogs are important in terms of relevant mentions. However, there are a number of influencial non-travel specific blogs with relevant conversations taking place across a broader spectrum of special interest areas including Lifestyle, Food, Music, and Sport. This indicates a strong connection between travel and other interest areas, providing an opportunity for destinations to actively engage beyond traditional travel boundaries.
- This use of SMM tools is only the first stage in assessing key influencers, especially given definition and measurement issues as above. A more detailed manual review is also required to understand the context or main theme of the source and whether there is a good match with the destination. It involves degrees of involvement from first joining or viewing an 'Influencer Source', then "listening" over a period of time before deciding when and how to interact and engage.
- Table 22.3 is based on an evaluation of key blog influencers. A similar analysis should be undertaken across multiple social media channels – Twitter, forums, news sites, video and image sites etc.

What?

One of the major benefits of using advanced Social Media Monitoring tools is that they provide an instant snapshot of what is being discussed, often presented as a tag cloud. This is shown in Figure 22.1 for the two cities examined in more detail. A more detailed analysis can then be undertaken of any of the key words shown.

Brand sentiment

SMM tools attempt to automate the analysis of brand sentiment using sophisticated algorithms which seek to determine whether key words are positive or negative. The quantified results are then presented as percentage ratings of overall sentiment (positive, negative and neutral) as illustrated in Table 22.4 for London and New York.

While sentiment analysis may be highly beneficial for marketers and PR professionals interested in how a destination is perceived by visitors, great care should be used in interpreting the results. The intricacies of language can often fool the most complex sentiment engines (e.g. sarcasm) and no SMM tool is 100 per cent accurate. The best levels achieved are cited in the region of 80-90 per cent accuracy. Some tools err on the side of caution preferring to rate most mentions as neutral with the exception of those which are very clearly positive or negative.

As users of these systems it is important to understand more precisely the context of a negative or a positive comment and their implications. In short, automated tools need to be viewed as filters for a more detailed manual review.

London

travel next family great show work End year soon think trip shopping world people best events city really meet summer UK stay tour England new 2010 love hotel us good tourists attractions weekend marketing visitors weekend Top I'll must offer Britain West fun friends free experience BT Asks Tower

New York

year travel best world hotels planning things people great love show NYC good reason trip top home stay tour even attractions life offer us Center think next help tourists art today Manhattan night located friends really enjoy shopping Street summer Queen food must area restaurants experience Island business American Museum

Figure 22.1 Key Word Tag Clouds

Actionable insights

The ultimate objective of Social Media Monitoring is to deliver actionable customer insights from the data analysed. Although the case example above has presented only a very top level analysis, the data presented should be sufficient to highlight the actionable insights that can be delivered from a more detailed SMM monitoring exercise. These are listed below in a series of questions that should be addressed by DMOs, travel, tourism and hospitality businesses:

- Does the volume of mentions/online conversations taking place relevant to our brand justify resource investment in on-going social media monitoring? Can we afford not to invest in this area?
- Where do our customers (actual and potential) 'hang-out' online and what are they saying about our brand and the competition? How can we best engage with them?

Table 22.4 Sentiment Analysis

	London			New York		
	Positive	**Negative**	**Mixed**	**Positive**	**Negative**	**Mixed**
% of Mentions	90	8	3	86	9	5

Word	**Category**	**Appears in % of London Mentions**	**Appears in % of New York Mentions**
like	Adjectives	23	38
problem	Negative	6	10
hate	Negative	2	5
difficult	Negative	4	5
concern	Negative	4	4
bad	Negative	5	9
perfect	Positive	9	18
great	Positive	30	33
good	Positive	23	32
fun	Positive	11	14
enjoy	Positive	19	26
best	Positive	30	40
beautiful	Positive	14	16

Source: The authors.

- Who are the key influencers and how can we best leverage positive word-of-mouth effects?
- What sentiments are being expressed about our brand? How can we best leverage positive brand sentiments? How should we respond to negative comments?
- How can we best use SMM Tools for measuring the overall performance and business impact of our on-going investments in social media?
- How can we best integrate the actionable insights delivered into our overall social media vision and strategy?

6. Recommendations

Based on the above, we would make a number of recommendations to travel, tourism and hospitality businesses considering the pro-active use of an SMM tool.

- Think strategically – the business benefits and ROI delivered from SMM will be improved the more closely activities in this area are aligned with a well defined and agreed Social Media Strategy; a strategy with clearly defined objectives, targets and key performance indicators. For organisations without a defined Social Media Strategy (unfortunately, the majority), SMM Tools can help to define the generic strategy to be followed in terms of where to engage (which channels to use) and the level/depth of engagement with each channel.
- Focus on 'actionable insights' – as should be clear from the case example presented, SMM tools can provide very useful analysis of relevant conversations taking place across diverse social media channels. However, the tools are not perfect and suffer from a number of major weaknesses. To avoid falling into the 'paralysis by analysis' trap, tourism and related businesses should focus on the 'actionable insights' being delivered, even from data which is not 100 per cent perfect. This supports Sigala (2011) who argues that the key issue in CRM 2.0 is to focus on how tourism businesses can best leverage user generated content, key influencers, customer-to-customer conversations etc.
- Performance framework – by evaluating the online 'buzz' being generated about a brand, SMM has become an essential element of social media performance measurement, business impact and ROI assessment. As above, the benefits derived in this area will be enhanced by using a robust Performance Measurement Framework, answering the two main questions what to measure and why? Our own '6Is' Performance Framework is summarised in Figure 22.2 and explained in more detail in Hamill and Stevenson (2010). The key features of the framework are as follows:

    - The '6Is' of social media performance – Involvement (the number and quality of customers involved in your various online networks); Interaction (the actions taken by online network members – read, post, comment, review, recommend etc.); Intimacy (the brand sentiments expressed, level of brand 'affection' or 'aversion'); Influence (advocacy, viral forwards, referrals, recommendations, retweets etc.); Insights (the level of customer/actionable insight delivered from monitoring online conversations); Impact (business impact of your social media activities benchmarked against core business goals and objectives).

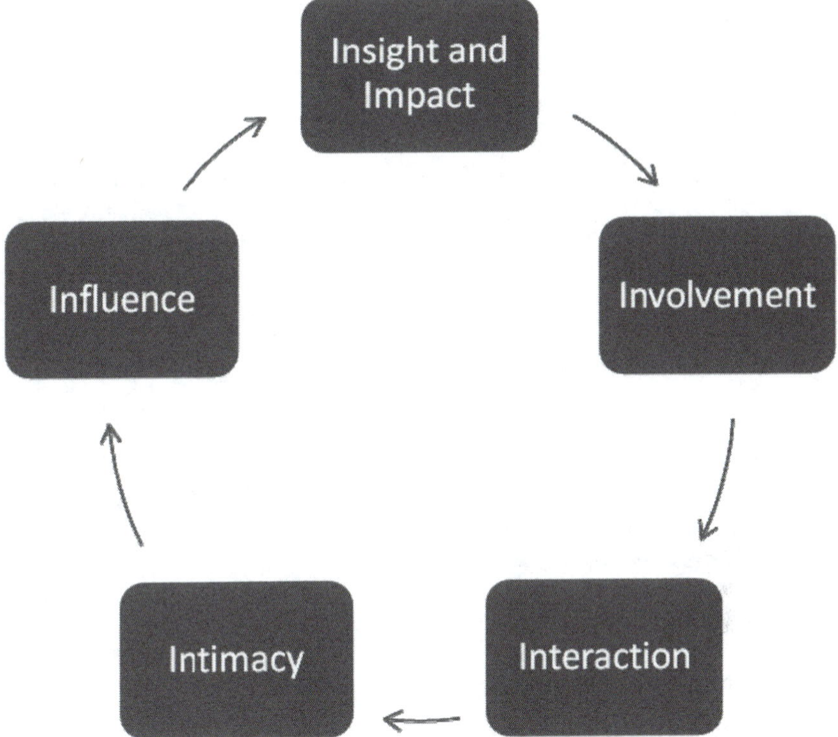

Figure 22.2 The 6Is Social Media Performance Framework

Source: Derived from Hamill and Stevenson 2010.

- The use of a simplified Balanced Scorecard (BSC) approach linking social media 'lead' measures (the first '4Is' above) to 'lag' performance measures i.e. ultimate business objectives. In a social media era, the '4Is' of social media involvement, interaction, intimacy and influence become the main 'drivers' of future business success.
- The three main levels of social media perfomance measurement – individual channels; overall 'buzz'; business impact. The '6Is' listed above are not intangible difficult to measure criteria. In fact, the complete opposite is the case. They can be measured to a very high degree of accuracy using the analytics provided by each individual social media channel (e.g. Facebook Insights, Klout for Twitter, YouTube Views etc.); SMM tools to evaluate the overall 'buzz' being created; and the Balanced Scorecard for linking 'lead' social media measures to overall business impact.
- The main stages involved in implementing a social media perfomance measurement system – agree business objectives, targets, KPIs,

customer segments, key initiatives and actions, on-going performance evaluation.

- Planning – undertaking a Social Media Monitoring exercise requires careful planning around the key issues discussed in previous sections – research questions addressed, key search phrases used, choice of software tool etc. As regards the latter, the limitations of even the most advanced SMM tools have been identified in this chapter. A robust monitoring exercise will normally involve the use of mutliple tools, including a manual search of networks closed to SMM tools.
- Resources – despite the growth of automated SMM tools, a large element of human intervention is still required to produce accurate actionable insights. While it is relatively easy to run a top level SMM search, automated results cannot always be trusted, specifically in determining which mentions or sources are more valuable or in the analysis of sentiment (where several limitations exist). The user must question the accuracy of automated results, especially with the growing amount of 'PR spam' in this area.
- Over hyped and over sold? – despite some clear benefits from the use of SMM tools, they are not a panacea. Considerable manual effort and expertise is involved in getting the best from even the most expensive tools. There are several limitations as previously identified which suppliers provide little information on, preferring to focus on (and possibly overstate) the benefits. A 'future agenda' for suppliers is listed below.

7. Future Agenda for Suppliers and Researchers

For suppliers of SMM Tools there are a number of issues to consider:

- Create serendipity (or finding outliers): Social Media Monitoring involves sifting through large quantities of information. This encourages the analyst to focus their attention on high value mentions. The current evolution of SMM tools helps to provide a view of value but is this accurate; does it exclude only non-relevant mentions? Are there potentially valuable mentions or outliers being missed? Could suppliers extend search features to return more valuable results? For example, services such as Stumbleupon have a different approach to finding relevance or value, focusing on outliers and producing an illusion of serendipity or happenstance.
- "Can" the spam: Spam is a growing issue in social media. Even the most advanced SMM tools do not deal with spam effectively. A significant level of human intervention is required to flag each instance, adding

considerably to the workload. Given the very expensive price of many SMM tools, should spam filtering be more effective?

- Turn down industry/PR generated noise: The above argument also applies to the growing number of industry or PR led messages being posted – often the same message posted on multiple social media channels. This represents 'noise' broadcasting rather than user generated content. It is a very labour intensive and exhaustive process to filter out this noise. Could suppliers of SMM tools more accurately identify and filter out industry noise and in doing so add value to the River of News?
- Recognise there is no universal adapter: SMM Tools are limited in the channels and sources they index. The analyst is often required to use multiple tools, including manual search, and to merge results. Whilst there are constraints on which sources an SMM tool can access (e.g. Facebook makes little information available outside of its own platform), could SMM suppliers make the integration of additional research easier?
- Differentiate the user experience: SMM tools should be compared (and compete) on some of the aforementioned features in addition to the more standard functionality available from almost all of the tools.

For researchers in this area, the growing importance of Social Media Monitoring creates a number of exciting opportunities:

- Understanding adoption and use: Research is needed to better understand SMM adoption levels and existing barriers to use. Despite clear business benefits, few travel, tourism and hosptiality businesses (especially SMEs) are actively engaged in this area. Potential barriers include: lack of understanding of the benefits; lack of awareness of the tools, their features and functions; a perception that Social Media Monitoring tools are expensive and the reserve of big brands; a very complex, fragmented and confusing supplier marketplace.
- Examining the relationship between use of SMM tools and practices and business impact: Research is needed to explore more deeply the relationship between use of SMM tools and related Social Media Monitoring and Measurement practices and underlying business performance. This could be in terms of sustained competitive and customer advantage but also more granularly at a business objective level.
- Exploring the relationship between broader social media mentions and business impact: An exciting "potential" relationship may also exist between the level and quality of Social Media Mentions and underlying business performance e.g. how an increase in Social Media mentions of a destination translates to an increase in visitor numbers. More specifically this research should explore the relationship between the type (e.g. User Generated versus Industry mentions) and timing of mentions and business indicators (e.g. trends around visits to a destination, sales, website visits or enquiries).

References

Band, W. 2008. *The CRM 2.0 Imperative – Look to New Solutions to Keep Pace with the Emerging Social Customer*. Available at: www.forrester.com/rb/Research/crm_20_imperative/q/id/43991/t/2?src=45543pdf [accessed: 12 February 2011].

Buhalis, D. 2000. Marketing the competitive destination of the future. *Tourism Management*, 21, 97-116.

Buhalis, D., Nininen, O. and March, R. 2007. Customer empowerment in tourism through consumer-centric marketing (CCM). *Qualitative Market Research: An International Journal*, 10, 265-281.

Dinnie, K. 2004. Place branding: Overview of an emerging literature. *Journal of Place Branding*, 1(1), 106-110.

Egan, J. and Harker, M. 2005. *Relationship Marketing: Three-Volume Set*. SAGE Library in Business and Management. London: Sage Publications.

Fan, Y. 2006. Branding the nation: What is being branded? *Journal of Vacation Marketing*, 12(5), 5-14.

Förster, M. 2010. *Social CRM Requires a New Marketing Skill: Having a Conversation*. Available at: www.peppersandrogersgroup.com/blog/2010/07/customer-strategist-martin-for.html [accessed: 12 February 2011].

Frow, P. and Payne, A. 2007. Customer relationship management: A strategic perspective. *Journal of Business Market Management*, 3(1), 7-27.

Gertner, R., Berger, K. and Gertner, D. 2006. Country-dot-com: Marketing and branding destinations online. *Journal of Travel & Tourism Marketing*, 21(2/3), 105-116.

Gnoth, J. 1998. Branding tourism destinations, *Annals of Tourism Research*, 25(3), 758-760.

Govers, R., Go, F.M. and Kumar, K. 2007. Promoting tourism destination image. *Journal of Travel Research*, 46, 15-23.

Gugjonsson, H. 2005. Nation branding. *Journal of Place Branding*, 1(2), 283-298.

Hamill, J. and Stevenson, A. 2010. Step 3: *Key Performance Indicators (Post 1)*. Available at: www.energise2-0.com/2010/06/27/step-3-key-performance-indicators-post-1/ [accessed: 12 February 2011].

Hankinson, G. 2004. Relational network brands: Towards a conceptual model of place brands. *Journal of Vacation Marketing*, 10(2).

Holger, E. and Hoyer, W.D. 2010. Customer relationship management and company performance: The mediating role of new product performance. *Journal of the Academy of Marketing Science*, 39(2).

Hosany, S., Ekinci, Y. and Uysal, M. 2005. Destination image and destination personality: An application of branding theories to tourism places. *Journal of Business Research*, 59(5), 638-642.

Kahn, J. 2006. A brand-new approach. *Journal of Place Branding*, 2(2), 90-92.

Kevork, E. and Vrechopoulos, A. 2009. CRM literature: Conceptual and functional insights by keyword analysis, *Marketing Intelligence & Planning*, 27(1), 48-85.

Kim, Y.M. and Hawamdeh, S. 2008. Leveraging customer knowledge: A comparative study of eCRM functionality and its use in e-commerce websites. *International Journal of Electronic Customer Relationship Management*, 1(4).

Lebedenko, V. 2004. Opinion Pieces, Where is Place Branding Heading? *Journal of Place Branding*, 1(1), 12-35.

Liao, C.C.Y., Chen, Z.H. and Deng Y.C. 2010. Mining customer knowledge for tourism new product development and customer relationship management, *Expert Systems with Applications*, 37(6), 4212-4223.

O'Shaughnessy, J. and O'Shaughnessy, N.J. 2000. Treating a nation as a brand: Some neglected issues. *Journal of Macromarketing*, 20(56).

Papadopoulos, N. 2004. Place branding: Evolution meaning and implications. *Journal of Place Branding and Public Diplomacy*, 1(1), 36-49.

Parkerson, B. and Saunders, J. 2004. City branding: Can goods and services branding models be used to brand cities? *Journal of Place Branding*, 1, 242-264.

Payne, A., Storbacka, K. and Frow, P. 2008. Managing the co-creation of value. *Journal of the Academy of Marketing Science*, 36(1), 83-96.

Peters, L. and Pressey, A. 2010. Networks as learning organisations, Special Edition of the *Journal of Business & Industrial Marketing*, 25(6).

Richards, K.E. and Jones, E. 2008. Customer relationship management: Finding value drivers, *Industrial Marketing Management*, 37(2), 120-130.

Sanad, A., Fidler, C. and McBride, N. 2010. Critical success factors for customer relationship implementations, *UK Academy for Information Systems Conference Proceedings* 2010.

Sigala, M. 2011. eCRM 2.0 applications and trends: The use and perceptions of Greek tourism firms of social networks and intelligence. *Computers in Human Behavior*, 27, 655-661.

WTO. 2010. *Tourism Highlights 2010 Edition*. World Tourism Organization.

Index